Acknowledgements

The UNESCO International Bureau of Education is very grateful to the following individuals for so generously giving their time to support this project in at least one of the following variety of ways: commenting on earlier versions of the introductory chapter, providing detailed critical feedback on the final draft version of one or more of the studies, facilitating communication between the IBE and the authors in the face of occasional technical challenges, and offering opportunities to share ideas on the project as it developed.

Abdeljalil Akkari, University of Fribourg; Munir Bashshur, American University of Beirut (AUB); Desmond Birmingham, Department for International Development (DfID, London); Barbara Bruce, Social Science Research Council (SSRC); Peter Buckland, the World Bank in Washington DC; Deo Byanafashe, Faculty of Arts and Human Sciences at the National University of Rwanda; Roy Carr-Hill, Institute of Education at the University of London; Michel Carton, Graduate Institute of Development Studies (IUED) Geneva; Peter Colenso, the World Bank in Sri Lanka; Nat Colletta, Institute for Peacebuilding and Development in Washington; Sundaram Divakalala and E.B. Ekanayake, German Technical Cooperation (GTZ) in Sri Lanka and Pakistan respectively; Adnan El Amine, Lebanese University and Lebanese Association for Educational Studies (LAES), Tony Gallagher, School of Education at Queen's University in Belfast; Vincent Greaney, the World Bank in Washington; Gerhard Huck, German Development Co-operation (GTZ) in Sri Lanka; Colin Kaiser, UNESCO Office Sarajevo: Kenneth King, Center for African Studies at the University of Edinburgh, Christiane Kohser-Spohn, the Georg Eckert institute (GEI); Lidija Kolouh–Westin, Stockholm University; Dick Lageweg, Netherlands National Commission for UNESCO; Fabienne Lagier, Swiss Development Cooperation (SDC); Ellen Lange, Ministry of Education and Research in Norway; Angela Little, Institute of Education at the University of London; Anna Obura, consultant; Falk Pingel, Organisation for Security and Co-operation in Europe (OSCE) Sarajevo; Margriet Poppema, International Development Studies at the University of Amsterdam; Verena Radkau García, Georg Eckert Institute (GEI); Moritz Rosenmund, Pädagogische Hoschule in Zurich; Jamil Salmi, the World Bank in Washington; Margaret Sinclair, UNESCO Education Sector; Alan Smith, University of Ulster (UU); Harvey Smith and Richard Webber, Coordinators (CfBT) Rwanda; Chris Talbot (UNESCO: IIEP); Deirdre Watson, Department for International Development (DfID) Rwanda; Sue Williams, UNESCO Bureau of Public Information; and Duncan Wilson, the Right to Education Project.

Special thanks to Lucy Shaw at UNESCO: IBE for her tireless, cheerful, and creative contributions.

This book was made possible thanks to institutional support that the Swedish International Development Agency (SIDA) has been generously providing the International Bureau of Education.

Education, Conflict and Social Cohesio

Edited by
Sobhi Tawil and Alexandra Harley

International Bureau of Education

I

ISBN: 92-3-103962-8

Preface

Conflict has recently emerged as one of the challenges for reaching Education for All goals. International attention, initially concerned with the destructive and disruptive impact of armed conflict on education systems, has now turned to the more subtle and complex relationships between education and conflict. There is a growing international awareness of the potential for educational governance, schooling structures, as well as teaching and learning content and methods to act as catalysts for the outbreak of violent conflict.

The studies presented in this volume examine the role of educational policy change in social and civic reconstruction and the redefinition of national citizenship within the context of identity-based conflicts. The underlying assumption is that if educational change is to be a meaningful contribution to processes of national reconciliation and peace building in the context of civil strife, the complex linkages between schooling and conflict need to be explicitly recognised and explored. How do forms of educational governance, processes of curriculum policy-making, and of curriculum development contribute, either to a shared sense of national identity and inclusive citizenship, or, to an exacerbation of social divisions, tensions, and identity-based conflict?

These questions are explored by national educational decision-makers and researchers in Bosnia-Herzegovina, Guatemala, Lebanon, Mozambique, Northern Ireland, Rwanda, and Sri Lanka. By focusing on processes of curriculum policy change in the wake of civil strife, the studies provide a more nuanced understanding of the relationships between schooling, social divisions, and political violence. In examining the role of curriculum policy in eroding or reinforcing social cohesion in divided or conflict-affected societies, the studies demonstrate how such issues are relevant to efforts at peace building education in all societies.

The seven studies are the result of the collaborative *Curriculum Change and Social Cohesion in Conflict-affected Societies* project coordinated by the UNESCO International Bureau of Education during 2002-2003. The project is an integral part of the support provided by the International Bureau of Education for the strengthening of national capacities in the areas of curriculum policy dialogue, research and development.

CECILIA BRASLAVSKY
DIRECTOR

Contents

Chapter 1

Education and Identity-based Conflict: Assessing curriculum policy for social and civic reconstruction

Sobhi Tawil

Alexandra Harley

About the Authors

Sobhi Tawil has been co-ordinating the Capacity Building for Curriculum Development programme at the UNESCO International Bureau of Education (Geneva) since 2002. He was formerly the head of the Exploring Humanitarian Law project (1999–2001) at the International Committee of the Red Cross (ICRC). He also lectures in Education, Conflict and Development at the Graduate Institute for Development Studies (IUED) in Geneva. Alexandra Harley assisted in developing and managing the *Curriculum Change and Social Cohesion in Conflict-Affected Societies* project at the International Bureau of Education (2002–2003). Prior to her work on this project, Ms. Harley taught environmental education in Nicaragua (1998–2000) where, following Hurricane Mitch, she founded and directed a small NGO to support populations affected by the disaster.

EDUCATION AND CONFLICT

The link between education and conflict is now squarely on the Education for All (EFA). Already in the 1980s, the declining enrolment patterns observed in many developing countries were often associated with situations of political instability and armed conflict (Berstecher & Carr-Hill, 1990). In 1990, the World Declaration on Education For All referred to "war, occupation, [and] civil strife" as significant elements of the "daunting problems" that "constrain efforts to meet basic learning needs" and reaffirmed the right to basic education for "children and adults affected by armed conflict:" With the end of the bipolar world in the early 1990s, there appears to have been a continuation, if not an accentuation of the trend towards greater social instability, political violence, and armed conflict.

During this same period, international attention progressively shifted from a concern with violent conflict solely as an obstacle to ensuring access to basic education for all, to an awareness of the more subtle, complex, and often disturbing linkages between education and conflict. An exploration of the experiences of Cambodia, Colombia, Palestine and Sierra Leone by the UNESCO International Bureau of Education in 1997 reflected this growing international concern with the targeting of education in situations of political violence, as well as with the ways in which the contents and processes of schooling may actually contribute to precipitate the outbreak and development of violent conflict (Tawil, 1997). The investigation recognised that there was a need to distinguish between education as an "accomplice to rebellion" and the outbreak of armed conflict, and education as a victim of overt violence with the sources of the conflict lying elsewhere.

The UNICEF Innocenti Research Center has explored and identified the positive and negative faces of education in relation to ethnicity and conflict, focusing on the potential role of school education in amplifying social divisions, and as a precipitating factor in the outbreak of political violence (Bush and Saltarelli, 2000). They argue that destructive educational practices—when combined with such causal factors as economic tensions, poor governance, and perceived threats to cultural identity—may fuel suspicion, hostility, ethnic intolerance, and violence. In convincing support of this argument, they identify a number of ways in which education has exacerbated hostility, including: the uneven distribution of education; education as a weapon in cultural repression; denial of education as a weapon of war; the manipulation of history for political purposes; the manipulation of textbooks; and segregated education that tends to reinforce inequality, lowered self-esteem, and stereotyping.

The World Bank has also explored the role of education both as a determinant of direct and indirect forms of violence, and as an instrument to reduce societal violence (Salmi, 2000). Salmi proposes an analytical framework in order to understand the different forms of violence, and applies it to the examination of the positive and negative role of education in situations of violence. He notes that while education can be an effective instrument to reduce violence, "schools are violent environments and the education process or lack thereof, are important determinants of violence."

The observation that educational content, structure, and delivery systems may, in themselves, be *catalysts* of violent conflict is now an explicit concern of the international community within the framework of the Education for All goals. The *Education in Situations of Emergency and Crisis* thematic assessment study prepared for the World Education Forum in Dakar (UNESCO, 2000) recognised that "weaknesses in educational structure and content may have contribut[ed to] conflict" and that "an education system that reinforces social fissures can represent a [

source of conflict." This idea is re-iterated in the 2002 EFA Monitoring Report, which stated that a "major concern in post-conflict situations is to avoid replication of educational structures that may have contributed to conflict."

The issues paper *Education, Conflict and International Development* produced by the U.K. Department for International Development (DfID) goes one step further. Smith and Vaux (2003) not only reiterate that education can be part of the problem as well as part of the solution, but also promote the adoption of a long-term perspective based on analysis of education policies and practice in terms of their potential to aggravate or help resolve conflict. The authors argue that it is crucially important to consider the linkages between education and conflict not only in times of overt violence, but also as "a routine ingredient of development thinking within the mainstream education sector."

The fact that development thinking has neglected to systematically analyse the possible "negative face" of education may be partly explained by the apolitical and a-historical character of mainstream educational development and EFA discourse. Such discourse has largely overlooked the fact that social and cultural conflict – both intrinsic components of any schooling process – shape educational policy-making. One clear way to recognise the more politicised role of education and to recover critical historical perspective, is through an assessment of the process of educational policy change in societies affected by identity-based conflicts.

EXPLORING CURRICULUM POLICY IN IDENTITY-BASED CONFLICTS

Examining educational policy change within the context of identity-based conflicts was the focus of the *Curriculum Change and Social Cohesion in Conflict-Affected Societies* project coordinated by the UNESCO International Bureau of Education (2002–2003). The aim of the project was to gain a better understanding of the role of education policy in shaping social and civic identities and in redefining or reconstructing national citizenship within the context of identity-based conflicts. The underlying assumption is that for processes of educational change to be meaningful contributions to national reconciliation and peace building in the context of identity-based conflicts, the complex linkages between schooling and conflict need to be explicitly recognised and explored. Of central concern were the policy issues that determine the role of schooling in the formation and transmission of collective identity, memory, and sense of citizenship and of shared destiny. The exploration and documentation of these issues in Bosnia and Herzegovina (BiH), Guatemala, Lebanon, Mozambique, Northern Ireland, Rwanda, and Sri Lanka is guided by the following question:

How do the forms of educational governance, processes of curriculum policymaking, and of curriculum development contribute to either (1) a shared sense of national identity and citizenship which is inclusive and respectful of diversity or (2) exacerbate social divisions, tensions, and identity-based conflicts?

The studies presented in the following chapters of this volume explore this central question. In doing so, some of the authors examine the extent to which the education system itself has been a potential source of the very conflict it is expected to prevent and remedy. The challenge facing all of the authors was to explore not only the way schooling relates to violent conflict, but also to understand how this relationship is rooted in contested and/or changing conceptions of national cohesion and how it impacts on identity formation.

Figure 1: The seven project cases

Learning from societies emerging from civil strife

Focusing on processes of curriculum policy change in the wake of civil strife arguably provides a more nuanced understanding of the nature of the relationships between formal schooling, social divisions, and political violence, where such issues are more apparently explicit than in other contexts. Assessing the ways in which formal schooling may be seen to have undermined social cohesion in such cases helps to delve more fully into the question of how education can also contribute to reconstructing and renewing social peace based on justice. Moreover, understanding the role of education in general, and of curriculum policy in particular, in their capacity to erode or reinforce social cohesion in the context of conflict-affected societies, is relevant to efforts at peacebuilding education in *all* societies.

Approach and methodology

In designing this project, an attempt was made to link each study to on-going processes of educational research, which aimed to strengthen local research capacity and policy dialogue. Thus, where possible, the seven studies presented in the following chapters were prepared by national educational decision-makers and researchers. It is hoped that the compilation of these studies in one volume shall similarly allow for increased opportunities to explore problematic areas of educational policy in divided or conflict-affected societies in a comparative and constructive fashion. The framework grew out of a set of guiding questions that was developed by the project team at the start of the project. Preliminary versions of the seven studies were presented and discussed at an international seminar organised in Geneva, providing the authors with an opportunity to share their work with each other, as well as with an international audience. The critical input collected was used by the authors to improve and finalise each of their studies, and by the project team as a whole to refine the analytical framework. Throughout the process, group reflection and dialogue helped overcome difficulties and challenges inherent to comparative work and analysis while at the same time trying to avoid prescriptive and rigid formulas. Additional critical feedback was gathered through the presentation of the project in its entirety, and/or selected cases at a number of international forums[1]. Finally, the completed drafts of the seven studies were circulated to a number of national and international experts for comment. The entire process has thus sought to promote dialogue and raise awareness concerning important questions relative to identity, violent conflict, and social cohesion that are being addressed in educational reform in societies in both the North and the South.

Situating the seven studies

The first study, on ***Bosnia and Herzegovina*** (chapter two), was developed by an international expert closely involved in establishing the inclusive consultative structures and mechanisms that led to the development of the Education Reform Strategy Paper in November 2002. Moreover, the study was prepared based on the in-country experience and expertise of the UNESCO field office in Sarajevo with which the author had been closely involved in providing technical advice for an unofficial core curriculum team representing the diverse educational authorities within the Federation of Bosnia and Herzegovina, as well as the Ministry of Education of the Republic of Srpska.

Prepared jointly by the national coordinator and the chief technical advisor for the Project to Mobilise Support for Mayan Education (PROMEM), the ***Guatemala*** study (chapter three) is embedded in the process of curriculum development for the inclusion of Mayan culture and language in the national Curriculum for Basic Education. The development of the study was part of a process of dialogue with key stakeholders in Guatemalan education and was thus linked to the work of the Consultative Commission for Education Reform and the Accompaniment Commission for Compliance with the Peace Accords.

Chapter four, on ***Lebanon***, reviews the ways in which curriculum policy was framed during key moments in the historical development of schooling, including following the reestablishment of peace in the early 1990s after the end of fifteen years of civil war. This exploration into curriculum policy formulation and the issue of Lebanese identity, history, and sense of citizenship is presented by the former president (1999-2002) of the Educational Centre for Research and Development (ECRD), who was in charge of the Civics Education Project and the development of history curriculum in the postwar period.

The ***Mozambican*** team was composed of three experts from the National Institute for the Development of Education (INDE) and the University Eduardo Mondlane in Maputo. The study (chapter five) focuses on the impact of a series of politico-ideological shifts in education policy "exploring the possible links between the experience of armed conflict, recent political change (…) and the reinforcement of national identity through curriculum change." In addressing the "competitive co-existence" between the former colonial Portuguese language and the twenty-one indigenous languages, the chapter traces the ways in which language policies have attempted to define national cohesion. In doing so, the team reviewed official documentation produced by the Ministry of Education, interviewed a range of stakeholders involved in educational reform, and conducted a limited number of observations and interviews among students in a pilot school in Maputo.

Chapter six, on ***Northern Ireland***, was developed as part of the ongoing evaluation work of the pilot Social, Civic and Political Education Project. Formerly director of the project at Ulster University, the author was also the principal officer at the Northern Ireland Council for the Curriculum, Examinations and Assessment. The study was supplemented by interviews with individuals from a range of organisations with both policy and academic orientations who have been involved in shaping or implementing education policy in relation to the conflict. Additionally, the study draws on existing research that explores the views of young people on the relevance of educational experiences in Northern Ireland with regard to the social and political environment of conflict.

In the case of **Rwanda** (chapter seven), the study "is part of the whole process of curriculum change and review underway" and the methodology used "is in line with the current process of educational policy development" in which the team of three from the National Curriculum Development Centre and the Kigali Institute of Education consulted with teachers, head teachers, students, Ministry of Education officials, donors, and representatives of religious groups. The study addresses two main questions: 1) What was taught in schools in the past, and how has that contributed to social divisions and conflict; and 2) What values should be taught in Rwandan schools to bring about social cohesion?

Finally, chapter eight, devoted to **Sri Lanka**, was prepared by three senior professionals who have been associated with the development of school and teacher education curriculum over the past three decades. The study focuses on the link between education reform and political violence in Sri Lanka. In attempting to present a comprehensive and balanced record and analysis of educational policy against the backdrop of twenty-five years of conflict, the authors accessed a wide range of studies and printed documents. They also consulted and interviewed relevant persons and authorities in order to document views on the way in which curriculum change may contribute to foster social cohesion and peace in the country.

Assessing curriculum policy from a social cohesion perspective

The common analytical framework attempts to provide a coherent way of approaching a range of key issues associated with processes of curriculum policy reform following a protracted period of civil strife. The principal concept guiding this assessment is that of social cohesion, and supplements pedagogical, socio-economic, or other logics of curriculum evaluation. The practiced strength of the framework has proven to be the flexibility with which specific sets of issues and questions proposed can be highlighted and explored in widely differing historical, cultural, socio-economic and political contexts, as well as in policy development processes at very different stages of reform. The framework is organised around five main categories of guiding questions relating to: (1) the background to the conflict, (2) educational governance, (3) curriculum paradigm sifts, (4) difficult policy issues, and (5) the role of research (see Appendix 1 for more detail). In practice, different structures of educational governance and resulting patterns of policy dialogue, and differing models and phases of curriculum change tend to dictate varying logics of framing the issues. Figure 2 is a simplified representation of the analytical framework and the remaining discussion of this chapter will be organised around these more generalised categories, beginning with the central concern of social cohesion and social and civic reconstruction. Each category will be introduced by a brief selection of guiding questions from the original framework and will be illustrated by a discussion of the ways in which some of the primary concerns are taken up by the authors in the chapters that follow.

Figure 2: Assessing curriculum policy from a social cohesion perspective

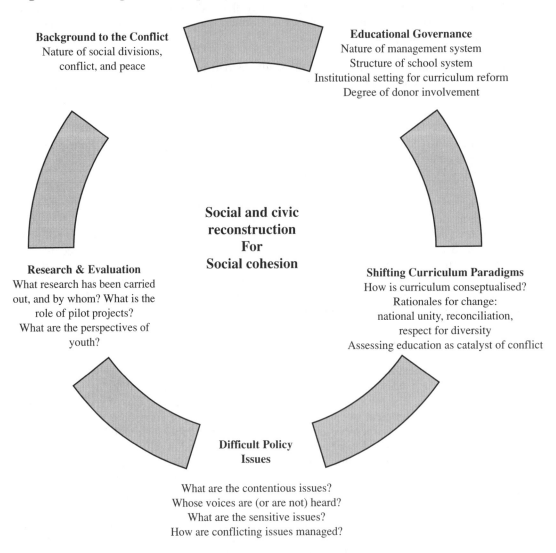

Background to the Conflict
Nature of social divisions,
conflict, and peace

Educational Governance
Nature of management system
Structure of school system
Institutional setting for curriculum reform
Degree of donor involvement

**Social and civic
reconstruction
For
Social cohesion**

Research & Evaluation
What research has been carried
out, and by whom? What is the
role of pilot projects?
What are the perspectives of
youth?

Shifting Curriculum Paradigms
How is curriculum conseptualised?
Rationales for change:
national unity, reconciliation,
respect for diversity
Assessing education as catalyst of conflict

**Difficult Policy
Issues**

What are the contentious issues?
Whose voices are (or are not) heard?
What are the sensitive issues?
How are conflicting issues managed?

SOCIAL AND CIVIC RECONSTRUCTION FOR SOCIAL COHESION

The studies that follow have prioritised social cohesion as the prism through which they assess curriculum policy change. It is therefore clearly important to begin our discussion with a closer look at this term. While efforts to define social cohesion have generated numerous models and typologies, a single agreed definition remains rather elusive. Recent scholarship, however, argues that the real utility of the term "social cohesion," is precisely that it can function "as a *framing concept* for thinking through the complexity of policy issues" (Beauvais and Jensen, 2002). We also endorse this understanding of social cohesion as less a concept that begs a single fixed definition, and more the idea of a paradigm—an umbrella concept or governing principle—under which public policy can be constructed and assessed. Moreover, like all paradigms, it is capable of shifting. The term denotes an awareness of social exclusion and inclusion that can be applied to a wide range of policymaking contexts aimed at responding to diverse social challenges. Social cohesion, in other words, is neither a given entity nor a thing in itself. The way it is perceived translates into the way it is defined. The way it is defined, in turn, determines the types of indicators used for the assessment that serves to inform policy formulation. As an organising idea, it may delineate the crucial elements that should not be excluded from the process of policy dialogue, of the framing and reframing processes of reflection and debate, and of policy formulation. In reading the studies presented in this volume it will therefore be salutary to keep the following questions in mind: 'How is the question of social cohesion approached?' and 'How are policy-makers approaching curriculum policy change in view of social and civic reconstruction?'

Exploring curriculum policy as part of a broader process of social and civic reconstruction implies a developmental perspective. As such, the social and political environments in which educational policy reform aimed at social and civic reconstruction can take place are of a decidedly different nature than those encountered in emergencies and acute conflict situations. The latter has, nevertheless, been the main referent for much of the education and conflict discourse to date, and has important implications as to the relative roles of international, national and local partners in educational policy formulation. Implicit in the chapters that follow, on the other hand, is the conviction that education policy reform is likely to be most effective and sustainable when initiated by a sovereign national education authority in a context of relative security and political stability. The need for a national educational authority, socially acknowledged as legitimate, which can construct and define education and curriculum policy at the nation state level, places this discussion in the framework of education and development, rather than that of education in emergencies.

Figure 3: Conflict status and type of educational initiative

Conflict status	Nonconflict; relative "peace"	Internal trouble; social unrest; "pre-"conflict	Armed conflict	Transition out of violence; peace process	"Post-" conflict
Type of educational initiative	Education for prevention (development)		Education in emergencies		Education for social and civic reconstruction (development)

It is important to stress that education functions in a political domain and understanding this is to understand that very little about it is neutral. The implications of this for educational policymaking relate to the process of determining and defining legitimate knowledge that serves to define the nation-state in any given context. Schooling has played a key role in the historical development of nation-states. "The nation," it should be recalled, "is an imagined political community" (Anderson, 1991) for which compulsory public schooling is an essential mechanism of integration. The development of schooling as part of the formation of modern nation states has often embodied a violent process of destruction and reconstruction of social relations and structures. Given the importance of schooling in nation-building, it has been argued that the monopoly of legitimate education in modern nation-states may be more important than the monopoly of legitimate violence (Gellner, 1983). While recent political globalisation has challenged traditional national sovereignty, it has also curiously strengthened the *idea* of the nation state (Meyer et al, 1997), and the number of civil wars seen in the latter part of the twentieth century demonstrated the intensifying degree of political violence necessary to preserve it. As the relationship between violence and the construction of the nation state shift, so too does the relationship between schooling and violent conflict. The discussion that follows is an assessment of that changing relationship.

BACKGROUND TO THE CONFLICT

In attempting to understand any process of educational policy change, it is important to examine the social and political context. Given our focus on social cohesion, it is important to consider cultural, social, and political factors in a historical perspective in order to understand the nature of social divisions, of identity-based conflict, and of the peace. The main guiding questions proposed in the framework are the following (see Appendix 1 for more detail):

- *Nature of social divisions*: What is the nature of social divisions? What is the nature of group identity? What is the role of language, religion, and ethnicity in defining cultural identity? How is group identity articulated with social/political divisions?

- *Nature of conflict*: What is the type of conflict? What are the scale, intensity, duration and recency of the violence? To what extent is the conflict identity-based?

- *Nature of peace*: What is the nature of the political agreement (if any) that has ended the conflict? How is the role of education/curriculum reform articulated in peace agreements (if at all)?

In exploring these questions, it is possible to develop a critical and historic awareness of the shifting role of education with regard to social cohesion. Interestingly, the attention given to a narration of the background to conflict in each context reflected the difficulties in undertaking this critical exercise. The authors of the various studies have remarked how difficult it was to endeavour to present an historical overview in light of the fact that versions of "official history" are often integral to the roots of the conflict, thus making history a highly charged concept. They further mentioned that the exercise of documenting the contextual background provided a direct opportunity to experience the difficulties of selecting appropriate historical information in an effort to communicate more or less objective information that would seem accurate to both national and international readers. The necessity of confronting this in the opening pages of the each study, therefore, had an impact on the presentation and discussion of policy change that followed.[2]

The nature of conflict

The term "conflict" is used here to refer to situations of violent armed conflict. More specifically, the term here refers to internal conflicts and, particularly, to situations of civil war. From the "troubles" in Northern Ireland to the civil wars in Lebanon and Mozambique; from the separatist armed struggle in Sri Lanka to the genocide in Rwanda; from what has been alternatively called the "civil war," the "war of aggression," and the "ethnic cleansing" in BiH to the centuries of cultural repression in Guatemala—these dramatic experiences of political violence of varying scale, intensity, and duration are essentially all conflicts at national or subnational levels, even if they have sometimes been integrated into wider regional or international conflicts.

Discussions within the project team pointed to uncertainties about the relevance of using terms such as "ethnic conflict" as a means of describing the nature of the conflict in these societies. The authors of the Rwandan study, for example, present an analysis of the inadequacy of the various theories of ethnic conflict as a means to fully understand the tragedy of the 1994 genocide. They point to serious academic debate, which questions the validity (and racist conception) of the origins of the term. They go on to argue that

> [...] it is not the existence or nonexistence of ethnic groups that is important. The problem is that people believe in them and then behave accordingly. Therefore, if Rwandans want to find solutions to social divisions, it is important to talk about ethnic categorizations, ethnicity, and ethnic groups, in order to express a consensus as to the truth about them as they are experienced and defined.
>
> (Rutayisire, Kabano, and Rubagiza)

The concept of "ethnic conflict" appears inadequate to understand situations of violent conflict because it overlooks, diverts attention from, or obscures the political, economic, and social issues at stake. We propose "identity-based conflict" as a term that appears to be both more accurate and more appropriate, as it makes the central question of identity more explicit. This is important because

> a certain form of identity—be it individual, social, cultural, professional, religious, or political – constitutes the point of departure for any and all relations with others. Identity is what makes us what we are and who we are. And yet, the experience of identity invariably evokes codes of exclusion, difference and distinction. Belonging to a collectivity always concerns the delimitation of that collectivity and the application of a logic of conflict and contention.
>
> (Burgess, 2002)

The preceding quote suggests that different forms of identity represent potential sources of social division. However, it may be argued that social divisions also result from exclusion from employment, means of production, and land (economic exclusion), as well as exclusion from education, health care, housing, and other social services (social exclusion). Cultural identities and social and economic exclusion may overlap and represent an important source of identity-based conflict when associated with forms of political exclusion that imply the denial of security, representation, citizenship, and other basic political and cultural rights. Viewed this way, the range of conflicts explored in the seven studies can be further understood on the basis of issues of legitimacy of the nation-state and associated conceptualisations of citizenship and national identity.

In Guatemala and Mozambique, for example, where the legitimacy of the nation-state is not in question, each society is undertaking a radical reconceptualisation of citizenship at the national level. In the case of Guatemala, this involves a shift from a hegemonic and monocultural assimilationist tradition to a multilingual and multicultural conception of Guatemalan national identity based on the principle of "unity in diversity." Contemporary Guatemala challenges the traditional conception of identity as a dualistic "self"/"other" and goes beyond the juxtaposition of "integrated" multiple identities in the definition of national citizenship, to arrive at a vision of *"el otro yo"* — a fusion of self and other as complementary and simultaneous. Mozambique is rediscovering a national (African) identity that was partly recovered at the end of its war for independence (1964–75). The current efforts to incorporate cultural and linguistic diversity have been long delayed by the civil war between FRELIMO and RENAMO (1976–92).

While the existence and legitimacy of the nation-state in its existing contours is not in question in the cases of Lebanon and Rwanda, both societies are seeking to strengthen a central national identity that will hold the nation together. If there is consensus on the reality of a "pluralistic" Lebanese nation-state composed of seventeen official communities, the 1975–89 civil war reflected the lack of agreement on the definition of a common Lebanese national identity and a sense of civic loyalty. As for the case of Rwanda, the fact that the post-1994 government of national unity defines "peace and reconciliation" as a "life skill" reflects an explicit attempt to overcome a long tradition of division and discrimination by endeavoring to strengthen a common national identity.

In BiH, Sri Lanka, and Northern Ireland, on the other hand, the contours of the nation-state and the idea very idea of the nation itself, are being critically questioned. This is clearly reflected in the Tamil separatist struggle in Sri Lanka, at least until the recent signing of the ceasefire agreements in 2002, as well as in Northern Ireland, where the "legitimacy of the state is still in question, with no consensus as yet as to its nature (and) with a range of identities."[3] Similarly, in BiH, a nation-state that emerged in 1995 as a result of the disintegration of the former Yugoslavia, the fact that the constitution speaks of "three constituent peoples" politically organised into two "entities" reflects the lack of any basic consensus on the nature of the state and of citizenship.

In each case, the specific nature of the conflict has implications for the conceptualisation of citizenship and a direct incidence on the challenges posed to educational policy reform in terms of (re)defining national culture and identity through methods of governance and sensitive learning areas.

The nature of peace

The nature of the cessation of hostilities and of the peace achieved is crucial to defining the possibilities for social and civic reconstruction through education policy. The nature of the political settlement, whether internally developed or externally imposed, has implications for the nature of political will to reform education, as well as for the construction or consolidation of legitimating mechanisms which give education policymakers a mandate for change. In the case of Northern Ireland, for instance, the Good Friday or Belfast Agreement (1998) "created a new political context in which issues like the constitutional status of Northern Ireland, policing, and the role of human rights suddenly became open to debate. Society was challenged to define what democracy means or could mean in Northern Ireland". In Lebanon, the 1989 Taef Agreement that brought an end to fifteen years of civil war in Lebanon articulated the need "to unify history and civic education textbooks" as part of declared efforts to counter political sectarianism. Finally, the case of Guatemala is particularly rich in establishing the links between socially constructed peace accords, negotiated over a period of many years, and the perceived need to undertake a process of educational and curriculum policy reform. The authors insist on the 1995 Accord on the Identity and Rights of Indigenous Peoples because of the fact that it "established the right to a cultural identity" and of the importance of the peace accords in general for the acknowledgment not only of the enduring exclusion of the indigenous people but also of the enduring resilience of the Mayan experience in spite of it.

This is the main reason why the peace accords and the national dialogue and consensus entrusted the education of new generations in a culture of peace and intercultural dialogue to the education system.

(Salazar Tetzagüic and Grigsby)

EDUCATIONAL GOVERNANCE

After an examination of the background to the conflict, it is necessary to analyse the context of the education system in which curriculum reform is being undertaken. More specifically, analysis of the context of educational governance implies an examination of the nature of the management system, the structure of the school system, the institutional setting for curriculum development, the nature of donor involvement (where relevant), and their combined implications for reform. The guiding questions listed below are a representative sample of those that were identified to guide this contextual scan of the educational system.

- What is the *nature of the management system* (centralised, decentralised, fragmented) and where is the locus of decision-making authority?

- What is the *structure of school system* (segregated, assimilated, integrated, other; school types and share of each)

- What is the impact (if any) of *dependency on donor support* on curriculum policy choices (rationales and direction of change, as well as modalities for consultation)?

Fragmented decision-making in Bosnia and Herzegovina

The case of Bosnia and Herzegovina is a unique example of the fragmentation of educational governance in which the uncoordinated, supervisory presence of the international community -- including the unique Office of the High Representative -- functions as the "ultimate constitutional authority in BiH, superior to that of democratically elected governments." The "unhealthy levels of political involvement," fostering strong distrust and lack of confidence, and the creation of "thirteen education policymaking authorities with no state-level mechanism or framework for inter-authority, countrywide policy dialogue," have translated into the development of three parallel school curricula, reflecting the distinct, often inflexible, and mutually exclusive ideologies of the country's three constituent peoples. A major obstacle to curriculum reform then is that there is no identifiable and widely accepted national education authority. In the absence of a strong national identity, and the presence of a partisan environment characterised by a fierce defence of cultural autonomy, curriculum policy reform in learning areas such as history and geography, language and literature, and religious instruction, or what is referred to as the "national group of subjects", is strongly resisted:

> [a]t a systemic level, the high number of people with a professional education—particularly holders of university degrees—ensures that there is a keen awareness of the importance of education as a means of defending cultural identity and disseminating politico-cultural ideology. Moving from "socialist" education (with the interests of the state as its underpinning ideology) to "ethnic-nationalist" education (with the interests of an ethno-political group as its underpinning ideology) has been conceptually a simple matter.

(Stabback)

Parallel school systems and diversified curricula in Lebanon

The case of Lebanon implicitly questions the degree to which schooling could possibly serve as a unifying mechanism, given the existence of parallel public and private school systems and of diversified curricula. Not only did the private education sector historically precede the public one, but it continues to represent the overwhelming share of school enrolments with over 60 percent of students at all levels. The efforts of the Lebanese government since 1946 to unify school curricula may therefore be seen as a way of countering the fragmentation embedded in the legacy of private schooling and the right of religious groups to manage their own schools as enshrined in Article 10 of the Constitution:

> [e]ducation is free in so far as it is not contrary to public order and good morals that it does not affect the dignity of the several faiths. There shall be no violation of the rights of the religious sects to have their own schools, subject to the general prescription concerning public education which is decreed by the state.
>
> (Frayha)

Efforts made in 1946, 1969 and more recently in the 1990s following the end of the civil war, have all aimed to centralise the education system, reinforce the supervision and control of the private sector, and strengthen the supervision of textbook design and production and the renewal of school curricula. Recent efforts of the Ministry of Education to develop and introduce civics education at all levels of school education are to be seen as an effort to overcome the divisive effects of parochial schooling.

Curriculum responses to segregated schooling in Northern Ireland

The complex structure of the parallel school systems in Northern Ireland, characterised as it is by segregation essentially on the grounds of religion and class, reflects the divisions in the society as a whole. The fundamental question in such a context is the impact of segregated schooling and of parochial socialisation on the nature of relations between communities. The debate that emerged following the outbreak of the violence in 1969 as to the extent to which the causes of the sectarian violence could be attributed to the segregated school system have remained inconclusive. Despite this lack of evidence, the Department of Education Northern Ireland in the 1980s clearly stated its position relative to the responsibility of public policy:

> [t]he Department wishes to emphasise that it is not questioning the right to insist on forms of education in schools which amount to segregation. It considers, however, that this right is coupled with an inescapable duty to ensure that effective measures are taken to ensure that children do not grow up in ignorance, fear or even hatred of those from whom they are educationally segregated.
>
> (Arlow)

Although a promising alternative to the segregated educational structure in Northern Ireland, integrated primary and post-primary schools developed since the early 1980s to educate Protestant and Catholic students together represent only approximately 4 percent of total school enrolment. Given the limited scope of decreasing the segregated nature of the school system, an array of curricular responses, ranging from official Education for Mutual Understanding and Cross-Community Contact schemes, to pilot projects (discussed further below) such as Social, Civic and Political Education, have thus also been developed to overcome the negative and divisive socialising impact of the segregated schooling structure.

The impact of donor support in Mozambique

In addition to fragmented education authority structures and the highly segregated education systems of parallel school systems, the nature of educational governance on which curriculum policy choices depend may also be linked to the degree of donor involvement. In this regard, Mozambique stands out as one of the most aid-dependent countries in the world. This reality makes it difficult to determine to what extent "aid dependence and indebtedness have undermined Mozambique's sovereignty so that the conditions attached to aid have forced the country to accept some controversial policy changes" (Balegamire Bazilashe, Dhorsan, and Tembe). Moreover, the fragmented coordination of aid has further undermined the government's capacity to set priorities and design its own programme. Unable to devote adequate funding to curriculum reform, the government is dependent on priorities set by donors which appear to provide more support for pilot monolingual programmes than they do for bilingual programmes. Finally, implementation of decisions made within the national project of curriculum reform is set back by lengthy administrative procedures to access funds needed for implementation.

SHIFTING CURRICULUM PARADIGMS

What is meant by curriculum?

Although there is no agreed definition of the term "curriculum," a broad definition often adopted in the literature refers to the organisation of sequences of learning experiences in view of producing desired learning outcomes. The official planned intended school curriculum is articulated in a series of documents that include legislative decrees, policy documents, curriculum frameworks or guidelines, standards frameworks, syllabi, textbooks, and other instructional materials. Many rightly argue that while officially prescribed curricula clearly define the content, methods, and structures of intended learning experiences, they fail to account for the actual conditions of implementation (or "real" curricula) that ultimately shape learning experiences and define learning outcomes. In addition, examination of official curriculum overlooks the importance of the unplanned learning of the hidden curriculum in which meanings are conveyed indirectly by the way language is used, the behaviour and attitudes of teachers, the interactions that occur in the classroom, and the assessment methods practiced. From this perspective, curriculum may be broadly conceived to encompass educational philosophy, values, aims and objectives, organisational structures, teaching and learning materials and methods, student experiences, assessment, and learning outcomes. It is a process that includes both intended or officially prescribed curriculum, as well as actually implemented or real curriculum.

Curricular renewal as a reflection of changing approaches to social cohesion

Curricular renewal is the crux of the process of reform of school education. A social cohesion approach to processes of curriculum development would see these processes as "related to the prerequisites of societal integration—specific to a given society—to be realised on both the levels of material conditions and symbolic representations" (Rosenmund, 2000). Processes of curricular change are often introduced on the basis of a recognised weakness in school education. This weakness is defined in terms of the weak relevance of existing curricula in reflecting the ways in which society has changed as a result of conflict, and/or in promoting the types of social changes perceived as being necessary to ensure transition out of civil strife, reconciliation, and the consolidation of peace. The types of knowledge, skills, values, norms, attitudes, and behaviours that encourage *respect for human dignity and diversity* are mainly located within often sensitive areas of learning that touch upon the often sensitive issues of collective memory or collective amnesia, identity, sense of citizenship, and of shared destiny.

- How is curriculum conceptualised?

- What are the rationales for change?

- Has there been any assessment of the role of schooling, in general, and of curriculum, in particular, in the exacerbation of social divisions and/ or in the tensions leading to the outbreak of conflict?

- If the conflict has provoked a shift in curriculum paradigms, what is the nature of that shift? Does this reformulation move toward reinforcing a common national identity or toward the recognition of multiple identities in the process of reconciliation and of social reconstruction?

How is curriculum conceptualised?

Conceptualisations of curriculum as contained in this volume vary somewhat in each context. On the one hand, this includes a traditional and narrow view of curriculum as simply a list of subjects, as is the case in Bosnia and Herzegovina, where

> There would appear to be no commonly agreed definition of "curriculum" as an overarching concept. This absence of a consensual definition, compounded by the fragmented nature of educational responsibility, explains the absence of any broad curriculum statements or documents and the lack of a countrywide curriculum policymaking body.
>
> (Stabback)

Conversely, other conceptualisations are based on very broad definitions that encompass unplanned learning and the hidden curriculum. Advantages of such broad definitions can be particularly useful in contexts of highly segregated school systems, as is the case in Northern Ireland, where the complex structure of the education system reflects the divisions in the society as a whole, and could arguably be considered to be part of the hidden curriculum. One level of curriculum defined in that particular context is that of:

> Structured learning experiences that are supported and informed by curricular documents, resources, training, assessment, and evaluation. These experiences may or may not take place in the classroom; and may derive from the informal socialising impact of school life and human interaction.
>
> (Arlow)

Despite variations in the way in which curriculum is conceptualised in each of the studies presented here, there is a general consensus around the idea that curriculum is to be defined in relation to "structured series of intended learning outcomes" (Sri Lanka) that are planned and which, according to the context, may or may not go beyond the classroom or the school environment and encompass other institutionalised education settings. An essential aspect referred to explicitly in some of these approaches is that of "*desired*" knowledge, skills, and attitudes (in Guatemala and Rwanda), which emphasises the crucial issue of the authority to define and select legitimate knowledge.

Clarifying how curriculum is conceptualised in each context is important in that it determines curricular paradigms and the way in which these relate to educational/pedagogical tradition(s) and how these may be changing. To a very real extent, the societies discussed in the seven studies are undertaking curriculum change as a process of social self-reflection, pointedly reflecting the links between curriculum and identity noted by Popkewitz and Brennan (1998):

> curriculum is continually a practice of inclusion/exclusion, of constructing reason and nonreason that have critical moments in the construction of 'self' and the world.

Reconceptualising the nation through inclusion in Guatemala

The case of Guatemala makes explicit the systematic exclusion that has resulted from the homogenising nature of monolingual and monocultural policies, rooted in the official denial of multilingual and multicultural reality of national society. In addressing this legacy, there has been a critical examination of educational policies in a broad public debate that has necessitated a fundamental paradigm shift, moving away from the previous hegemonic educational vision and reconceptualising national identity. Educational paradigms are explained as having shifted from principles of assimilation in the pre-1944 era, to acceptance and integration in the post-independence years, and finally, to the current paradigm of interculturalisation based on the 1985 political constitution, and in which the concept of national citizenship is based on the acceptance of multiple cultural identities. The education reform of 1998 that followed, "established the foundation and profile of a new form of education whose source would be the specific cultures of the peoples of the nation, as well as universal knowledge and cultural values" (Salazar Tetzagüic and Grigsby). In a radical departure from the centuries of repression...

> Education is now considered to be a decisive factor for promoting the cultural identity of each of the peoples that make up the country and for affirming the national identity. It is through education that a peaceful and harmonious coexistence between the people and communities is fostered—a coexistence based on inclusion, tolerance, solidarity, respect, equality, equity, and a mutual enrichment that eliminates all discriminatory manifestations.
>
> (Salazar Tetzagüic and Grigsby)

Undoubtedly, however, it is a promising way of framing the fundamental national debates about identity mentioned previously. Policymakers in Guatemala, for example, are clearly acting to construct their vision of social cohesion through curriculum reform:

> Beyond the paradigm shift in curricular theory, curricular changes introduce a reconceptualisation of the school, not only in the reorganisation of its structures to adapt to what is known as modernity, but also—and especially—in the perspective of building a new multiethnic, plurilingual, and multicultural nation that has emerged from an armed conflict that fragmented and polarised the society.
>
> (Salazar Tetzagüic and Grigsby)

From failing the nation to promoting national unity and reconciliation in Rwanda

There is a view among key education stakeholders in Rwanda today that the pre-1994 curriculum was characterised by a lack of values and that it is precisely through the recovery of and redefinition of social values that social and civic reconstruction can move forward. Rutayisire, Kabano, and Rubagiza describe a pre-1994 political environment, which

> heavily influenced an education system that did not do much in terms of the prevention of conflict. The Rwandan system was characterised by injustice based on ethnicity, regionalism, gender disparity, and religious discrimination, all of which could certainly have contributed to the 1994 genocide.

While the authors acknowledge the progress made thus far in educational development in Rwanda, they nevertheless note that:

> ... a closer look at the education system before the 1994 genocide reveals that the education system—and specifically the *school curriculum*—failed the nation. How else would one explain the criminal activities of teachers, doctors, lawyers, priests, nuns, bishops, and any other profession one could think of? What had gone wrong with the education system?

The study suggests that learning content, teaching and learning methods and school structure has historically exacerbated and fuelled social tensions and even created social fissures. Mention is made of the more or less arbitrary mechanisms of identification that were a function of a colonial legacy that had little to do with a "true" Banyarwanda identity. The critical and deeply reflective questioning of the relationship between the education system, group identity, and the causes and the extreme violence is informing the nature of curriculum policy change in Rwanda based on the premise that

> [t]he curriculum is the heart of any education system and that the establishment and delivery of effective curricula will contribute significantly to achieving both quantitative and qualitative targets including reconciliation, social cohesion, and national unity.
>
> (Rutayisire et al)

Education reform and political violence in Sri Lanka

In discussing the education reforms of 1972 and 1981 the authors note that while they may have been initiated in response to socio-political crises that surfaced in the course of the war, the reforms did not appear to be grounded in any "conscious effort" to address the pressing issue of national cohesion. The reforms did represent an attempt to correct perceived imbalances in educational provision, but altering forms of access did little to address the fundamental problems of inequity in the system. Only the most recent (1997) reforms have struggled directly to identify the

> major divisive systemic features such as segregation of children by ethnicity, the need to enable children to become bilingual and thereby facilitate communication among them, and the need to introduce a multicultural perspective in designing curriculum.
>
> (Perera, Wijetunge, and Balasooriya)

Despite this more profound understanding of the challenges facing the education system, the authors caution that the crucial areas of assessment and accountability must not be neglected in determining the effectiveness of the envisioned reform. They note that, as yet, any concrete investigation of the extent to which the reforms "have been designed to facilitate, and have actually facilitated, the achievement of the national goals and competencies for social cohesion has not been examined adequately and qualitatively."

DEALING WITH DIFFICULT POLICY ISSUES

Curriculum policy change as a process of social dialogue in divided societies

In the context of social divisions, there are strong arguments in favour of focusing on the process of policy development of the official national curriculum. The important issue in using the social cohesion approach to curriculum development "is the *bargaining* that occurs about the shape of education with respect to the society's structure and symbolic representations" (Rosenmund, 2000). It follows that this process of *negotiation* and *social dialogue* about the way in which national school education is seen as having to change is context specific, and would have to be rooted in analysis of the historical, social, and cultural context. Indeed, we have seen above how the specific nature of the conflict implies particular challenges for educational policy reform in terms of reframing national culture and identity through language policies, social studies, and the teaching and learning of history, geography, civics, literature, and religion. The broader the process of consultation and social dialogue that is implemented to elicit and define the aims and goals of education to translate the vision of the citizen of tomorrow, the more extensive will be the links that connect diverse social actors. Examining the process of reaching consensus on the definition or reformulation of sensitive learning content in conflict-affected societies is indeed of great value in understanding how education may contribute to social cohesion and how this contribution can be promoted and strengthened through focused educational policymaking processes. National curriculum guidelines and frameworks may therefore be seen as *social contracts* resulting from processes of social dialogue, bargaining, negotiating, and reaching consensus. What, then, are some of the main questions that can guide an understanding of how difficult policy issues are dealt with?

- What are the sensitive or contentious policy issues relative to questions of history, collective memory, national identity, and sense of citizenship?

- Who is consulted and who is consulting in the process of reviewing and changing curriculum policy? What is the nature of their participation? Whose voices are heard, and how are they expressed?

- How are conflicting views dealt with? How is consensus reached? What are the risks of polarisation? Might it be counterproductive to discuss certain issues at certain times?

Linguistic and cultural issues in Guatemala

Multiple ways of thinking about questions of national inclusion are dependent on multiple forms of expression, both at a "practical" level involving linguistic parity (between and among indigenous languages and Spanish), and at socioeconomic and sociopolitical levels that insist on just educational policies, which are understood to include and be defined by just legislative practices. Characteristic of the recent reform in Guatemala is the effort to build a participatory and representative consultation process, reflecting a crucial extension and application of the political promises made in an effort to bring an end to the civil war. Salazar Tetzagüic and Grigsby note that the reform is fundamentally "a social movement inclusive of and coordinated with other processes of social transformation, which aim at the construction of a plurilingual, multiethnic, and pluricultural state." Thus, bilingual and intercultural curriculum reform is seen as both belonging to the community and also as the means of transforming that community. It prioritises and insists on the source of social transformation as one that has grown out of the process of dialogue:

> …the cultural and social resurgence of the Mayan People and of other indigenous peoples, is leading Guatemala to redefine itself as a nation and reorganise itself as a state. It is a dynamic process that is moving along a path of justice and equity, towards unity in diversity, whose source and support is the new education and intercultural dialogue.
>
> (Salazar Tetzagüic and Grigsby)

Language policies and national unity in Mozambique

Schooling in Mozambique was subject first to the assimilationist policies of the colonial authorities and then, after independence, was inscribed within the broader ideological changes in the socialist world. Thus, desired curriculum reforms after independence (in 1975) languished throughout the subsequent civil war (1976–92) and have only recently been given united national attention. Segregation, while first institutionalised under the colonial administration of schooling as a physical separation, took on a linguistic form after independence, as Portuguese persisted as the nation's official language. Even as the current introduction of local language curriculum is working to ease this form of social division, economic disparities persist in reinforcing challenges of equal access. Despite the continued dominance of the colonial Portuguese tongue, ambitious mother tongue language reforms are the strongest feature of the current policy change.

As Mozambique has only recently undertaken to incorporate cultural and linguistic diversity, it is also seeking to recover a national (African) identity. Yet the challenges of constructing a new curriculum able to integrate a southern African outlook and reinforce local identities, without weakening the idea of a national identity, are significant, and focus mainly on language policy reforms. As expressed by Helge Rønning, in Mozambique:

> there existed, and still exists, an attitude in political circles of equating the development of African language with tribalism, and that raising the question of a different language policy is tantamount to questioning the project of national unity.
>
> (Balegamire Bazilashe et al)

The new language policy and the current introduction of local languages as media of instruction during the first years of primary education mark a clear departure from the past. Local languages, (once considered to be possible causes of division) and local cultures (previously considered to be elements of obscurantism and obstacles to the construction of the modern socialist citizen) are now beginning to be considered by policymakers as a key means to reinforce national identity.

History in Sri Lanka

History is arguably the most contentious area of learning in Sri Lankan school education. In the aftermath of the protracted conflict, the content of history teaching has been seriously debated and such key questions as "Whose history is it? Who should select it? For what purpose?" have been the subject of public discussion. However, the polarisation of views on these fundamental issues of collective memory has obstructed any possible national consensus on the content of history to be taught in schools, and highlights all too clearly the close linkage between such curriculum policy issues and the wider political issues related to the cessation of violence, the resolution of political conflict, and the nature of the peace

> Historiography has significantly influenced the conflict, and the painful collective memories and group animosities that have become increasingly polarized over time stand in the way of reconceptualising or rewriting history as a school subject that could facilitate social cohesion and national integrity. [...] the challenges posed by some of the most contentious issues seem to threaten the very foundation of the curriculum framework, indicating that the processes of negotiation and consensus building on the political realm will be crucial, in the final analysis, to how decisionmaking is dealt with at the level of reorganising and restructuring school knowledge.

> (Perera et al)

National identity and social studies in Lebanon

One of the main educational challenges in postwar Lebanon was to mould a new generation of Lebanese youth that would have a common national identity based on a set of shared social and civic values and an acceptance of the pluralistic and unified nature of Lebanese society. While educationists considered social studies to be an appropriate vehicle for the transmission and the formation of such principles and values, the process of translating these ideas into the development of common history and civics curriculum was problematic. In addition to conceptual problems around such terms as political sectarianism, pluralism and diversity, one of the central problems faced by the Consultative Committee in the mid 1990s was reaching consensus on Lebanese identity. This was perhaps most clearly reflected in the problematic development of history curricula, where

> The question was then how to combine and balance divergent historical narratives, which place a greater emphasis either on the Phoenician or the Arab legacy of Lebanon, and on what sets Lebanon apart from the rest of the Arab world as opposed to what embeds it within that tradition.

> (Frayha)

The development of civics education curricula has been based on the implicit assumption that school education "can positively address the sectarianism, clannishness, and regionalism, entrenched during the war, and thereby contribute to national unity." While the process of developing civics education curriculum has been accompanied by difficulties, compromises and controversies, it has now been effectively integrated at all grade levels. This has not been the case with history where the suspension of the newly designed common primary textbooks for grades 2-6 reflects the persistent difficulties in reaching consensus on Lebanon's national identity and history. In recent years, the difficulties encountered in the development of social studies curriculum has been compounded by the recent demand, voiced by both Christian and Muslim clergymen, for the integration of religious education in the official public school curriculum.

RESEARCH AND EVALUATION

> - What is the role of pilot programmes and what are the ways in which these may (re)inform curriculum policy decisions?
>
> - What evaluation has been undertaken on recent curriculum change? If so, what type, with what results, and with what implications for (re)informing policy and implementation of curriculum changes?
>
> - How do youth/students perceive reform? How do they see education in relation to conflict?

While important as a source of innovation and experimentation in all educational systems, pilot projects at the grassroots level take on particular significance in the context of more challenging policy contexts. It is true that pilot projects in a fragmented educational authority structure such as that of BiH may have limited scope for mainstreaming and informing curriculum policy, particularly as there is no locus for national decision-making for school education. On the other hand, in the context of civil strife with as yet unresolved political conflicts, as is the case in Northern Ireland and Sri Lanka, pilot projects can play a crucial role. They not only in inform educational policy change to foster social cohesion, but also offer the possibility, as in Northern Ireland, to create a context in which policy change becomes possible.

The role of pilot projects in Northern Ireland

> Northern Ireland's society still seems to be characterised by a lack of consensus around issues of central importance in any democratic society. [...] Historically, civic life and the law enforcement and legal system had been experienced, by some, as sectarian. A sense of shared ownership of these crucial areas of public life is, at best, only beginning to emerge.
> (Arlow)

Prior to 1998, the political impossibility of discussing and addressing segregation at a policy level was circumvented through pilot grassroots efforts undertaken by committed volunteers and individuals who envisaged social reconciliation through educational initiatives. Furthermore, had the curriculum reforms been undertaken in the area of civics/citizenship (in particular) as a standard "top-down" development exercise by the educational authorities, there would likely have been "accusations of social engineering." The crucial importance, therefore, of the ("bottom-up") pilot initiatives is that they have been credited with having changed "the nature of discourse in Northern Ireland" by introducing a language that "allows people to express their support for cultural pluralism and political dialogue rather than sectarianism and political violence."

The revision of civics curricula within a wider social context is a way of allowing for the emergence of alternatives to contentious issues by no longer taking their irresolution for granted.

> It is not accidental that concepts contained in the thematic areas are difficult. The difficulty of the language reflects the nature of citizenship education and the complexity of the issues we are asking young people to engage with. In Northern Ireland, the very concept

of citizenship is problematic; it is therefore important that the conceptual areas be seen as problematic as well, in that they give rise to issues that are open to multiple, conflicting, and changing interpretation.

(Arlow)

The pilot projects promote an analysis of the multiple, conflicting, and changing interpretations of contentious issues—in other words, making the definitions and codes themselves problematic inspires a different kind of shared civic ownership in vital areas of public life.

Critical examination of established scholarship

In other cases, such as Rwanda, research is crucial to defining fundamental questions relative to the experience of violence before any significant effort may be made to promote reconciliation and national cohesiveness through formal education. Because Rwanda is, as yet, engaged in relatively early stages of curriculum policy reform, much of the discussion in chapter seven is a blend of both early data analysis and conceptual rigor, mapping out questions and facilitating consultation for possible responses. From the very beginning, the study's authors question the blind importation of "scholarship," including (as mentioned previously) the relevance of theories of race and ethnicity in explaining the genocide, thus raising the fundamental question of the responsibility of scholars in the dynamics of identity-based, or so-called "ethnic conflict." Such questioning leads to the search for a valid response to the authors' concerned refrain of "Why Rwanda?" The current challenge to write an official national history whose purpose is to strengthen a common national identity, requires a redefinition of citizenship, which, in turn, requires, at least partly, a redefinition of scholarship and its incumbent responsibility.

> We maintain that in contrast to the robust efforts to restore security and infrastructure following the devastation in 1994, not enough critical attention has been focused on analysing and assessing the ways in which schools understand and teach about the Rwandan genocide. This is true with respect both to analysing and assessing how schools develop this understanding and also to the means that they have at their disposal. Education has clearly been used to divide the Rwandan society. However, the authors are convinced that through restoring memory and reconstructing history as objectively as possible, Rwandans can gradually be helped to draw together as one nation.
>
> (Rutayisire et al)

CONCLUSION AND PERSPECTIVES

The studies presented in this book focus on the (political) process of reconciliation and of social and civic reconstruction embedded in (sovereign) educational policy reform. The central question is to determine how societies are reconstructing themselves regarding sovereign and sensitive issues related to the (re)definition of national identities, memory, sense of citizenship, and shared destiny. Who has the power to define what official identity is or includes at the level of the nation-state? And, equally crucially, how is this done? In terms of the direction of curriculum policy reform, such questions imply uncovering the power structures that determine who is in a position to define policy, who continues to be excluded, and how this political dynamic functions.

> The construction of national imaginaries provides a way to think about the discourses of educational reform and research. They should not be thought of as descriptive of change

but as embodying a deep reshaping of the images of social action and consciousness through which individuals are to relate to the multiple global and local contexts in which they participate.

(Popkewitz, 2000)

In each of the seven societies presented in this book, the specific nature of the social divisions has implications for the conceptualisation of citizenship and a direct influence on the challenges posed to educational policy reform in terms of (re)defining national culture and identity through language policies, social studies, and the teaching of subjects such as history, geography, civics, literature, and religion. The examination of education and conflict in these societies demonstrates the ways in which schooling can be the primary and contested terrain within which the structure of national identity is formed. Each of the contexts of conflict may be characterised as identity-based in which national monocultural state or subnational sectarian identities have been claimed as the legitimate basis for political violence. Questions of identity, as they relate to social cohesion, are essential to investigate given that they relate to inclusion/ exclusion, and often to division and conflict.

How social cohesion is defined with regard to educational policymaking in the wake of violent political conflict is largely linked to the way in which the goals of schooling are conceptualised. In examining education policy in the seven societies presented here, there are three things being asked (more explicitly in some cases than in others) of the curriculum development process, namely, that it[4]

1. become aware of its own potential role in having served as one of the underlying causes of the conflict (assessing language policies, history curriculum, and pedagogical and structural approaches adopted concerning identity formation);

2. attempt to deal with the legacy of the conflict (incorporating reconciliation and peace-building philosophies and practices); and

3. attempt to prevent any further outbreak of violent conflict (promoting tolerance, critical thinking, and values commonly esteemed by society).

The resulting aims of curriculum reform reflect different aspects of social cohesion. Furthermore, as it is by no means a static concept, in considering these questions social cohesion is shown to have undergone a conceptual evolution over time in the context of each education system. For example, in the case of Mozambique,

> The new curriculum nevertheless introduces important changes as it redefines Mozambican national identity in terms of a multilingual and multicultural society. The continuing effort to "preserve national unity," in other words, is not in doubt. It is the definition of what constitutes national unity that is undergoing a transformation.

(Balegamire Bazilashe et al)

It is worth bearing in mind while reading the chapters that follow how the different perception of what social cohesion means and how it functions plays out in the national policy arena. The study of Rwanda, for instance, demonstrates the possible tension between the aims of the economic policies and the aims of the education policies, both of which are ostensibly operating under a paradigm of social cohesion.

> [I]n spite of the emphasis on increasing the access to and improving the quality of education for young Rwandans, very little attention has been paid to investing in an assessment of how schools understand and teach about issues related to values that reinforce social cohesion, citizenship, human rights, peace, unity, and reconciliation.
>
> (Rutayisire et al)

Are policymakers and other stakeholders operating under the same national paradigm of social cohesion when determining different policies? How are assumptions framing consequences? In developing education policy under the paradigm of social cohesion, the majority of these seven societies are redefining and reconceptualising what "diversity" and inclusive policies are able to contribute as inputs. Examining these processes enriches our understanding of social cohesion. In the cases of Rwanda, Sri Lanka, and Guatemala, there appear to be clear steps in the process of reflecting on what social cohesion has meant in the past, how that definition has itself been exclusive, what the dangers and consequences have been, and how the concept has thus transformed and evolved along very similar lines to those of education policies in societies emerging from civil strife. Social cohesion, which is also described as "national unity," "national cohesion," "social harmony," "internal social peace" (*salam ahli*), "unity in diversity," and "unity and reconciliation" is thus increasingly understood as an idea that acknowledges and legitimates the presence of multiple national identities. Its effective meaning can be seen in processes of curriculum development.

Endnotes

[1] International workshop organised by the World Bank devoted to *Curricula, Textbooks, and Pedagogical Practices and the Promotion of Peace and Respect for Diversity* (Washington, March 24–26, 2003); OECD brainstorming meeting devoted to *Promoting Social Cohesion Through Education* (Paris, July 3, 2003); UNESCO IBE regional seminar on *Curriculum Reform and Social Cohesion in Central America* (San José, Costa Rica, November 5–7, 2003); International Conference organised jointly by the European Centre for Conflict Prevention and the Netherlands National Commission for UNESCO on *Conflict Resolution in Schools: Learning to Live Together* (Soesterberg, The Netherlands, September 15–16, 2003); International summer school on *Post-Conflict Reconstruction in the Education Sector* organised jointly by the UNESCO International Institute for Educational Planning and the World Bank Institut Paris (July 7–15, 2003); internal seminar at the UK Department for International Development (DfID) devoted to *Education and Conflict* (London, December 5, 2002); and UNESCO international experts meeting on *Textbooks and Learning Materials: Component of Quality Education That Can Foster Peace, Human Rights, Mutual Understanding and Dialogue* (Paris, December 12–13, 2002).

[2] It is also to be noted in this respect that Chapter 2 on Bosnia and Herzegovina does not provide a historical context both because the author is not from the region nor specialised in the history of the Balkans, and because the recent history of the region and the analysis of armed conflict in the Balkans in the 1990s remains highly controversial.

[3] Michael Arlow, statement made during international seminar (Geneva, April 3, 2003).

[4] The authors would like to thank Nat Colletta at the Institute for Peacebuilding and Development (Washington) for his comments in this regard.

References

Anderson, B. (1991.) *Imagined Communities: Reflections on the Origin and Spread of Nationalism*. Revised and extended edition. London: Verso.

Beauvais, C., and Jenson, J. (2002.) *Social Cohesion: Updating the State of the Research*. Canadian Policy Research Networks Discussion Paper No. F/22. Ottowa. Available at http://www.cprn.org.

Burgess, P. (2002-2004.) Network on Identity-Based Conflict, International Peace Research Institute (PRIO) Research Project. Oslo. http://www.prio.no/page/Project_detail/Staff_alpha_ALL/9244/37853.html

Bush, K., and Saltarelli, D. (2000.) *The Two Faces of Education in Ethnic Conflict: Towards a Peace-Building Approach to Education*. UNICEF Innocenti Center.

Gellner, E. (1983.) *Nations and Nationalism*. Ithaka, New York: Cornell University Press.

Heyneman, S. (2001.) *Measuring the Influence of Education on Social Cohesion*. Paper presented to the Oxford International Conference on Education and Development.

Hobsbawm, E. J. (1992.) *Nations and Nationalism since 1780: Programme, Myth, Reality*. 2nd ed. Cambridge: Cambridge University Press.

Isaacs, A. (2000.) Education, Conflict and Peacebuilding: A diagnostic tool. Ottawa: Canadian International Development Agency.

Mehta, U. (1997.) "Liberal Strategies of Exclusion." In: F. Cooper and A. Stoler, eds., *Tensions of Empires: Colonial Cultures in a Bourgeois World*. Berkeley: University of California Press.

Meyer, J., Boli, J., Thomas, G., and Ramirez, F. (1997.) *World Society and the Nation-state*. American Journal of Sociology, 103 (1), 144-181.

Popkewitz, T. S., Pereyra, M. A., Franklin, B. M. (2001.) "History, the problem of knowledge, and the new cultural history of schooling." In:, Popkewitz, T.S., Franklin, B.M., Pereyra, M.A., eds., *Cultural History and Education: Critical Essays on Knowledge and Schooling*. New York: Routledge Falmer.

Popkewitz, T., S. (2000.) *Educational Knowledge: Changing relationships between the State, Civil Society, and the Educational Community*. State University of New York Press, Albany.

Rosenmund, M. (2000.) "Approaches to international comparative research on curricula and curriculum-making processes." In: *Journal of Curriculum Studies* 32(5): 599-606.

Salmi, J. (2000.) *Violence, Democracy and Education: An Analytical Framework*. LCSHD Paper No. 56, Human Development Department. Washington: World Bank.

Sinclair, M. (2002.) *Planning Education in and After Emergencies*. Fundamentals of Educational Planning 73. Paris: UNESCO International Institute for Educational Planning.

Smith, A., and Vaux, T. (2003.) *Education, Conflict and International Development.* DFID Issues Paper, London.

Tawil, S., and Harley, A. (2003.) "Education and Conflict in EFA Discourse," *Norrag News* (13): 43-47.

Tawil, S., ed. (1997.) *Educational Destruction and Reconstruction in Disrupted Societies.* Final report of meeting, May 5–6, 1997. Geneva: UNESCO International Bureau of Education.

UNESCO. (2002.) "Education for All: Is the World on Track?" EFA Monitoring Report. Paris, UNESCO.

———— . (2000.) Dakar Framework for Action, Education for All: Meeting our collective commitments. Dakar, April 2000.

————. (2000.) "Education in Situations of Emergency and Crisis." Thematic Assessment Study Prepared for the World Education Forum in Dakar, Paris: UNESCO.

UNESCO. (1990.) World Declaration on Education for All: Meeting our basic learning needs. Jomtien, Thailand, 1990.

UNESCO. IBE. (2002.) Report of the August 29–30 Technical Meeting on Curriculum Change and Social Cohesion in Conflict-Affected Societies, unpublished, Geneva.

UNICEF. (1999.) Peace Education in UNICEF, Working Paper Series. Education Section, New York.

Wieviorka, M. (1998.) "Le nouveau paradigme de la violence," *Culture et conflits,* 29–30.

Appendix 1: Analytical Framework

1. Background to conflict	
Nature of social divisions	• Nature of social divisions • Nature of group identity (language, religion, "ethnicity") • How group identity is articulated with social/political divisions • Issues of "cultural defensiveness" and inflexibility.
Nature of conflict	• Type of conflict: internal armed conflict/disturbances; political violence; sectarian violence; "ethnic conflict"; civil strife—"identity-based conflicts" in which very existence of communities is perceived to be under threat • Difficulties in naming the conflict • Scale and intensity of violence • Duration of violence/recency
Nature of peace	• Nature of political agreement • Nature of external involvement • How the role of education reform/curriculum change is articulated in peace agreements (if at all)
2. Characteristics of present-day education system (with historical background as relevant)	
Management system	• Degree of centralisation/decentralisation • Level of democratisation of policy structure • Fragmentation?: potential difficulties in identifying locus of decisionmaking authority • "Real" decisionmaking power
School system	• Structure of school system (segregated, assimilated, integrated, other) • School types: public, private, community, other • Share of overall enrolment in each school type
Institutional setting for curriculum development	• What is/are the department(s) that translate policy decisions and develop curricula materials ? (institutional mechanisms & structures) • What is the relative degree of authority/autonomy of this/these department(s) with regard to central education authorities?

Educational/curricular traditions	• What is being built on?
	• What are the national pedagogical traditions?
	• What are the curriculum traditions?
	• What has been done in the past?
	• What are the characteristics of the examination system?
	• What is the pedagogical style?
Implications for reform	• How do these traditions impact on possibilities for effective curriculum changes/innovations?
	• To what extent do educational traditions influence present policy decisions?
	• What are the implications for teacher training?

3. Economic context of reform (internal and external)	
Resource assessment	• How does economic context determine possibilities for consultation (languages, translation, evaluative research, surveys, national workshops/debates)?
	• How do resource assessments (textbook development, teacher training) impact on the scope of policy change?
Nature of donor involvement	• What is the degree of dependency (if any) on external funding, expertise, and/or initiatives for implementation of curriculum change?
	• What impact (if any) does this have on curriculum policy choices (rationales and direction of change, as well as modalities for consultation)?

4. Rationales for curriculum policy change: Schooling as a factor of conflict and reconciliation	
Rationales for curriculum change (why change?)	*Change is introduced on the basis of a recognised weakness in the relevance of existing curricula in reflecting the ways in which society has changed as a result of conflict and/or in promoting the types of social changes perceived as being necessary in order to ensure transition out of armed conflict and political violence and the consolidation of peace.*
	• What assessment (evaluative research, surveys, national workshops) of the relevance of curricula have informed the need for change?
	• What has been identified as having potentially contributed to the conflict in the first place?
	• How has this been identified and by whom?
	• What is the level of political will to undertake change?

5. Rethinking what is "legitimate" knowledge (understood broadly as "learning content")	
Changes in curricular paradigms	• Has the conflict provoked a shift in curriculum paradigms? • If so, how has the curriculum paradigm shifted from the "pre-conflict" period to the present? • How has the curriculum model or approach changed? • What philosophical premises are these decisions based on? • How is curriculum conceptualised and by whom? • What is curriculum policy reform thought/assumed to be capable of in terms of its contribution to peace-building, stability, reconciliation, social cohesion etc ? • Does hope (future orientation) play a role?: Is the curriculum reform asking the present to confront the future, the past, both?
Direction of curriculum change	• What needs to change as a result of the paradigm shift? • In what ways are the aims and principles of education reformulated? • Does this reformulation move toward reinforcing a common national identity (through assimilation) or toward the recognition of multiplicities in reconciliation/reconstruction?
6. Policy dialogue, consensus building, and resistance: **Challenges posed by sensitive learning areas**	
Modalities of consultation and participation in policy reform	• Who is consulted in the process of reviewing and changing curriculum policy (stakeholders)? • What is the nature of their participation? • Whose voices are heard, and how are they expressed? • Whose voices are not heard? • What is the process of consultation? • How does it emerge after prolonged period of conflict? • What are the motives and levels/degrees of influence of stakeholders? • The quality of their input? The genuineness of the consultation? • Who is undertaking to consult?

Identifying difficult issues with regard to sensitive learning areas	• Are there any contentious/sensitive/difficult issues to resolve? (particularly in areas of learning such as languages, social studies, civics, religious studies, history, etc., that touch upon collective memory, identity, sense of citizenship?). Which ones? • What are the different viewpoints/conflicts of interest among stakeholders with regard to the learning areas listed below? ***Culture and Languages*** • Status of official national language(s) • Language(s) of instruction • "National" literature **Civics/citizenship** • Thematic, multidisciplined approach or discrete subject? • Degrees of flexibility • Questions of contradictions between content and methodology **History** • Rewriting of official history. • Does the curricular reform perpetuate tradition/status quo or introduce a critical historiography? (necessary preconditions for the latter? Recency of conflict, etc.) • Is the reform questioning a founding myth of a national identity (as opposed to a more "recent" history)? **Religion** • Religious instruction versus culture of religions
Consensus building: Dealing with difficult issues	• How are conflicting views dealt with? • How is consensus reached? • How does consensus building come about or change throughout the distinct phases of policy dialogue, policy formulation, and policymaking? • Ids there any risk of polarisation? • Might it be counterproductive to discuss certain issues at certain times? • What are the processes of negotiation and of consensus building adopted in drafting and approving curriculum frameworks and subject curricula? • What strategies are employed to deal with these difficult issues?

Curriculum balance	• How is learning content reorganised and restructured? • What decisions are involved? • How is a new curriculum balance defined? • How is the issue of overcrowded curriculum approached? • Infusion and cross-curricular models vs. separate subjects. • In an effort to create space for additional content, what is reduced (removed, left out, rejected)? • How does this impact explicit policies about teaching methods?
7. Research, monitoring, and evaluation	
Pilot programmes	• Role of pilot programmes and way in which these may (re)inform curriculum policy decisions (What is the scale of pilot programs? Who is involved? Is evaluation taking place?)
Monitoring policy & practice: Identifying indicators of change (if applicable)	• Has any evaluation been undertaken on recent curriculum change? If so, what type, with what results, and with what implications for (re)informing policy and implementation? • Research carried out to identify gaps, obstacles, limitations, etc. • Role of evaluative research in identifying degree of receptivity/resistance in the implementation of curriculum changes. • What is the nature of the resistance that may be encountered?
Perspectives of youth	• How do youth/students perceive reform? • How do they see education in relation to conflict?

Chapter 2

Curriculum Development, Diversity, and Division in Bosnia and Herzegovina

Philip Stabback

About the Author

The author is an experienced Australian education administrator who was attached to the UNESCO field office in Sarajevo as a senior education expert from August 2001 to June 2002, and was then the interim director of education in the Organisation for the Security and Cooperation in Europe (OSCE) during July and August 2002. In this latter role, he was responsible for establishing the inclusive consultation structures and mechanisms that led to the development of the Education Reform Strategy Paper (November, 2002) described later in this chapter.

On a methodological note, and as a part of documenting this study, in February 2003 the author also conducted a research study in BiH to test a number of the hypotheses that were forming the basis of this study. (The report of the research study is referenced among the "Key Reference Documents" at the end of this chapter.) In addition, this study has been developed using the in-country experience and expertise in the UNESCO field office in Sarajevo.

List of Acronyms

BAM	Bosnian Convertible Mark (ISO currency code)
BiH	Bosnia and Herzegovina
EC	European Commission (European Union)
EC-TAER	European Commission—Technical Assistance to Education Reform
FBiH	Federation of Bosnia and Herzegovina
FRY	Federal Republic of Yugoslavia
GFA	General Framework Agreement for Peace
IBE	International Bureau of Education
OECD	Organisation for Economic Co-operation and Development
OHR	Office of the High Representative (in Bosnia and Herzegovina)
OSCE	Organization for Security and Cooperation in Europe
RS	Republika Srpska
SFRY	Socialist Federal Republic of Yugoslavia
SMS	Shared Modernisation Strategy
SWOT	Strengths, Weaknesses, Opportunities, Threats
UNDP	United Nations Development Program
UNESCO	United Nations Educational, Scientific (and) Cultural Organization
UNHCR	United Nations High Commission for Refugees
UNICEF	United Nations Children's Fund (formerly United Nations International Children's Emergency Fund)
VET	Vocational Education and Training

INTRODUCTION

Background

The social fabric and infrastructure of Bosnia and Herzegovina (BiH)[1] were devastated by the war that raged in the country from 1992 to 1995 and which marked the final disintegration of the former Yugoslavia. Over 250,000 BiH citizens were killed, with very high casualties among civilians, including children, and millions sought refuge either in other countries or other parts of BiH.

The educational system also suffered, with more than half of the country's school buildings sustaining significant damage, a great many classrooms left uninhabitable, and resources badly depleted. While valiant attempts were made to continue schooling during the war, often under very difficult and dangerous circumstances, it is clear that education services generally were severely disrupted.

Given the extent of the damage, it is understandable that the primary focus of postwar reconstruction was on infrastructure and hardware rather than on issues of curriculum and teaching quality. In recent years, however, the importance of these latter issues has become apparent. BiH has demonstrated, through its application for accession to the Council of Europe, a desire to be recognised as a unified, democratic state. Its citizens want to understand and enjoy the freedoms of modern democracies and to achieve the standard of living experienced elsewhere in Europe. Education, and curriculum in particular, has much to contribute to this transformation.

Change in BiH since the war, particularly in the education sector and more specifically in curriculum and curriculum policy, has been a complex and laborious process. The following factors have contributed to this complexity:

- The emergence during the war and the post-conflict consolidation of three parallel curricula, each one purporting to represent the heritage and ideology of one of the country's three constituent peoples—Bosniaks, Croats, and Serbs—and accompanied by deeply entrenched, ideologically based policy positions.
- A high level of political involvement in education and a fundamental and pervasive lack of trust among politicians and political parties of each other and each other's motives.
- The creation by the General Framework Agreement for Peace (GFA), generally referred to as the Dayton Agreement, of a complex administrative structure in the country, consisting of two entities, one of which (Republika Srpska, or Serb Republic) is highly centralised and one of which (Federation of BiH) is a highly decentralised federation of ten cantons, some of which are predominantly Croat, some of which are predominantly Bosniak, and some of which are "mixed."[2] Ethnic allegiances exist between some cantons. This structure has resulted in twelve education policymaking authorities (thirteen if the separately administered Brcko District is included) with no state-level mechanism (such as a ministry) or framework for interauthority, countrywide policy dialogue.
- The increasing rate of refugees and internally displaced persons (IDPs) returning to their prewar homes as minority populations. These returnees are frequently unable to

access an acceptable curriculum and sometimes are unable to attend local schools or are segregated within those schools.

- The existence of a large international community (IC) effort in the education sector that was, at times, internally competitive and, until recently, was purely project based with no coordinating strategy. The relationship between the IC and local authorities is colored by the existence of the high representative, whose mandate is the implementation of civilian aspects of the GFA. The high representative is the ultimate constitutional authority in BiH, superior to that of democratically elected governments.

Definition of "curriculum"

Within this context, curriculum remains old-fashioned, and curriculum development processes and policy are highly centralised and controlled by each educational authority. There would appear to be no commonly agreed definition of "curriculum" as an overarching concept. This absence of a consensual definition, compounded by the fragmented nature of educational responsibility, explains the absence of any broad curriculum statements or documents and the lack of a countrywide curriculum policymaking body.

In fact, there is no equivalent word for "curriculum" in any of the three official languages, and it is normally translated as *plan i program*—"plan and program." In understanding the context in BiH, it is therefore important to distinguish between the concepts of "curriculum" and "syllabus." Curriculum development and curriculum policy in BiH focuses almost entirely at the level of syllabus (perhaps a more accurate interpretation of "plan and program"), with little or no connecting framework of objectives, learning outcomes, or guiding principles.

Syllabi themselves consist of detailed lists of facts and other information (referred to in translation as "factography") to be learned and memorised. This approach has led, in turn, to syllabi being overloaded (as more information is added) and disconnected from each other. Another frequent criticism is that the information prescribed in them is often repeated in later grades.

BACKGROUND TO THE CONFLICT

The nature of social composition

The Balkans region, and particularly the central part that now comprises the country of Bosnia and Herzegovina, has a long history of cultural diversity and richness, and also of conflict and conquest. This derives in large part from its geographical position as a major route for cultural and trade exchange between Europe, to the west and north, and the eastern Mediterranean and Asia, to the south and east.

Over the centuries, the area has been part of the Roman, Byzantine, Ottoman, and Austro-Hungarian empires, the kingdom of Yugoslavia, and, in the period after World War II, the Socialist Federal Republic of Yugoslavia. This succession of profound cultural and social influences has created a society in BiH that is quintessentially multicultural, and, in social terms, both rich and complex.

The population of BiH is comprised of three cultural groups, or "constituent peoples"[3]—Serbs, Croats, and Bosniaks—as well as "others," including Jewish and Roma minorities.

Table 1: Population Figures[4]

Population before the war (according to 1991 census)	4,377,033
Religious/ethnic distribution	43.4% Bosnian Muslims 31.2% Bosnian Serbs 17.3% Bosnian Croats
Estimated deaths during the war	250,000–300,000
Persons displaced within one entity	1,000,000
Total number of internally displaced persons	1,500,000
Refugees in other countries	1,250,000

Source: UNESCO, 1996.

The impact of the 1992–95 war on the demographic profile of BiH was profound. Of particular importance were the exodus of business leaders, academics, and teachers, and the number of persons displaced both internally and internationally. The increasing rate of return of refugees and IDPs to their prewar homes has placed a great deal of pressure on authorities in the social sector. Significant changes in the ethnic composition of major centres, such as Sarajevo, have also impacted the social and political life of those communities.

It should be noted that there was a religious dimension both to the conflict itself and to various post-conflict political and social arrangements. The targeted destruction of religious buildings and icons during the war is evidence of this dimension. While it should not be assumed that religion is a central organisational ideology, the Bosniak constituency is, broadly speaking, Muslim, the Croat constituency is Roman Catholic, and the Serb constituency is Orthodox Christian.

The three major nationalist political parties, each of which represents one of the constituent peoples, all exert great influence in the political, economic, and social life of the country. This is illustrated through, for example, the emergence of three recognised official languages in BiH—Serbian, Croatian, and Bosnian, variants of the single Serbo-Croat language that existed prior to the 1992–95 conflict—and a distinct education system aligned to each people.

The existence of three major constituent peoples[5] has given rise to a partisan environment characterised by a fierce defence of cultural autonomy, often resulting in costly and inefficient administration of education and other institutions and processes. For example, the insistence that school textbooks be printed in three languages, necessitating smaller and more costly print runs, places a burden on education resources that the various systems can scarcely afford.

The nature of the conflict

A bitter three-sided war was fought in BiH from 1992 to 1995, and caused widespread devastation across the country, including the destruction of numerous school buildings and significant interruption to the provision of educational services. Millions of people were displaced, both to various areas of BiH and to other, mainly European, countries. The rate of return of these displaced people to their prewar homes has increased significantly in recent years, and many challenges relating to the education of returning children have emerged. In addition, significant redistributions of the populations of the three main constituent peoples occurred during and immediately following the war.

It has been commonly estimated that 258,000 people, representing 5.9 percent of the population, were killed in the war, including disproportionately large numbers of civilians, especially children. Of the three constituent peoples, the Bosniak population was hurt the worst, accounting for well more than half of all casualties.

Education facilities across the country were very badly affected:

> Well over half of all school buildings in Bosnia and Herzegovina have been seriously damaged, destroyed, taken over by the army or used to house people displaced by the war. In the remaining available spaces pupils, students and teachers occupy many classrooms that have been poorly maintained and have no glass in the windows, no doors and no heat.[6]

While claims have been made by education authorities in BiH that all children continued to receive basic education during the years of the war, it has become clear that this was not the case. There is no doubt that many teachers continued to provide, often at great personal risk, basic teaching under enormous duress. It is also true, however, that a great many teachers left the profession and even the country during this period, resulting in the necessary employment of large numbers of untrained teachers. This is especially true of instructors of foreign languages, many of whom sought refuge outside BiH or acquired employment with international organisations. In addition, changes to school routines were introduced to meet the accommodation emergency, including the introduction of two or even three school shifts a day and a shortening of the school year.

It is also clear that the education process for many people was severely disrupted or terminated during the war. By way of illustration, in the period 2000–02, the Central Bosnia Canton authorities, encouraged and supported by the UNESCO office in Sarajevo, identified more than 640 people,[7] mostly between the ages of sixteen and twenty-five, who had not completed elementary school. As a result, these people have until now been excluded from further education and employment as well as from, for example, obtaining a driver's license. A simple extrapolation based on this canton would suggest that more than ten thousand young BiH citizens may not have received a basic education because of the conflict.

The ethnic "cleansing" of many areas of the country, the long siege of Sarajevo, and other war-related events have left deep social, physical, and psychological scars on BiH. Whether it was, in fact, a civil war, a war of aggression, or some other type of conflict will no doubt be debated for many years. What is presently very clear is that the legacy of the conflict is a divided, even fragmented, country whose leaders, in many cases, see education as a means of sustaining ideology and promoting politico-cultural identity, and who focus far more vigorously on differences than on similarities.

The nature of the peace

As a result of the signing of the General Framework Agreement (GFA) for Peace in 1995, two entities were established in BiH: the Republika Srpska (with a centralised administration), which is predominantly Serb; and the Federation of BiH, which consists of ten cantons, each having a constitutional responsibility for education. As indicated on Map 1, some cantons are predominantly Bosniak, some are predominantly Croat, and some are mixed. A separate district of Brcko was also created, and is administered under international supervision. Consequently, there are thirteen individual education jurisdictions of three different types in the country.

Other than listing education as a fundamental human right to which all citizens are entitled, the GFA and its annexes made no specific reference to education, and consequently gave it no official status or priority in postwar reconstruction activities. Under the BiH Constitution, no powers in education rest with the state-level government, although some efforts have been made to interpret the jurisdiction of the Ministry of Civil Affairs as including some responsibility for education.[8]

Early postwar reconstruction in education concentrated on the rebuilding of infrastructure, particularly school buildings. However, since 1999, attention has increasingly been given to such matters as curriculum modernisation and harmonisation, and pedagogy.

Nevertheless, some of the rationales of the GFA have combined with persistently contentious politics to particularly ill effect for education. The situation, as described below in a report by the OECD in September, 2001, remains much the same today:

> The decentralising logic of Dayton has made education a hostage to latent nationalism in BiH. Politically, education is seen largely as a vehicle for creating three separate national histories, languages and cultures, rather than as a way to develop a common State identity. Although there are few substantial differences in policy or practice across the Entities or cantons, the politics of separation make co-ordination difficult. A second constraint is the lack of clarity in the relative powers of the four levels of governance, particularly in the FBiH.

The implementation of the GFA is supervised and monitored by the high representative, whose authority derives from the agreement. The high representative is described in Annex 10 of the GFA as the final authority "in theatre" to interpret the agreement and to supervise the implementation of civilian aspects of the peace settlement. The high representative is nominated by the steering board of the Peace Implementation Council, and is endorsed by the United Nations Security Council.

The Office of the High Representative (OHR) exerts significant influence in all aspects of reconstruction, and the high representative has broad powers to impose legislation as required. This supervisory role of the international community (IC) over the elected government of the country is unusual, and has contributed to a dynamic between the IC and local authorities and between members of the IC itself which is perhaps unique among countries emerging from periods of conflict.

The IC has played a significant role in all facets of rebuilding the country. The UN mission to BiH focused largely on the rebuilding of civil police forces and the judiciary, while the mission of the Organisation for Security and Co-operation in Europe (OSCE) concentrated on the areas of human rights, security, elections, and democratisation. Immediately following the war, sixty thousand NATO troops were deployed across BiH as a peacekeeping force, and approximately twelve thousand remain there today as a stabilisation force.

Other major organisations, including UNESCO, UNDP, UNICEF, the World Bank, and various European organisations (most notably the European Union and the Council of Europe), have also been active in reconstruction activities. Bilateral donors have helped to rebuild all aspects of the social and physical infrastructure, and almost three hundred NGOs working in BiH list "education and training" among their areas of interest.

It is important to note, however, that significant tensions between members of the IC have manifested themselves at various times and over various issues. It is most likely that these tensions are due to markedly different, although not necessarily contradictory, priorities— those that seek immediate, even imposed, solutions to urgent problems, and those that seek sustainable, locally supported redevelopment and modernisation of systems, including education systems and curriculum. These divisions have been exacerbated by the fragmentation of education decisionmaking in the country, and by the inability of governments to articulate to the IC clear directions and priorities for education reform.

Further pressure is brought to bear on this environment by the requirements placed on BiH for its accession to the Council of Europe. These requirements include "the fundamental reform of the existing parallel education systems of Bosnia and Herzegovina."[9]

Map 1: Federation of Bosnia and Herzegovina and Republika Srpska

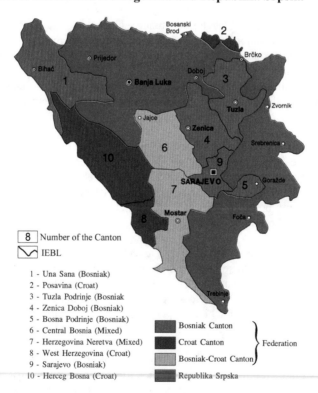

8 — Number of the Canton
IEBL

1 - Una Sana (Bosniak)
2 - Posavina (Croat)
3 - Tuzla Podrinje (Bosniak
4 - Zenica Doboj (Bosniak)
5 - Bosna Podrinje (Bosniak)
6 - Central Bosnia (Mixed)
7 - Herzegovina Neretva (Mixed)
8 - West Herzegovina (Croat)
9 - Sarajevo (Bosniak)
10 - Herceg Bosna (Croat)

Bosniak Canton
Croat Canton   } Federation
Bosniak-Croat Canton
Republika Srpska

Source: http://www.ohr.int/ohr-info/maps/images/federation-of-bih.gif.

CHARACTERISTICS OF THE PRESENT-DAY SYSTEM

The present education system in BiH derives much of its practice from the system of the former Socialist Federal Republic of Yugoslavia (SFRY). During the socialist era (1945–90), education was a high priority for the SFRY government, and concerted efforts were made to provide free and compulsory education for all citizens. However, the system experienced the following problems:

- education gradually became a lower priority for government;
- a high level of "ideologisation and politicisation" of curricula developed;
- educational governance became more centralised; and
- there were high levels of uniformity, and a lack of diversity.[10]

These factors are critical influences on the education systems that were developed in BiH following the 1992–95 war.

Management system

General

As mentioned above, responsibility for education administration in BiH rests with thirteen distinct authorities: the government of the Republika Srpska (RS); the government of the Federation of BiH, which has a role in coordinating the functions of the cantons; the ten canton governments within the federation; and the district of Brcko. Each of these authorities has its own education legislation.

There is considerable variation in size and structure among these authorities, from the RS government administering education for approximately one-third of the country's children to the Education Ministry in Bosna Podranje Canton (Gorazde), which has responsibility for just ten schools.

With regard to resources, it should be noted that, with the exception of the Brcko District, whose budget has been heavily subsidised by the international community, all education authorities have great difficulty meeting expenditure commitments. It is generally agreed that teachers are poorly paid, and it is common for salary payments to be several months in arrears, despite levels of public expenditure on education in BiH being "significantly high compared with European norms."[11]

Wide disparities also exist in education expenditure across the country, in both per capita and per pupil terms, resulting in significant inequities in educational opportunity. For example, the annual expenditure per student is BAM 285 (approximately US$169) in Sarajevo Canton, and BAM 99 (approximately US$58) in Bosna Podranje Canton.[12]

Of critical importance is the lack of any countrywide framework for policy development in the education sector generally, or for curriculum, standards, teaching quality, assessment, and certification in particular.[13] All administration procedures and educational policy are prescribed in "books of rules," a vestige of the former SFRY regulatory system, on which schools and local authorities rely heavily. It is equally clear, however, that such a system does not result in equity of opportunity or outcomes.

Republika Srpska

The administration of the RS is highly centralised and reflects to a very large degree the structures and practices of the former SFRY. Government offices, including the Ministry of Education, are located in Banja Luka, in the western RS, which in itself presents serious challenges of geographical distance from isolated regions in the east. (See Map 1 above.) The RS Education Ministry is responsible for curriculum and policy development across the sector in the RS, although administration and financing responsibilities in secondary schools are devolved to municipalities.

Federation of Bosnia and Herzegovina

Within the federation, responsibility for education resides at two levels. The central, federal government has a coordinating function only, with no direct responsibilities for delivery of educational services. There are varying curricula in use in the federation's ten cantons, along the lines of the three characteristic divisions between the cantons themselves. Thus, a "Bosniak curriculum" is used in the five cantons with a Bosniak majority, a "Croat curriculum" is used in the three cantons with a Croat majority, and both curricula are used in the two "mixed" cantons where both Bosniaks and Croats are essentially equally represented. The situation is rather more complex, however, as none of the federation's cantons are totally uniform. Anytime there is a municipality dominated by a cantonal minority (as is the case, for example, in the Bosniak-majority cantons that include Croat-majority municipalities), the "minority" curriculum is used. "Where there is no constituent group of sufficient size to justify its own school, the children are free to attend classes in the dominant curriculum of the local community, which is a common occurrence throughout BiH, including RS" (OECD, 2001).

Until recently,[14] the education minister and deputy minister each represented one of the two dominant constituent peoples in the federation (Bosniaks and Croats). Fulfilling the coordinating function has proved difficult, chiefly due to the lack of willingness on the part of the Education Ministries in the cantons to relinquish any authority to the federation government, compounded at times by disagreement between the entity minister and the deputy minister. It could also be argued that the nature of the "coordinating role" of the entity ministry has never been clearly or fully elaborated.

Responsibility for the management and delivery of education, including matters of curriculum and quality teaching, are the direct responsibility of individual cantons. In cantons where there is a clear Bosniak or Croat majority, the minister and deputy minister are appointed from within the majority political party. In the three mixed cantons, a Croat minister always has a Bosniak deputy minister, and vice versa.

It should be noted that a number of inefficiencies arise from such arrangements. For example, in mixed cantons, parallel structures of institutions and administrative units have developed, "producing not only further fragmentation but also inefficiency and lack of transparency."[15] Matters of curriculum, appointment of school directors and boards, and the provision of education appropriate to minority returnee and refugee children are matters of ongoing contention and concern in all areas of the country, but are particularly complex in mixed cantons.

It is clear, however, that a phenomenon of "ethnic centralisation" exists in the federation. The influence of ethnically based political parties, not the Constitution, ensures the fragmentation of education authority and policymaking. This can be seen particularly, but not only, in Croat areas.

Pedagogical institutes

Reflecting the former SFRY structures, the RS and some cantons maintain pedagogical institutes (PI). The role of the PI is largely inspectorial and focuses on uniformity of curriculum, programming, and delivery as an indicator of quality. Due primarily to lack of resources, the functions themselves, as well as the capacities of PIs to carry them out, are very limited.

The school system

Throughout BiH, eight years of education is compulsory, commencing in most parts of the country at six years of age.[16] Following elementary school, three types of secondary education are available to students: a four-year "academic" education in gymnasia, a three-year vocational education, or a four-year technical or "professional" education, each conducted in specialised schools. There are also a number of more specialised "streams," in, for example, arts education, teacher training (for teachers of early primary grades), and religious education. Private schools are permitted by law in BiH and do receive state funding, but they constitute a very small part of the sector. For example, in the federation only three of the 1,026 elementary schools and six of the 204 secondary schools operating in 2000 were private.[17]

In 2001, the estimated enrolment rate of students in all types of secondary schools was 72.6 percent.[18] In terms of OECD norms, a disproportionately low number of students enrol in gymnasia (around 26 percent in the federation and 17 percent in the RS, compared to the OECD average of 51 percent). To compound this problem, the extent to which vocational and technical schools are meeting the needs of industry and the economy is doubtful. The vocational curriculum remains dominated by specific skills determined largely under the planned labour market regimes of the former SFRY, and teaching and learning are largely theoretical rather than practical. Vocational education and training (VET) curriculum generally was developed to meet the needs of an economy based on now largely dysfunctional heavy industry. As a result, it is unlikely that graduates of the VET system operating in BiH today are well equipped to seek employment or to contribute significantly to the economic recovery of the country.

The school system in BiH remains highly politicised. Political parties play a significant role in the appointment of school directors and members of school boards. At a systemic level, the high number of people with a professional education—particularly holders of university degrees—ensures that there is a keen awareness of the importance of education as a means of defending cultural identity and disseminating politico-cultural ideology. Moving from "socialist" education (with the interests of the state as its underpinning ideology) to "ethnic-nationalist" education (with the interests of an ethno-political group as its underpinning ideology) has been conceptually a simple matter.

As a result of this politicisation, the formation of working groups in curriculum development projects, for example, has frequently been characterised by disagreements about the ethnic constitution of groups and by the defence of established cultural positions.

Of particular concern to many progressive educators is the absence of any standardised and reliable assessment of outcomes or system of certification of student achievement, particularly at the crucial milestones—the end of elementary school, and the end of secondary education. There is concerted resistance, particularly but not only in the RS, to the establishment of any curriculum, accreditation, or certification agency at the state level. Certification and issues related to quality teaching and learning remain the responsibilities of individual schools. Schools apply largely unstated and probably inconsistent standards in the issuing of school certificates.

With regard to "standards," it would appear that, until relatively recently, the term was used synonymously with "uniformity." Little attention has been given to that notion of standards relating to student learning—that is, to the standard and quality of student learning and the comparability of grades awarded from one school to another. With the establishment of the Standards and Assessment Agency, work is being done to establish benchmarks of learning achievement, albeit in language and mathematics only and in a limited number of grades.

Of most concern to both the IC and many educators in BiH, however, is the continuing trend toward ethnic separation and alienation through the development of three distinct school and curriculum structures. Because responsibility for education rests with authorities and administrations with clear ethnic allegiances, it is understandable, if not inevitable, that those authorities, led by ethnically based political parties, have developed policies and approaches that reinforce and enhance their respective ideologies. Consequently, there is a Serb school system and curriculum in the Republika Srpska; a Croat school system and curriculum in several cantons, particularly in Western Herzegovina; and a Bosniak school system and curriculum.

Such structures inevitably have complex consequences. In mixed cantons, for example, both Croat and Bosniak schools exist, administered by two distinct and cost-inefficient systems. This divisive arrangement is complicated further by the return of refugees from within BiH and abroad to their prewar homes. Returning minorities are frequently presented with an education system that is inappropriate and even offensive to their cultural or religious beliefs.

Crude attempts to accommodate the needs of children from different socio-ethnic backgrounds have included the "two schools under one roof" system, in which two ethnically separate schools were established in one school premises, usually with separate entrances. This policy essentially institutionalises differences through the implementation of two curricula and the effective separation of children according to their ethnicity.

The trend toward ethnic separation became critical with the distribution by the federal Ministry of Education of a circular supporting these practices throughout the federation in 1997. This paper resulted in a marked increase in interest among members of the IC in education policy and in finding sustainable and acceptable policy solutions.

In the absence of a strong national identity in BiH, ill-conceived education policy can promote social division and, in many cases, alienation and intolerance. Since the end of the war, there has certainly been little evidence of any willingness on the part of political or educational leaders to compromise or to relinquish any responsibility for educational policy in order to achieve either improved administrative efficiency or enhanced educational opportunities for young people. It could further be argued that as "nationalists" and "nationalist" political parties have lost influence in other areas of public policy, education has become increasingly important to them.

The institutional setting for curriculum development

As described earlier, Republika Srpska and the canton ministries have responsibility for curriculum within their respective jurisdictions. Traditionally, ministers rely on pedagogical institutes for technical expertise in curriculum development, and it is common for cantons without pedagogical institutes to use the curriculum created by other, "allied" cantons. For example, Posavina Canton, a Croat-majority canton in the far north of the country, uses the Croat curriculum issued by the pedagogical institute in Mostar, in the southwest.

To draft new curriculum materials or syllabi, the ministry or pedagogical institute would most commonly establish a "commission" in, for example, a particular subject, under the supervision of the ministry. There is no responsibility for curriculum at the state level; consequently, there is no curriculum agency charged with developing a curriculum framework or common sets of standards with which the various authorities should comply.

Educational/curricular traditions and implications for reform

Standards of student learning achieved in the former Yugoslavia are generally considered to have been relatively high, and that significant reform and expansion of education occurred during the 1980s. However, those standards were achieved within a system characterised by

- "centralised" authority over curriculum, teaching methodology, and textbooks, with no authority delegated to regional authorities or schools;
- curriculum that consisted of vast bodies of information and facts with no attention given to the development of skills (such as skills of analysis and synthesis, research and problem solving) and attitudes;
- teacher-dominated methodology in which the teacher was seen to be the conveyor of knowledge and the students the recipients; and
- a relatively high level of isolation from other countries in Europe.

It is of significance that current policymakers in BiH were the successful products of this environment. In addition, they have had few opportunities to be exposed to other education systems and practices, because

- the war created specific and urgent reconstruction priorities;
- data from other countries are not as readily available as might be expected;[19] and
- little information about modern trends in curriculum is available in local languages.

Policymaking in curriculum and education generally is therefore based firmly on old models. Unsurprisingly, curriculum remains old-fashioned, dominated by decontextualised information and knowledge and with little recognition of skills, values, and attitudes as desirable learning outcomes. Teachers rely heavily on lecture and didactics, and on single, state-endorsed and state-produced textbooks.

General characteristics of curriculum

As alluded to in previous sections of this study, general education curriculum at both primary and secondary levels in BiH is very prescriptive and reflects in documentation, content, and implementation of the models common in the former SFRY. The notion of the discrete subject dominates the curriculum across the country, with little (if any) effort to integrate learning through cross-curriculum themes or broader content areas.

Each subject is assigned a number of hours or teaching lessons per week. This is strictly implemented and monitored, as far as resources allow, by the pedagogical institutes or the Ministries of Education. In general terms, sixteen lessons per week are required for grades one and two, twenty-six lessons for grades seven and eight, and up to thirty lessons for gymnasia. Quality of the curriculum is controlled through ensuring uniformity of inputs, defined largely in terms of time and content rather than on any detailed statement of outcomes and standards of learning that students are expected to achieve at each level and in each subject.

In describing content, curriculum across the country focuses almost entirely on knowledge and recall of facts. It is not surprising that, in such a context, learning is frequently by rote, and assessment tends to consist of students recalling and reciting factual details. When compared to contemporary curriculum paradigms and European trends in curriculum development and design, this model is seriously deficient. It pays little attention to the development of generic skills—including the skills of research and information gathering, of synthesis and analysis, of critical and lateral thinking, of communication, of information technology, and of forming and defending personal opinions and judgements—or to subject-specific skills and applications that underpin modern curriculum. Nor does it address the development of creativity and imagination, or values and attitudes, in any explicit or detailed way.

Curriculum policy decisions across BiH are made at the central authority level. Schools or groups of schools have little if any opportunity to design or adapt curriculum to local circumstances, such as to local social, economic, or geographical conditions. In such an environment, it is difficult for schools to consider or address the particular learning needs of individual students, or to capitalise on the resources available locally.

The national group of subjects

The ministerial agreement of May 10, 2000,[20] confirmed a category of subjects in the primary and general secondary curriculum known as the "national group of subjects" that had existed since the socialist era. While there is no evidence that the curriculum in these subjects in the former SFRY contributed to the breakdown of social cohesion, it is clear that it did little to prevent the breakdown that led eventually to conflict across the region.

The national group of subjects are those that are most closely connected to cultural identity and that call for personal, subjective judgements and interpretations. Consequently, they are of strategic interest to political parties, which, in most cases, represent cultural and ethnic interests and are therefore the most sensitive and controversial.

The national subjects are

- language and literature,
- history,
- music and art,
- religious instruction, and

- geography/nature and society (in elementary schools).

Interestingly, sociology and philosophy, studied in secondary schools and similar in nature to those listed above, are not included in the national group. It is difficult to establish the true rationale for the maintenance of this separate category of subjects in the curriculum of a modern state. However, possible reasons include

- their capacity for entrenching and sustaining ethnic differences;
- perceived threats to cultural identity and survival in a fragmented state in which the IC has ultimate authority; and
- a new affirmation of cultural identity as a reaction to earlier socialist curriculum in which the values of the state were paramount.

It is certainly likely that the various education authorities, encouraged by political parties, realise that these subjects provided the clearest opportunities for educating young people in the ethno-cultural ideologies of each of the three constituent peoples. Education authorities have defended stoutly their right to develop their own curriculum in these areas. In doing so, it could be argued that they are using the curriculum as a means of enshrining and sustaining social division in curriculum areas that would, in more stable circumstances, lend themselves most productively to encouraging social cohesion.

What is clear is that the categorisation of these national subjects presents a very real challenge for liberal thinkers and educators in BiH. In modern curriculum and school systems, these subjects are used to strengthen social cohesion, to encourage debate, to promote tolerance and understanding of students' own and other cultures, and to ensure the development of informed, critical, personal views of the world. It could also be argued, however, that the creation of the category of national subjects in BiH gives narrow-minded ethnic ideologues the opportunity to stifle debate, to use education to promulgate narrow, "nationalist" philosophies, and to present young people with inappropriate and sometimes inaccurate views of other cultural groups.

Textbooks

As was and largely remains the norm in Eastern European countries, curriculum and teaching in BiH relies heavily on textbooks. Generally a textbook is produced by the state (i.e., by an acceptable Ministry of Education) for each subject at each grade level, and is commonly written by a curriculum developer. It is expected that classes across each education jurisdiction will work through the textbooks at common rates and in common sequences. As a result, teaching is uniform and unresponsive to learning needs and styles of individuals, and learning is generally passive.

The nature and production of textbooks has been a source of continuing concern for the Office of the High Representative in BiH, and numerous attempts have been made to ensure that textbooks are free from offensive or inflammatory material. To achieve this, an inter-entity ministerial agreement was signed in Banja Luka on August 20, 1999. Through this agreement, ministers gave undertakings that offensive material would be removed from existing textbooks, that new textbooks would contain no offensive material, and that processes would be established that gave other Education Ministries opportunities to comment on textbooks and to object if necessary.

Implementation of this agreement has proved difficult, most frequently because ministries failed to comply with timelines (in making their textbooks available to ministries in other jurisdictions, for example). This gave rise to a new agreement, initiated by the OHR in December 2001, which required the establishment of new ministerial textbook commissions, as well as an OHR commission to oversee those of the entity ministers, and to act as final arbiter in sensitive matters. Responsibility for this process has recently been transferred to the OSCE.

Various Conferences of Entity Ministers[21] have addressed matters of offensive materials in textbooks. However, as recently as the school year 2001–02, a textbook supporting the Serb curriculum in primary-level social science was produced by the RS Education Ministry. On the cover of the book was a map purporting to depict "Greater Serbia," including the RS, with the clear implication that the RS was not part of Bosnia and Herzegovina. It would therefore seem that limited progress in policy terms is being made.

Similarly, little progress has been made in a transition toward the production of textbooks in a commercially competitive way. While this might in part be due to lack of resources in schools and systems to purchase commercially produced textbooks and by the underdeveloped nature of the publishing industry, it could also be explained by the unwillingness of education authorities to relinquish control over a powerful educational tool.

With regard to curriculum resources, there remains a heavy dependence on single, state-produced textbooks that restrict effective teaching and learning. Teachers are not trained to use their own creativity in devising teaching-learning activities and are not encouraged to supplement textbooks with other contemporary stimulus material. One recent development has been a tendering process for new textbooks for the 2003–04 school year, instigated by the federation. This has resulted in the approval of more than one textbook series and might signal a move to an open, competitive textbook market in some cantons.

Assessment

Assessment practices are similarly out of date. Assessments, even at the university level, are frequently oral, and the criteria for passing and failing assessments are unstated and inconsistent. There is no single or standardised examination or certification system at any stage of schooling, which, although understandable in the fragmented context, makes moving between schools difficult for students. The lack of a matura examination continues to frustrate attempts to have the education system respected by other countries.

Teacher training and future curriculum development

The implications of these traditions for future curriculum development and for teacher training are significant. The high levels of politicisation of curriculum development, the lack of experience and expertise in modern curriculum design and curriculum development processes, and the continued exclusion of experts, parents, and other stakeholders from curriculum processes will continue to inhibit progress.[22] Similarly, the development in teachers of a wider range of teaching strategies and shifting focus from teaching to learning—characteristics of modern school and curriculum systems—will place increasing demand on both preservice and in-service teacher training programs.

Any curriculum change requires an implementation strategy that recognises both the needs and the limitations of teacher training capability. It is unlikely that large-scale, extensive programs will be available in the near future in BiH. An integrated approach was certainly a fundamental principle of the Shared Modernisation Strategy (SMS) described below, which included a strand of pre- and in-service teacher training being developed concurrently with the curriculum framework strand. It is to be hoped that future phases of this project will adopt a similar approach.

Because resources for teacher training will be limited, whatever curriculum changes are introduced to BiH schools will need to accommodate, to the greatest extent possible, current practice. For example, in developing new syllabi for each subject, it will be important to minimise change to content itself, but to focus on the rearrangement of content to increase flexibility. This can be achieved, for example, through the application of a modular syllabus design incorporating a core and elective structure.

Nevertheless, it is likely that teachers will need to receive some introduction to the concept of a state-level curriculum framework (should one be developed), and be provided with opportunities to understand their responsibilities, if a more flexible syllabus design is adopted.

The resource implications for ministries of new curricula should be taken into account during the development phase, and should also be noted by governments as they undertake the reform of education budget processes.

The nature of current activities of the international community in education and curriculum

The incapacity of local authorities to find satisfactory solutions in such areas as the national group of subjects, and continuing lack of clarity in the use of such terms as core/joint/ common/harmonised/unified curriculum, has led to the IC becoming involved in curriculum and curriculum policy from a particular perspective. The IC role has become one of leader and initiator of curriculum reform, although its approach to such a role has sometimes lacked strategic focus.

Central to current reform efforts are the terms "harmonisation" and "modernisation," both of which appear in the Education Reform Strategy Paper adopted by the education ministers and approved by the Peace Implementation Council in November 2002. The OHR and, more recently, the OSCE have focused on harmonisation, which is perceived as a short-term alignment of current curriculum. This alignment of content, ensuring that topics in subjects are taught in the same grade in each of the three existing curricula, would facilitate mobility between systems which would be of particular advantage to returnee children.

The term "modernisation" is one used by agencies focusing on longer-term objectives, such as the European Commission (through the EC-TAER project described below) and some UN agencies, including UNESCO. This process would deliver a curriculum that is consistent with contemporary European practices, including being more relevant to contemporary and future society, being more flexible and responsive to student needs, and delivering outcomes for students in a range of domains.

This is not to say, however, that the terminology and descriptors employed by the IC have been clearly defined for all stakeholders. By way of illustration, in its recently published tender documents for the next phase of the EC-TAER project, the EC introduced the notion of a "decentralised core curriculum," the nature of which is not specified. While the support of the IC has been and remains vital, it has generally not pursued a coordinated and strategic approach to curriculum reform activities. It is possible that this deficiency will be addressed through the coordination efforts of the OSCE described below.

OSCE

In August 2002, the OSCE, supported by the OHR, assumed a coordinating role in the education sector among members of the IC. The OSCE established an education department within its mission to BiH, and was immediately charged by the high representative with responsibility for the development of an education reform strategy. In response, the OSCE developed a structure of representative working groups, regional groups, and a public education forum, all responsible to the Education Issues Set Steering Group, comprising the heads of major international organisations concerned with education. The working groups, regional groups, and forum attracted significant membership of local experts.

The strategy was developed during September and October of 2002, signed by the entity and cantonal ministers of education in November, and presented by them to the Peace Implementation Council in Brussels on November 25. It is anticipated that this document will provide a road map for reform of the education sector.

With regard to curriculum, the reform strategy paper describes a dual approach to reform: the development of a "harmonised, common core curriculum" for introduction in all education jurisdictions in the country for implementation at the beginning of the 2003–04 school year, and the development of a "modernised" curriculum by 2010.

The introduction of a harmonised curriculum is clearly seen as a short-term measure to facilitate the availability of an acceptable interim curriculum to all children, especially minority returnee children. The common core curriculum has recently been developed and is defined as a set of common topics for each subject and grade, and includes the national subjects (with the exception of religious instruction). It should be noted, however, that it is based on the existing syllabi and does not yet represent a "modernised" curriculum.

OHR

The OHR has transferred responsibility for education coordination to the OSCE. While it remains represented on all relevant committees and working groups, the OHR has closed its education department. The OHR does retain an executive authority to force local education authorities to comply in matters that it considers of particular concern.

UNESCO

UNESCO is involved in a range of activities in BiH and has been especially active in providing support to curriculum reform. This support has included commissioning research on the quality and acceptability of the curriculum in the national subjects (1999), a curriculum symposium in 2000 that was designed to suggest ways forward for BiH, significant technical support to the curriculum strand of the Shared Modernisation Strategy (2001–02), and a number of discrete curriculum-related activities. The UNESCO office in Sarajevo closed on September 30, 2003. However, UNESCO is continuing its support of curriculum reform in BiH through a capacity-building project designed to enhance the knowledge and skills of curriculum developers in the country. This project will train up to seventy curriculum experts in modern curriculum design and curriculum-making methodology. The project is being managed and implemented by the IBE.

UNICEF

UNICEF is managing a major project in BiH entitled Child-Friendly Schools. The project focuses on the training of teachers in modern, mostly interactive teaching methodology through which it is anticipated that schools will be managed and teaching and learning conducted in a child-friendly and effective manner. UNICEF also provides active leadership in the area of quality and modernisation of general education within the reform framework proposed and managed by the OSCE and described above.

European Commission

During 2001–02, the EC implemented a major reform project, which included the modernisation of primary and general secondary education. This reform came to be known as the Shared Modernisation Strategy. The amount and nature of activity of the project changed significantly in the autumn of 2002. The project's recent work has been directed at refining the recommendations contained in its first report. This led to the publication of a Green Paper (final recommendations) for consultation in April 2003 and a White Paper (agreed policy and strategy) in October 2003.

Council of Europe

The Council of Europe continues to support the Conference of Entity Ministers of Education as well as specific initiatives in curriculum, most notably in approaches to the teaching of history. The council has also played a leading role in the drafting of modernised education legislation.

World Bank

The World Bank is playing a key role in providing advice to the governments of BiH regarding efficient financing and administration of the education sector. Of particular relevance to curriculum development is the financial support provided by the bank to the BiH Standards and Assessment Agency. The Bank is currently developing the Education Restructuring Project to facilitate the implementation of the reforms in the strategy paper described below.

ECONOMIC CONTEXT OF REFORM

Resource assessment

As noted above concerning the general aspects of the management system, expenditure on education in BiH is significantly higher than European norms, but there are obvious inefficiencies in the way education funding is spent. It is not uncommon for cantons to exceed their budgets, sometimes quite early in the budget period, resulting in payment of teacher salaries being months in arrears, textbooks not being replaced, and plant and facilities being poorly maintained.

The precise nature of these inefficiencies remains unclear. It is frequently argued by some members of the IC that the major inefficiency is associated with the existence of three "parallel" curricula and there being three education systems in operation. While this might be a contributing factor in the context of BiH, it is probably not the only cause. Unsustainably large bureaucracies, the existence of large numbers of branch schools in rural areas, unproductive administrative practices, and lack of accountability and audit processes are likely to be significant contributors to inefficiency.

The Una-Sana Canton, for example, has a single curriculum, and the highest education expenditures both as a proportion of GDP (11.3 percent) and as a share of total expenditure (33 percent), in the federation.[23] While the existence of a very small university and the general level of poverty accounts in part for this relatively high expenditure, it should also be noted that the region's economy has virtually collapsed. In spite of these circumstances, the traditional administrative structures remain, and have even been expanded to fulfil the canton's responsibilities within the federation structure. On the other hand, the Neretva Canton, with two curricula and two universities, has the lowest GDP expenditures on education in the federation, but is a relatively wealthy canton.

As part of the Education Reform Strategy, the governments of BiH have undertaken to "establish financially sustainable budget allocations based on per pupil/student funding methods for all education levels . . . that promote a more efficient use of human resources . . . , school facilities and material support."[24]

Until such reforms take effect, there is unlikely to be sufficient funding available for the new textbooks or the teacher training required to support extensive curriculum reform.

The nature of donor involvement

In the absence of a solid and reliable funding base and sound management practices, BiH will continue to rely on the international community for both funding and technical assistance across the education sector. This dependency creates a relationship between local authorities and the IC that is somewhat complex.

Local authorities are generally proud of the educational traditions of the country and of the significant improvements that were made throughout the former Yugoslavia during the 1980s. However, they do recognise that little progress was made during the 1990s, and that the divided and ethnically driven systems which now exist represent a decline in standards. They also understand that the IC will be central to future reform.

The IC's initial postwar focus in BiH was on the rebuilding of schools and classrooms. In the late 1990s, when its attention turned to curriculum and the quality of education provision, its efforts lacked strategic vision and direction. However, renewed attempts at effective coordination were initiated by the OSCE in mid-2002, and the IC is now working in a coordinated and more strategic manner to achieve reform.

It is clear to the IC, as well as to local authorities, that a modern and efficient education system is central to the future development of BiH as a cohesive and prosperous state:

Our education system is crucial to the development of our country's intellectual capital. Our young people must be confident that they can receive the quality education that they require to open the door to the future—here at home.

We know that the education system here in BiH is in urgent need of modernisation. It has fallen behind the rest of Europe. We need to make a combined and sustained effort to enhance the quality of education across the board. Bosnia and Herzegovina's last and best chance for a viable future hinges on its young people.[25]

It cannot be claimed, however, that the local education community has unqualified trust in IC efforts. While the IC has been successful in brokering a number of inter-entity agreements and has generally promised a great deal, no countrywide, structural reform has been delivered, and the agendas of the different elements of the IC have often confused and overloaded local education authorities. The fragmented nature of education responsibility in BiH has made it impossible for entity and canton authorities to coordinate the country's reform efforts or to provide any consolidated strategic leadership to the IC. Exacerbating this problem is that the IC, until recently at least, has all too often shown little capacity to coordinate itself.

The relationship between local authorities and the IC also has been coloured by the supervisory capacity and function of the Office of the High Representative. Suspicion and recalcitrance on the part of local authorities at all levels have characterised numerous interactions with the IC, and have frequently led to interventions by the OHR to ensure fairness in and access to education services.

It is possible that, with the existence now of an agreed strategy, reform, including curriculum reform, will proceed with greater urgency and efficiency, and with increased levels of cooperation and coordination between local authorities and the IC.

ASSESSMENT OF SCHOOLING AS A FACTOR OF CONFLICT

Curriculum evaluation in BiH

A major weakness in the strategic approach to curriculum policy reform since the war has been the absence of an agreed and negotiated plan based on a systematic evaluation of the current curricula. Without such a plan, quality improvement, especially in such a complex political and social environment as that in BiH, is very difficult. Nevertheless, a number of significant evaluations have been conducted.

Evaluation of curricula of the "national subjects"

One noteworthy attempt to initiate an evaluation and planning process was undertaken in 1999 when UNESCO commissioned a curriculum evaluation team led by Professor Volker Lenhart of the University of Heidelberg. The primary focus of this evaluation was the "politically socialising intentions" of the various curricula in the national group of subjects. A secondary task was to evaluate the "technical quality" of the syllabi of those subjects. Subsequent to this evaluation, UNESCO and OHR convened the Symposium on the Curricula of the National Subjects in Bosnia and Herzegovina, held in Sarajevo on February 7–8, 2000.[26]

In his opening remarks, Professor Lenhart provided the following summary of the findings of the 1999 evaluation:[27]

Politically socialising intentions of the Bosniak curricula

The Bosniak curricula contain a lot of neutral and tolerable components. There are several desirable aims, objectives and units especially where other nationalities of Bosnia and Herzegovina are taken into consideration. The not acceptable objectives and content items refer to active military training of school students and to a view of history in which Bosniaks are mainly seen as victims of aggression, genocide, ethnic cleansing in past and present. Though the events which are described with these terms have to be treated in a school curriculum the underlying concepts implicitly define the other nationalities of the country as aggressors and instil into Bosniak students an attitude which is not helpful for peace building and reconciliation.

Politically socialising intentions of the Croat curricula

The Croat Curricula in Bosnia contain several neutral and tolerable elements. There are some desirable aims, objectives and units, especially where an international outlook is presented. However, there are aims, objectives and content items which are not acceptable due to a narrow orientation towards the Republic of Croatia. There is also a far reaching tendency to ignore the other nationalities of Bosnia and Herzegovina. This trend is especially visible in the language and literature or history curriculum of primary schools.

Politically socialising intentions of the Serb curricula

The curricula of RS contain a lot of desirable and tolerable units, for example if the history curriculum deals with the other South Slavic peoples. On the other hand the curricula show a few items that have to be considered as offensive and not acceptable content (for example: the active participation of students in firing the air-rifle and throwing the "school hand-bomb" prescribed in defence and protection and a view of recent history with demands to remove sanctions against Serbia without mentioning the causes of such restraints). It should be noted, that the "region of reference" in the curricula of RS is Serbia and the Federal Republic of Yugoslavia. RS, although seen as an entity of its own and as a geographical part of BiH, is clearly described as one of the "Serbian countries" in the "Serbian geographical area." However, RS is one of the two entities that comprise BiH and so a stronger orientation of the curricula of RS to BiH will be necessary. It is particularly important for the curricula of RS to take the other two nationalities of the country into consideration. The analysis showed a great insufficiency concerning this matter, with the Bosniak and Croat population of the country being practically ignored (this is especially the case in language and literature, music, nature and society and geography). This attitude is latently offensive and therefore not acceptable.

With regard to the technical quality of the curricula, the evaluation team found the following:[28]

The Bosniak curricula do have on the average a sufficient technical quality according to curriculum design standards. Possibilities for improvement are especially open concerning reducing content overload, hints on teaching methods, and elements of curriculum organisation, like more openness, horizontal linkages and spiral elements.

The Bosnian Croat curricula do have in their majority a sufficient technical quality according to curriculum design standards. However, in some cases the relationship of the program documents and the annex is not clear. The secondary history curriculum is poor because it is not elaborated but contains only some headlines. The fully worked out plans are understandable and practicable but open for improvement concerning content overload, organisational patterns, like openness, horizontal linkage, and hints on media and evaluation techniques.

The overall technical quality of the Bosnian Serb curricula can be assessed as good. In some cases, the co-ordination of aims and units, objectives and content can be improved. In a few cases, the aspired level of achievement is too high. Content overload is a very visible feature. The plans can be improved concerning curriculum organisation, like allowing for more openness, including spiral elements and indicating horizontal linkages.

The intentions of the symposium that followed this evaluation and that are referred to above were to

1. define a curriculum structure (such as "framework, core, unified, or parallel," providing any "parallel" curriculum was consistent with the Dayton Agreement), noting that whichever model was adopted must solve the problems of mutual recognition of certificates and those associated with the education of local minorities, especially returnees;

2. remove bias from the curricula and state principles for reform; and

3. establish a curriculum revision mechanism that would have among its terms of reference the improvement of technical quality of the syllabi.

The symposium was presented with a number of models of curriculum current in the following European contexts: Northern Ireland, Switzerland, Germany, and Greece. Recommendations from the UNESCO Conference on History Textbooks of South-East Europe were also presented. The symposium reached the following conclusions:

1. The curriculum model best suited to the needs of BiH is the Swiss model. That means parallel curricula with a high level of coordination between the authorities of the Entities.

2. Coordination mechanisms, such as a Standing Conference of Ministers of Education, need to be established by the three communities, with the involvement of the Ministries, pedagogical Institutes, OHR, UNESCO and the Council of Europe.

3. There needs to be mutual exchanges of information on changes and developments in the respective systems.

4. Each constituent people should offer curricular modules to be integrated in the curriculum of the others, especially in the areas of culture and language.

5. Certificates should be mutually recognised in order to facilitate cross-entity mobility. Legislation should be adopted that would permit the integration of children from other areas and groups, including minority groups, especially returnee children. One highly desirable possibility is the hiring of teachers from the other constituent peoples, in order to meet the needs and rights of the returnee children in terms of cultural and linguistic distinctiveness.

6. Both alphabets should be taught throughout the country, and the children should be exposed to the literary heritage of the other constituent peoples. They should also be made aware of the common and distinct features of the three linguistic variants present in BiH.

7. Textbooks imported from Croatia and the FRY will no longer be tolerated if the country of reference is not BiH; most textbooks should be produced and printed in BiH.

8. There should be some shared core elements in the curricula, such as a common Human Rights and Civic education. To this end, high quality teaching and teacher-training materials have already been developed by the Council of Europe, UNESCO and CIVITAS. Other consentiently developed and agreed upon units should be integrated into the curricula of the other constituent peoples.[29]

By 2003 little progress had been made toward the implementation of the conclusions of the symposium, particularly the application of the recommended curriculum model, namely "parallel" (presumably three) curricula with a mechanism to ensure "coordination" between them. As noted earlier in this chapter, a standing conference of entity ministers was established, but largely does not function as an effective mechanism for coordination. Similarly, a Curriculum Harmonisation Board was formed but, because of procedural inefficiencies and the entrenched positions of its members, was similarly unsuccessful.

A number of speculative questions arise from this process. Was the "Swiss model," favoured by the symposium participants, particularly the element of a coordination mechanism, an achievable outcome for BiH? Was the model favoured by BiH participants in the symposium simply because it maximised the potential for the retention of the status quo—that is, separate curricula? Was any system of parallel curricula really acceptable to the international community, in particular to the OHR? Would such a model, regardless of the effectiveness of any "coordination mechanism," solve problems confronting minorities and returning minority children? Whatever the true answers to such questions, the model favoured by the symposium, the "Swiss model," has, in general terms, been abandoned.

SWOT analysis: European Commission
Technical Assistance to Education Reform (in BiH) (EC-TAER)

At its initial conference at Jahorina in June 2000, the EC-TAER project carried out an evaluative survey through a SWOT (strengths, weaknesses, opportunities, threats) analysis. Participants in this activity included curriculum policymakers and curriculum developers from all constituencies in BiH. The summarised results of this activity can be found in Table 2.

Table 2: Summary of EC-TAER Project (2000)[30]

Negative sides of present curriculum—WEAKNESSES	Positive sides of existing curriculum—STRENGTHS
Lack of modern structure: Does not adequately consider: • working and learning as a permanent process throughout one's life • learning for work and employment • learning communication skills • learning life skills	*Present curriculum gives broad basics for education insofar as it is:* • "good" • extensive (detailed) • many-sided (creativity) • integrated
Too centralised: • does not allow creativity • is not flexible	*Scientifically based:* • aims are scientifically based
Does not allow the development of democracy and learning "for" democracy: • curriculum delivered from the "top" (not from participants who are directly involved in the teaching process) • does not allow democracy in any structure (neither pupils, teachers, principles, nor parents can contribute inputs in the curriculum-making process) • principles of democracy should be involved in each subject	*Provides a good basis for:* • continuation of education (to chose the school where pupils want to go) • making possible a broad selection of occupations
Not adapted to the needs of children: • does not accept differences • does not develop differential abilities • does not develop skills	
Too much information that is: • not systematised toward complexity • repeating • not balanced theory and practical knowledge • targets are not clear and too generalised	
Lack of coherence: • among school subjects • within the contents of subjects	

While it could be argued that this activity did not fully and accurately capture the views of the entire education community, the SWOT analysis did represent an attempt to articulate the strengths and weaknesses of general curriculum in BiH in a systematic way.

Democracy in education in Bosnia-Herzegovina and FR Yugoslavia (FRY)

This extensive study was conducted from 1996 to 1999 by the Institute of International Education at Stockholm University in Sweden. The study focused on "democratic transition" and sought to establish whether or not BiH (among other countries in similar situations) had undergone a transition to democracy, and the extent to which that transition was facilitated by and reflected in its education system.

The report of the project also makes a number of observations about curriculum in general in BiH and, at least by implication, about curriculum policy and policymaking. For example, it asserts that: "In the two countries (FRY and BiH), the education systems were—during the research period—never used to implant democratic attitudes and values. Instead, they were used to defend, even reinforce, specific ethnic interests."[31]

With regard to the nature of schooling and its impact on democratisation in BiH, the report concludes that "the school as an institution without internal democratisation, and without autonomy, cannot seriously contribute to democratic education (even with the best curricula)."[32] Such findings have clear implications for the effectiveness of "stand-alone" syllabus development that purports to educate young people about democratic principles, but is not supported and reinforced by the general school environment. They also underline the importance of democratising curriculum decisionmaking—of ensuring that teachers and students are empowered, through applying contemporary curriculum models, to make some choices about what is taught and learned.

Perhaps of most significance is the report's conclusion that

> The teachers are not given any professional freedom, nor do they actively participate in influencing the contents. They are given a list of "tasks" that have to be fulfilled within a given timeframe. School inspectors are evaluating whether or not the curriculum is being followed as planned. Against this background, it is difficult to imagine an engaged student with critical thinking skills who is actively participating in the process.[33]

The devaluing of initiative, liberal and critical thinking, creativity, and problem solving that this finding implies is a challenge that BiH curriculum developers must overcome if the nation's children are to be well prepared for the twenty-first century.

Policy survey

In gathering data and opinion for this study, an evaluative questionnaire was compiled and distributed through the UNESCO field office in Sarajevo, to forty-one key curriculum policymakers in BiH.[34] The results, compiled following analysis of the nineteen completed questionnaires and follow-up consultations, show that there is unanimous or almost unanimous agreement that

- changes to general education curricula in BiH are necessary;

- changes to the processes of and structures for curriculum development and curriculum policymaking are necessary;
- there should be a core curriculum common to all parts of the country;[35]
- the current curricula are "overloaded";
- the current curricula do not contribute sufficiently to social cohesion and a peaceful BiH; and
- the current curricula do not prepare young people adequately for the future.

Conclusions

Evaluation activities illustrate clear and broad-based general agreement among the education community and observers in BiH that the general education curriculum is out of date. Studies such as those cited above indicate the following issues:

- There continue to be significant obstacles to curriculum reform in BiH, particularly the "politicisation" of curriculum development processes.
- Curriculum development processes are not transparent, and exclude consultation with teachers, parents, students, and, in many instances, local experts.
- The curriculum paradigm on which current curricula in BiH are based concentrates far too heavily on memorisation and the recall of facts. Concomitantly, there is too little emphasis on the development of skills, values, and attitudes, and on creativity and the development and valuing of personal opinions and viewpoints. Such a curriculum model also discourages modern teaching methodologies, such as multi-perspective approaches to history.
- The curriculum is "overloaded." It is a very commonly held view that there is insufficient time available to teach and learn the requirements of current syllabi.
- There should be some form of common core curriculum across the country. While the development of a common core would represent significant progress, it is unclear whether that core would only include "noncontroversial" subjects (such as mathematics and computer sciences) or what are currently described as "national subjects" (such as language, literature, art, and history). It could be argued that, for a common core curriculum to make any contribution to social cohesion and stability, these latter subjects would need to be included. There is also no current consensus about the definition of the term "common core curriculum" and whether it should consist simply of subjects or of values and perspectives integrated across the curriculum.
- There is considerable difference in opinion regarding the teaching of recent history. Some curriculum policymakers, including history specialists, argue that teaching about the 1992–95 war should not be included at all in school curriculum on the grounds that "the society is not ready to deal with the issues," and that "more time is required."

Rationales for change

Emerging from the evaluations and surveys described above are (at least) three rationales for significant change to current curriculum. It should be noted that local authorities have not articulated these rationales, nor is there any evidence that any locally initiated reforms are due to the findings of the evaluations listed above.

Rationale 1: To ensure flexibility in curriculum design

The current curriculum design model in BiH is inflexible (a "one-size-fits-all" curriculum), based on the belief that every student in any given system should learn the same things at the same time. This approach relies on uniformity as an indicator of quality. This model fails to acknowledge, among other things,

- the strengths and weaknesses of individual students;
- the strengths and weaknesses of individual teachers;
- the learning styles of individual students; and
- local conditions, including the cultural perspectives that might differ from community to community, local economic and employment conditions, and local resources that might be available.

Rationale 2: To ensure that curriculum is relevant

Current curriculum is unable to provide a relevant and contemporary set of knowledge, skills, attitudes, and values to students. The curriculum is characterised by a disproportionate concentration on information with little if any attention given to the application of that knowledge, the development of useful skill sets, and outcomes in the affective domain.

Relevant to contemporary global society:
Curricula in BiH have remained largely unchanged for decades. Much of the knowledge expected to be learned by students is not current, and other significant outcomes domains found in contemporary curricula (skills, values, and attitudes) are not sufficiently addressed. Curricula therefore do not prepare students adequately to become citizens of the twenty-first-century world.

Relevant to contemporary society in Bosnia and Herzegovina:
Like all societies that have suffered traumatic conflict, BiH has undergone enormous change. Curriculum must reflect the social realities of contemporary BiH. The country's curricula do not adequately prepare students to become citizens of a peaceful and cohesive BiH.

Relevant to the economy of Bosnia and Herzegovina:
School curriculum is multifunctional, and cannot be detached in theory or practice from economic imperatives. Social stability in BiH, as elsewhere, is linked with the financial and economic security of individuals.

BiH is moving from a centralised heavy-industry-based economy planned according to the perceived needs of the former Yugoslavia to its own national economy, building on its strengths and attempting to cope with its weaknesses. Consistent with trends in the global context, BiH is seeking to privatise many inefficient, state-operated enterprises and to develop the service industry sector. Curriculum policymakers in BiH have an obligation and an opportunity to ensure that young people learn generic work skills of value in this economic environment, including problem solving and entrepreneurial skills. There is no significant recognition among curriculum policymakers in BiH that general education, not just vocational and technical education, can provide young people with valuable, employment-related skills.

Rationale 3: To contribute to the elimination of cultural prejudices

There is little doubt that current administrative and policymaking arrangements in education provide opportunities for authorities to go their own way. Given the ethnic dimension of the 1992–95 war and its vicious nature, it is perhaps not surprising that authorities would use their autonomy in education and curriculum to devise ways to promote ethnocentric views. In BiH, each education authority is able to promote a culturally inappropriate curriculum that in the end is socially divisive and unregulated by any agreed framework of curriculum standards or "rules."

School curriculum should be redesigned in ways that acknowledge constitutional responsibilities but eliminate the use of education to promote distorted or unacceptable political-cultural ideology. Curriculum should be designed in a manner that promotes informed decisionmaking by students about social and cultural issues and provides optimistic and balanced views of the future.

RECONCEPTUALISING CURRICULUM: CHANGING CURRICULUM PARADIGMS AS A RESULT OF CONFLICT

Changes in curricular paradigms

The paradigm on which the current curricula in BiH are based is one that was, until recently, common to much of Eastern Europe and has historically been part of the education history of most countries. It is narrowly focused on the memorisation and recall of facts, with little if any attention given to the development of skills, values, and attitudes, including those relating to the new national identity of BiH as a sovereign state. Teaching methodology is similarly narrow, being didactic and instructive. Interactive discourse is rare in the classroom, and students are given few opportunities to develop and express opinions.

What is the effect of such a paradigm? This type of curriculum stresses uniformity over individualism, conformity over creativity, and the value of learning the acquired knowledge of previous generations over the skills of inquiry and problem solving. It fails to model the principles of democracy and, most importantly, does not develop the potential of the individual. The power of curriculum lies in its potential to capture the core values of society. The public rhetoric of political leaders in BiH expresses the country's desire for a stable, prosperous, peaceful, and democratic society. Modern curriculum and new curriculum development processes must facilitate and reflect these aspirations. In doing so, curriculum development must be transparent and consultative, and the curriculum itself must focus on individual learners as the building blocks of the future society.

Efforts at reform in BiH, which commenced in June 2001, have attempted to address these problems. Most notably, the reforms envisaged by the Shared Modernisation Strategy developed within the European Commission reform project EC-TAER and supported by UNESCO have attempted to create a more contemporary curriculum paradigm, one that is more flexible, devolves some decisionmaking to regions or schools, and more effectively meets the current and future needs of individual students. The development of curriculum consistent with this paradigm is based on two fundamental concepts: first, an initial focus in the curriculum development process on *learning outcomes*; and second, curriculum as a *framework*. The following explanatory text relating to these concepts was agreed to by the SMS Working Group on Curriculum:

Outcomes

An outcomes approach to curriculum takes, as its primary focus, <u>what students should learn</u> rather than what teachers should teach. The starting point of this approach is the desired learning outcomes for students in a range of domains. Content is then formulated and organised in ways that will enable students to achieve these outcomes.

Within such a process, content is still important. However, outcomes curriculum focuses clearly on the purposes of teaching that content by specifying the learning outcomes that students should achieve.

To be equipped for the modern world, students need to acquire knowledge, but they also need to develop a range of skills and competencies and to develop values and attitudes that will make them good employees, citizens and community members.

This approach to curriculum promotes the achievement by students of all these outcomes.

Curriculum as a framework

A framework is a way of organising curriculum. It is an alternative to the notion that all students must learn all things, and allows schools and teachers, within certain guidelines, to choose content (topics, units, themes) that best suit the needs of their students. It devolves a level of decision-making to schools while retaining a set of prescribed outcomes as the common goal of all teaching.

This model is illustrated in Diagram 1. It responds to the difficulties that curriculum developers have faced in BiH in achieving consensus at the level of "inputs" or "content." To address this problem, this model takes "outputs" or "learning outcomes" as its primary point of consensus—recognising that agreement on the knowledge, understandings, skills, values, and attitudes that young people should have acquired at the end of particular stages of schooling provides a sound base on which to build a curriculum. It can also provide a set of criteria for judging the relevance of subjects and directions for their reform, and can shift the focus in teaching methodology from *teacher-dominated instruction* to *student-centred learning*.

Diagram 1: Curriculum Development Model
Agreed On by the Curriculum Working Group of the Shared Modernisation Strategy

Broad learning outcomes at particular stages of schooling

Within each stage of schooling, a set of subjects or integrated learning areas that have relevance to the broad learning outcomes

Subjects organised into core + elective + optional or other appropriate structure

Learning outcomes for each subject consistent with broad learning outcomes above

Subject content (topics/units/modules) organised to provide flexibility (such as core + elective + optional topics)

It should be noted, however, that this is an initiative of an international organisation. While entity ministers of education signed an inter-entity accord (the Jahorina Agreement) supporting the strategy, and while the working groups in the project were comprised entirely of local experts, it should not be assumed that this represents a substantive shift in curriculum theory or curriculum policy for BiH. There is much work yet to be done. Nevertheless, a recently released EC-TAER White Paper confirms the importance of such a model, claiming that

> a consistent approach to the development of the curriculum in BiH is not possible without an initial, framework curriculum. A framework curriculum and (subsequent) syllabus should contain learning outcomes as its primary focus. A curriculum that has its focus on learning outcomes represents a change of education paradigm centring on what students should learn and not on what teachers should teach.[36]

Direction of curriculum change

Education system management and curriculum policy formulation in BiH is fractured and politically manipulated. Ministers of education are appointed by political parties that represent the interests of dominant ethnic groups. In the Republika Srpska, the minister and senior officials are Serbs. In predominantly Croat and Bosniak cantons, the minister and senior officials are Croat and Bosniak respectively. In the mixed cantons, the minister and deputy minister are appointed, one from each of the two ethnic groups within the constituency.

What does this mean for policymaking in education generally, and for curriculum in particular? In general terms, policy in Republika Srpska, Croat cantons, and Bosniak cantons reflect the political interests of the dominant sociopolitical group, and policy is made accordingly. In mixed cantons, little progress is made as deputy ministers frequently undermine the policy decisions of their ministers. In all cases, attempts at reform rarely seek to build a national identity and rarely have a socially cohesive state as an underpinning philosophical aim.

An illustration of this can be seen in the ministerial reaction to the notion of a state-level curriculum development agency. It is clear to most informed observers that some delegation of responsibility for curriculum to the state level is required if consistent curriculum quality, as well as standardised credentials and mobility for students, are to be realised. Ministers from the RS and Croat cantons object strenuously to even a discussion of such concepts, seeing them as a significant intrusion on their authority, a threat to the cultural base of their curriculum, and vehicles for ethnic domination by Bosniak interests.

Of particular interest is their attitude to different categories of subjects. It has been agreed for some time that there is significant commonality in noncontentious subjects (such as mathematics, natural sciences, and computer science) in the three curricula. Even so, nothing has been achieved in agreeing to single or harmonised syllabi in these subjects, and no agreement has been reached on producing single textbooks. This in itself could be interpreted as a lack of goodwill and real intent on behalf of education authorities. In such circumstances it is understandable that agreement on the national group of subjects has made no significant progress.

With regard to language, BiH has reached a complex situation of three postwar languages (Serbian, Croatian, and Bosnian) having replaced a single prewar language (Serbo-Croat). Each school system espouses its own language and insists that textbooks be produced in that language, regardless of cost—despite the fact that, with a few exceptions, the languages are so similar that students can understand all of them.

It would seem that there is a clear advantage in considering language as not a single issue, but as issues around at least two quite distinct matters: language as a means of instructional discourse, and the acquisition and study of language. With regard to the language of discourse, it would seem that an acceptable solution has been found in Brcko District, where it is claimed that both teachers and students converse in the language of individual choice. With regard to the study of language, however, separate classes are still conducted.

In summary, the aims and fundamental principles of education are yet to be reformulated in BiH. Local authorities have made little progress toward defining or acknowledging a common national identity or toward the accommodation of multiplicities in reconciliation and reconstruction. Clear ethnic differences between curricula remain, particularly in the national subjects, and are reinforced by fragmented education administration and a lack of effective systems and processes.

Recent initiatives in this regard are, however, worth noting. The report *A Message to the People of Bosnia and Herzegovina*, also referred to as the Education Reform Strategy Paper, was initiated by the OHR and the OSCE, and supported by major international organisations. Its production followed a series of working group and consultation meetings, each of which sought to involve as many local experts and stakeholders as possible. The result was a series of "pledges" representing a commitment to reform in education, signed by entity and canton ministers. With regard to curriculum, the main pledge is to develop

> a modern curriculum framework for all levels of primary and general secondary school education, encompassing the entire range of subjects, and focussing on relevant and contemporary knowledge, skills and attitudes to enable students to face the challenges of the 21st century.[37]

A second major reform initiative is the production of a new Law on Primary and Secondary Education, led by the Council of Europe with the strong support of OHR and OSCE. With regard to curriculum, the proposed law envisages a "common core curriculum" (Article 41),[38] and the Curriculum Agency, which is described as "an independent expert body responsible for establishing a common core curriculum for all levels of education" (Article 47). It is to be hoped that these initiatives will bring greater focus to curriculum reform in BiH, and will contribute to the creation of a strong national identity and reconciliation.

POLICY DIALOGUE, CONSENSUS BUILDING, AND RESISTANCE: CHALLENGES POSED BY SENSITIVE LEARNING AREAS

Modalities of consultation and participation in policy reform

The notion of consultation as it is generally conceived does not exist in curriculum development processes in BiH. As noted earlier, there is no state-level curriculum framework or curriculum ministry or agency. Consequently, any revision of curriculum is undertaken at the level of the canton or, in the case of the RS, the entity. The recent research study sponsored by UNESCO and described above in relation to the evaluation of curriculum as an aspect of the rationales for curriculum change, noted the following in relation to consultation:

> Some interviewees pointed to serious deficiencies or even absence of true consultation processes of the type that exist in other democracies. It was recommended that greater attention be given to listening and responding to the concerns of teachers, parents and students.[39]

Traditionally, ministries have relied on the expertise of pedagogical institute staff to develop curriculum. This remains the case, but it is clear that progressive educators and curriculum developers in these institutes do not have a strong voice in curriculum design and content. While some recent curriculum initiatives, such as that in the RS, have included teachers in the development process, there is no systematic mechanism for consulting with teachers at large, parents, students, employers, or other relevant stakeholders.

Of interest in this context is the public education campaign launched late in 2002 by the OHR and OSCE. Using the slogans "We deserve better education" and "All for schools, schools for all," the campaign aims to raise awareness about the need for education reform, and to interest the broader community in reform activities. Greater consultation and participation in curriculum development and other processes might result from the campaign.

Identifying difficult issues with regard to sensitive learning areas

Difficult issues in BiH curricula are generally contained within the category "national group of subjects." As mentioned above, these subjects include history, language/literature, geography/ nature and society, music and art, and religious instruction. Currently there are Bosnian, Croat, and Serb syllabi in these subjects. In the questionnaire part of the UNESCO: IBE (2003) research study, respondents were asked the following question, and were invited to elaborate on their answer:

> Do you think changes in the "national subjects" (History, Language and Literature, Geography, Nature and Society, Art, Music, and Religious Instruction) are necessary?

All respondents answered "yes" to the question, and their comments were summarised as follows:

> Respondents generally believed that the National Subjects provided opportunities to encourage national identity, democracy, reconciliation and co-existence. They generally argued for a focus on the quality of literature, art and music rather than on achieving a balance between the three cultures. It was also suggested that the term "National Group of Subjects" is unhelpful and should be discontinued, and that Religious Instruction should be removed from public schools. One respondent recommended that ecological awareness be more prominent in these subjects, and another that these subjects should be combined into broader learning areas in Grades 1-3.

In the second phase of the research, interviews were conducted with respondents. The report contains the following summary of opinions regarding national subjects:

> It was generally felt by interviewees that the traditional category of "National Group of Subjects" should be removed from curriculum policy dialogue. This categorisation of subjects was generally seen as unhelpful and unnecessary, although all interviewees acknowledged the importance of cultural sensitivities. The general feeling was that these subjects should be treated, as far as possible, like all others.
>
> With regard to the teaching of History, there was a relatively consistent view that a study of the history of the last decade in BiH should not be included in the curriculum. A number of interviewees qualified this view suggesting that a "basic outline" of events since 1992 should be provided to students. In addition, one interviewee expressed the view that "our history textbooks are histories of destruction, not of creation—we should explain destructive events but we should focus on the creation of a new culture. Children have the power to create a multicultural future that our leaders do not have."
>
> A number of interviewees used literature to illustrate their responses in this area and consistently rejected the current approach of numerical balance of authors in the curriculum in favour of a focus on the quality of literature. Many interviewees stressed the necessity

for concentrating on the skills of literary appreciation and analysis rather than on the current obsession with literature as cultural heritage. All however stressed the need for all students to study authors from all cultures in BiH, as well as the literature of other countries.

Comment

It should be noted that no interviewee volunteered multi-perspectivity as a solution to problems in the teaching of history, despite extensive work in this area in recent years by the Council of Europe and Euroclio. Rather, the common view was that a greater distance in time as well as a "social maturity" was required before this period is included in the curriculum.

The strongest voice dissenting from this view was that of students. Although a far from representative sample, the twelve students interviewed were adamant that the war should be studied and discussed if lessons are to be learned by future generations and if there is to be an end to the "fifty year cycle of wars in the Balkans."

One trend suggested by the consultations is an increasing distance between the opinions of practitioners (especially teachers but including Pedagogical Institute representatives) and "official" government positions on the issue of culturally "sensitive" subjects.

Consensus building—dealing with sensitive issues

The current initiative in BiH to create a common core curriculum will clearly need to confront issues related to the national group of subjects. In discussing the notion of a common core curriculum, the research report indicates considerable disagreement about whether and how those subjects should be treated. This is a matter of vital concern to all future curriculum reform efforts.

With regard to the following individual subjects:

Languages

The SFRY education system recognised three official languages and nine "nationality" languages although, in practice, only one of these three official languages, Serbo-Croat, was spoken before the war. One outcome of the 1992–95 war was the development of a separate language for each of the three constituent peoples, which then replaced the single Serbo-Croat language. As a result, there are now three national languages and two official scripts in BiH, Latin and Cyrillic, with the latter still used extensively in the RS.[40]

In the context of BiH, it is clear that the politics of language serve as a vehicle for promoting national divisions. Each of the three languages is used as the language of instruction and is part of the curriculum in the relevant education system. This gives rise to obvious problems wherever students from minority ethnic groups attend schools, and has been exacerbated in areas of minority returns to prewar homes.

Civics/citizenship

Civics/citizenship is taught as a discrete subject, and was introduced through a Civitas-sponsored project to replace the civil defence subjects that existed prior to and immediately after the war. Although to a large extent the teachers of this subject were recruited from the ranks of civil defence teachers, training in appropriate "interactive" teaching methodology was provided as part of the project. Some of the Civitas courses have recently been included in the common core curriculum.

History

Although varying from grade to grade, history curricula in BiH have some content in common, especially at the level of world history. Teaching about the history of the country and the region, and of each constituent people, however, varies, as would teaching about the 1992–95 war. While a redesigning of the curriculum to introduce a greater focus on historiographical skills and multi-perspective teaching would be long-term approaches, there appears to be no short-term solution to this problem. The general view regarding teaching about the 1992–95 war appears to be that it should not be included in the school curriculum at this time.[41]

Religion

"Confessional" or "catechism" religious instruction is included in all three curricula. While there is some opposition to this and a suggestion that schools should become secular institutions, the Churches still exercise considerable influence in this area. The subject "Culture of Religions," a new syllabus focusing on religion as a historical and cultural study, is currently being piloted.

The recent Implementation Plan for the Interim Agreement on Accommodation of Specific Needs and Rights of Returnee Children, agreed to by entity ministers, adopts the following approach to these subjects:

> III. National Group of Subjects
>
> 3. In regard to the so-called "national group" of subjects . . . , parents shall be given the possibility to opt for Entity/Canton or the curriculum of their own choice,
>
> a) All schools shall organise classes from the national group of subjects . . . provided that parents and students opt to have the national group of subjects taught according to a curriculum that is different from that already being taught. All schools shall be requested to organise these classes in the following manner:
>
> - In schools where there are 18 or more students in a grade (or the minimum number prescribed by the law required for combined grades), schools shall be required to organise regular classes for the said subjects to replace the current national subjects taught.
> - In schools where there are fewer than 18 students in a grade, schools shall be required to organise classes according to the decision of the competent Ministry.[42]

It is clear that this is an administrative rather than a curriculum-based solution. It is to be hoped that, in the forthcoming development of a common core curriculum, permanent solutions will be explored.

Curriculum balance

Reorganising and restructuring the curriculum

Attempts have recently been made by some education authorities to "rebalance" their curricula. In Tuzla Canton, students in the last two years of secondary school are now expected to study a smaller core of material in most subjects, and are being offered the opportunity to elect pairs of subjects for specialist, in-depth study. This introduces a relatively high degree of flexibility, although it should be noted that it applies to two grades only, and that the syllabi themselves still consist of lists of facts to be memorised.

In Sarajevo Canton, a similar arrangement was introduced for the 2002–03 school year. However, it appears that, to achieve this level of specialisation, two years' content was compressed into one year, and nothing was removed from the syllabus.

In the RS, a new curriculum was introduced in 2002–03 that, according to the minister, reduced content by 30 percent. This figure was queried by some participants in the recent UNESCO: IBE research,[43] who also claimed that the curriculum failed to implement any principles of modern curriculum design.

Curriculum in the Brcko District has for some years been harmonised to encourage ethnically mixed classes. No independent study of the success of this curriculum and its implementation, particularly its modernisation, has been conducted. However, in some circles of the international community the "Brcko model" has been recommended as at least a stopgap measure to realise harmonisation of curricula.

The overcrowded curriculum

There can be no doubt that "overcrowding" is the most commonly raised criticism of BiH curriculum. This could understandably and accurately be interpreted as both too many subjects and too much content within each subject, and is clearly related to the nature of syllabi themselves—that they consist entirely of lists of facts and information to be memorised, frequently by rote. This problem was a particular subject of the UNESCO: IBE research study.[44]

> The overburdening of students with detailed lists of "facts" to be learned by heart, exacerbated by content being repeated in subsequent years, was by far of most concern to all interviewees. There was also a very high degree of consensus that this problem could be "easily overcome" if subject experts were given the opportunity to eliminate unnecessary material. Suggestions for achieving this included simply deleting material, as well as more imaginative methods of arranging topics within subjects, allowing students to pursue their own interests, and a greater use of project-based teaching. Examples cited of subjects where this problem exists suggest that it is a problem across the curriculum.[45]

It would seem that this problem arises from a fundamental principle of BiH curricula that, to achieve quality, all students must study all topics in all subjects. Over time, subjects have been added to the curriculum, but little attention has been given to rationalising the range of subjects or the content of individual subjects in a consistent and systematic way.

RESEARCH, MONITORING, AND EVALUATION

Research

Pilot programs

There have been several projects in BiH in recent years that have produced or are in the process of producing reformed curriculum at the subject level, including two that have specific elements of creating a peaceful and cohesive society: Culture of Religions, and a civic education program sponsored by Civitas and supported by the U.S. embassy.

While Culture of Religions is still in the pilot phase, the latter program has introduced curriculum in Foundations of Democracy in grades one through eight and Democracy and Human Rights in secondary schools. These curricula are part of a broader program that includes an annual, countrywide, project-based competition. The project has delivered training to fourteen thousand teachers since 1996 and has provided textbooks, teacher guides, and other materials to schools across the country.

Despite the success claimed by this civic education program, a question remains regarding its impact on the rest of the curriculum. For example, it remains open to debate whether the teaching of the national subjects is consistent in principle and practice with this program. A challenge for curriculum developers in BiH is to ensure that syllabi developed as "stand-alone" subjects fit within a curriculum framework or comply with an agreed set of standards, and are consistent to an appropriate degree with other subjects.

Perspectives of youth

Extensive consultations with young people were limited by the aims and scope of this study. Detailed responses of young people to a series of questions related to democracy and democratic processes can, however, be found in Lidija Kolouh-Westin, ed., *Democracy in Education in Bosnia-Herzegovina and FR Yugoslavia*, Institute of International Education, Stockholm University, Sweden, May 2002.[46]

Chapter 7 of this report contains a very detailed and clear analysis of student responses, which need to be read in the context of the report. However, some findings of the study have very important implications for curriculum developers in BiH, including

- Students believe that they learn most about democracy by watching television and from parents, rather than from school experiences.
- Students generally favour authoritarianism. (It is likely that this preference would include authoritarian approaches by teachers.)
- A significant number of students do not believe that students should take part in decisionmaking at school. (It is likely that this belief would include curriculum-related decisions.)

Monitoring policy and practice

With few exceptions,[47] there has been no comprehensive evaluation of the current curricula in BiH, nor has any set of criteria or standards for acceptable curriculum design or content been developed. Nevertheless, terms such as "modernisation" and "European standards" are used frequently in BiH, but have not been elaborated or widely understood.

One way forward and, in particular, to resolve the difficulty of constitutional responsibilities, is to develop a National Curriculum Framework and create an effective mechanism for endorsing the various curricula developed by the Republika Srpska and cantonal authorities. To be successful, however, this strategy would need to be supported at both the central and local levels, and include the development of clear standards for acceptable syllabus design and content based on an agreed set of criteria.

Resistance to this approach could emanate from either the local authorities or the international community or both. As a matter of principle, local authorities might not be willing to surrender ultimate authority over their curricula to another body, even if they are adequately represented on that body. For its part, the IC might not have confidence that adequate levels of regulation and monitoring of standards, particularly at the school level, would be achieved through this framework approach.

Resolution of such objections could only be achieved through consultation and negotiation, and by the development of adequate mechanisms for monitoring and evaluation.

Needs identified for future development

Professional curriculum development

Curriculum development in BiH is highly politicised and ad hoc, and largely excludes a wide range of education stakeholders such as parents, employers, and students. It suffers from unacceptable levels of direct influence by political and, in some cases, religious interests. Further, curriculum is conceptualised exclusively as *products* (syllabi) rather than *processes* of evaluation, consultation, development implementation, and review.

These matters need to be addressed as a matter of urgency. Curriculum development professionals should be identified and trained in methodologies of curriculum development so that future curriculum is developed through a transparent, inclusive, professional process based on best practice.

Modern syllabus design

Current BiH syllabi fail to acknowledge in any meaningful way the diversity of outcomes that should be the goal of any modern syllabus: the application of knowledge and the development of skills (both practical and intellectual), values, and attitudes. It is critical that, as soon as possible, a full range of learning outcomes be elaborated and utilised in syllabus design, including outcomes related to human rights, if curriculum is to make any real contribution to economic prosperity, personal satisfaction for students (and teachers), and a stable, peaceful, and cohesive society in BiH.

Developing a strategic approach

It is clear that a great deal of effort, money, and goodwill has been expended by the IC in attempting curriculum reform in BiH. It is equally clear that little has been achieved. It must be understood by all stakeholders that curriculum reform is much more than revising a syllabus or introducing a new subject. Substantive reforms to curriculum processes and curriculum design will be required if education is to make a meaningful contribution to prosperity and stability.

To achieve this, the IC and local authorities must develop both a shared vision for curriculum and curriculum processes in BiH and also a set of objectives that build on current practice and reflect the realities of the resource environment. It is to be hoped that the Education Reform Strategy Paper alluded to earlier will provide a foundation for focused and expeditious progress.

The need for recognition

Certificates issued by schools in BiH are not widely recognised within the country by other school systems. Student achievement is not measured in any standardised way, and there is no final or matura examination that can give reliable information about what has been learned. Consequently, there is little recognition of education attainment or of the quality of BiH education outside the country.

Ways of measuring student achievement in reliable, standardised ways must be developed as a matter of urgency. While public examinations at the end of elementary and secondary education should be considered as a basis for issuing standardised certification for students, other assessment regimes and models that are affordable and achievable within the BiH context should be examined.

Deciding on one curriculum or three

Fundamental to all curriculum reform is the need for a decision about the future "shape" of curriculum in BiH. Local authorities (the RS, and the cantons within the federation) seek to retain their constitutional right to develop their own curricula, while acknowledging the benefits of consistency and a degree of commonality across the country. The IC has introduced notions of "common core curriculum," "harmonised curriculum," "modernised curriculum," and "curriculum framework," but has been unsuccessful in negotiating an agreed and detailed model.

A solution to this primary issue might lie in the establishment of a representative curriculum agency with countrywide responsibility for the quality of curriculum. This agency would be charged with developing a standards framework, a set of quality standards with which every curriculum must comply if it is to lead to the issuing of standardised school certificates. The agency would also be responsible for "endorsing" each curriculum as having met the required standards. In this way, systems could retain responsibility for curriculum development but within an agreed guiding framework.

Endnotes

[1] Bosna i Hercegovina. The common abbreviation in English-language documents is BiH, although technically it should be BaH.

[2] As noted in a report by the OECD, September, 2001: "some, but not all, of these ten cantons allow further devolution of education authority to the municipal level, particularly if there are disputes over access by a national group to education in its own language" (p. 7).

[3] Preamble to the BiH Constitution.

[4] Adapted from Kolouh-Westin, Lidja, ed., May 2002, *Democracy in Education in Bosnia and Herzegovina and the FR Yugoslavia*, Sweden: Institute of International Education, Stockholm University, p. 106.

[5] Constituent peoples were officially recognised during Tito's SFRY period.

[6] UNESCO, May 1996, *Review of the Education System in the Federation of Bosnia and Herzegovina*, Paris.

[7] During 2000, UNESCO BiH successfully supported one school district near Travnik in providing basic education for 114 local people whose education had been interrupted by the war. As a second phase of this project, UNESCO continues to seek funding to provide such opportunity for more than 530 people across the canton who have identified themselves as wanting to complete their elementary schooling. It is likely that these figures represent minimum numbers. This work is being conducted in active partnership with the Middle Bosnia Education Ministry.

[8] For example, in its efforts to achieve consistent, modern education legislation across BiH, the Council of Europe sought the sponsorship of proposed laws by the state-level Ministry of Civil Affairs, relying on the reference in the GFA to education as a fundamental human right.

[9] Extract from the declaration made by the Conference of Ministers of Education of BiH, May 10, 2000, available online at www.ohr.int.

[10] Kolouh-Westin, May 2002, pp. 6–7.

[11] World Bank, 2002, *Bosnia and Herzegovina—From Aid Dependency to Fiscal Self-Reliance: A Public Expenditure and Institutional Review*, p. 88.

[12] Ibid., p. 95.

[13] It should be noted that the Standards and Assessment Agency, established by the authority of an inter-entity agreement, has commenced work in the establishment of performance standards and their assessment in mother tongues and mathematics in some grades of primary school.

[14] Following the elections held in October 2002, the position of deputy minister has been abolished at the entity level.

[15] World Bank, 2002, p. 88. It should be noted that a transition to nine years of schooling has been signalled in the new state-level framework law, and that this transition has been initiated in the RS. However, this process has not included any significant revision of curriculum content.

[16] In some cantons, compulsory schooling begins at age seven.

[17] Federation of BiH, Ministry of Education, Culture, Science and Sport, Education in the Federation of BiH—A Brief Description, Sarajevo, 2000.

[18] World Bank, 2002, p. 90.

[19] With regard to limitations on information available on the Internet, for example, some studies indicate that computer usage in BiH is the second lowest, after Albania, in Europe.

[20] There is broad consensus that the May 10 Agreement is a seminal document and the authority for a number of reform initiatives, although there has been ongoing debate as to its interpretation. The text of the agreement is included as an Appendix to this chapter.

[21] The Conference of Entity Ministers of Education was established in 1998 by the Council of Europe with the support of the OHR. While the conferences give the ministers opportunities to conduct a policy dialogue with each other and with the IC, it is doubtful that they have contributed to substantive progress in policy implementation. A range of matters, including textbooks, are continuing agenda items. This in itself is evidence that few contentious policy issues have been successfully concluded.

[22] It should be noted that a UNESCO-sponsored training program for curriculum developers in BiH, managed by IBE, is currently being considered for 2004.

[23] World Bank, 2002, Table 4.13, p. 96.

[24] *A Message to the People of Bosnia and Herzegovina: Education Reform*, p. 20, available online at www.oscebih.org.

[25] Ibid., p. 7.

[26] It should be noted that how widely the findings and conclusions of the symposium were disseminated by education authorities is unclear. Given subsequent events (such as the signing of the May 10 Agreement), it

could be concluded that the symposium had considerable impact on the thinking of ministers of education, but had little immediate impact on curriculum development practice.

[27] UNESCO Sarajevo, 1999, *Report on the Symposium on the Curricula of the "National" Subjects in Bosnia and Herzegovina*, p. 6, compiled by Stefanie Lessmann.

[28] Lenhart, V., Kesidou, A., and Stockman, S., August 1999, *The Curricula of the "National Subjects" in Bosnia and Herzegovina: A Report to UNESCO*, Heidelberg.

[29] UNESCO Sarajevo, 1999, p. 23.

[30] Please note that the table has been annotated by the author for greater clarity. EC-TAER, October 2001, *A Shared Strategy for the Modernization of Primary and General Secondary Education in BiH*, Report of the Inaugural Conference, pp. 11–12.

[31] Kolouh-Westin, May 2002, p. iv.

[32] Ibid., p. 182.

[33] Ibid , p. 149.

[34] A full report of this study (Stabback, Philip, February 2003, *Curriculum and Curriculum Policy Reform in Bosnia and Herzegovina*) can be obtained from the UNESCO field office, Sarajevo, BiH, or from the IBE.

[35] It should be noted that, while it is encouraging that all respondents to the questionnaire agreed that there should be a common core curriculum, there was, at the time of the questionnaire, no agreed definition of a such a curriculum, nor did all respondents agree as to its contents.

[36] *White Paper—Reform of Primary and General Secondary Education in Bosnia and Herzegovina*, produced by BiH Educational Authorities (assisted by the EC-TAER Programme and funded by the European Union), October 2003, p. 3.

[37] *A Message to the People of Bosnia and Herzegovina*, p. 12.

[38] It should be noted that the common core curriculum is not necessarily consistent with the notion of a "modern curriculum framework," a commitment contained in the reform strategy paper cited above. It is not yet clear how these differences will be reconciled.

[39] Stabback, February 2003, pp. 20–21.

[40] OECD, September 2001, p. 7.

[41] As noted in the 2001 OECD report: "In BiH, the main function of the curriculum (especially in history and mother tongue) is political—not the improvement of education quality. . . . [T]he curriculum is used mainly to support nationalist issues and consolidate the balance of power" (p. 25).

[42] "Implementation Plan for the Interim Agreement on Accommodation of Specific Needs and Rights of Returnee Children" can be found online at www.oscebih.org.

[43] Stabback, February 2003.

[44] Ibid.

[45] Ibid., p. 17.

[46] A further study of interest on this topic can be found in the UNDP, *Human Development Report—Youth*, 2000, available online at http://www.undp.ba/Publications/NHDR%20-%202000%20eng.pdf.

[47] The evaluations and research projects that have been carried out are described above.

Appendix 1: Key Reference Documents

Bosnia and Herzegovina—From Aid Dependency to Fiscal Self-Reliance:
A Public Expenditure and Institutional Review

This review was conducted by the World Bank in 2002 and contains a detailed analysis of expenditure and management practices in the education sector in BiH. It is available online at www.worldbank.org.

Constitution of Bosnia and Herzegovina

The BiH Constitution can be found at Annex 4 of the GFA.

Documents related to the European Commission project EC-TAER (Technical Assistance to Education Reform), and the Shared Modernisation Strategy (SMS)

Detailed information about this project is available online at www.ec-taer.org.ba. Of particular significance is the *First Report to Ministers of Education* of June 2002, which summarises the outcomes of the first phase of the project.

The project has recently published its Green Paper, "a set of policy recommendations presented for consultation to key constituencies at a stage when amendments … can be made" (p. 7). This document is expected to guide future reform in a number of areas, including curriculum.

General Framework Agreement for Peace (GFA)

This is the peace agreement negotiated to end the war in 1995, and is also known as the Dayton Peace Accord or the Dayton Agreement. It is available online at www.ohr.int.

Kolouh-Westin, Lidija, ed. (May 2002.) *Democracy in Education in Bosnia-Herzegovina and FR Yugoslavia*, **Institute of International Education, Stockholm University.**

This is available online at http://www.interped.su.se/publ_yellow.asp.

A Message to the People of Bosnia and Herzegovina: Education Reform

In November 2002, the entity ministers of education in BiH, strongly supported by the Office of the High Representative and the Organisation for Security and Cooperation in Europe mission to BiH, outlined their objectives in education reform to the Peace Implementation Council. This document, also known as the Education Reform Strategy Paper, has, for the first time, clearly defined a set of strategic objectives and timelines that had been negotiated between the IC and local authorities. It is available online at www.oscebih.org.

OECD. (September 2001.) *Thematic Review of National Policies for Education—Bosnia and Herzegovina*, **Stability Pact for South Eastern Europe, Table 1: Task Force on Education (English).**

Stabback, Philip. (February 2003.) *Curriculum and Curriculum Policy Reform in Bosnia and Herzegovina.*

The most recent research into and analysis of curriculum and curriculum policymaking was undertaken as part of the preparation of this study. A full report of the research study can be obtained from the UNESCO field office in Sarajevo, BiH, and the IBE.

Appendix 2: The Inter-Entity Ministerial Agreement of May 10, 2000

Declaration

We, the Federal Minister of Education, the Deputy Federal Minister of Education and the Minister of Education of the Republika Srpska, gathered for a meeting of the Conference of Ministers of Education of Bosnia and Herzegovina convened by OHR and the Council of Europe, and co-chaired by the Senior Deputy High Representative, Ambassador Dr Matei Hoffmann, and Mr. Gabriele Mazza, Council of Europe, on 10 May 2000 at OHR, Sarajevo, declare our commitment to the fundamental reform of the existing parallel education systems of Bosnia and Herzegovina as a matter of high priority, as requested by the Council of Europe within the process of accession of BiH, as well as by the International Community as a whole. We unanimously adopt the following principles:

1. The highest quality of education based on genuine European standards and norms should be sought for all children and young people of Bosnia and Herzegovina, the single most valuable resource that the country has in order to shape its future;

2. Education must no longer be used to divide and fragment the communities of Bosnia and Herzegovina; on the contrary, it should be used to bring them together and live in tolerance with one another. Any existing forms of segregation must be removed from the parallel education systems in the Federation and Republika Srpska, and co-ordination assured in order to facilitate the return of refugee families throughout the whole of Bosnia and Herzegovina;

3. While each constituent people of Bosnia and Herzegovina is entitled to preserve and develop its own cultural and linguistic heritage, common and shared elements which facilitate intercultural understanding and communication should be stressed and reflected in all curricula and relevant textbooks. Measures to be taken throughout the country include the teaching of both Cyrillic and Latinic alphabets, the teaching of the shared literary and cultural heritage of the three communities, and teaching about all major religions practised in BiH;

4. Curricula and textbooks for the national subjects must use Bosnia and Herzegovina as their country of reference. The names of the two entities, the Federation of Bosnia and Herzegovina and the Republika Srpska will also be taught and used in textbooks where appropriate;

5. All certificates and diplomas must be recognised and accepted throughout the country in order to facilitate the mobility of pupils, students, teachers, teacher trainers and other educators;

6. Sustained and coordinated efforts to reform and renew the different education systems should immediately address the pervasive overload of subjects in all curricula.

Fahrudin Rizvanbegovic
Minister of Education, Science, Culture and Sports
Federation of Bosnia and Herzegovina

Nenad Suzic
Minister of Education
Republika Srpska

Ivo Miro Jovic
Deputy Minister of Education, Science, Culture and Sports
Federation of Bosnia and Herzegovina

Appendix 3: Fact Sheet - Bosnia and Herzegovina

Population before the war (according to 1991 census):	4,377,033
Population:	3.7 million
Population under 15 years of age .	:18.3%

(An estimated 258,000 people, representing 5.9 percent of the population, were killed in the war)

Persons displaced within one entity:	1 million
Total number of internally displaced persons:	1.5 million
Refugees in other countries:	1.25 million
Life expectancy at birth:	73.8 years
Purchasing Power Parity GDP per capita:	US$ 5,970
Gross national income per capita:	US$ 1,175
Adult literacy rate (age 15 and above):	93.0%
Structure of education system:	4 + 4 + 4

Compulsory education: eight years, commencing in most parts of the country at six years of age.

Administrative organisation: Serb school system and curriculum in the Republika Srpska, a Croat school system and curriculum in several cantons, particularly in Western Herzegovina, and a Bosniak school system and curriculum.

Religious/ethnic distribution:
Bosnian Muslims (43.4%); Bosnian Serbs (31.2%); Bosnian Croats (17.3%).

Official and recognised languages: Serbian, Croatian, and Bosnian, variants of the single Serbo-Croat language that existed prior to the 1992–95 conflict. There are two official scripts in BiH, Latin and Cyrillic with the latter still used extensively in the Republika Srpska.

Sources: The author and the UNDP Human Development Report 2003.
Note: All figures for 2001 except if otherwise stated.

Chapter 3

Curriculum Change and Social Cohesion in Multicultural Guatemala

Manuel de Jesús Salazar Tetzagüic

Katherine Grigsby

About the Authors

Manuel de Jesús Salazar Tetzagüic is the national coordinator for the Project to Mobilise Support for Mayan Education (PROMEM) and, in this capacity, is now contributing to the development of the curriculum proposal requested to PROMEM by the Ministry of Education for the inclusion of Mayan culture and language in the National Curriculum of Basic Education. He is a member of the Parity Commission in charge of the implementation of the peace accords, as well as a member of the Parity Commission for Educational Reform, and he is a well-respected Mayan scholar. He is supported by his colleague, Katherine Grigsby, UNESCO Guatemala chief technical adviser for PROMEM, in charge of the implementation of innovative practices of Mayan bilingual and intercultural education and of the preparation of the curriculum proposal to include Mayan culture and language in the National Curriculum of Basic Education. She has collaborated with UNESCO in various positions since 1994 and has authored education materials and several articles.

List of Acronyms

ALMG	Academia de Lenguas Mayas de Guatemala
	(Academy of Mayan Languages of Guatemala)
AVANCSO	Avance de las Ciencias Sociales en Guatemala
	(Association for the Advancement of Social Sciences in
	Guatemala)
BEST	Mejoramiento de la Educación Básica
	(Improvement of Basic Secondary Education)
BIE	Bilingual Intercultural Education (see also EMBI)
CACIF	Comité Coordinador de Asociaciones Agrícolas, Comerciales, Industriales y
	Financieras
	(Chamber of Agriculture, Commerce, Industry and Finance)
CCRE	Comisión Consultiva de la Reforma Educativa
	(Consultative Commission for Education Reform)
CEDIM	Centro de Investigación y Documentación Maya
	(Centre for Mayan Documentation and Research)
CENALTEX	Centro Nacional de Libros de Texto y Material Didáctico
	del Ministerio de Educación (National Textbook Centre)
CNEM	El Consejo Nacional de Educación Maya
	(National Council of Mayan Education)
CNPRE-COPMAGUA	
	Comisión Nacional Permanente de Reforma Educativa—Coordinacion De Organizaciones Del Pueblo Maya De Guatemala (Permanent National Commission of Education Reform of the Coordination of Mayan People's Organisations of Guatemala)
CONALFA	Comité Nacional de Alfabetización
	(National Literacy Training Committee)
COPARE	Comisión Paritaria de Reforma Educativa
	(Parity Commission for Education Reform)
DICADE	Dirección de Calidad y Desarrollo Educativo
	(Directorate of Educational Quality and Development)
DIGEBI	Direccion General De Educacion Bilingue Intercultural
	(General Directorate of Bilingual Intercultural Education)
EGP	Ejército Guerrillero de los Pobres (Guerrilla Army of the Poor)
EMBI	Educación Maya Bilingüe Intercultural
	(Mayan Bilingual Intercultural Education)
FAR	Fuerzas Armadas Rebeldes (Rebel Armed Forces)
FEBIMAM	Formación en Educación Bilingüe Intercultural Maya Mam
	(Mayan Mam Bilingual Intercultural Training in Education)
FEBIMAM	Fortalecimiento de la Educación Bilingüe Intercultural en el Area Maya Mam
	(Strengthening of Intercultural Bilingual Education in the Maya Mam Area)
MINUGUA	Misión de Verificación de las Naciones Unidas en Guatemala
	(United Nations Verification Mission in Guatemala)
MR–13	Movimiento Rebelde 13 de noviembre (13 November Rebel Movement)
OREALC	Oficina Regional para América Latina y el Caribe de la UNESCO (UNESCO Regional Office for Education in Latin America and the Caribbean)
ORPA	Organización Revolucionaria del Pueblo en Armas
	(Revolutionary Organisation of People in Arms)
PAEBI	Programa de Acceso a la Educación Bilingüe Intercultural

	(Programme for Access to Bilingual Intercultural Education)
PDP	Professional Development Programme
PEB	Programa de Educacion Bilingue (Bilingual Education Programme)
PEMBI	Proyecto de Educación Maya Bilingüe Intercultural
	(Mayan Bilingual Intercultural Education Project)
PROASE	Programa de Apoyo al Sector Educativo en Guatemala
	(Programme of Support for the Education Sector in Guatemala)
PROMEDLAC	Projeto Principal de Educação na América Latina e Caribe
	(Regional Intergovernmental Committee of the Major Project in Education in Latin America and the Caribbean)
PROMEM	Proyecto Movilizador de Apoyo a la Educación Maya
	(Project to Mobilise Support for Mayan Education)
PRONEBI	Programa Nacional de Educación Bilingüe Intercultural
	(National Programme of Bilingual Intercultural Education)
SEGEPLAN	Secretaria De Planificacion Y Programacion
	(Secretariat of Planning and Programming)
SIMAC	Sistema de Mejoramiento de los Recursos Humanos y Adecuación Curricular
	(System of Human Resources Improvement & Curricular Adaptation)
ULEM	Unidades Locales de Educación Maya (Local Mayan Education Units)
UNESCO	United Nations Educational, Scientific and Cultural Organization
URNG	Unidad Revolucionaria Nacional Guatemalteca
	(Guatemalan National Revolutionary Unity)
USAID	United States Agency for International Development

INTRODUCTION

Guatemala is the northernmost country of Central America. It covers an area of 108,889 square kilometres in the central and southern part of Mesoamerica, the cradle of many different languages and cultures, and an ecological corridor between the north and south of the American continent. It shares a border to the north and west with Mexico, to the east with Belize, the Caribbean Sea, Honduras, and El Salvador, and to the south with the Pacific Ocean.

The system of government is republican, democratic, and representative, with a political organisation consisting of twenty-two departments and 331 autonomous municipalities. The country has a population of 11.9 million inhabitants, of whom 50 percent are indigenous. The inhabitants living in rural areas—grouped in 19,600 communities of fewer than two thousand individuals—comprise 60 percent of the total population.

At present there are twenty-one Mayan linguistic communities in Guatemala; together with Garífuna and Xinca, and the official state language of Spanish, these communities make up the multilingual and pluricultural configuration of the nation.

Linguistic Map of Guatemala

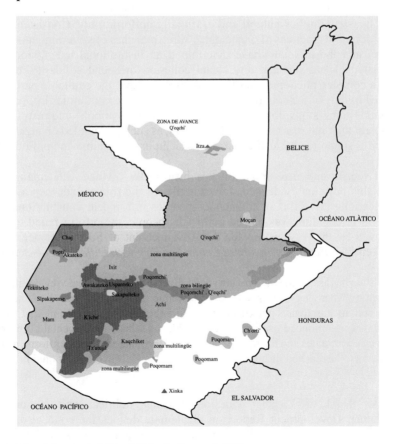

Source: Linguistic Atlas of Guatemala, Michael Richards, Guatemala 2003

The challenges of social cohesion

In the text of the *Popol Wuj* (sacred book of the Maya K'iche'), the Mayan grandmothers and grandfathers advised: "Arise all, call on everyone, so that no one remains behind the others."

They meant by this that all human beings have our *K'ojlem* (being, nature, and dignity) and that at the same time we bring with us our *Ch'umilal* (star, mission, and vocation), and that with the help of our *Wach q'ij* (guidance of the lunar calendar), we can develop fully, without harming others but, on the contrary, walking together in harmony and solidarity.

We feel it is most appropriate to begin this chapter by considering the concepts of social cohesion and curriculum change in light of their application to a Guatemalan society that has only recently emerged from a protracted internal armed conflict lasting thirty-six years. In doing so, we begin by highlighting the historical causes of the phenomenon of social disintegration, the policy of state homogenisation by way of the education system, and the maintenance of racism and discrimination against the indigenous peoples. We then examine the way in which educational reform is both reflecting and contributing to shifting conceptualisations of citizenship, national identity, and social cohesion.

Guatemala is a multiethnic, multilingual, and pluricultural nation. In contrast, the legal definition of the state implies natural and essentially uniform unity. Consistent with this, the political traditions and practices of Guatemala's three branches of government—the legislative, the executive, and the judicial—have determined an institutionalised monoculturalism. As a nation, Guatemala has not had any social cohesion or social solidarity, but instead has experienced a complex phenomenon of coexistence, without the equitable participation of all citizens in the building of the country. Each of the peoples or communities in Guatemala has the basic elements, values, signs, forms of social organisation, symbols, and institutions that help them to maintain their internal cohesion. The nation, as such, is founded on legal principles and standards, and is supported by institutions that sustain its geographic and political unity.

A culture of racism and discrimination has historically divided Guatemalan society, and it persists to this day—as evidenced, for example, in the propaganda deployed against the proposal concerning the rights of indigenous peoples in a recent constitutional amendment. When the 1999 referendum was placed before the people, the reform failed to be ratified. A study conducted by the Association for the Advancement of Social Sciences in Guatemala (AVANCSO) entitled *Homogeneous Images in a Country with Different Faces* concludes that:

> The State has assumed Guatemalan social diversity from an ideal viewpoint, standardising, forgetting—denying—the social and economic complexity typical of the country. This state activity has always placed society before secular duty, something that, as a hegemonic vision, has reproduced itself uninterruptedly, and whose fundamental purpose has been to convey civic values and formative elements that are standardising, uniform; an ideal concept which is to be reached through, among other means, formal educational processes.
>
> (AVANCSO, 1998)

Another factor that hinders social cohesion is social, political, and economic exclusion. The 2000 Human Development Report on Guatemala defines the concept of exclusion as: "The existence of groups that see the enjoyment of economic, social, cultural and political opportunities offered by society, as being very limited." It identifies three dimensions in which exclusion is evident:

1. the economic dimension, including structural limitations that hinder access to and participation in the markets, which, at the same time, curtails access to resources and income;

2. the political-judicial dimension, implying that the traditional mechanisms of social participation are inadequate to express the interests of the most vulnerable groups and, rather, impose barriers that prevent citizens from exercising their rights; and

3. the social exclusion dimension, ranging from a lack of knowledge of identities and particularities regarding ethnic groups, gender, and religion, to the preferential treatment of certain individuals and social groups.

In this struggle to build an all-inclusive society, the following aspects of exclusion will have to be overcome:

- the divide between rural and urban societies;
- differences in income;
- the gap between indigenous and nonindigenous communities;
- gender inequalities; and
- different degrees of political participation.

In its conclusions, the report proposes an educational and cultural revolution by means of three strategies (United Nations System in Guatemala, 2000):

1. inclusion through education;

2. the elimination of illiteracy in Guatemala by the year 2020; and

3. primary education for all.

The country is in the middle of a vortex of a diverse nature. The Guatemalan population is characterised by its social fragmentation, which was accentuated by the protracted internal armed conflict. However, educators are in the process of building new educational policy through dialogue and consensus. At the same time, communities and parents are raising their voices, demanding social justice and improved governance. The families and communities still hope for a better life as they continue to work, produce, and trade (to the extent permitted under current national economic conditions). Throughout history, Guatemala's peoples and communities have been able to cope with and solve injustices and inequalities through creative work, in spite of the chronic weaknesses of the state.

The social reconstruction and recovery process—with justice and fairness, and unity in its diversity (moving beyond unity in inequality)—would fundamentally rest on four political commitments of the state as contained in the peace accords:

1. the historical vindication of human rights violations (responsibility in the face of the truth);

2. reconceptualisation and reform of the state (recovery of identity);

3. recognition of and respect for the social, ethnic, and cultural makeup of the nation and for democratic values (governance); and

4. the complete reform of the educational system (consolidation of the community, construction of nationality, and participation in the global sphere).

The fundamental questions of this study seek to articulate the relationship between education policy, curriculum change, and social cohesion in multicultural Guatemala: How has education been identified as a factor of conflict? Why is education considered the central issue of the peace-building process, and how are new education policies building on the peace accords? What technically feasible and politically viable measures can be and have been taken to reform the education system in order to realise the rights safeguarded in the Constitution and the peace accords? How is education policy contributing to the national debate that is centred on the rethinking of concepts of nation, citizenship, multiculturalism, and national identity? How is curriculum change being developed through consultation and dialogue with all stakeholders? How are education policies and curriculum reform contributing to greater social inclusion and the identification of factors of social cohesion?

Methodology and organisation

The study is based on data collection, an analytical review of important texts and reports, and a process of dialogue established through interviews with key stakeholders in Guatemalan education. It is important to mention that information was obtained from the Consultative Commission of Education Reform (CCRE) and the Accompaniment Commission for Compliance with the Peace Accords. Other relevant sources for the study are the conclusions and recommendations of the Third National Congress of Mayan Education (August 2002) and the Congress on Educational Quality (October 2002).

The first section of the study presents a brief historical description of Guatemala and its cultural and linguistic origins, including the emergence, formation, and consolidation of Mayan culture. Succinct treatment is also given to the Spanish invasion and the colonisation that followed, described as an epoch that set the conditions for the institutionalisation of exclusionary social, cultural, and economic policies vis-à-vis the indigenous peoples, whose determined cultural resistance has, in turn, allowed for their survival up to the present. The historical overview is provided in order to clarify some of the causes of the internal armed conflict that emerged during the second half of the twentieth century and to highlight the difficulty of building a full democracy based on principles of justice and equity, equality and reciprocity, and respect and interculturalism. The section concludes with a brief description of the dialogue and negotiation processes that accompanied the peace accords.

The second section describes the characteristics of cultural and educational policies that developed during the colonial and republican eras, in which a monocultural approach prevailed over a multicultural one. Conceptually, the rationales for recent and ongoing education reform are seen as having shifted, from those based on a paradigm of assimilation to those evolving toward a paradigm of acceptance, and eventually arriving at an intercultural paradigm. The section includes a summary of the phase of complying with the commitments that the accords established, particularly with regard to education reform.

In the third section we focus on the central element of bilingual and intercultural education (BIE) in the process of curriculum reform. The strategies that have been adopted to realise this new policy vision are described, as is the crucial work of both national and international agencies and institutions in its piloting and implementation.

The fourth section engages in an overview of the ways in which mechanisms for dialogue and consultation were set up as a key aspect of education reform in order to comply with the commitments that the peace accords established. The function and results of the CCRE are summarised, as are the issues that were put on the national education agenda for debate.

The fifth section is a discussion of the process of curricular transformation, the main challenges it faces, and the type of support it receives. It concludes by outlining the proposal concerning the relevance of Mayan belonging in curriculum design, which the Ministry of Education has adopted for strengthening Mayan BIE policy in education reform.

The chapter concludes by identifying factors that contribute to the achievement of social cohesion, and in particular those that result from having complied with the peace accord commitments and implemented recommendations agreed to by both civil society commissions and the government relative to the issues of specific parameters for elaborating land policy and the fiscal pact, strengthening the justice system, ensuring civil participation at all levels, making indigenous languages official, and reinforcing the power of civil society in a democratic society. What stands out within the broader education reform is the particular curriculum transformation process as it was designed by the Parity Commission and implemented, followed up, and evaluated by the Consultative Commission. The final points indicate critical future steps to be taken and areas to be reinforced in order to fully realise the new policy directions.

HISTORICAL OVERVIEW OF GUATEMALA

Pre-Columbian history

The cultural history of Guatemala has its sources and foundations in the native cultures of Mesoamerica—a region of approximately 350,000 square kilometres in which the Mayan culture has long been prominent, with a history dating from approximately the fifteenth century BC, the epoch when the early preclassical period began. The area is occupied at present by the Mexican states of Chiapas, Yucatán, Campeche, and Quintana Roo, in addition to the nation-states of Guatemala, Belize, and the western regions of El Salvador and Honduras. Its linguistic history dates back to the twenty-sixth century BC, a period during which, according to the linguist Norman A. McQuown,

> a small group of American Indians, the Mayanos, with a quite uniform way of speaking, and who spoke a language whose relatively close relations (Totonaco and Mixeano) were to be found in another part of Mesoamerica, settled near the highlands of the Cuchumatanes in the northwestern region now called the Highlands of Guatemala.
>
> (Gallo, 2001)

Having managed to discover and cultivate corn—the "American cereal"—in the Archaic Mesoamerican period (6000 BC), groups of people came together in gradually more organised settlements until they established well-developed cultures, such as the Olmeca (predecessors of the Mayans), who lived on the southern coast of Guatemala and Mexico.

The preclassical Mayan period lasted from 1500 BC to AD 250 in the lowlands of Petén, the central highlands, and the southern coastal plain of Guatemala. Cities such as Uaqxaqtun, Tikal, Ceibal, and Kaminal Juyu' were built; the knowledge and use of ceramics, agriculture, and astronomy began to develop; and the Mayan civilisation began to take shape.

In the classical period (AD 250 to 900), cultural expression flourished in all aspects, agriculture was developed, technology increased, trade grew, and politics became consolidated. Large ceremonial centres and complex cities were built with architectural refinement, connected by wide *saqb'e*—roads made of lime and stone—which also served as routes to guide religious and spiritual events as determined by the calendars, such as the *tzolkin* ritual and the *jaab'* agricultural ritual. Art, sciences, and history flourished as well, together with mathematics, astronomy, and philosophical thinking. Noteworthy during this period was the splendour of the cities—Tikal, Palenque, Copán, Ceibal, Quiriguá, Nebaj, Kohunlich, Bonampak, Dzibilchaltœn, Uaxactœn, Altun Ha, R'o Bec, Comalcalco, Chicaná, Chinkultik, Xunantunich, Edzná, Yaxchilán, the sacrificial altar of Piedras Negras, Uxmal, Kabah, Labná, Tulum, and others.

The postclassical period began at the end of the ninth century AD, when, because of political and economic crises and various conflicts, people started to abandon the cities in the central area and to prosper in the northern area (Yucatán and Quintana Roo in Mexico, and Belize and Honduras), in the cities of Chichén Itzá, Mayapán, Tulum, Lamanai, Izamal, Akalán or Chakanputœn, Tankaj, Xelja', Corozal, Nito, and others. Toward the south, on the Pacific coastal plain and in the highlands, additional realms prospered, such as the K'iche', Mam, Kaqchikel, Tz'utujil, Poqomam, Q'eqchi', Itza', and Achi, as well as the Tayasal and Itzá in Petén (all heirs of the Mayan culture), with the Pipil and Xinca areas and other linguistic families in the southeast of what is present-day Guatemala.

One characteristic of this period is that Mayan culture was greatly influenced by other societies of the central area of Mexico, mainly the Toltec, who had emigrated to the south from Tulán toward the end of the tenth century. It was during this period that Quetzalcoatl, "the feathered serpent"—known in Mayan as Kukulkán, and in K'iche' as Q'uq'kumatz—was an influential, legendary figure, the civilising hero of the Toltec, a people whose culture radiated out from its centre, the city of Teotihuacán. Pyramids and ceremonial and scientific centres, including astronomical observatories, continued to be built, and river trade and sea trade—with routes ranging from the area of the Gulf of Mexico to the coasts of Nicaragua and Costa Rica—increased.[1]

Spanish invasion, conquest, and colonialism

The Spanish invasion of Guatemalan territory began in the southwestern region (Soconusco and Zapotitlán) at the end of 1523. The conqueror Pedro de Alvarado, an audacious and ruthless man, led the expedition sent by Hernán Cortés to subdue the areas and *caciques* of the territory known by Mexican peoples as Quautemallán (which in the Nahuatl language means "land of many trees").

The first people to face the Spaniards in defence of their territory and culture were the K'iche's. The succession of battles—Zapotitlán (Xetulul), Olintepeque (Xekik'el), and Quetzaltenango (Xelajuj)—in which the Mayan-K'iche'n cities became allies demonstrated to Alvarado that in spite of their military defeat, the indigenous peoples were determined to resist and survive on their own. The next people confronted were the Kaqchikels, who had at first made an alliance with the Spanish in the hope that they would be able to enjoy some autonomy in the new order. After suffering cruelties at the hands of the Spaniards, they too rose against the invaders. The third people invaded were the Tz'utujils, whose territory was in the southern part of Lake Atitlan, where they coexisted like siblings of a single culture with the K'iche's and Kaqchikels, in spite of their rivalries. The next town to be invaded was Izcuintepeque, followed by other cities and towns. Alvarado then headed for Mixco Viejo, the capital of the Pokomams. After finishing his campaign in the central highlands and the southern coastal plain of Guatemala, the invader went to the Mam region in the northwest, where some of the oldest Mayan peoples lived. After several confrontations, their last stronghold, Zaculew, fell.

The conquest of the Mayans was not totally complete until almost two centuries later, in 1697, when the stronghold of Kanek, in Petén Itzá, fell. It is important to note, however, that the start of Spanish colonisation in 1517–18 was also the beginning of indigenous resistance, and that the characteristics of the economic and political foundations laid during those two hundred years have made it difficult to build a full democracy and a firm and lasting peace in Guatemala.

The first capital of the kingdom of Guatemala was founded on July 25, 1524, in Iximchá (or Tecpán Cuautemallan). It was the start of the colonial regime through which the systematic suffering of indigenous peoples began. Among the elements and institutions that guaranteed Spanish colonial domination were

- slavery;
- the *encomienda*;[2]
- the institutionalisation of the concept of personal services (characterised by a master-servant relationship);
- land distribution, ownership, and use;
- the administration of the public treasury; and
- the exclusive development of the technology, trade, and crafts industries.

The second capital was founded in Almolonga (or Ciudad Vieja), although this was later destroyed by an avalanche of water and mud. The third capital was Antigua Guatemala, in the Panchoy Valley—recently declared a cultural heritage site of humanity by UNESCO—and the fourth was the city of Guatemala de la Asuncion, which has remained the capital to the present day.

With respect to culture and education, the enterprise of conquest and colonisation was supported fundamentally by the native people's evangelisation, considered to be the central pillar of the whole process. As a result of this practice, the indigenous people were obliged to accept the new doctrines and abandon their own religion and ancestral world vision. Two indigenous positions resulted from this policy. The first was one in which they adapted to conditions imposed by the invaders while continuing to interpret things through their own worldview. The second was an attitude of cultural resistance manifested through the persistence of traditional religious practices with their own principles, values, and customs. The religious orders in Guatemala were consolidated during this period. The Catholic Church, organised in curacies and parishes, was responsible for the evangelisation and education of the people, though it did experience some interference in its implementation of the new judicial, political, social, and economic order. Some missionaries chose to defend the indigenous people from abuses committed by the Spanish, denouncing the latter and facing them in court. Still others were interested in studying the languages and culture of the native peoples.

Faced with the adverse situations introduced under colonialism, Mayan people took refuge in their culture, sustaining an educational ideal based on

- spirituality;
- work;

- their mother tongue;
- their religious calendar;
- the oral transmission of culture;
- the determination and transmission of knowledge by means of ideographic writing (glyphs);
- the generation and transmission of their knowledge of science and technology from one generation to another;
- the creation and re-creation of art;
- the practice of the ball game with its high spiritual content; and
- the vigesimal mathematical system.

The essential requirements of education were to become a person (that is, to have dignity), have wisdom and knowledge, develop understanding, cultivate and protect nature as the whole in which we coexist, and learn to work.

Formal education, as introduced by the Spanish, was available only in the cities; later, as the curacies were consolidated, it was extended to large settlements. In the capitals, large schools were established, such as Santo Domingo (1550), San Francisco (1575), Santo Tomás (1620), and San Lucas (1620). In 1676, San Carlos University was founded, obtaining in 1687 the title "Royal and Pontifical University of San Carlos." At present it is the only state university in Guatemala. The adoption of a colonial educational model inspired by Christianity largely destroyed the traditional Mayan forms of education as well as their institutions and customs, giving rise to a gradual process of assimilation and the adoption of the other culture that has prevailed up to the present.

Another important social phenomenon during the colonial period was the emergence of the *mestizo* population (*ladinos*). The *ladino*[3] culture in Guatemala has its origins in the sixteenth century; it began a little after the emergence of *mestizo* families, principally as a result of the often violent but sometimes peaceful mixing of indigenous and Spanish blood.

> Probably the mixing of the races started to occur at the same time as the conquest. As a consequence, a few years after this, there was already a large generation of mestizos. Over 500 years ago indigenous women were conceived of as being valuable spoils of war, with the result that the conquerors believed they had rights over them.
>
> (Claudia Dary, 1995)

Reviewing the history of conquest and colonialism is crucial to understanding how—during the first half of the sixteenth century, in the midst of an avalanche of violent actions and the breakup of the political, economic, social, and cultural organisation of native peoples and nations—new forms of social organisation and cultural identities emerged.

The history of the republic

On September 15, 1821, Guatemala—together with the other Central American provinces that made up the General Captaincy of the Kingdom of Guatemala—declared its independence from the Spanish crown. Three years later, the country embarked on its republican life, with the Constitution of the Federal Republic of Central America. One characteristic of independence was that it was carried out by persons belonging to the educated urban sector from the territory's capital and by groups of *criollos*,[4] people with political and economic weight. These individuals were following a "peaceful plan," which would avoid harmful popular unrest and keep the same authorities operating in the same system. This was done so seamlessly that the last political leader of the colonial regime became the first political leader of the independent government. The social, economic, and cultural conditions of the people would likewise remain unchanged, with the same duties and obligations.

During this period, important events occurred that have, to a great extent, moulded the Guatemalan education system that prevails today. One example of current pedagogical practice with respect to the colonial period is that it has recognised and been able to outline the monocultural and monolingual foundation of Guatemala's formal education system. Likewise, as the discriminatory treatment of the indigenous majority was made increasingly evident, it contributed to the worsening of the conflict and implicitly pointed to education as a factor of the tensions. In 1824, the Assembly passed a decree that promoted the *ladino* settlement of indigenous villages for the purpose of eliminating native languages, which were considered to be an obstacle to progress. (In this context, the education proposals presented by Antonio Larrázabal to the Courts of Cadiz in his speech on February 14, 1812, had declared him to be "in favour" of indigenous education, recommending that in all the "Indian" villages, places be built where Spanish could be taught, in addition to reading, writing, counting, and Catholic catechism. He considered the ignorance of the "Indians" to be so deeply rooted that it called for rapid, active, and effective measures to be taken.)

From 1821 to 1944 the political dynamic of Guatemala was in the hands of liberals and conservatives, with some periods of democratic government and long periods of dictatorship, such as those of Rafael Carrera in the nineteenth century, Manuel Estrada Cabrera (1898–1920), and Jorge Ubico (1931–44). Governance during these dictatorships rested on the absolute centralisation of public administration, police control of citizens, and the exploitation of the indigenous people, especially as it related to agricultural exports, the building of roads, and compulsory military and domestic services. It further was based on the control of freedom of expression and political activity, and on a low level of interest in education.

The liberal revolution of 1871 brought reform to the country's education; it reestablished the secular, free, and compulsory nature of education introduced in 1832, and it reformed the curriculum in accordance with the principles and objectives of the liberal policy for which the institutes for studying the baccalaureate and teacher training schools were created. More funds were allocated to teaching and textbook production, and specialised centres were created, such as the Agricultural School, the Music Conservatory, the School of Crafts and Trades, and an institute for indigenous people.

A political, economic, and social movement with popular participation—mainly from urban areas, students, and the military—produced the October Revolution of 1944, which put an end to the fourteen-year-old dictatorship of Jorge Ubico. Achievements during this period of history include the autonomy decrees of the municipalities and the National University, in addition to the establishment of a system of respect for civil liberties and the fundamental rights of the individual. Components of the latter were the establishment of legal conditions for

- the organisation and operation of political parties;
- the rights of women and minorities to participate in civil life;

- the right to freedom of expression; and
- a process of modernisation of the state.

The 1945 constitution established the basis for a new stage in the political life of the country.

The first government of the new order, with Juan José Arévalo as president, promoted popular education, a national literacy campaign, the itinerant missions of Initial Culture, the Popular University, and the founding of rural teacher training schools. It also created the Peasant School Nuclei and renewed education programs, the Seniority Law for the fair remuneration of national teachers, and the opening of secondary institutes. It is important to highlight the creation of federation-type schools in furthering autonomy in the classroom and in the whole school, in addition to the founding of a publishing unit within the Ministry of Education and the creation of the Faculty of Humanities at the National University.

The post-revolution democratic period lasted ten years. In 1954, the National Liberation movement defeated the government of President Jacobo Arbenz Guzmán; the 1945 constitution was repealed and replaced with a political statute, and a new constitution was passed in 1956. Trade union activity was temporarily prohibited, as well as any political party activity if the party had been supportive of Guzmán regime. This period, from 1954 to 1986, marked a phase in which the possibilities for pluralistic democratic political party participation were closed off and the army controlled the direction of the country.

At the beginning of the 1960s, there was a military uprising in reaction against the authoritarian nature of the regime and the corruption of the government. It was brought under control, but it gave rise to the establishment of the 13 November Rebel Movement (MR–13) and the beginning of an internal armed conflict that lasted for thirty-six years. As a consequence of the 1963 coup, the Constituent Assembly was convened, and it passed the 1965 political constitution that remained in effect until March 1982.

The earthquakes of February 4–6, 1976, which resulted in 27,000 dead, 77,000 wounded, and one million homeless—the majority of victims being indigenous inhabitants of rural areas—shook the social and political conscience of the country, and had a significant economic impact. The catastrophe and its fallout demonstrated to the country and to the world the striking economic and social inequalities that existed, but it also awakened a spirit of solidarity among Guatemalans and prompted support from other countries. The Catholic Church, through the Episcopal Conference, issued the Pastoral Letter "United in Hope," which denounced exploitation, poverty, and the repression of the majority of the population. During this period, popular and peasant organisations were reinforced, and the guerrilla movement in the regions of the central and western highlands of the country—with organisations such as the Guerrilla Army of the Poor (EGP), the Rebel Armed Forces (FAR), and the Revolutionary Organisation of People in Arms (ORPA)—also started to gain strength.

Between 1978 and 1983, Guatemala's people suffered many serious human rights violations. State repression and massacres of indigenous and other rural people were systematic. Leaders and directors of opposition political parties, members of cooperatives and social communicators, teachers, religious leaders, thinkers, and trade union leaders were routinely persecuted and eliminated. The internal armed conflict flared up again and again during this time. In 1982, the different factions of the insurgency movement joined together to form the Guatemalan National Revolutionary Unity (URNG). Thousands of families in the rural and indigenous areas had to flee and seek refuge in Mexico.

A coup in 1982 repealed the 1965 constitution, which was substituted with a fundamental government statute. There was another coup in August 1983, this time in favour of a return to democratic institutions with a Supreme Electoral Tribunal and the convening of a National Constituent Assembly, which was established in August 1984 after free elections. On May 31, 1985, the new Political Constitution of the Republic was passed. In the history of constitutional reform in Guatemala, no constitution has had broader participation of political parties and civil society organisations than this one. Even though it lacked the involvement of indigenous peoples (who constitute over half the population of the country), it did recognise the multilingual, multiethnic, and pluricultural nature of the nation and the right to the cultural identity of individuals and communities according to their values, language, and customs. It also created bodies that would guarantee democratic order, such as the Constitutional Court, the Ombudsman's Office, and the Supreme Electoral Tribunal.

The nature of internal armed conflict

The origin of armed conflict in Guatemala can be found in the persistence of social inequality, economic and political exclusion, ethnic, cultural, and linguistic discrimination, and the domination of the indigenous people by the *mestizos* and *criollos*. For the indigenous people, the conflict of 1960–96 was aimed at overcoming the conditions of social inequality and economic and political exclusion.

It is important to note that, at the beginning of the conflict, the antigovernment revolutionary forces were not demanding an end to ethnic, cultural, and linguistic discrimination. However, as the struggle evolved, more profound causes for violent political protest began to be identified, such as the impoverishment, exclusion, and exploitation of indigenous people *as* indigenous people and irrespective of their peasant or class status. Indeed, the nation as imagined or conceived by liberal and conservative Guatemalan Republicans was based on the exclusion of indigenous people and maintained by the practice of ethnic segregation. The issue of the exclusion and oppression of the indigenous people emerged as a central theme in the last phase of the process of dialogue and negotiation for the peace accords, because it had to do with the sources and foundations of Guatemalan identity and with equity, justice, and social equality.[5]

The conflict in Guatemala was both a class struggle and an effort to oppose the cultural repression of the indigenous people. The two issues were inter-related, because indigenous people were historically relegated to the lower classes as a result of the various entrenched forms of social exclusion that had been established under the racist colonial paradigm. Thus, it was all too easy for the links between social and economic discrimination and cultural and linguistic discrimination to fuse. Bringing these issues out into the open has engendered hope for building a firm and lasting peace in Guatemala, starting with the right to cultural identity, opening the space for participation at all levels and adopting a national pact to eradicate all kinds of discrimination, especially cultural and gender discrimination.

Peace dialogues

In 1986 the first government to follow the newly written (1985) constitution took office. It was a time of hope, especially in relation to political stability, the protection of human rights, economic recovery, and local development. During this period, urban and rural development councils were created at the national, regional, and provincial levels. The Central American Presidential Summits (Esquipulas I in 1986, and II in 1987) were held, during which agreements were reached that established the bases for the process of democratisation and pacification in the countries of the isthmus. Entities for guaranteeing democracy were established, including the Constitutional Court and the Ombudsman's Office. In the same vein, the General Attorney's Office was reinforced with the creation of the General Prosecutor's Office, and the independence of the Supreme Electoral Tribunal was strengthened. In the process of complying with the Esquipulas II peace plan, the National Reconciliation Commission was created, and initial conversations about reestablishing peace began between the government and the URNG.

The process of peace dialogues involved the participation of different national stakeholders, organisations, and institutions, as well as the support of representatives from friendly countries and the United Nations. It should also be noted that some influential sectors of the country opposed the negotiations.

Four phases of the process were identified between 1986 and 1996.

1. *Phase of opening up and of political will due to the urgency for peace in the region:* [6] This phase was marked by the presence of regional and international interest in establishing peace in countries with internal conflicts. Guatemala received support from friendly countries trying to begin a dialogue to settle the conflict; the country was not able to do this alone because the combating parties were determined to continue the confrontation. The citizens who were promoting dialogue toward an agreement found, in this international interest, the support conducive to its development.

2. *Phase of internal negotiations for making the dialogue process viable:* [7] After the signing of the Esquipulas II agreement, the government began to comply with the agreed-upon commitments, among them:

   - forging a destiny of peace for Central America;
   - fighting for peace and eradicating war;
   - making dialogue prevail over violence, and reason over rancour;
   - concentrating more on the youth of Central America, whose legitimate aspirations for peace and social justice, and for freedom and reconciliation, have been frustrated for many generations; and
   - invigorating peace efforts.

The process encompassed the following aspects:

   - national reconciliation;
   - the exhortation to cease hostilities;
   - democratisation;
   - free elections;
   - cessation of aid for irregular forces;
   - not using the territory in order to attack other states;
   - negotiation on security;
   - arms control and regulation;
   - refugees and displaced persons;
   - cooperation, democracy, and freedom for peace and development; and
   - international verification and follow-up.

The agreement established a broad framework in addition to precise guidelines, and this contributed to the involvement of civil society in the process.

3. *Phase of negotiation between the government and the URNG on the agreed-upon subject areas*:[8] This was marked by the achievement of the substantive accords considered at present to be the national agenda for peace and development. The assembly of civil society presented the basic reference texts (although they were not binding) for negotiation and signing. The role of the United Nations as moderator between the parties strengthened the commitments adopted at the national level and provided them with international validity.

4. *Phase of compliance with the commitments established in the operational and substantial accords relative to peace building*:[9] This current phase of the peace-building process is marked both by progress in complying with the commitments and by setbacks. The involvement of civil society organisations is carried out thematically through the commissions, and serves as the basis for reform or for passing laws that guarantee the continuity of policies and programmes established in the accords.

EDUCATIONAL POLICY REFORM AND PEACE BUILDING

Guatemalan cultural and educational policy models in the twentieth century

During the twentieth century, the evolution of trends in cultural, linguistic, and educational policy in Guatemala went through several phases. In a study on trends in such policies, Norma Tarrow (UNESCO, 1992) identified three paradigms that national, pluricultural, and multilingual states have used in order to deal with the phenomenon of languages, multiculturalism, and human rights. The three paradigms that can be applied to the case of Guatemala are those of assimilation, acceptance, and interculturalism.

Assimilation was the dominant paradigm in Guatemala from the beginning of the century to 1944. It was the model of a monocultural society that neither recognised nor accepted the reality or existence of multiculturalism, nor the principle of equality between the dominant and dominated groups. It sought to attain the ideal of development through the imposition of cultural and linguistic uniformity. Consequently, the use of indigenous languages was persecuted and prohibited, those who contributed to the universal use of Spanish and the adoption of the Spanish culture by the indigenous people were rewarded, and the nationalistic conscience was ashamed of the multilingual and multiethnic nature of the nation.

The second paradigm of acceptance emerged and was promoted when the 1945 constitution, which included an indigenist policy for the first time, was passed. Compensation programmes began to be developed to deal with the needs and values of the dominated groups, even though the objective was still to assimilate or integrate them into the dominant model of the society. During this phase, community development programmes, the National Indigenist Institute (of the Inter-American Indigenist system), and Spanish programmes with bilingual educational promoters (in Mayan languages and Spanish) were introduced.

The third phase came after the passing of the 1985 constitution, a judicial instrument with a pluralistic approach, in which the right to cultural identity and social organisation of the indigenous communities was recognised, as well as the use of their languages, Mayan clothes, values, and customs. The paradigm that resulted from this document is one of interculturalism;

with it, as a national objective, a dialogue is being initiated between cultures. Furthermore, the concepts of interaction, interdependence, exchange, and reciprocity are emerging; programmes to combat prejudice and racial discrimination, and to support human rights education and basic quality education for all, are also being promoted. Guatemala is still in this third phase, and its citizens are hopeful but also mindful of setbacks, such as the failure to ratify the constitutional reforms (1999) that included articles on indigenous rights and other social and cultural rights.

Table 1: Cultural Paradigm Shifts in Guatemala During the Twentieth Century

Historical Period	Dominant Paradigm	Features
1900–44	Assimilation	Monocultural model Multicultural reality denied Use of indigenous languages prohibited
1945–85	Acceptance	Indigenist policy Compensation programmes
1985–present	Interculturalism	Recognition of right to cultural identity Intercultural dialogue Combating prejudice and discrimination

The cultural and social resurgence of the Mayan people and other indigenous peoples is leading Guatemala to redefine itself as a nation and reorganise itself as a state. It is a dynamic process that is moving along a path of justice and equity, toward unity in diversity, whose source and support is the new education and intercultural dialogue.

In search of a new cultural and educational model: Building on the peace

At the beginning of the 1990s, Guatemala initiated a process of rethinking the concepts of nation, citizenship, multiethnicity, multiculturalism, and national identity. The process of shifting from a monocultural ideological approach to a pluricultural one was influenced by

- the concepts developed in the Constitutional Articles (1985) on social and cultural rights;
- the role of the indigenous movement and other social sectors in preparing the 1992 commemoration of the fifth centennial of the discovery of America; and
- the declaration of 1993 as the International Year of Indigenous Peoples of the World by the United Nations.

In 1990 the Congress of the Republic created the Academy of Mayan Languages of Guatemala through official decree. Two of the most important events occurred in 1994—the negotiation of the Accord on the Identity and Rights of Indigenous Peoples in the Peace Dialogues, and the celebration of the First National Congress of Mayan Education, convened by the National Council of Mayan Education (CNEM) and the Ministry of Education.

One of the characteristics of the process leading up to the peace accords is that the negotiating groups—the government of Guatemala, the URNG, and representatives of the United Nations (as a moderating agency)—used the text of the Constitution as a basic reference point for the whole process. This has given the adopted commitments a solidity, a legal disposition, and a sense of continuity in the midst of the political contradictions that characterise Guatemalan society.

Some of the accords' essential points pointed out the necessity of reforming the Constitution, because these reforms

> are substantive and fundamental conditions for the reconciliation of the Guatemalan society in the framework of the rule of law, democratic coexistence, full observance and strict respect for human rights, the eradication of impunity and, at the national level, the institutionalisation of a culture of peace based on mutual tolerance, reciprocal respect, concerted agreement on interests and the broadest social participation at all levels and with all institutions in power; that the reforms mentioned will contribute to political stability, to the strengthening of the civil power and the redefinition agreed upon in relation to the functions of the army for the new historical stage of the country; and that these systematise and develop, furthermore, the spirit and meaning of the commitments signed institutionally, politically, economically, socially, ethnically, in relation to human rights, their strict observance and the fight against impunity.
> (Accord on Constitutional Reforms and the Electoral System, 1996)

The commitments on education reform contained in the accords, which served as the basis for consultation and consensus for the parity and consultative reform commissions, are described below. Most relevant among these are the 1995 Accord on the Identity and Rights of Indigenous Peoples and the 1996 Accord on Socio-economic Aspects and the Agrarian Situation.[10]

As stated in the Accord on the Identity and Rights of Indigenous Peoples, the education system is one of the most important vehicles for the transmission and development of cultural values and knowledge. It should respond to the cultural and linguistic diversity of Guatemala, recognising and strengthening indigenous cultural identity, Mayan values and education systems and those of the other indigenous peoples, and access to formal and informal education. Additionally, it should be inclusive of the indigenous educational concepts in the national curriculum.

It is within this context that the government is committed to educational reform, including

- decentralising and regionalising the system in order to realistically adapt to linguistic and cultural needs and particularities;
- valuing the leadership role of communities and families in the definition of the curriculum and the school calendar as well as in the appointment and removal of teachers in order to respond to the interests of educational and cultural communities;
- incorporating Mayan educational concepts and those of the other indigenous peoples, in their philosophical, scientific, artistic, pedagogical, historical, linguistic, and political-social components, and reinforcing and extending bilingual intercultural education; and
- reinforcing the world vision, knowledge, and technologies of indigenous peoples as the basis for their development and for the recovery and preservation of the environment.

> ### Principles and Commitments Set Out in the
> ### *Accord on the Identity and Rights of Indigenous Peoples*
> ### That Served as References for Educational Reform
>
> Mayan Culture is the original basis of Guatemalan culture, and, together with the other indigenous cultures, it is an active and dynamic factor in the development and progress of Guatemalan society.
>
> Language is one of the pillars upon which culture is supported, inasmuch as it is a vehicle for the acquisition and transmission of the indigenous world vision, of its knowledge and cultural values.
>
> The recognition of the identity of indigenous peoples is fundamental for the construction of national unity based on the respect and exercising of political, cultural, economic and spiritual rights of all Guatemalans.
>
> The identity of peoples is the combination of a set of elements that defines them and, at the same time, allows them to be recognised as such. When dealing with Mayan identity, which has shown a capacity for secular resistance to assimilation, the following are fundamental elements:
>
> - Direct descent from the ancient Mayas and self-identification as such.
> - Languages which come from a common Mayan root.
> - A world vision which is based on the harmonious relation of all the elements of the universe, in which the human being is simply another element, land is the mother which gives life, and corn is a sacred sign, the centre of the culture. This world vision has been transmitted from generation to generation through material and written production and through oral tradition, in which women have played an important role.
>
> A common culture based on the principles and structures of Mayan thinking, a philosophy, a legacy of scientific and technological knowledge, Mayan artistic and aesthetic organisation, a collective Mayan historical memory, community organisation supported by group effort and respect for peers, and a concept of authority based on ethical and moral values.

Through the education plans, the commitments also included promoting the principle of unity in diversity and the right to receive instruction in one's native language and culture as the basic conditions for respecting and reinforcing cultural identity and self-esteem. In the context of education reform, the commitments of the accord took the different Mayan educational experiences very much into account. The commitments that resulted included the continued promotion of Mayan schools, the strengthening of the bilingual intercultural education programme for indigenous peoples, and the inclusion of a Mayan language and culture segment for the entire Guatemalan school population. Likewise, commitments were made regarding the creation of a Mayan University or the promotion of other indigenous higher education institutions, as well as the operation of the National Council of Mayan Education. It was also agreed to reinforce the system of study scholarships and grants. Teaching materials will be corrected if they present cultural or gender stereotypes. In sum, it will be a new education system in which children will be taught not to discriminate but rather to build a new nation together.

The 1996 Accord on Socio-economic Aspects and the Agrarian Situation also devoted an important component to commitments to education and training, setting down the following objectives as a guiding framework.

1. To affirm and disseminate moral and cultural values, concepts and behaviour which will be the basis of democratic coexistence, respectful of: human rights, of the cultural diversity of Guatemala, of the creative work of its people and of the protection of the environment, as well as of the values and mechanisms of participation and consensus among citizens on social and political issues, which is the basis of a culture of peace.

2. To avoid the perpetuation of poverty and social, ethnic and geographical discrimination, and discrimination against women, particularly that which results from the rural-urban divide.

3. To contribute to the incorporation of technical and scientific progress and, therefore, to the achievement of growing levels of productivity, of better employment generation and improved income for the people and of an advantageous insertion into the world economy.

The accord was based on the concept that education and training fulfil fundamental roles in the economic, cultural, social, and political development of the country. They are thus essential for a strategy of equity and national unity, and are determining factors in economic modernisation and international competitiveness. This is why it is necessary to reform the education system and its administration, as well as to apply a state policy that is coherent and dynamic with regard to education. The accord also established commitments such as

- a significant increase in resources allocated to education;
- the adaptation of educational content, using as a basis the results of the reform commission established under the Accord on the Identity and Rights of Indigenous Peoples;
- an extension of coverage at all levels, specifically in bilingual education in rural areas;
- training for social participation;
- a programme of national civic education for democracy and peace, the renewal of the political culture, and the peaceful solution of conflicts;
- community-school interaction and community participation;
- the training of educational administrators; and
- the establishment of a consultative commission to implement reform in support of the Ministry of Education.

Following the 1995 Accord on Indigenous Peoples, the General Directorate of Bilingual Intercultural Education (DIGEBI) was created, and the curriculum for primary teacher training was revised, incorporating Mayan cultural elements into the subject areas of philosophy, language, and didactics.

The year 1996 saw the signing of the firm and lasting peace (marking the end of the civil war) and the ratification of the International Labour Organization's Convention 169 on Indigenous and Tribal Peoples in Independent Countries. With the peace accord signed, 1997 was characterised as the year of the commissions (parity and specific), which were set up to comply with the peace commitments in relation to a number of issues:

- strengthening of the judicial system;
- recognition of indigenous languages as official languages;
- land rights;
- reform and participation at all levels;
- indigenous sacred places;
- a historical vindication of human rights violations;
- a specific education plan for uprooted people; and
- general education reform.

It was a year of intense dialogue and mutual recognition among Guatemalans from different cultures and social levels.

The following year, 1998, the conclusions and recommendations reached concerning each of the abovementioned issues were disseminated to the different social sectors and cultural communities of the country. The Parity Commission presented the Conceptual Framework and Design of Education Reform to the Ministry of Education and educational stakeholders, and the current Consultative Commission for Education Reform (discussed further in the section on Consultation and Curriculum Policy Formulation) was established.

In 1999, the country embarked on learning about, discussing, and ratifying proposed reforms to the Constitution through a referendum. Despite the fact that the year seemed to be of key importance in the process of strengthening and securing the commitments laid out in the peace accords, the results of the referendum were negative. Four factors explain this failure:

1. the dominant economic and political groups had opposed the reforms because they impinged on their historical privileges;

2. the leaders of the peace movement were overconfident because the issue was of such immediate importance and they were unable to influence urban areas in order to translate the importance of the reforms into votes;

3. control of the mass media was in the hands of the dominant economic sector; and

4. the votes of the indigenous society were divided into at least three groups—one in favour of reforms, one that abstained for fear of reprisals by the sectors that had persecuted them and destroyed their villages in the past, and one that had failed to receive clear information about the reforms.

As a result, it was feared that 1999 would represent the "burial" of the peace accords. However—and this is characteristic of Guatemalan society—something unpredictable occurred:

the accords were relaunched in the third quarter of 1999. Significantly, education reform has been considered to be the central issue of the peace-building process ever since.

In 2000, there was a change of government; during the inauguration ceremony, the new president declared that the peace accords constituted the political commitments of the state, with a renewed promise to the process of educational reform as one of those policy priorities. In its plan for the sector, the Ministry of Education had stated that its mission was to: "Transform the national education system, making it participatory in compliance with the Peace Accords, in the framework of the process of Education Reform and the Governance Pact, prioritising the strategies of (1) expanding access, and (2) an improvement in the quality of services" (MINEDUC Plan, 2000–04). The plan was based on the policies of Equity and Justice, Interculturalism, Quality/Excellence, Democratisation, and Sustainability.

Basic education policy framework

The Political Constitution of the Republic establishes that the of main objective of education is the integral development of the individual through knowledge of national and universal reality and culture. It declares that education, instruction, social training, and the systematic teaching of the Constitution and of human rights are of national interest. It also makes initial, pre-primary, primary, and basic secondary education compulsory.

The Education Law (Legal Decree 12-91) defines the national education system as an orderly and interrelated set of elements, processes, and subjects, through which educational action is developed in accordance with the characteristics, needs, and interests of the historical, economic, and cultural reality of Guatemala. Education should be participatory and decentralised in management, delivery, and decisionmaking at the regional level.

The administration of the system is the responsibility of the Ministry of Education, and organised at the levels of

- *the directorate*: the Ministerial and Vice Ministerial Offices and the National Council of Education;
- *coordination and execution*: the General and Provincial Directorates;
- *advice and planning*: the Directorate of Quality in Educational Development and the Improvement of Human Resources; and
- *support*: support programmes for educational development.

In the municipalities and the area jurisdictions, the system is supported by the technical-administrative coordination offices and pedagogical guidance teams.

At the beginning of the 1980s, the Latin American and Caribbean governments, with the support of international agencies, agreed to promote, in their respective countries, the Major Project in the Field of Education for Latin America and the Caribbean, PROMEDLAC.[11] This had a positive influence on the Guatemalan education system, particularly in the areas of extending access to basic education, improving educational quality, and eradicating illiteracy. The project supported improvements in the administration of the system and in teacher training, as well as the reinforcement of research and educational planning and evaluation. In addition, the first experiences of bilingual education of the Bilingual Education Programme (PEB), were introduced in pilot schools in the K'iche', Mam, Kaqchikel, and Q'eqchi' linguistic communities.

Educational indicators in 2002 registered a net rate of schooling of 47 percent at the pre-primary level, 88.5 percent at the primary level, 30.5 percent at the basic secondary level, and 17.5 percent at the diversified secondary level. The illiteracy rate is still 32.4 percent (SEGEPLAN, 2003). Primary education—the seven- to twelve-year age group—is the level that has received most attention in the last fifteen years, and an average school enrolment of 65 percent in 1988 has increased to 84 percent in 2000. It is hoped that with a 2 percent growth in enrolment each year it will be possible to achieve universal access to primary education in the country by 2013. In order to reach this goal, it is essential to improve the quality of teaching.

It is also crucial to ensure a sustained increase in the state budget allocation for public education such that it might reach 4 percent of the gross domestic product (GDP) in 2005. The funding of education is one of the problems that the Guatemalan state has had to solve gradually in order to comply with national laws, the peace accords, and international agreements on education, science, and culture. Between 1990 and 1999 the share of annual GDP allocated to education varied between 1.7 and 2.0 percent, which is far below the Central American average and the goals established in the World Declaration on Education for All in 1990. Guatemalan state budgetary allocation for education in relation to the GDP in 2002 was 2.3 percent, one of the lowest in Central America.

Based on data from the 2000 school year, the dropout rate in primary education remains at an average of 11 percent, while grade repetition is at 12 percent. Knowledge gaps remain an unresolved and persistent problem; there is a gap between girls' and boys' enrolment ratios at each level, with an average 7.1 percentage point difference in favour of boys and a generally urban bias. Finally, with respect to the multilingual and pluricultural nature of the country, only 18 percent of the indigenous population receives bilingual and intercultural education.

The education reform of 1998

Rationales: Cultural stereotypes and social solidarity

In Guatemala, social, cultural, ethnic, and gender relations still retain signs, gestures, attitudes, and expressions that show the persistence of discrimination and a lack of equity and solidarity. This culture of discrimination was, for many years, expressed through stereotypes that appeared in school texts and educational materials. An analysis made by the Linguistics Institute of Rafael Landivar University on stereotypes in school textbooks, and published between 1984 and 1992 by the national textbook centre, CENALTEX, concluded that textbook materials contained cultural and gender stereotypes and prejudices, in addition to distortions and omissions about the pluricultural, multilingual, and multiethnic nature of Guatemalan society and about the history of the country.[12] It was through these materials that the national conscience of many generations was formed.

Education is now considered to be a decisive factor for promoting the cultural identity of each of the peoples that make up the country and for affirming the national identity. It is through education that a peaceful and harmonious coexistence between the people and communities is fostered—a coexistence based on inclusion, tolerance, solidarity, respect, equality, equity, and a mutual enrichment that eliminates all discriminatory manifestations. It is for this reason that the design of the reform, and other documents derived from it, explain that it is necessary "to teach not to discriminate." The educational system must have as its mission not replicating any type of discrimination within the school setting, and should, moreover, promote this idea of nondiscrimination in Guatemalan society as a whole. To achieve this,

- programmes, contents, classroom practices, textbooks, and other materials must be reviewed to eliminate discriminatory beliefs, attitudes, and procedures;

- respect for equal opportunities in school and in other educational settings must be promoted; and

- educational legislation must be reviewed to eliminate discriminatory provisions and to incorporate standards that will make such legislation operational.

This is a struggle against gender, ethnic, social, cultural, linguistic, and geographic discrimination. The design of the current educational reform established in its philosophical framework that "The cultural phenomenon is the best defined and specific face of a nation because it encompasses the treasures of its life and its history, of its spirit and of its present and future aspirations" (COPARE, 1998).

Background

Prior to the current reform, the educational reform of 1987 was undertaken within the framework of the 1985 constitution. The policy of decentralisation at the root of the reform engendered two strategies: (1) administrative regionalisation based on politico-geographical and not cultural-linguistic criteria; and (2) curriculum reform aiming to adapt national education objectives and learning content to regional characteristics. Generally, this reform is appreciated for having set up local workshops on curriculum change in order to contribute to the formulation of a pedagogical project in each educational community. The process was interrupted in 1989 by a teachers' strike that lasted ten weeks and led, among other consequences, to 100,000 children dropping out of school, mainly in rural and indigenous areas (MINEDUC, 1990). This interruption in the reform process led the Ministry of Education and the teachers' association to discuss and promote a new Education Law (1991), which currently regulates the national education system.

Aims

The education reform of 1998 established the foundation and profile of a new form of education whose source would be the specific cultures of the peoples of the nation, as well as universal knowledge and cultural values. It would promote regionalisation in accordance with linguistic criteria and, in doing so, would formally include the community's mother tongue into the teaching-learning process. It would reinforce the Spanish language as the lingua franca of the country, reconceptualising the national identity as the result of an intercultural dialogue. Finally, it would espouse an education that might help to eradicate discrimination and exclusion, strengthening educational communities and the awareness of moral, social, civic, and environmental values. The fundamental dimensions of the education reform are

- the individual as the source of the rights and duties of the human being;

- the family as the keeper and creator of the values of life; and

- the culture as an expression of the originality and freedom of each community and people, as a human right.

Objectives

According to the document "Design of Education Reform," the objectives of the new Guatemalan education are the following:

- To reflect and respond to the characteristics, needs and aspirations of a multicultural, multilingual and multiethnic country, respecting, reinforcing and enriching personal identity and the identity of its peoples, as the basis for unity in diversity.

- To provide a sound technical, scientific and humanistic education, including enhancing performance for productive work, the development of each people, and national development.

- To contribute to the systematisation of the oral tradition of the nation's cultures, as a basis for endogenous strengthening, which will be conducive to their own growth and the achievement of positive and useful exogenous relations.

- To instil respect and the practice of human rights, solidarity, democratic life and a culture of peace, the responsible use of freedom, and compliance with obligations, overcoming individual interests in the search for the common good.

- To contribute to the capacity for the critical and creative adoption of knowledge and of indigenous and western science and technology in favour of rescuing and preserving the environment and integral and sustainable development.

- To generate and put into practice new educational models which respond to the changing needs of the society and its development model.

Guiding principles

In response to the social, cultural, economic, and political context in which Guatemalan society lives, attentive to regional and world agreements on education, science, and culture, and in compliance with the peace accords, education reform is guided by four central guiding principles:

1. *Life in democracy and a culture of peace*: this is a fundamental element of education for a society that has historically suffered from political violence, social and economic injustice, and an eventful democracy with low levels of participation. It is an element around which it is necessary to build and reinforce a culture of participation, dialogue, peaceful conflict resolution, an awareness of human rights, and the practice of social and spiritual values of the cultures in the country in agreement with universal values.

2. *Unity in diversity*: this is a central principle around which the spirit of a new nation is to be built, supported by its diversity, based on respectful and supportive relations, and aimed at the integral education of new generations for their active participation in national and international life.

3. *Integral and sustainable development*: this central principle aims at building a model of sustainable development with an identity that is economically feasible, politically viable, ecologically sustainable, humanly acceptable, socially and ethnically fair, and culturally relevant. The aim is to contribute to achieving an improvement in the quality of life through the elimination of poverty and a concern and care for health and the environment, within a framework of justice, legality, and equity. It considers the development of an education that respects and cultivates the natural environment of each microclimate to be of vital importance.

4. *Science and technology*: this central element corresponds to guaranteeing sustainable development in complete harmony with nature, raising productivity and fighting poverty, and valorising Mayan science and technology and that of other indigenous peoples. The education process should thus promote, while always maintaining cultural identity:

- the systematic exercise of scientific thinking;
- the stimulus of creativity;
- the capacity to learn how to learn and how to undertake;
- self-criticism and the continuous search for a scientific explanation for natural and social phenomena;
- the analysis and solution of problems and the development of critical thinking,
- scientific research and experimentation; and
- permanent updating in relation to global technological developments.

Strategic areas of the reform

The reform has been characterised throughout as a participatory and representative process that has been built gradually. The Parity Commission organised dialogues and consultations with different sectors, institutions, communities, and key education actors in the country, and formulated the design for education reform, which was presented to the Guatemalan society to be executed by the Ministry of Education and supported by the Consultative Commission. Fundamentally, it is a social movement inclusive of and coordinated with other processes of social transformation, which aim at the construction of a plurilingual, multiethnic, and pluricultural state. As a process, it includes political, technical, scientific, and cultural aspects; by nature it is integral, gradual, permanent, and futuristic; in its dynamics it is flexible, open to evaluation, feasible, and accumulative. Having carried out the consultation and gained national consensus, the Ministry of Education and the Consultative Commission identified seven strategic thematic areas for education reform (see Table 2).

Table 2: Strategic Areas of Reform

AREA	IMPLICATIONS FOR SOCIAL COHESION
Equity	Compulsory basic education for all Overcoming social, economic, and cultural inequalities
Quality	Cultural relevance and responsiveness of curriculum to education demand
Human Resources	Responding to traditionally overlooked needs in indigenous regions, uprooted communities, and among disabled persons
Multiculturalism and Interculturalism	Recognition of multiculturalism and the promotion of intercultural dialogue as a means of establishing respect and overcoming inequalities
Decentralisation and Modernisation	Responding to local and regional needs in formal and informal education
Sustainability	Enhancing the involvement of local government
Monitoring and Evaluation	Community participation and social audits

1. *Equity*: refers to the obligation of the state to provide compulsory initial pre-primary, primary, and basic secondary education for all as stated in global commitments made at Jomtien (1990) and Dakar (2000). Complying with these commitments implies solving the problem of social, economic, and cultural inequalities, through systematic transformation and modernisation of education.

2. *Quality*: refers both to issues of cultural relevance and education demand, in addition to questions of relevance referred to when discussing to what degree education is able to substantially inform the integral development of the individual. It involves political, ideological and technical, and pedagogical dimensions of the curriculum vis-à-vis its relationship to the community and the society; modalities of evaluation; textbooks and other learning materials; pedagogical orientation and educational supervision; the pre- and in-service training of teachers, and research and evaluation.

3. *Human Resources*: refers to the improvement of the processes of education, selection, training, updating, evaluation, and remuneration and incentives concerning educational personnel. There is particular emphasis on the creation of a teaching service to respond

to needs that have been traditionally overlooked, specifically in indigenous regions neglected by the system, in uprooted communities, and among disabled people.

4. *Multiculturalism and Interculturalism*: refers to the need to redesign the traditionally monocultural and monolingual nation through the education system. Recognition of the multiculturalism of the country and the building of interculturalism is a central pillar of the education reform. A dialogue that results from the different world visions and is mutually enriching for all the people and communities because of its potential to lead to respectful encounters will contribute solutions to national problems and aid in overcoming inequalities.

5. *Decentralisation and Modernisation*: involves the integral transformation of both formal and informal education subsystems in order to adapt to the diverse nature of the nation and to the geographical and ecological regions, as well as to the challenges inherent in the dynamics of global development. It will respond to the needs for local and regional management established in the recent laws on urban and rural development and decentralisation, paying attention to municipal autonomy.

6. *Sustainability*: refers to the need to agree on education policies as state-level policies. It also relates to advancing the involvement of local governments and development councils in education development and influencing the demand for education services. It further serves to maintain the principle of state subsidy for public education.

7. *Monitoring and Evaluation*: refers to indicators proposed for the execution and implementation of the reform plan and the verification of the achievement of goals. It can rely on having community participation and be strengthened by social audits.

Translating the reform policies into curriculum

We will briefly turn now to the ways in which the education reform and its strategies have been concretely incorporated into the curriculum. Curricular integration of preschool education, for example, is being implemented in order to take into account not only the particular features and characteristics of children's developmental stages, but their sociocultural and linguistic background as well. The curricular change at this level is fundamental to establishing the foundations of social cohesion through educational communities, since it is based on such criteria as family and community involvement, attention to local environments and cultural relevance, and communication in the mother tongue (DICADE/MINEDUC, 2002).[13]

During the first phase of National Implementation of the General Framework of Curricular Reform and the Basic Curriculum for Primary Education, in rural and urban areas of the public, private, cooperative, municipal, and community sectors of the country, bilingual and intercultural modes of teaching and learning in early childhood education were implemented.

The Ministry of Education established and disseminated the new two-cycle primary education curriculum through the provincial directorates of education and the municipal and zone coordinating offices. The first cycle covers the first, second, and third grades; the second cycle covers the fourth, fifth, and sixth grades.

Table 3: Organisation of Curricular Areas into Cycles

Fundamental Areas (first cycle)	Training Areas
• Communication & Language L1 Native Language • Communication & Language L2 Second Language • Communication & Language L3 Third Language • Mathematics • Social & Natural Environment • Artistic Expression • Physical Education	Learning Skills Civic Education Productivity & Development

Fundamental Areas (second cycle)	Training Areas
• Communication & Language L1 Native Language • Communication & Language L2 Second Language • Communication & Language L3 Third Language • Mathematics • Social Sciences • Natural Sciences & Technology • Artistic Expression • Physical Education	Learning Skills Civic Education Productivity & Development

The conceptual framework, the profiles for admission and completion of the basic secondary education level, and the organisation and development of the fundamental and formative areas contain and cover principles, objectives, and strategies that facilitate the integral development of human beings. The framework recognises, respects, and nurtures cultural identity that is oriented toward an experience of human rights and a culture of peace, and promotes intercultural life as elements of harmonious coexistence and social cohesion.

Another important result is the implementation of the first phase of a programme addressed to teachers at a national level, the Professional Development Programme (PDP). The purpose of the PDP is

- to improve the pedagogical and technical quality of preschool and primary school teachers;
- to disseminate the new concepts of Guatemalan education;
- to improve traditional educational practices; and
- to fulfil the commitments assumed by the country in global and regional education agreements.

Fifty-five thousand teachers from the 331 municipalities of the country participated in the first phase. The subject areas developed were Mathematics and Logical Thought, Communications and Language, Cultures and Languages of Guatemala, Social-Cultural Context, and Educational Reality. Three universities (the state university and two private universities), in coordination with the Ministry of Education, implemented the programme.

BILINGUAL AND INTERCULTURAL EDUCATION

As was mentioned in the historical overview of Guatemala, twenty-one of the country's linguistic communities are Mayan in origin.[14] In addition to these, Garífuna and Xinca also exist, the first being of Afro-Caribbean origin and the second from another Mesoamerican linguistic family. Spanish is Guatemala's official language. According to the text of the Universal Declaration of Linguistic Rights, a linguistic community is

> any human society established historically in a particular territorial space, whether this space be recognized or not, which identifies itself as a people and has developed a common language as a natural means of communication and cultural cohesion among its members. The term language proper to a territory refers to the language of the community historically established in such a space.
>
> (Barcelona, Spain, 1996)

The struggle of the indigenous peoples of Guatemala is expressed in this declaration, and the strategy, which allows for the technical feasibility and political viability of realising this right in the education system, is that of bilingual and intercultural education (BIE).

Strategies adopted for BIE

The important thematic emphasis placed on multicultural and intercultural elements characterises the latest reform efforts. The Ministry of Education has, therefore, established that bilingual and intercultural education be a fundamental strategy of the new Guatemalan education model.[15] To realise the incorporation of BIE, the ministry has adopted the following specific strategies and policy changes.

First and foremost, the ministry is betting on the strategy of training bilingual intercultural education teachers. Seventeen BIE teacher training schools have been created, in which young men and women are trained to develop their teaching skills for the preschool and primary education levels, in view of their application in schools located in regions that are predominantly inhabited by an indigenous population.[16] Furthermore, the ministry has established that from now on, education in all schools in indigenous communities shall be bilingual and intercultural, and shall be intercultural in all of the schools in the country.

Secondly, the rural teacher training schools (created in the years 1947–75 under the paradigms of assimilation and acceptance) have been transformed into teacher training schools in BIE. In regions with a predominantly *mestizo* population that is primarily Spanish speaking, the Ministry of Education has created intercultural preschool and primary education teacher training schools. It is expected that in the medium term this policy will result in having teachers who have been trained in accordance with the new educational concept being promoted through the current educational reform.

The final result of this reform that we will discuss is the linguistic policy defined by the Ministry of Education for application in preschool and primary education. The levels of language proficiency of the school-age population of the country are diverse. Therefore, the ministry has established flexible strategies oriented toward developing both the mother tongue and a second language, in a gradual and progressive manner, until students are able to reach a stable social bilingual status.

Table 4: Profile of Bilingual Proficiency for Preschool and Primary Education[17]

Preschool Education	First Cycle	Second Cycle
L2	L3	L3
	L2	L2
L1	L1	L1

Key: L1 = native language; L2 = second language; L3 = third language

The profile is a guiding framework for social-linguistic development in the classroom and the school community. At the preschool level the mother tongue is the language of communication and learning; it is the language in which boys and girls bring their prior familial and cultural knowledge to school. In the school setting the linguistic proficiency is broadened by new actors, new situations of communication, and new purposes. The second language starts to develop, mainly through oral expression.

The mother tongue is defined as the language in which a child learns to speak. The profile presents the mother tongue as the language of communication and learning and as the object of study in the two primary school cycles. The area of communication and language in the mother tongue enables the development of linguistic capacities and the skills to organise thoughts.

The profile presents the development of the second language as a gradual and progressive learning process that begins at the preschool level and continues until the primary level has been completed. Proficiency in a second language is fundamental in this multilingual and pluricultural nation. The learning of a second language is enabled by the phenomenon of the transfer of acquired abilities in the mother tongue—in other words, the thinking and communication skills are acquired only once (DICADE, 2002). Starting with the second cycle, the profile presents an idiomatic parallelism between L1 and L2. English, the third language (L3), is incorporated as an object of study with which the linguistic and cultural horizon of children is broadened and enriched. In the first cycle the third language is mainly developed through oral expression and then advances to reading comprehension and writing.

The greatest challenges facing bilingual intercultural education lie both in raising the awareness of personnel in the education system and in contributing to more informed national opinion. The importance and relevance of bilingual education is based on the argument that educating the child in the mother tongue and culture is a matter of respect for the dignity of the individual and particularly relevant for success at school. A further challenge is to demonstrate to the society, and particularly to parents, that bilingual education not only improves the indigenous people's progress at school but also manages to disseminate intercultural values and attitudes within the school community.

Bilingual and intercultural education in practice

National Programme of Bilingual Intercultural Education

Because of the positive results obtained in the bilingual education project (1980–84), particularly as reflected through the reduction of the dropout rate, improved motivation due to the use of the mother tongue and culture, and the improved quality in teacher training, the Ministry of Education created the National Programme of Bilingual Intercultural Education (PRONEBI) with the support of USAID and national counterpart funds. The forty pilot schools have been increased to four hundred schools in the four linguistic areas of K'iche', Mam, Kaqchikel, and Q'eqchi', with a progressive extension to another nine linguistic areas (Tz'utujil, Pokomchi', Q'anjob'al, Ixil, Achi, Chorti, Pokomam, Popti, and Awakateko), especially at the level of bilingual pre-primary school. The methodologies for bilingual teaching have been updated, with sixteen hundred teachers trained along with twelve hundred education promoters with teaching certificates as bilingual pre-primary teachers. Eighty-five curriculum development specialists and educational supervisors have specialised in bilingual intercultural education at the university undergraduate and teaching degree levels.

The goal of the programme in an initial five-year phase (1985–89) was to reach 160,000 monolingual indigenous Mayan children at the pre-primary and primary (grades one to four) levels with bilingual education methodologies and an intercultural approach. The programme continued for another five years (1991–95) in association with the project BEST—Improvement of Basic Secondary Education (USAID-MINEDUC).

General Directorate of Bilingual Intercultural Education

As a consequence of complying with the commitments established in the Peace Accords on the Identity and Rights of Indigenous Peoples (March 1995) and on the Socio-economic Aspects and the Agrarian Situation (May 1996), in addition to the recommendations of the First Congress of Mayan Education convened by the National Council of Mayan Education, CNEM, the government issued Resolution 736-95, through which it created the General Directorate of Bilingual Intercultural Education (DIGEBI) as part of the national education system. According to the Education Law, the general directorate has a high level of coordination and execution at the national level, and consequently has the considerable challenge and responsibility of promoting and leading the process of generalising bilingual and intercultural education in the country, which will contribute to solving the many deficiencies in the education of indigenous peoples in the future.

During the 2002 academic year, bilingual and intercultural education was implemented in 3,808 pre-primary and primary schools, by 7,570 teachers, reaching close to 270,000 indigenous children (DIGEBI-MINEDUC, 2002). It should be noted that this coverage represents 20 percent of the total school population reached during that academic year, a very low percentage when compared to the provisions established in the National Education Law and the peace accords.

The Institute of Linguistics and Education of Rafael Landivar University

The Institute of Linguistics and Education of Rafael Landivar University was founded in 1986 with the objective of carrying out research and development in linguistics and sociolinguistics of the Mayan languages and other indigenous languages (Garífuna and Xinca), as well as studying Spanish as a second language in the schools located in indigenous regions. As a result of this, there have been twelve hundred publications released, including

- pedagogical grammars;
- judicial glossaries;
- texts and literature for primary and pre-primary education in twenty-one Mayan languages;
- manuals for training bilingual teachers;
- children's literature in Mayan languages and Spanish; and
- modules and booklets for bilingual literacy.

An extensive debate on Guatemalan education and linguistics has developed, supported by the Consultative Commission for Education Reform. The institute, through its director, Guillermina Herrera, contributed substantively to the creation of the Academy of Mayan Languages of Guatemala (1990) and the Commission for Making Indigenous Languages Official.

Mayan Bilingual Intercultural Education Project

This project was designed in response to the new policies of the Ministry of Education (1993–95) and to the Accord on the Identity and Rights of Indigenous Peoples. The project aims to contribute to the renewal of both the school curriculum in areas with a predominantly indigenous population and the bilingual teacher training in schools in the central and western highlands of the country. It was initiated in 1995 and continues to support rural and bilingual education at the time of writing.

Programme of Support for the Education Sector in Guatemala, PROASE/European Community

The project supports quality improvement and cultural relevance in pre-primary and primary education in the Verapaz region (Q'eqchi and Pokomchi). It also supports the teacher training schools of Cobán and Salamá, with curriculum reform as well as a refresher programme for bilingual teachers.[18]

Contribution from the Support Mobilisation Project for Mayan Education, PROMEM/ UNESCO/NETHERLANDS for Mayan Bilingual Intercultural Education and Education Reform

This project was designed as a concrete response to the commitments of the Peace Accord on the Identity and Rights of Indigenous Peoples, and to the recommendations of the First National Congress on Mayan Education (1994). One of its objectives is to put into operation the Local Mayan Education Units (ULEM), in which quality improvement and cultural relevance in pre-primary and primary education are being progressively developed. This is being done through mother tongue and second-language learning, Mayan mathematics, Mayan values, Mayan calendar and spirituality, aesthetics and art, and additionally through changes in classroom and school management. The impetus the project has given to Mayan language and culture in the curriculum has influenced the Ministry of Education to pay more attention to bilingual intercultural education. Furthermore, the project has developed the important activity of research and the systematisation of Mayan science and culture, as well as teacher training at the level of teaching and undergraduate degrees that support bilingual intercultural education in teacher training colleges. The project has been active since September 1995 and concluded its second phase in October 2002. An extension phase was developed in 2003 in order to promote the dissemination of Mayan pedagogical innovations to other educational communities and the scaling up and adoption by the mainstream education system.

CONSULTATION AND CURRICULUM POLICY FORMULATION

Institutional framework of curricular change

Since July 1989, the entity responsible for implementing curricular policies has been the System of Human Resources Improvement and Curricular Adaptation (SIMAC). It was created by Resolution 470-89 for the purpose of implementing a permanent training policy for management, technical, and teaching staff in the education system, in addition to being responsible for curricular design and development and pedagogical research and evaluation. As of 2001, its functions were redirected with the creation of the Directorate of Educational Quality and Development (DICADE). DICADE's objectives are to develop the curriculum transformation process and improve human resources in the education system, the two main components of education reform, and to further work in educational research and development in the country.

The activities and functions of SIMAC-DICADE are carried out in coordination with the Consultative Commission for Education Reform and the specialised departments of the Ministry of Education, such as the General Directorate of Bilingual Intercultural Education, the General Directorate of Extra Curricular Education, the Education Innovation Unit, the Education Planning Unit, the National Education Self-Management Programme, the Education Development Units of the Provincial Directorates of Education, and the Provincial Head Offices for Bilingual Intercultural Education.

The Ministry of Education, within the framework of state reform, has established as one of its policies the modernisation and decentralisation, in terms of management, delivery, and decisionmaking, of the education system. In following this policy, it proposes to promote the participation of the education community and civil society in educational work, decentralise administrative and technical functions, and redistribute and reorganise financial functions. To achieve this technically, it has been proposed that quality monitoring in education services be decentralised through reintroducing the pedagogical support and orientation system at the local level.[19]

Although some advances have been made in the transformation of the education management model such as the substitution strategic planning for detailed programming and the greater use of teamwork and control by results, state decentralisation and reorganisation have progressed slowly, and education management, in its core aspects, continues to be marked by a centralised administration operating along rigid and hierarchical lines. By the same token, the intermediate levels, with regard to technical functions and quality processes, continue to be transmission chains for the hierarchy, and the schools are the executors of uniform educational actions directed by the central levels.

Nevertheless, the curriculum reform policy promoted in the framework of education reform clearly proposes curricular decentralisation as a direct consequence of its stated objective to pay greater attention to the characteristics and demands of the student population within the framework of the country's cultural and linguistic diversity. Therefore, the intention is to develop a flexible, significant, and relevant curriculum with the participation of the educational community and civil society.

Given the above discussion, three levels of implementation for curricular planning have been proposed:[20]

1. *The national level*, which prescribes the guidelines and objectives of national education as well as the common elements of the curriculum, and establishes learning aptitudes for all Guatemalan children in the framework of unity in diversity.

2. *The regional or intermediate level*, for which the curriculum is contextualised in accordance with the characteristics and individual features of the sociolinguistic regions of the country, with the aim of strengthening identity and interculturalism in conditions of equality and equity.

3. *The local or school/education centre level*, for which education projects and classroom curricular programmes are prepared, based on national curricular guidelines and the regional sociolinguistic and cultural curricular context, in accordance with local characteristics and the most intensely felt interests and needs of the children.

One of the limitations faced by the Ministry of Education in putting this curricular decentralisation policy into practice is its dependence on the current distribution of national zones of governance. The political and administrative division of Guatemala into provinces or municipalities, which does not correspond to the cultural and linguistic diversity of the country, is nonetheless reflected in the present organisation of the education system's administration. The CCRE presented a proposal for educational regionalisation that would use sociolinguistic criteria for decentralising the curriculum. As a result, Regional Socio-linguistic Councils were established and are currently in the process of being structured. In principle, it is hoped that these councils, which integrate Ministry of Education authorities and officials with representatives of both the education community and civil society, will participate in curricular preparation at the regional level.

Even once the process of establishing the councils within the education system's administration has occurred, qualitative progress in the administrative decentralisation of the state—progress in accordance with provisions concerning the economic, social, cultural, linguistic, and environmental criteria in the Accord on the Identity and Rights of Indigenous Peoples—will not have been similarly achieved. Because of this, educational regionalisation based on sociolinguistic and cultural criteria will face operative delays. Beyond the crucial challenge of realising decentralised curricular transformation, other structural problems need to be overcome, such as the lack of qualified personnel, the more effective use of appointed personnel, and an insufficient budget for implementing the different components of education reform.

Forms of consultation and participation: Constructing national dialogue

The Consultative Commission for Education Reform

The process of education reform resulting from the 1996 peace accords generated new spaces for impact in decisionmaking processes, with one of the most important being the establishment of the Consultative Commission for Education Reform (CCRE). The CCRE was an outgrowth of the Parity Commission for Education Reform (COPARE) and was formally established April 2, 1997, comprised of five government delegates and five representatives of indigenous organisations. One result of the work done by the CCRE was the elaboration of a new Design for Education Reform. This document integrates more than forty-three education proposals presented by civil society, and also serves as a philosophical and conceptual framework for the transformation of the education system, providing strategic guidelines for an integrated education project for the Guatemalan nation which is in harmony with the country's multiethnic, pluricultural, and multilingual characteristics. The envisioned participation of the Mayan, Xinca, Garífuna, and *ladino* peoples occupies a central position in the document.

The CCRE is a decisionmaking body with broad representation from among different sectors, including Mayan organisations, women's organisations, teachers' unions and associations, students, journalists, Churches, universities, private education centres, and private enterprise,[21] with the responsibility of setting the guidelines for implementing education reform. It obtained legal status on October 24, 1998, through Resolution 748-97, and has obtained several extensions to its effective operation (currently through July 31, 2004) due to the important role it plays in the process of education reform. The Ministry of Education is responsible for its general coordination, though it operates with an executive council, made up of five regular members elected from the general assembly, and has a representative function. It also has a technical secretariat that provides the support necessary for developing its different activities.

In accordance with the priorities and fundamental components of the Design for Education Reform, the CCRE established five subcommission working groups:

1. Juridical Framework;
2. Curricular Transformation;
3. Human Resources;
4. Social Mobilisation; and
5. Multi- and Interculturalism.

These groups are made up of CCRE members and external consultants, contracted mainly through international cooperation funding, and charged with the task of preparing technical proposals. Once the proposals have been improved upon and approved by the CCRE, they represent a fundamental input for decisionmaking on the implementation of education reform.

The results of the CCRE's work during its five years of operation are impressive.[22] One effort worthy of special mention was the realisation of the process of National Dialogue and Consensus on Education Reform. In 2001, for example, the process concluded with the following expressed aims having been reached:

- curriculum transformation with the effective participation, at all levels, of the teachers and members of civil society who make up the Councils of Education, with geographical, ethnic, cultural, linguistic, gender, and productivity relevance in accordance with the National Education Law and in the framework of a culture of peace, in order to generate sustainable development.
- provision of education to all those being educated in their mother tongue and culture, strengthening and developing their identity at all levels, areas, and educational modalities, aiming at building stable social bilingualism for intercultural coexistence in all the communities (CCRE, 2001).

The discussions served the purpose of validating and legitimating the reform's central elements and fundamental strategies. The reform of education policies required, on the one hand, legitimisation by those who were to implement it and, on the other, broad social support among key actors and those involved in some way with work in national education. Among these actors it is necessary to draw attention to the teachers and their professional organisations and unions, whose opposition to the education reform proposed at the end of the 1980s prevented its implementation.

One of the lessons learned from this experience was that it was essential to carry out a broad consultation process, especially when taking into account the variety of important national issues (see Table 5) that were placed on the national education agenda, whose relative merits were debated with a view to building a democratic and inclusive society following armed conflict.

Table 5: Issues Placed on the National Education Agenda for Debate

Guatemalan identity based on a hegemonic culture	versus	national identity based on cultural diversity.
Traditional inherited knowledge	versus	scientific modern knowledge.
A monocultural education system	versus	an intercultural education system.
Biased official history	versus	history representative of all the nation's peoples.
Monolingual education for all	versus	bilingual education for indigenous people.
Educational materials reproducing the ways of thinking of the dominant culture	versus	educational materials representative of the world visions and cultures of different peoples.
Teacher training for the adoption of a single culture	versus	teacher training for cultural diversity and multi- and interculturalism.
Unifying pedagogical practice	versus	diverse pedagogical practice in accordance with cultural contexts.
A uniform and centralised curriculum	versus	a diversified and flexible curriculum.
Centralised education management in accordance with the political and administrative divisions of the country	versus	decentralised education management in accordance with the sociolinguistic and cultural diversity of the country.

The process of dialogue and reaching consensus had the fundamental objectives of preparing a National Education Agenda by means of the participation of different sectors of Guatemalan society and of establishing a system of Education Councils in view of making them permanent participation structures for the education community and civil society in actions related to education reform.

Thus, this process was developed from the bottom up—or, in other words, from the base to the summit—with its point of departure at the municipal level and on up to the provincial and national levels, holding 331 municipal meetings, eleven meetings in the different zones of the capital, and twenty-two provincial dialogues in addition to constructing what was termed the "Great National Dialogue."[23]

The dialogues and consensus reached at the different levels, beyond legitimating and validating education reform in its fundamental elements, represent a sound point of departure for their translation into education policies. The most significant areas of consensus (see Table 6) represent a real leap in quality for Guatemalan education.

Table 6: The Most Significant Areas of Consensus During the "Great National Dialogue"

The equal extension of quality coverage for all Guatemalans at the different levels of the education system without distinction due to gender, ethnic group, or social class.

The extension of bilingual intercultural education, in which the native culture and mother tongue occupy their corresponding central position in the educational experience.

A state guarantee of the right of Guatemalan children to secular, free, and compulsory education, in the framework of the provisions of the Political Constitution of the Republic, the Education Law, and the peace accords.

Professionalisation of teachers and their advancement through the improvement of their working conditions.

Decentralisation of the education system, making education administration more efficient and effective through reinforcing local and municipal organisation.

An increase in the budget allocated to the education sector, as an essential condition for overcoming the difficulties caused by the armed conflict in Guatemala.

The promotion of education reform with the real and effective participation of the education community and civil society, so that they might assume a new role of co-responsibility for this process.

Improvement in the quality of education and absolute backing for curricular transformation with the participation of the education community and civil society, in which new educational content is incorporated in accordance with the cultural and linguistic diversity of the country and the requirements of the local, regional, and national reality.

More specifically, regarding the improvement in educational quality to be guaranteed through the incorporation of Guatemala's cultural and linguistic diversity, it is absolutely necessary to guarantee the following through curricular transformation:

- Respect for and promotion of different cultural identities, through dialogue and the elimination of discrimination, racism, and gender (among other) stereotypes.
- The development of multi- and intercultural education so that all Guatemalans recognise, respect, and appreciate the linguistic and cultural wealth of the country.
- Civics education to guarantee educational experiences that will build a culture of peace on the basis of democratic values and in accordance with human rights, ensuring the participation of the education community and civil society.
- The participation of girls and women in the education system in a framework of equitable gender relations.
- The development of forms of education directed at work and the diversification of training in aptitudes and capacities required for work and professional performance, in the context of a global economy and in relation to the potential for regional and local development.
- The promotion of education with excellence, in accordance with the progress of science and technology, in which learning to do, to know and think, to be, to live together, and to learn and undertake are the fundamental pillars.
- The development of an education in which contents are incorporated for improving the quality of life, specifically in reference to health and sex education.

Beyond the transcendent impact on national life that the consensus on education reform signified, according to Dr. Bienvenido Argueta Hernández, general coordinator,

> the most significant achievement of this process is the coordination of a system of education councils (municipal and provincial) . . . and the basis for establishing a National Education Council, which represents the extraordinary magnitude of this process. Interpreting all this effort in the national context, we can say that the problem of building democracy in this country and generating conditions for governance, requires the generation of mechanisms and structures capable of promoting the organised participation of society at all levels. Beyond the consensus on education reform, the coordinated structure contributes the ideals of reconstructing a democratic and peaceful state.[24]

In spite of the outstanding discrepancies awaiting resolution, there is no doubt that a national consensus was achieved in relation to the significant issues of education, establishing, in its turn, the basis for reforming education policies and for democratising the national education system. However, the provisional establishment of the Education Councils at different levels failed to become institutionalised, and therefore they did not continue working in support of the education reform process.

As was to be expected, the absence of these opportunities for participation made it impossible to take advantage of the enthusiasm and commitment generated by the education community and civil society in favour of education reform. Instead, a kind of immobility and discouragement among the different involved sectors was produced. Likewise, the redirecting of available resources is still pending on the agenda of the Ministry of Education, as well as institutional reorganisation, the reinforcement of national capacities for education management, and the mobilisation of new resources required for putting into practice the policy reform agreed upon in the national dialogue and consultation process.

However, from the technical-administrative viewpoint, curricular transformation followed its course from the structures of the Ministry of Education through SIMAC-DICADE. In coordination with the other technical bodies of the ministry, temporary spaces were organised for selective and restricted technical consultation on the different components of the new curricular proposal and on the professionalisation of teachers. This was done through workshops that brought together programme and project specialists, officials from the provincial and local education entities, teachers' representatives, and parents who had been previously selected. The groups consulted, which were considered by the Ministry of Education to be representative of both the education community and civil society, validated the proposals presented according to established criteria.

Likewise, the Consultative Commission for Education Reform continued to meet and deliberate once every two weeks on the direction of the process of implementing the reform and the preparation of the proposal for the Long-Term National Plan 2000–20, for transforming the education system with a twenty-year vision that encompassed not only the country but the citizenry and society at large.

Preparation of the Long-Term National Plan was begun in 1999 with the participation of the CCRE and the Ministry of Education, for which they organised nine sectoral and two multisectoral workshops, and in which important consensus was reached on the vision of Guatemalan citizens for the year 2020, its medium- and long-term components, its goals and strategies, and its basic qualitative-quantitative indicators. Four years later, the formulation of the plan is still at the stage of being concluded, approved, and made official, with the understanding that in its final version it will incorporate the studies, projections, and other work that has been done in the meantime by the Education Planning Unit of the Ministry of Education.

It is vital to emphasise the importance of planning in the implementation of education policies for the achievement of the objectives proposed in education reform. In this context, it is significant to note that although essential changes have been legitimated through broad backing from the education community and civil society, and with the fundamental policy decisions readily available, medium- and long-term planning and implementation has still not been carried out. Once the plan has been concluded and made official, it will, among other things, extend the possibilities for obtaining an increase in the budget allocation for national education, and the mobilisation of a greater financial contribution from the international cooperation sector for education.

The National Education Campaign

In 1999 a joint media initiative emerged in favour of increasing the national budget allocated to education. A mere 2.2 percent of GDP is designated to education, meaning that Guatemala continues to be one of the few countries of Latin America with below-average spending on public education, and falls well short of the 7 percent allocation established by the National Education Law. More than forty institutions, entities, and organisations joined this initiative, including the media, religious entities, indigenous organisations, entrepreneurial organisations, academic and research institutions, and higher education and international-cooperation bodies and agencies.

Over 150,000 signatures were collected to back the petition for increasing the education budget, which was presented to the president of the Congress of the Republic in November 1999. In principle, the increase requested was approved by the legislature. However, in real terms, this increase did not become effective, because funds that had already been committed through loans and social funds, intended for programmes that other state entities were responsible for, were added to the global education budget to inflate the figure.

The initiative grew over subsequent years until it became an important civil society movement, with the participation of sixty-six institutions, entities, and organisations. In 2002 a document entitled "Education, a Challenge for Guatemala: Proposal for an Increase and Quality in Ministry of Education Spending in 2002, with a Long-Term Vision"[25] was published, and action to communicate the message was intensified through various media (press, radio, and television) in addition to increased lobbying efforts with the parliamentary blocks of the different political parties.

In spite of the initial participation of the Ministry of Education in the official opening of the Great Campaign, it was not possible to achieve a systematic synergy, with the result that coordination with the Consultative Commission for Education Reform, assigned to that ministerial portfolio, was not possible.

Despite efforts made between 1999 and the present (2003), it has not been possible to achieve the necessary increase in the national education budget. The lack of success is partly due to a conflict of political interests, the failure of the fiscal pact, and the national political and economic crisis. Likewise, a lack of cohesiveness in the legislature in relation to issues of national interest, such as education, has had a deleterious effect on the objectives of the Great Campaign.

In spite of progress, certain aspects of the reform—its internal contradictions, divergences, and antagonisms; the institutional fragility of the education system it aims to change, its vulnerability, and its incapacity to satisfy generated expectations; the insufficient available resources; the few tangible results and, perhaps most important, the lack of opportunities for the organised, real and effective participation of the education community and civil society—have all contributed to the slow progress and occasional stagnation of the education reform process.

Thus, it is not difficult to understand either the prevailing feeling of discouragement or the loss of credibility resulting from key actions and decisions made by the Ministry of Education. This situation, further associated with the different problems that must be faced in implementing education reform, has created a tense and conflictive relationship between ministerial authorities and the national teachers' organisation.

THE PROCESS OF CURRICULAR TRANSFORMATION: A DISCUSSION

The curriculum paradigm shift and its foundation

As mentioned earlier, curricular transformation in Guatemala has undergone a profound paradigm shift, not only in relation to curricular theory, but also and especially in the conception of the education system itself, transcending conventional curricula and supply systems and depending instead on the best existing educational practices. An attempt is being made to stop doing more of the same, introducing a broad vision of education and a new way of thinking and doing in education.

There can be no doubt that the educationists and others who questioned the notion of the country as a homogenous national culture—an idea that has long served to legitimise the physical and cultural violence against the Mayan people—allowed for the understanding needed for the new vision. This conceptual shift was an extremely significant contribution to the reconstruction of the country during the post-conflict period. The desire for quality education with cultural and linguistic relevance that is stated in the new education policy demonstrates the importance now given to what was ignored by the national development agencies, whose focus was historically on the urban monocultural schools.

The Guatemalan curricular proposal, having as its frame of reference the prospective vision—of the nation, the society, and the citizen—is intent on a new humanist and sociocognitive paradigm, in which the education process is centred on the human being as a social being, a creator and bearer of culture, with specific characteristics and identity and the capacity to transform the world. Beyond the paradigm shift in curricular theory, curricular changes introduce a reconceptualisation of the school, not only in the reorganisation of its structures to adapt to what is known as modernity, but also—and especially—in the perspective of building a new multiethnic, plurilingual, and multicultural nation that has emerged from an armed conflict that fragmented and polarised the society.

In this context, curricular changes aim at strengthening the values of the peoples of the Guatemalan nation for the sake of democratic coexistence and the development of a culture of peace. In accordance with the building of a democratic state that is inclusive and respectful of diversity, the promotion of an education project is proposed for the whole society seeking to reinforce equality among cultures, insofar as they are all creative and genuine expressions of humanity and represent the meaning of and ways of interpreting the world.

With the implementation of the new curriculum it is hoped that the children of Guatemala, besides being the protagonists of their learning and developing the necessary aptitudes for living as full individuals and citizens, can come to understand and accept differences among individuals and peoples, as well as the common features among them, and recognise *others* as they are, with their visions and ways of acting in the world, for the sake of tolerance, respect, peaceful coexistence, and conflict prevention.[26]

Interculturalism is also incorporated as one of the new curriculum's main components, taking into account the linguistic and cultural rights of the peoples of Guatemala against the frame of universal culture. In this context, interculturalism in the educational act is presented in the perspective of knowledge and respect for other cultures; an appreciation of the sociocultural diversity of the Guatemalan nation; and an overcoming of the distrust, fear, prejudice, and stereotypes that are a result of the discrimination and intolerance that has prevailed historically and which became more acute during the thirty-six-year armed conflict.

To make this new education paradigm a reality, new pedagogical practices must be formed in order to overcome rigid patterns of learning, promoting processes through which the methods, procedures, and techniques are based on cultural contexts and on the existing knowledge of children. In this context, an effort is being made to recover the dialectical relationship between teaching and learning, giving centrality back to the act of learning as the fundamental objective of the education process, and at the same time opening the possibility of rethinking the education model that is currently in force.

The curricular proposal of the Ministry of Education is based on the resignification of the concept of "contents," understanding them to be the learning of procedures, attitudes, concepts, values, and standards that characterise culture of all kinds—the culture to which the children belong, the culture of other peoples, and culture that is universal. This is concentrated on

- *central axes*:[27] thematic issues derived from the conceptual framework of education reform;
- *fundamental areas of education*:[28] those that constitute the organisation of learning based on different disciplines in accordance with the needs, demands, and aspirations of children; and
- *competencies*: understood as being complex capacities with different degrees of integration which are demonstrated in different areas of people's lives, express different degrees of personal development and active participation in social processes, and constitute a synthesis of the experiences that people have accumulated over time.

The challenges of curriculum change

Interculturalism, insofar as it is a dialogue among equals, is the right path in the culturally and linguistically diverse reality of Guatemala. In this sense, curricular changes should deal with at least seven fundamental challenges:

1. The use of the mother tongue as a learning tool and means of social communication, for which it is necessary to adopt a linguistic policy that advocates for the promotion, recovery, and development of the languages of the different peoples in conditions of equality and equity.

2. The recognition of the cultures of the different peoples and of their evolutionary and dynamic nature, as well as their translation into educational content, their incorporation into the national curriculum, and their inclusion in the act of education through significant learning experiences for all Guatemalan children.

3. The initial and continuous training of teachers for greater sensitivity to issues of diversity and multi- and interculturalism, in addition to the improvement of their working conditions.

4. Educational regionalisation based on sociolinguistic criteria as an option that recognises the cultural and linguistic diversity of the country in the education system for achieving the objectives of education reform.

5. A recognition of the fact that the success of education reform does not depend solely on curricular transformation but, rather, should be combined with the development of a set of education policies guaranteeing access to quality education for all and the successful completion of basic primary education for all Guatemalan children, and particularly for indigenous children, who usually only manage to finish the initial grades of schooling.

6. The building of integral regionalised education plans stemming from the Long-Term National Plan, as a strategy for the practical application of education reform, which should (Torres, 2000):

   a. respond to a broad and systemic vision of education—that is, contemplate the whole set of educational scenarios, practices, and agents actually operating within the country (or in the different sociolinguistic regions of the country);

b. start with the detection, analysis, and appreciation of people's basic needs for learning;

c. be profoundly participatory in nature, in preparation as well as in development and direction;

d. clearly establish the commitments and responsibilities of all educational entities and agents involved;

e. have one single entity for planning, leading/management, and supervision, charged with integrating those responsible for the different levels and sectors of the administration;

f. enjoy a high degree of autonomy in implementation and development;

g. include evaluation procedures and strategies in their definition; and

h. secure the necessary economic and technical resources.

7. The acceptance that it is not enough to have education policies for implementing education reform, since for this implementation to be effective it must have the backing, support, and definite commitment of teachers and other actors in the education community, as well as different sectors of society. Therefore, it is necessary to establish and implement well-conceived strategies aimed at allowing dialogue and reaching consensus.

Education policy reform in Guatemala runs the risk of being just a declaration of good intentions that are based on a set of curricular documents and standards that fail to be executed and produce real change in the classroom. Were this to happen, it would generate more discouragement and scepticism among actors of the education community and society concerning the advantages of reforming the education system, especially when one takes into account the fact that while it is from within the education apparatus that the desired change is being promoted, key actors in the education process are nonetheless failing to play their real role.

As has already been stated, it is now necessary to close the gap that exists between the ministerial entities at the central level (who formulated the new curricular proposal) and those who in principle should execute it (i.e., the intermediate and local entities). At the same time, a process of enrichment and ownership should be promoted for and among the experts and teachers, parents, and the different key sectors of the society. In this context, it is worthwhile to incorporate the lesson learned in other experiences of reform: to achieve essential consensus, one must experience necessary dissent, since conflict is an essential and inevitable ingredient of change.

The proposal cannot be judged as ideal solely on the basis of its conceptual consistency, coherence, and technical criteria, but must above all be assessed with respect to its relevance and viability when placed against the existing conditions and demands of reality. In the same way, it is risky to believe that, insofar as the curricular proposal is already available, the difficulties faced must relate to its practical application when, in reality, they refer to the challenges of both planning its implementation and creating the conditions necessary for that implementation to be successful.

This includes the coordination of the policies for education reform with those for economic and other areas of social reform, since one should not forget that schools are often the place where the effects of poverty on children and their families become manifest. Furthermore, it is necessary to have a holistic and systemic vision of reform, in which the different components of education—curriculum, pedagogical processes, initial and in-service teacher training, educational resources and materials, education management and administration, equipment and infrastructure—form part of a planned global strategy of development and educational change.

Even when curricular changes aim at responding to the cultural, linguistic, and social diversity of the communities, it is important to venture beyond curricular, pedagogical, and administrative adaptations, in order to make room for the incorporation of forms of education differentiated according to the particular contexts and realities.

As previously stated, it is of extreme importance not to give in to the temptation of thinking that reform *is* the proposal, which is to say, that the documents containing the basis and guidelines for change constitute the reform. The existence of a new curriculum and new textbooks, the professional teacher training programmes, the proposal to transform the teacher training schools, the opening of a teacher training programme for pre-primary bilingual intercultural education and for primary bilingual intercultural education, to name but a few, are certainly all important steps in the process of reform—but they are not the reform itself. Reform is a gradual process, not a specific event.

The role of the international community in curriculum change

In this process of the awakening of communities in their quest for a relevant, quality education, projects and programmes such as Schools Without Frontiers, Mayan Bilingual Intercultural Education (EMBI/GTZ), Primary School Teachers Bilingual Intercultural Training of Totonicapán, and Cooperation Between Dutch Universities for the Development of Primary Education (HOB-Holland) have participated, bringing a technical and pedagogical accompaniment. All of them have opted for building their own models to respond to the strongly felt educational characteristics and needs of the communities in their areas of influence, within the framework of national educational policies and educational reform.[29]

International cooperation has given the most support to Mayan and bilingual intercultural education, in terms of both funds and technical advisory assistance. For example, in 1998 international cooperation funded 90 percent of EMBI's actions in the country, while the Ministry of Education covered the teachers' salaries as a condition established in cooperation agreements. The loans negotiated by the government with organisations such as the World Bank and the Inter-American Development Bank include BIE components, but they do not represent the significant share of the total indigenous population. Furthermore, the loans will have to be repaid.

In accordance with the UNESCO/PROMEM *Study on the Best Practices in Mayan Bilingual Intercultural Education in Guatemala,*

> all agree that the present educational models can be improved, that they have undergone substantial changes on the ground as their implementation has evolved and in accordance with the lessons learned that they record. This implies an evolution of their own concept of educational work in their areas of influence.
>
> (Rivera Alvarez, 2002)

The support of projects and programmes funded by international cooperation to the educational system in sociolinguistic regions has substantially influenced the reorientation of education policies and strategies for a multilingual and pluricultural society. In addition, where education has been adapted to the communities of the students, it has achieved the demonstrable relevance and fundamental nature of local culture and mother tongue instruction to the entities of the national education directorate. This is where the decision to promote an intercultural and bilingual education for all the people of Guatemala emerged. To date, the relevant nature of bilingual intercultural education for the indigenous peoples and an intercultural education for the entire Guatemalan population has been confirmed. Nonetheless, one of the problems identified in this process is that of the temporary nature of the projects. In light of this situation, the Ministry of Education has declared its intention to ensure the continuity of the objectives that were developed through international cooperation.

According the abovementioned study, the experiences of educational innovation that have been systematised in the communities with the accompaniment of the different projects and programmes have the following aspects in common:

1. Children have problems when their education is not developed in the language and codes of their cultural community. This is the first and biggest barrier that a child must face, because it touches his or her thought structures and ways of creating, recreating, and constructing. According to Vygostky, language is just a synthesis of the thought-construction process.

2. Teachers must get to know the community and the immediate reality of the child through the maintenance of an ongoing dialogue; they must carry out an immersion exercise before judging the capacities of the children.

3. The focus of the general framework of each of the projects and programs involved in Mayan bilingual intercultural education coincides in considering that there are no more propitious conditions for building and developing the knowledge of Mayan children than those of their own cultural context, in their own idiomatic codes. It is in their own language and environment that children will best develop the logical process of constructing knowledge, and this is where the educational community will be called on to play an extremely important role and provide the learning process of the new generations with significant contents.

4. The school must represent the conjunction of the best contributions of the community, as the intent is for the children to be nourished from their own culture. This will allow them not only to reaffirm their own identity but will prepare them to confront and cope with adverse and diverse scenarios.

5. The projects agree that the treatment of Mayan mathematics (the vigesimal numerical system) is called on to play a leading role, as it is through its pedagogical treatment that the students' logical thinking will be developed, because both thought and language are merged. They also find the development of Mayan values, complemented by universal values, to be of equal importance. Similarly, they attach value to the expression, re-creation, and creation in the area of aesthetics and Mayan arts in the school experience serving, at the same time, to complement the additional three areas of language (mother tongue and second language), mathematics (universal and Mayan), and observance of the Mayan calendar.

Mayan culture and language in the national curriculum:
A proposal of the Support Mobilisation Project for Mayan Education

As mentioned previously, among the most important changes of the Guatemalan educational reform process is the recognition and incorporation of the cultural and linguistic diversity of the country as the central element for the transformation of the educational system. The formal incorporation of the Mayan culture into the national curriculum—a culture whose nature serves as a foundation for nationality—has come to complement the basis, contents, worldview, interpretation of social and natural phenomena, and principles and values of human coexistence, with which the curriculum is constructed and developed. Another significant change is the acceptance of the community's mother tongue in teaching and learning in the linguistic regions of the country within the framework of bilingual and intercultural education.

One of the central elements of educational reform is the curricular transformation, together with the reorganisation of the different components of the educational system, that makes its implementation possible in the educational work developed in education centres. This has represented an important paradigm shift insofar as the intention is to go from a centralised concept of the curriculum to a decentralised concept in which responsibility is shared with the intermediate levels of educational management, with the educational communities, and, specifically, the directors of educational centres. The idea is to go from a standardising curricular model to a more open and flexible one that allows the national educational objectives to be placed within the context of the linguistic, cultural, and socio-educational realities of the country, and of the characteristics of each particular educational context. At the same time, this enables the creative involvement of teachers in the elaboration of broad curriculum design for educational centres, and specific curriculum planning for the classroom, participation that assumes a level of professional training commensurate with the demands and requirements that this task implies (UNESCO/PROMEM, 2002).

The UNESCO/PROMEM Support Mobilization Project for Mayan Education, in developing the experience of Mayan education in the K'iche', Mam, Tzœtujil, Ach', and Q'eqchi linguistic communities and in the multilingual zone, identified essential criteria for Mayan bilingual and intercultural education in the national education system (see Table 7).

Among the essential criteria, the Ministry of Education has incorporated those related to Mayan values, Mayan math, and Mayan aesthetics and art into the bilingual intercultural education curriculum. PROMEM's curricular proposal, with a view to constructing an intercultural education system for all, maintains that all children in Guatemala, irrespective of their ethnic origin, spiritual or religious beliefs, social status, or gender, should develop a significant body of knowledge concerning the fundamental elements of Mayan culture by way of educational content incorporated into the national curriculum whose origins can be traced back to the criteria previously mentioned. In other words, it is proposed that from these criteria will be derived, as a bare minimum, the content of the bilingual and intercultural education curriculum from the indigenous peoples, and as a maximum, the curriculum of the national education system.

The importance of developing these areas and values in the national curriculum is based on the logics of position and calculation, as well as the order and meaning of numerical values of the Mayan vigesimal system, which contribute to the configuration of thought and strengthen the development of intelligence. When complemented by the universal decimal system, it broadens and deepens the field of logical reasoning and problem solving.

Table 7: Essential Criteria for Mayan Bilingual and Intercultural Education in the National Education System as Proposed by UNESCO/PROMEM

Two languages: the community's native language and Spanish as lingua franca of the country.
Two mathematical systems: the international decimal system and the Mesoamerican Mayan vigesimal system.
Two value systems that are complemented in the educational system: Mayan values and universal values.
An integral set of values and expressions of aesthetics and art: Mayan and universal.
An integral set of nomenclatures for classification and interpretation of nature and the universe: Those of Mayan origin and those of the universal culture.
Two systems for recording and counting time: As expressed in the Mayan (Tzolk'in or Cholq'ij) calendars and in the universal calendar.
The history of the Mayan people and of other indigenous peoples in the history of Guatemala and of the world.

In view of the crisis of values in Guatemalan society, it is essential and unavoidable that Mayan values be formally incorporated into the national curriculum, and that universal values, which are complementary to Mayan values, and the values of other indigenous peoples be recovered. The values are categories of thought and the basis for the behaviour of people and groups within the sphere of their culture. They are considered to be the foundation for the conception of the world and of life, and form part of spirituality and social life. In Mayan thinking, value means the heart and energy of thoughts and wisdom.

Mayan aesthetics and art are the expression and making of the spirit and thinking of people who live within this culture; they can be found in all environments in Guatemala, and only need to be formally incorporated into the school setting of the educational system. Mayan aesthetics and art can be heard, seen, and touched. They are felt in the family the moment a child is born; they are the language of the future of Guatemalan society facing the world.

The elements of the curricular framework that support the PROMEM proposal are detailed in the following paragraphs. The contextual framework in which this curricular proposal was made took as its point of departure the educational practices of the Local Mayan Education Units, which are rooted in the peace process and the commitments contemplated in the Accords on the Identity and the Rights of the Indigenous Peoples, and the educational reform process.

In its work, the Support Mobilization Project for Mayan Education has addressed its efforts to the appreciation of the language and culture of the Mayan people, to build up from the community and jointly with the actors of educational work a proposal of educational guidelines, policies, and strategies with cultural and linguistic relevance.

To give continuity to the processes initiated during the first phase of implementation (1995–98), a large part of the efforts during the second phase (1999–2002) have been geared toward the pedagogical technical accompaniment of the educational experiences of the Local Mayan Education Units in developing the essential criteria of Mayan and bilingual intercultural education and their impact on the national curriculum.

At the request of the General Directorate of Bilingual Education, and taking into account the characteristics of the project and the progress made on the subject of Mayan education, in 2003 PROMEM developed "Mayan Relevance in the National Curriculum." This proposal develops, in terms of curriculum, three of the "Essential Criteria"—also known as the "non-negotiables"—of Mayan bilingual intercultural education for the purpose of developing and strengthening the country's multicultural and intercultural nature in the educational reform process. The proposal was formed from an analysis of best practices in education promoted by the Ministry of Education and by the programmes and projects related to the building of competencies and educational contents of EMBI. The purpose of this was to bring out substantive elements that could subsequently be used in a general fashion.

The fundamental assumptions of the proposal are the following:

1. It is based on the resignification of the "contents," these being understood as the learning of procedures, attitudes, concepts, values, and standards that characterise the culture to which the children belong.

2. It places children, learning, and teachers at the centre of the curriculum. It gives emphasis to significant learning—that is, to the process of constructing meanings as the nucleus of the teaching-learning process, through which the children learn a concept, a procedure, a value, an attitude, or a standard, if there is a possibility of attributing a meaning to it.

3. It takes into account that the attribution of meanings depends on the capacity of a child to establish substantive relations between what is new and still to be learned, and what he or she already knows (prior knowledge), in which process his or her culture and mother tongue play a determining role. It assumes that the relationship between teaching methodology (the teacher) and the results of the learning process (the children) is influenced by the setting of priorities of the thought-building processes of the students.

4. It is supported by the link between culture, learning, education, and schooling contents, through which "any element of the culture of a specific social group who considers that this element must be assimilated by its members, is susceptible to becoming a teaching content" (C. Coll).

5. It takes into consideration the areas of knowledge that relate to the teaching of values, mathematics, art, and aesthetics, derived from the knowledge of the Mayan people and their way of conceiving, classifying, and interpreting the world, and situating them in the place due to them in the national curriculum—that is, as official curriculum (or learning content) in the national education system.

6. It develops the contents of Mayan values, Mayan mathematics, and Mayan art and aesthetics in the three levels of curricular planning established by the Ministry of Education, namely, the national, regional, and local levels.

7. It establishes links with the fifteen Framework Competencies of the Basic National Curriculum of Basic Secondary or Primary Education prepared by the Ministry of Education and approved by the Consultative Educational Reform Commission.

8. It treats the teaching of values in its double dimension: as a cross-cutting theme and a learning area in itself.

9. It considers the Common Basic Contents (CBC) as the central matrix from which regional and local curricular designs, varied but related, must be prepared.

10. The CBCs, as conceived in the proposal, are oriented to the teaching of competencies seen as complex capacities with different degrees of integration that are made evident in different spheres of people's lives. These express the different degrees of personal development and active participation in social processes and are a synthesis of the experiences that human beings have been able to develop throughout their lives.

11. The proposal stems from a new meaning of the concept of contents, so that these may embrace different cultural forms. They also include scientific knowledge, methods and procedures, and standards, values, and attitudes. The CBCs are organised according to the following criteria:

    a. cultural and linguistic relevance and social meaning;
    b. scope and depth;
    c. integration and aggregation;
    d. horizontal and vertical linkage;
    e. updating;
    f. opening;
    g. hierarchical order; and
    h. simplicity and clarity.

The curricular proposal is structured in accordance with the National Basic Secondary Education Curriculum. The different areas of knowledge of the proposal, Mayan values, Mayan mathematics, and Mayan art and aesthetics were developed at the level of curricular implementation: macro (national), meso (regional by linguistic communities), and micro (local or of educational centre), taking three linguistic communities as an example: the K'iche', Mam, and Kaqchikel.

The curricular design at the regional and local levels of the three areas mentioned are structured around the following elements:

-   the educational objectives of the region in question, both of a general nature and for each of the teaching levels it serves;
-   the general competencies of the region, taking the framework competencies of the national curriculum as a basis;
-   the competencies per area and per cycle;
-   the contents of each of the learning areas (conceptual, procedural, and attitudinal);

- the sequencing of contents;
- the methodological strategies and the educational materials in support of curricular development; and
- the guidelines for assessing the learning processes and for passing from one grade to the other and from one cycle to the other.

Although the curricular proposal described in the above paragraphs has been structured according to the different levels of application defined in the curricular planning process established by the Ministry of Education, its incorporation into the process of curricular change and its consequent implementation and application in schools are still part of the ministry's pending agenda. In this sense, one of the central preoccupations regarding education innovation and best practices developed by the international cooperation projects in support of curriculum change policy, such as PROMEM, is the determination of effective strategies to influence policymaking so they can be generalised and institutionalised in the education system. In other words, it is necessary to establish the required "bridges" or links between educational innovations and best practices, and the decisionmaking of the Ministry of Education, so they can be incorporated into the curricular change process at the national level.

However, it is important to underline that efforts such as those of PROMEM and other international cooperation projects constitute a straightforward and consistent proof of the real possibility for change to the "nonbelievers," or to those who oppose curricular reforms. Through their results, these projects make the difference for children with respect to their access to quality and relevant education, as well as to their low dropout rates and successful termination of basic education.

CONCLUSION

Curriculum change and social cohesion

With regard to educational, cultural, and linguistic policies, Guatemala is showing itself to be engaged in a phenomenon of transition from a paradigm of assimilation to one of acceptance. This new vision of the country, one of social coexistence, has made it possible to set the foundations for harmonious coexistence between peoples and communities that make up the nation, mainly through an intercultural dialogue.

The Guatemalan educational system is in the midst of a constant and concerted dialogue to promote policies and strategies for curricular transformation and the improvement of human resources. The involvement of universities, teachers' unions, indigenous organisations, the private sector, and other educational organisations is providing significant support to the educational reform process.

Guatemalan society, made up of a diversity of communities and peoples, has pinned its hopes on the concept that the education of its children, under a new order of social and cultural relations, will be the principal means to achieve their integral development; that education will be conducted within the cultural, linguistic, and ecological context of the communities, guided by the vision of a civic and intercultural nation that participates in the dynamics of world development. A very significant experience that children have at school is when they realise that the most valued things in their culture, and the communication of those things in the mother tongue of their community, are an integral part of their curriculum.

During the last fifteen years of the country's history, the citizens have become aware of the plural and diverse nature of Guatemalan society, and of the principles of social and political coexistence derived from universal human rights. This is one of the bases for the process of social cohesion and peace building.

The factors that contribute to the attainment of social cohesion

Although there are influential sectors opposed to the peace accords, most people have adopted them as a national agenda. As we have seen, the educational system, on the recommendation of the Consultative Commission on Educational Reform, has designed a Long-Term National Education Plan, 2000–20, for the implementation of educational reform. This plan would ensure the continuity of the reform's objectives, goals, and strategic action, provided that the financial resources for its implementation are secured. Tensions here would be solved as long as there is a capacity for agreement between the government and the political parties, the entrepreneurial sector, the financial sector, the indigenous peoples, and civil society organisations.

The General Decentralisation Law

The recent approval of the General Decentralisation Law and the amendments to the Urban and Rural Development Councils Law and the Municipal Code represent an opening for participation at all levels, a need expressed by the people and included in the peace accords. The councils operate in local, municipal, provincial, regional, and national entities. Their natural use as negotiating bodies and their pluralistic makeup allow for making proposals, debating, solving, and promoting solutions to problems at their respective levels.

The new civic education programme

The new civic education program develops democratic values and promotes the practice of methods of conflict resolution. It is based on a new concept of the nation, beginning with an acknowledgement of the country's multicultural nature with a view to constructing intercultural acceptance, for the development of a new fundamental strategy in the process of consolidating social cohesion.

Promoting equality for women

The exclusion and marginalisation of women has been one of the most serious injustices in Guatemala. This is also true regarding the indigenous peoples. The persistence of these practices has limited the possibilities for solving problems, mainly poverty, illiteracy, and low political participation. The country has started to recognise, respect, and promote conditions of equality regarding the rights and obligations, of both men and women, in the development of the family and the community, and in the process of constructing nationality. At present, this is an unavoidable and irreversible theme in national debates and agreements.

Law on National Languages (2003)

A very recent event that has come to reinforce the foundations for social cohesion and solidarity is the approval of the Law on National Languages (May 2003). This law establishes principles, policies, and objectives that guarantee the right of peoples and communities to their native language and culture, particularly in health services, education, justice, and security. The law was passed in response to an indigenous social movement that started in the 1960s, buttressed by the peace accords in 1996, and reaffirmed in the dialogue and national consensus for educational reform in 2001. It is expected that the application of this law will provide a solution to prolonged social tension that dates back to the lack of linguistic rights of the early native peoples.

Spanish as lingua franca

Another factor of cohesion is the efficient development of a lingua franca in a multilingual society (by state law, it is the Spanish language in Guatemala), a language that does not impose itself or overwhelm but, rather, is an instrument of articulation, so that all ancestral linguistic territories become bilingual, using both an indigenous language and Spanish.

Integrating universal and Mayan values in curriculum

The universal values of truth, justice, equity, equality, fraternity, solidarity, brotherhood, and responsibility are complemented in the curriculum for social recovery, with the following values of Mayan thinking (UNESCO/PROMEM, 2002):

- *Qach'umilal* (recognition and respect for the star, mission, and vocation of each human being);
- *Kaqub'al K'ux* (a sense of internal harmony and responsibility);
- *Qäs tzij* (truthfulness of the word in all acts of life);
- *Ch'ajch'ojil* (values of beauty, pulchritude, and the integrity of nature and the universe, of people and objects);
- *Rumitijul qak'aslem* (devotion, meticulousness, and industriousness);
- *Tz'aqat* (fulfilment of the person, and compliance with one's work and commitments);
- *Poqonaxik* (esteem for and protection of everything that exists);
- *Nimanik* (respect);
- *Komonil* (a sense of community);
- *K'ulub'exik* (to take advice); and
- *Maltioxinik* (appreciation for people, nature, and the Heart of the Heavens).

Adoption of a culture of interculturalism

Finally, another identified factor of social cohesion is the gradual and progressive adoption of a culture of interculturalism, which is based on the concept of "a harmonious relation between cultures; in other words: a relation of positive exchange and social co-existence between culturally-different actors" (Giménez Romero, 2000). During 1999, intercultural dialogues were convened by the UNDP Q'anil B Project in Guatemala, on the basis of the following principles:

- *principle of citizenship*: this implies the full recognition and constant quest for real and effective equality of rights, responsibilities, and opportunities, as well as a permanent fight against racism and discrimination;

- *principle of the right to be different*: this entails respect for the identity and the rights of each of the peoples, ethnic groups, and sociocultural expressions of a country; and
- *principle of unity in diversity*: this is achieved by national unity, not imposed but built by all and assumed in a voluntary fashion.

Critical perspectives for the future

In the field of research, the curricular change and social cohesion processes make it necessary for the following to be promoted and strengthened:

- an in-depth study of the values of the cultures of the nation which, coupled with universal values, would contribute to the emergence of the new social, cultural, and political relations of the population;
- the standardisation of the knowledge of the indigenous peoples, particularly that of the Mayan people, regarding science and technology, art and aesthetics, philosophy and spirituality, linguistics and sociolinguistics, social organisation, and productive activity;
- studies on the pedagogical phenomenon in the classroom within the cultural and linguistic context and the processes of constructing knowledge; and
- studies on the behavioural relationships between teachers, parents, and the educational system, to ensure the stability of the educational services.

With regard to the right of the people and the communities to their cultural identity in accordance with their values, language, and customs, the Third National Congress on Mayan Education, convened by the National Council on Mayan Education—CNEM, reached the following conclusions:

1. There is an agenda in favour of quality education for the peoples with diverse cultures that make up Guatemala. The items in this agenda have been incorporated into the Educational Reform Design, the Long-Term National Plan, the conclusions of the Dialogue and Consensus for the Educational Reform, and other instruments. However, it is necessary to generate a sociopolitical movement that promotes, develops strategies, and demands the implementation of policies that enable the participation of the peoples and leading social sectors and actors, in order to satisfactorily achieve a profound transformation of society, the state, and, especially, the national education system.

2. This process of curricular transformation, led by the Ministry of Education, proposed a national, regional, and local (macro, meso, and micro) curricular project that is being progressively implemented for the different teaching levels. The educational centres of the Mayan people are concerned because they fear that the educational reform process promoted by the ministry will not take contents with a Mayan focus into account, and that the textbooks and educational materials will not equitably reflect the Mayan culture as the basis of Guatemalan culture (as recognised in the peace accords).

The historical memory of the internal armed conflict and the lessons learned by the families, communities, and our national society are still a source of debate, discussion, and negotiation, particularly with regard to issues of justice and pardon, forgetting and reparations. In view of this situation, it is essential to refer to the principles, values, worldview, and forms of peaceful coexistence of the native peoples and others who have confronted similar situations, and, in a similar fashion, to universal values and human rights, as the basis for mutual understanding, pardon, reparations, and reconciliation.

In this way, the country would be able to go from the "Memory of Silence" (CEH), to "Guatemala, Never Again" (ODHH). This is the main reason why the peace accords and the national dialogue and consensus entrusted the education of new generations in a culture of peace and intercultural dialogue to the education system. To be effective, it will entail a transformation of the curriculum and an integral reform process that includes the dynamics of participation for social development from the educational communities.

Endnotes

[1] Christopher Columbus, on his fourth trip, met Mayan traders to the east of the islands of Roatan in Honduras, and he describes in detail the products they were transporting and the size of the boats. Bernal Diaz del Castillo who accompanied Hernán Cortés on the expedition from Mexico to Honduras, describes the characteristics of the Mayan cities and population as well as their economic, political, and religious activity, with very important details for clarifying the real history of Guatemala (Chinchilla Aguilar, cited by Gallo, 2001).

[2] The *encomienda* was the institution by which the king granted to a private (Spanish) individual, for life, the right to collect, for his own benefit, a number of taxes from a village of "Indians"—that is, people indigenous to that particular area (MINEDUC, 1999). At first, the practice was like the granting of a prize to the conquerors and was specifically associated with slavery, and then it was more generally involved with all of the institutionalised practices of exploitation, discrimination, and economic, social, and political exclusion of the indigenous people.

[3] *Ladino*: a word that started to be used at the end of the sixteenth century to refer to the indigenous person who had learned Spanish and begun to dress in Spanish style; the *mestizos* are also called *ladinos*; at present anybody who is not indigenous is called *ladino*.

[4] People born in the Americas with Spanish parentage.

[5] A different case is what happened in 1820, when the Maya K'iche' indigenous people of Totonicapán, led by Atanasio Tzul, rose up to free themselves from oppression, not only from Spain but from the whole system of oppression and discrimination.

[6] Contadora Act on Peace (Panama, 1986); Message of Caraballeda for Peace, Security and Democracy, in Central America (Venezuela, 1986); Declaration of Esquipulas I and Esquipulas II (1986, 1987); Declaration of Alajuela (Costa Rica, 1988); Oslo Agreement (Norway, 1990), for the search for peace through political means; Agreement of El Escorial (Spain, 1990), Agreement of Mexico, procedure for the search for peace through political means and general agenda (Mexico, D. F., 1991).

[7] Agreement to create the National Reconciliation Commission (Guatemala, 1987); Total Peace Initiative of the Nation (Government of Guatemala, 1991); Global Proposal of the URNG (1992); Proposal of the Civil Sectors in Relation to Their Participation in the Peace Process (Guatemala, 1992); Agreement Signed Between the Permanent Commissions of Representatives of Guatemalan Refugees in Mexico and the Government of Guatemala (Guatemala, 1993); Agreement on the Integration of the Truth Commission or Commission of the Past (Mexico, 1993); Official Statement of the Civil Sector Coordination and of Civil Coordination for Peace (Guatemala, 1993); and the Conformation of the Civil Society Assembly.

[8] National Peace Plan, Government of Guatemala (1993); Human Rights Declaration (Government of Guatemala, 1993); Framework Agreement for the Resumption of the Negotiation Process Between the Government and the URNG (Mexico, 1994); Global Accord on Human Rights (Mexico, 1994); Accord for the Resettlement of Populations Uprooted by the Armed Confrontation (Norway, 1994); Accord on the Establishment of a Commission for the Historical Clarification of Human Rights Violations and of Acts of Violence That Have Caused Suffering to the Guatemalan People (Norway, 1994); Accord on the Identity and Rights of Indigenous Peoples (Mexico, 1995); Accord on Socioeconomic Aspects and the Agrarian Situation (Mexico, 1996); Accord on the Strengthening of the Civil Power and the Function of the Army in a Democratic Society (Mexico, 1996); Accord on the Definitive Ceasefire (Norway, 1996); Accord on Constitutional Reforms and the Electoral System (Sweden, 1996); Accord on the Bases for the Incorporation of the Guatemalan National Revolutionary Unity into the Legal System (Spain, 1996); Accord on the Schedule for the Implementation, Fulfilment and Verification of the Peace Accords (Guatemala, 1996); and Accord on a Firm and Lasting Peace (Guatemala, December 29, 1996).

[9] International and national negotiation for the establishment of the United Nations Verification Mission in Guatemala, MINUGUA; establishment of the Accompaniment Commission for compliance with the peace accords; establishment of the specific commissions and the parity commissions, by topic. In the commitments on education, the Parity Commission of Education Reform was established (COPARE) in 1997, and was responsible for the design of education reform; then the Consultative Commission of Education Reform was established (CCRE) in 1998, and this body is currently responsible for the process of national dialogue and consensus on education reform and the implementation of curriculum transformation.

[10] We could also mention the *Accord for the Resettlement of Populations Uprooted by the Armed Confrontation* (1994). In view of the effort made by the uprooted communities to improve the level of education of their people and the need to support and give continuity to this process, the government committed to:

1. Recognising the formal and informal education levels reached by uprooted persons, and using fast evaluation procedures and/or certification for this purpose; and
2. Recognising the informal studies of education and health promoters and giving them equivalent qualifications using the corresponding evaluation.

[11] In Spanish, *Principal de Educacion para America latina y el Caribe* (PROMEDLAC).

[12] In the study mentioned above, a stereotype is defined as a misconception or overly simplified conception of the characteristics and/or common behavior of a whole group without paying attention to their personal qualities. It also defines prejudice as the emotional attitude acquired before having acquired any proof or adequate experience, or as a belief or preconceived opinion imposed by the environment, the times, or by education. It infers that stereotypes implicitly imply the development of prejudices (ILE-URL, 1992).

[13] The following strategies are appreciated as specific actions of this strategy: the process of curricular renewal developed by the Escuela Normal de Maestras de Párvulos, "Alfredo Carrillo Ram'res," leading teacher training school in the country, as well as the implementation of the professional improvement plan jointly carried out by its teaching staff and the executive staff of universities with whom the academic program design was coordinated. Also participating in this activity were teachers from other public and private teacher training schools of the country.

[14] The Mayan languages are Akateko, Achi, Awakateko, Chort', Chuj,Iitza', Ixil, Kaqchikel, K'iche', Mam, Popt' (Jakalteko), Mopan, Poqomam, Poqomch'i', Q'anjob'al, Q'eqchi', Sakapulteko, Sipakapense, Tektiteko, Tz'utujil, and Uspanteko.

[15] As mentioned before, bilingual education (in an indigenous language and Spanish) has been promoted by the Ministry of Education since 1985 as a programme, and since 1995 in a significant sector of the schools under the coordination of one General Directorate. It was not until 2000 that the EBI received more institutional support from the ministry, when it began its process of generalising bilingual education in all regions of the country.

[16] According to the population census (1994) of the 331 municipalities, 166 have more than 50 percent indigenous population. Of the 166 municipalities, seventy-five have more than 90 percent. Seventy-eight municipalities have between 10 and 50 percent, and eighty-six have less than 10 percent. All municipalities in the country have a certain percentage of indigenous population.

[17] Sources: Proposal on sociolinguistic development in the classroom, General Directorate of Bilingual Intercultural Education, DIGEBI (2002); Kabul Iyom, Bilingual Intercultural Communities, UNESCO/PROMEM (1999); Studies on L1 and L2 in the classroom, the Linguistics and Education Institute, ILE-URL (2000).

[18] Other projects that support the development of bilingual education are the CEDIM Mayan bilingual intercultural schools; FEBIMAM/Belgian Cooperation; HOB/Holland, Regional Teacher Training School of Totonicapán; Refugee Children of the World, Ixil area; PAEBI/USAID, Province

of Quiché; EDUMAYA/URL/USAID, professional bilingual intercultural training at the levels of teaching, undergraduate, and master's degrees.

[19] Government Plan for the Education Sector 2000–04, July 2000, Ministry of Education, Education Reform Commission, Guatemala.

[20] National Curriculum for Primary or Basic Secondary Education, 2002, Ministry of Education.

[21] The Consultative Commission for Education Reform is made up of nineteen representatives: the National Literacy Committee (CONALFA); the Academy of Mayan Languages of Guatemala (ALMG); the National Council of Mayan Education (CNEM); the Permanent National Commission of Education Reform of the Coordination of Mayan People's Organisations of Guatemala (CNPRE-COPMAGUA); the San Carlos University of Guatemala; the Rafael Land'var University; the Mariano Gálvez University; the Del Valle University of Guatemala; the Francisco Marroqu'n University; the Rural University; the National Teachers' Assembly; the Episcopal Conference of Guatemala; the Evangelical Alliance of Guatemala; Private Education Institutions; the Chamber of Commerce and Finances (CACIF); the National Forum of Women; the Presidential Secretariat of Women; the National Students' Organisation of Guatemala; and Journalists' Organisations.

[22] The work to date of the CCRE can be summarised as follows: the presentation of the Education Reform Bill to the Congress of the Republic; a diagnostic assessment of the Ministry of Education's Human Resources in Teaching; the proposal for educational regionalisation based on sociolinguistic criteria; the preparation, through a participatory consultation process, of the documents: Citizen's Vision 2020; Vision of the Education System; the preliminary version of the Long-Term National Education Plan 2000–20 and a second version for the period 2004–23.

[23] According to reports on the conclusions of this process of dialogue, the participants ranged from: secondary and university students; mayors; representatives of the municipal community/organisation/institutions such as supervisors, technical-administrative coordinators, and technical-pedagogical coordinators; parents; teachers from the public and private sectors representing different grade levels; educators from the extra curricular and literacy programmes; representatives from churches, indigenous organisations, women s organisations and social and educational development organisations; provincial governors; provincial education directors; provincial NGOs; and representatives of the different linguistic communities of the country, and from the nineteen delegations of the Consultative Commission for Education Reform.

[24] Conclusions of the Dialogues on Education Reform, March 28, 2001, Chronicles of MINUGUA and the United Nations, United Nations Verification Mission in Guatemala, Spokesperson's office.

[25] In Spanish, *La educaci—n un reto para Guatemala: Propuesta para el incremento y la calidad del gasto del Ministerio de Educaci—n en 2002, con vision de largo plazo.*

[26] According to the Ministry of Education's proposal, the objects of curricular changes can be summarised in:

1. the improvement and integral development of the individual and of peoples;
2. knowledge, appreciation and development of the cultures of the country and of the world;
3. reinforcement of personal, ethnic, cultural, and national identity and self-esteem;
4. the promotion of peaceful coexistence among peoples, on the basis of inclusion, solidarity, mutual respect, and the elimination of discrimination;
5. an appreciation of the family as the basic social centre and as the first and primary educational entity;
6. education for participation and democratic exercise, a culture of peace, respect, and defence of human rights;
7. the transformation, resolution, and prevention of conflicts through a critical analysis of reality and the development of scientific, technical, and technological knowledge;
8. the internalisation of values and the development of ethical attitudes and behaviour for responsible interaction with the natural, social, and cultural environment; and

9. an improvement in the quality of life and the reduction of poverty, through the development of human resources.

[27] The central elements of the curriculum are the following:

- **Multi- and Interculturalism**: This gives rise to a real interaction among social groups, peoples, and cultures that coexist in the country.
- **Gender Equity**: This establishes a just relationship between men and women of different peoples. It means recognising as equal the values, rights, and responsibilities of all.
- **Education in Values**: This reinforces and disseminates personal, social and civic, ethic, spiritual, cultural and ecological values, for living in harmonious coexistence.
- **Family Life**: This promotes the stability and coexistence of its members.
- **Life as a Citizen**: This is for the development of a harmonious coexistence with the social and natural environment, beginning with an understanding of the personal, family, and social reality.
- **Sustainability**: This brings together permanent actions to guarantee conservation, rational use, and restoration of the environment and natural resources.
- **Security**: The presence of general conditions that allow people to feel protected against natural or social threats.
- **Guidance for Work**: This is a permanent process of integral training that allows people to become involved in improving the community's quality of life.
- **Technology**: This is aimed at strengthening curiosity, research, and the concern to find relevant technological responses to the reality of the surroundings.

[28] The areas of the curriculum are classified in:

- **fundamental areas**, focussing on basic skills that permit new knowledge to be generated autonomously, giving rise to the development of thinking skills and opening new spaces in education for students to relate to their natural and sociocultural milieu and to interact in the field of science and technology; and
- **training**, for developing the personal identity and self-esteem of children for building autonomous personalities and for developing cognitive processes of reinforcement in learning to learn. It also emphasises the skills that facilitate learning, aptitudes, and attitudes to productive work.

[29] Also participating have been projects such as the Mayan Mam Bilingual Intercultural Training in Education, FEBIMAM (Belgian Cooperation) in San Marcos; the Programme for Access to Bilingual Intercultural Education, PAEBI (USAID) in El Quiché; the Teacher s Training in Bilingual Intercultural Education, PEBI (PEMBI-GTZ)—Del Valle de Guatemala University in the Department of Sololá; a bachelor s degree project in bilingual intercultural education with an orientation to training of trainers (UNESCO/PROMEM/the Netherlands—Rafaél Landivar University of Guatemala) in Sololá and Huehuetenango; the training of professionals in bilingual intercultural education at the level of a teacher s, bachelor s, and master s degree, EDUMAYA-URL Project (USAID).

References

Bezmalinovic, Beatrice, Newman, Bruce, Nuñez, Gabriela, Tujab, Gloria, Nieves, Isabel, and Clay, Susan. (1991.) *First National Encounter: By Educating Girls, the Development of Guatemala Will Be Achieved*. Guatemala.

De Lara Galo, Carmen María. (1987.) *Conceptual Framework for Curricular Re-Adaptation*. Guatemala.

Educational Reform Consultative Commission. (2002.) *2004–2023 Long-Term National Education Plan*. Guatemala.

Gallo Armosino, Antonio. (2001.) *The 16th Century Mayan*. Guatemala: Rafael Landívar University.

General Directorate of School Education. (1998.) *Compilation of Education Laws*. Vol. IV. Guatemala.

Great National Campaign for Education. (2002.) *Education: A Challenge for Guatemala: Proposal for Increasing the Quality and Amount of the Ministry of Education's Public Expenditure in 2003, with a Long-Term Vision*. Guatemala.

Grigsby, Katherine. (2002.) *Theoretical Curricular Framework. Levels of Curricular Application. Mayan Relevance in the National Curriculum*. Vols. I and II. Guatemala: UNESCO/PROMEM, Ministry of Education.

Iturralve, Diego, Villoro, Luis, Castillo, Rolando, and Kymlicka, Will. (2002.) *Political Debate, Democracy, Citizenship and Diversity*. Guatemala: UNDP.

Ministry of Education, Guatemala. (2003.) *General Framework of the Curricular Transformation and the Basic Curriculum for Primary Education, National Implementation Level*.

———. (1999a.) *Education for All in the Year 2000: 1990/1998 Assessment Report*.

———. (1999b) *Synoptic History of Guatemala*. 1st ed.

———. (1991.) *Educational Philosophy, Policies and Strategies*.

National Council of Mayan Education—CNEM. (2002.) *Conclusions of the Third National Congress on Mayan Education, Results and Recommendations*. Guatemala.

National System for the Improvement of Human Resources and Curricular Adaptation—SIMAC. (1991.) *Education Journal, CEF Guide*.

Parity Commission for Educational Reform. (1998.) Design of the Educational Reform. Guatemala.

Rafael Landívar University and MINUGUA. (1997.) *Peace Accords: Signed by the Government of the Republic of Guatemala and the Guatemalan National Revolutionary Unity (URNG)*. Guatemala.

Rivera Alvarez, Otto Ricardo. (2002.) *Best Educational Practices of Mayan Bilingual Intercultural Education in Guatemala: Mayan Relevance in the National Curriculum.* Vol. I. Guatemala: UNESCO/ PROMEM, Ministry of Education.

Salazar Tetzagüic, Manuel de Jesús. (2001.) *Cultures and Intercultural Nature of Guatemala.* Guatemala: Institute of Linguistics and Education, Rafael Landívar University.

Torres, Rosa María. (2000.) *Education for All: The Pending Assignment.* Madrid: Editorial Popular.

UNESCO/OREALC. (1991.) *Major Project in the Field of Education in Latin America and the Caribbean.* Santiago, Chile.

United Nations System in Guatemala. (2002.) *2002 National Human Development Report, Guatemala: Human Development, Women and Health.* Guatemala.

———. (2000.) *2000 Human Development Report, Guatemala: The Inclusive Force of Human Development.* Guatemala.

University of San Carlos de Guatemala. (1995.) *Situational Analysis of Guatemalan Education 1994–2010.* Guatemala.

Appendix 1: Levels of National, Regional-Linguistic, and Communitary Curricular Implementation, Guatemalan Educational System

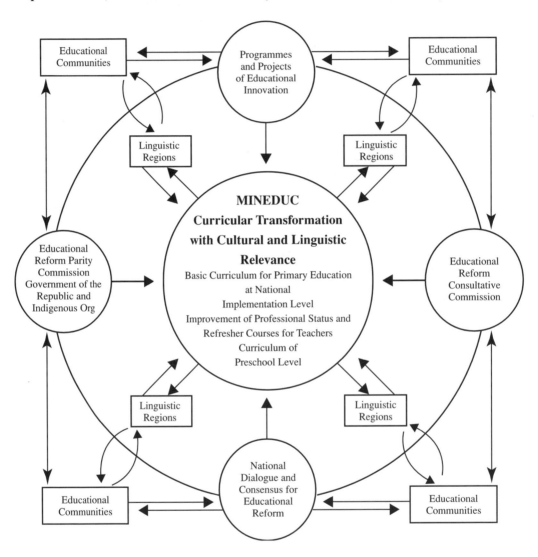

Source: UNESCO/PROMEM, June 2003

Appendix 2: Basics of the New Curriculum

The orientation of the curriculum by competencies (the capacity of a person to confront and solve everyday problems and generate new knowledge) strengthens the curricular development at the national, regional-linguistic, and local levels. To attain ownership and specificity in curricular decentralisation, framework competencies are established of Central Elements, Areas, Cycles, and Stages. This order allows the educational system to identify achievements and follow up the process at each level of development.

The Ministry of Education has established the following framework competencies for the level of Basic Secondary Education in the process of curricular transformation (MINUDEC, 2002).

Students who pass the Basic Secondary Education level

- promote and practice values, democracy, a culture of peace, and respect for universal human rights and the specific rights of the peoples and groups of Guatemala and the world;
- act with certainty, trust, freedom, responsibility, and honesty;
- use logical, reflexive, critical, purposeful, and creative thought in the building of knowledge;
- communicate in two or more languages of the country, one or more foreign languages, and in other forms of language;
- apply what they have learned—technology and knowledge of the arts and sciences inherent to their culture and other cultures, and focused on personal, family, community, social, and national development;
- critically use the knowledge of historical processes, from the diversity of the peoples of the country and the world, to understand the present and build the future;
- use dialogue and different forms of communication as a means to prevent, solve, and change conflicts, with respect for cultural differences and different opinions;
- respect and promote the culture and the concept of the world of the Garífuna, *ladino*, Mayan, and Xinca peoples and others in the world;
- contribute to the sustainable development of nature, and of the societies and cultures of the country and the world;
- respect and practice individual and collective social and environmental safety standards to promote the improvement of the quality of life, starting from their own concept of the world and from national and international regulations;
- exercise and promote democratic and participatory leadership and free and responsible decisionmaking;
- appreciate, practice, create, and promote the arts and other manifestations of the Garífuna, *ladino*, Mayan, and Xinca cultures and others in the world;
- express attitudes, abilities, skills, and habits for a permanent learning process;
- practice and promote physical activities, recreation, and sports, and make proper use of their time; and
- experience and promote unity in diversity, and social organisation with equity, as the basis of pluralistic development.

The framework competencies are based on the principles, policies, and objectives of the New Curricular Paradigm of Guatemalan education listed below (MINEDUC, 2002).

Principles of the New Curriculum:

- *Relevance*: This is a response to educational needs consistent with the social, economic, political, and cultural characteristics of individuals, peoples, and the country, according to the demands of the twenty-first century.
- *Participation and Social Commitment*: These are the basic elements of democratic life, including a capacity for and a possibility to communicate, a capacity for and a possibility to make decisions, and, with regard to social commitment, the shared responsibility of the different educational and social actors.
- *Equity*: This is based on a respect for differences, a basic condition for the eradication of social, ethnic, and gender discrimination, supported by interaction and equitable participation processes.
- *Pluralism*: This must facilitate the coexistence of the different political, ideological, educational, philosophical, and cultural trends; it is a set of values and positive activities derived from an intercultural education.
- *Sustainability*: This is a constant and progressive improvement of all human activities; a permanent development of knowledge, attitudes, values, and skills. Fundamentally, sustainability is a harmonious coexistence with nature.

Policies of the New Curriculum:

- to strengthen values for democratic coexistence and a culture of peace;
- to promote the development of each people and linguistic community, fostering intercultural relations;
- to promote bilingual and multilingual knowledge to support an intercultural dialogue;
- to promote equal opportunities of individuals and peoples;
- to train in productivity and industriousness;
- to promote and develop science and technology;
- to give emphasis to educational quality and innovative approaches;
- to establish curricular decentralisation;
- to pay attention to populations with special educational needs; and
- to promote the professional status and refresher courses for teachers.

Objectives of the New Curriculum:

- to improve and attain the integral development of individuals and of the peoples of the country;
- to have knowledge and appreciation and to promote the development of the cultures of the country and of the world;
- to strengthen personal identity and self-esteem, and ethnic, cultural, and national identity;
- to promote a peaceful coexistence between peoples on the basis of inclusion, solidarity, respect, mutual enrichment, and the elimination of discrimination;
- to appreciate the family as the basic social nucleus and as the first and permanent educational entity;
- to train for participation and democratic life, a culture of peace, and respect for and defence of human rights;
- to transform, solve, and prevent problems through a critical analysis of reality and the development of scientific, technical, and technological knowledge;
- to take ownership of the values and develop activities and ethical behaviour for a responsible interaction with the natural, social, and cultural environment; and
- to improve the quality of life and provide for the poor by developing human resources.

Appendix 3: Elements of the Vision of the World of the Mayan

The vision of the world of the Mayan is based on the concept of the harmony of the universe and the equilibrium of nature. *Uk'ux Kaj* is the heart of the heavens. *Uk'ux Ulew* is the heart of the earth. *Uk'ux Cho* is the heart of fresh water, and *Uk'ux Palouj* is the heart of salt water. *Uk'ux Kaj* is the factor of the energy of the universe and, together with the creators and builders Tz'aqol and B'itol, was responsible for the creation; with the help of the craftsmen grandfather Ixpinakok and grandmother Ixmukané *Uk'ux Kaj* created the first four men and the first four women. There were various attempts to create human beings, but it was not until they were created out of corn that they turned out to be perfect, because then they were also able to be thankful.

In the development and evolution of their culture the Mayan people created a vigesimal numerical system and relation of positions, organised counting, and recording of time in the 260-day Cholq'ij or Sacred calendar (lunar calendar), and the 360-day + 5 days of transition Ab' or agricultural calendar called Uayeb' (solar calendar). The characteristics of their scientific method were based on the process of observing, fixing, applying, and correcting. Their linguistic history is very old, and their languages, as well as their forms of social organisation, their productive systems, and a strong oral tradition that conveys the principles and values of their spirituality, knowledge, and methods of education have remained alive until today. Mayan aesthetics and art express, through their delicate embroidery, the ecological wealth and spirituality of their people. Women's *"guipiles"* are like codices that children learn and fix in their minds and senses since very young.

PRINCIPLES OF MAYAN THOUGHT

1. *The awareness of human beings of being immersed in the universe*: Human beings have, in this principle, the basis for including, both in education and training, that we are an element of and responsible for nature; that nature is our home and our mother. This is manifested in the profoundest sense of animism and trust in nawalism (everything has life and everything has its protector).

2. *Concern for the equilibrium of nature*: Living beings, the elements, and natural phenomena have an interdependent relationship. Human beings have to respect and at the same time try to maintain a balance with our closest natural surroundings. This is the reason we educate our sense of harmony.

3. *Art, sciences, and spirituality work as an interdependent whole*: In the Mayan concept of life, these three dimensions of human development are intimately linked. Art as a creative and recreational activity is also based on science and spirituality; science as an investigative and systematising discipline is based on art and spirituality; and spirituality, as a vital force inherent to humans and their harmony with the heart of the heavens and nature, is based on art and science.

4. *Corn is vital nourishment, a sacred sign, and the substance of our origin*: Corn is the vital and basic cereal of the Mayan culture. The *Popol Wuj* (Sacred Book of the Mayan K'iché) presents human beings made of corn by *Uk'ux Kaj*, heart of the heavens, and the craftsmen Ixpikakoke and Ixmukané. Agriculture and the solar calendar have corn as the focal point: it is a material element that has a spiritual protective force.

5. *All other people are my "alter ego" or other self*: The starting and arrival point in a relationship between human beings is to bear in mind that each person is a facilitator of individual and community life. All constructive or destructive actions taken by me regarding other people have direct repercussions for myself and for our society.

6. *There is a reason for knowledge to exist, provided such knowledge is passed on to the community*: Any discovery or intellectual finding is given to the community as a contribution to its development; the community recognises the efforts of people who provide knowledge, because they are improving life.

7.   *There is a natural compensation at work in all human acts or phenomena of life*: This is conceptualised as a point of equilibrium between individual human actions and social and natural phenomena.

MAYAN VALUES

The concept of a value identified in Mayan philosophy is *Ruk'ux Na'oj*, which means heart and energy of thought and wisdom. *Ruk'ux Na'oj* is the set of values that support the identity of a person in his or her social coexistence and relationship with nature; these values support the life of the family and the community, and foster the attitude to create, build, and solve; they are a manifestation of spirituality.

1.   *Laq'olaj ruwach'ulew*—the sacred essence of nature: This value is expressed in the concepts of Our Mother Earth, Our Father the Sun, and Our Grandmother the Moon, which appear in ceremonial prayers. It is made evident in the recognition of the *nahual* (protector) of the hills and valleys, the rivers and the lakes, the seas and the winds.

2.   *Loq'olaj kaj*—the sacred nature of the universe: From the universe comes life and the strength of our existence, and we are an element of it, together with nature.

3.   *Qach'umilal*—our star, our mission: This is based on the recognition of our star, which accompanies our mission and guides our vocation in this life.

4.   *K'awomanik*—the value of gratitude and thankfulness: People who practice the Mayan culture express their gratitude with great spirit for favours received, repressions, the coming of a new day, afternoon, and night; they also give thanks for advice received, the greetings and sharing with people at family and community gatherings. In Mayan social coexistence, thankfulness is a link of unity and solidarity; it expresses a value that, if practiced constantly, rejuvenates the person.

5.   *Rutz'aqat qak'asiem*—attainment of abundance and fulfilment of our work duties in our life: This is a value that expresses and permanently motivates people and communities to attain abundance, comply with their work duties, and fulfil their commitments and aspirations.

6.   *Kuqub'ab'äl K'ux*—sense and state of peacefulness, of responsibility: The spiritual force that produces peacefulness and peace is called *Kuqub'ab'äl k'ux*; it is the willingness to assume responsibility that a person develops in his education with the help of his family.

7.   *Tink'ulub'ej, tiqa k'ulub'ej*—I take advice, to take advice: *Tink'ulub'ej* is the value of giving advice and receiving advice; it also means to give advice or to guide another person.

8.   *Rumitijul aqk'asiem*—the value of work in our lives: *Mitij* is the quality of a diligent person, devoted to his or her work, being responsible and creative. *Mitijul* is the diligence and meticulousness that people put into the performance of their activities.

9.   *Tiqapoqonaj ronojel ruwach K'aslem*—the value of protecting everything because it has life: The concept of this value, from among the moral and social standards of Mayan spirituality, is very extensive in its scope and comprehension. *Tiqapoqonaj* is the force that helps maintain solidarity among the people of the community and with other peoples.

10.   *Niqa nimaj kitzij qate' qamama'*—respect for the words of our parents and grandparents: Respect for mother and father, grandmother and grandfather. This is a value based on Mayan family life; it supports the dignity of a person.

11.   *Ri qäs qitzil pan ruq'ajarik qatzij*—the true word of all our words: The word in Mayan society, as in other societies of the world, is the basis of their freedom and an instrument of their inter-relation and identity. The *Popol Wuj* starts the tale of the history of the creation of the world with the expression "*Taq xpe kut utzij w'aral*" (Here, then, is the word).

12.   *Tiqto'qi'*—to help each other, to cooperate with your neighbour and the community: One of the bulwarks of Mayan society regarding the subject of community development is cooperation, another way of showing solidarity.

13. *Ri ch'ajch'ojil, ri jeb'elik pa qak'aslem*—beauty and cleanliness in our life: *Ch'ajch'ojil* is a concept that is profoundly observed and appreciated in Mayan communities; it means clean. It is the cleanliness of people in their appearance, in their work, in the quality of the embroidery of their crafts or artistic work; in the order and cleanliness of their agricultural chores, in the quality of their ceremonial messages. *Jeb'elik* is that which is well done or well conceived.

14. *Awojb'anik*—to help maintain the vitality of the spirit in the body: This is the value that the Mayan cultural community gives to the action of helping to maintain the essential energy of the spirit in the human being; this is the reason a person must try, in all moments of life, not to let the force of the spirit become weak, or let it get away from the spirit.

Appendix 4: Fact Sheet - Guatemala

Total population   11.7 million

(50% are indigenous. The inhabitants living in rural areas, grouped in 19,600 communities of less than 2,000 individuals, comprise 60% of the total population.)

Population aged under 15:   43.3%

Gross domestic product: US$ 20.5 billion

Purchasing Power Parity GDP per capita: US$ 4,400

Life expectancy at birth: 65.3 years

Unemployment rate (1999):   7.5%

Public expenditure on education (as % of GDP) (1998–2000):   1.7%

Adult literacy rate (age 15 and above):   69.2%
Youth literacy rate(age 15–24):   79.6%

Net primary enrolment ratio: 84%
Net secondary enrolment ratio: 26%

Compulsory education: 7–14 (not enforced)

Structure of education system :

Primary: Length of program: 6 years (age 7–13)

General Secondary (Ciclo Prevocacional): Length of program: 3 years (age 13–16)

Diversified Secondary (Ciclo Diversificado): Length of program: 2 years (age 16–18)
Certificate/diploma awarded: Bachillerato

Upper Secondary (Technical Secondary School): Length of program: 3 years (age 15–18)
Certificate/diploma awarded: Perito Industrial, Agricola, Contador

Ethnic groups:
Mestizo (mixed Amerindian-Spanish or assimilated Amerindian—in local Spanish called *ladino*), approximately 55%; Amerindian or predominantly Amerindian, approximately 43%; whites and others, 2%.

Languages: Spanish, 60% (official language and predominant language of instruction); Amerindian languages, 40% (21 Mayan linguistic communities, Garífuna and Xinca).

(During the 2002 academic year, bilingual and intercultural education was implemented in 3,808 pre-primary and primary schools, by 7,570 teachers, reaching 269,375 indigenous children.)

Religions: Roman Catholic, Protestant, indigenous Mayan beliefs

Sources: The authors, UNDP Human Development Report 2003, and The International Association of Universities/UNESCO International Centre on Higher Education

Note: All figures for 2001 except if otherwise stated.

Chapter 4

Developing Curriculum as a Means to Bridging National Divisions in Lebanon

Nemer Frayha

About the Author

Nemer Frayha was the president of the Educational Centre for Research and Development (ECRD) in Beirut during the implementation of the Civics Education Project and the development of the history curriculum, from February 1999 to January 2002. The ECRD was established in 1971 and is in charge of educational planning, educational research and statistics, the revision and development of school curricula, and the writing of textbooks, as well as the in-service training of teachers. The centre was responsible for framing the Plan for Educational Revival in 1994 following the end of the civil war in 1989. Dr. Frayha is currently a professor in the Faculty of Education at the Lebanese University.

List of Acronyms

AUB	American University of Beirut
ECRD	Educational Centre for Research and Development (Beirut)
LAES	Lebanese Association for Educational Studies
PER	Plan for Educational Revival (1994)
PLO	Palestine Liberation Organization
UNESCO	United Nations Educational, Scientific and Cultural Organization
USJ	Université Saint-Joseph (Beirut)

INTRODUCTION

The history of Lebanon in the second half of the twentieth century is sometimes portrayed as a model of an open and creative social mosaic, exemplified by the country's seventeen communities living in mutual respect and tolerance, particularly during the rapid modernisation of the 1950s and 1960s. But the recent years in Lebanon have also seen a brutal civil war, referred to at times as marking the beginning of a wave of protracted internal armed conflicts at the global level. In these struggles, in Lebanon and elsewhere, issues of identity have superseded more traditional political ideologies as an important source of political mobilisation and violent confrontation.

This chapter does not attempt to analyse the multiple causes of civil strife in Lebanon in the mid-1970s and 1980s, nor does it attempt to review the range of analyses undertaken by a number of reputed historians and political scientists (see, for example, Corm, 2003, 1988; Salibi, 1988, 1976; Makdisi, 2000). The Lebanese civil war—or what has been referred to perhaps more appropriately as the "wars of Lebanon"—was embedded in regional and international conflicts, but sectarian identities, conflicting conceptualisations of national citizenship and loyalties, and the structure of the distribution of political power were all central issues both in the outbreak of conflict in 1975 and in the process of political and social reconstruction following the 1989 Taef peace accords.

This chapter focuses on these issues of identity and on the role of formal education in reproducing social divisions, or, conversely, in strengthening national cohesion. In order to better understand this role, the case of Lebanon presents the controversial issues related to the formulation of curriculum policy in sensitive learning areas linked to the definition of what constitutes Lebanese identity, history, and sense of citizenship. While the issues discussed are those associated with the process of curriculum reform that followed the reestablishment of peace in the 1990s, the case of Lebanon also reviews the ways in which curriculum policy issues were framed during key historical moments in the development of schooling in the country, including the establishment of the French mandate in 1920, independence in 1943, the 1968 reform at the height of the ideological conflicts within the wider context of the Middle East, and, finally, the postwar reform of the 1990s based on the orientations articulated in the 1989 accords.

In so doing, the study assesses the degrees to which the fragmented school structure, the weak coverage of public schooling, and curriculum content may have contributed not only to reflecting and reproducing, but also possibly to reinforcing, the sectarian divisions and political tensions that led to the collapse of the Lebanese state and the crisis of the Lebanese nation in 1975–90. This investigation is based on the underlying assumption that a critical examination of the dialectical relationship between schooling, curriculum, and conflict is crucial for informed policy formulation and the implementation of a social studies curriculum that may indeed strengthen social cohesion.

BACKGROUND TO THE CONFLICT

To understand the nature of civil strife in Lebanon, it is important to shed light on the history of the region referred to as Mount Lebanon, the comparatively recent process of state formation, and the development of an increasingly sectarian political system. While not intending to be exhaustive, this section provides an overview of the shifts in governance across the centuries (with their politico-economic implications), and the principal social factors that have contributed to what we now call a "Lebanese" identity. Contemporary Lebanese society reflects the diversity of an inherited mosaic of some seventeen different communities, of which the Maronite, Druze, Sunni, Shiite, Greek Catholic, and Greek Orthodox are the main religious groups. Each community can be seen to have possessed its own evolving sense of history, often coloured by political interpretations at the time (particularly throughout the nineteenth and twentieth centuries), related to regional ideological realities, and often resulting in conflicting interpretations.

Yet it is important to note that the projection into the past of modern political concerns, grounded as they are in the logic of the nation-state, fail to grasp the whole story. As Kamal Salibi noted in the introduction to *Lebanon: A History of Conflict and Consensus* (1988), a compilation of essays published the year before the end of the long civil war, "the concept of Lebanon as a historical country has been a highly controversial one ever since the State of Greater Lebanon, which is today the Lebanese Republic, was created within the present borders in 1920." While the notion of a Lebanese nation may no longer be at issue within the persistently sectarian structure of Lebanese society, issues related to the distribution of power and the confessional nature of the political system have posed important challenges to social cohesion over the second half of the twentieth century.

Conflict, state formation, and nation building

While the origin of Lebanon is generally traced back to the Phoenicians (3000 BC), the inhabitants of the region started to become Arab in culture and language following the Arab conquest of the region that took place in the seventh century AD. It is important to begin with this fact not only for motives of chronological convenience, but also in order to note that an Arab cultural and linguistic identity would be equally relevant for the Maronites (a Christian-Oriental sect with communion to the Roman Catholic Church), who, fleeing Monophisite persecution, settled initially in the northern reaches of Mount Lebanon during the fifth and sixth centuries,[1] as for the Druze (a sect with its roots in Shiite Islam), who first appeared and established themselves in the southern part of Mount Lebanon. Since the seventh and eighth centuries, the Sunnis and Greek Orthodox have constituted the bulk of the urban population of the coastal cities (Tripoli, Beirut, Sidon, Tyre). Significant Greek Orthodox and Catholic as well as Shiite communities also lived in and around Mount Lebanon, making it, at least in some areas, the home of a decidedly diverse religious population. These religious communities, sharing language, culture, and customs in common, should not, therefore, be mistaken for so called "ethnic" groups (Corm, 1988). The two culturally distinct groups that exist today in Lebanon, representing some 8 to 10 percent of the population, are the Armenians (7–8 percent) and the Kurds (2–3 percent). Described by Georges Corm as newcomers to the Lebanese land, they arrived at the beginning of the twentieth century as a result of Turkish persecution. These two large groups have their own languages and the Kurds have family and tribal traditions which are totally separate from the Arab structures in Lebanese society.

The sixteenth century marked a series of significant changes in the region. In 1516, the Ottoman armies invaded Syria and held control over the area until forced to hand it over to the French, four centuries later, at the end of World War I. European powers were able to take advantage of inter-religious wars in the Ottoman Empire through a series of capitulations granted them by Ottoman rulers, effectively allowing Western European countries to intervene in domestic affairs (Abouchedid and Nasser, 2000). The economic and cultural privileges that this engendered were reinforced, as we shall see later in this case, through the educational work of missionaries.

The historical use of the term "Mount Lebanon" to signify a coherent and separate social and political entity is a sensitive and potentially controversial issue. Nonetheless, there is general agreement that Mount Lebanon was a largely autonomous region that encompassed three Ottoman *vilayets*, or provinces, and that it became a privileged administrative unit in 1861, known as the *mutasarrifiyya* of Mount Lebanon. The latter occurred following nearly two decades of increasingly brutal violence between the Maronite and Druze communities when France, longtime champion of the Maronite community, who had suffered serious losses during the massacres of 1860, took the military and political initiative to intervene (Salibi, 1988). As a result, France, along with five other interested foreign powers (Turkey, England, Russia, Prussia, and Austria), signed the Règlement Organique (Organic Statute), resulting in the establishment of the semi-autonomous *mutasarrifiyya* of Mount Lebanon. Ultimate authority of the *mutasarrifiyya* still rested with the Ottoman rulers. The head of the entity (*Mutassaref*) was appointed by the sultan and assisted by a council whose membership was distributed among the religious sects. However, the *mutasarrifiyya* was under international guaranty, and internally, each sect had an outside guardian: the French sponsored the Christian Maronites, the British the Druzes, and the Russians the Greek Orthodox community. The Sunnis were not seen to need any outside protection, since the Ottoman sultanate was Muslim Sunni.

Arguably, the Ottoman authorities, during the period from 1840 to 1860, were the first to introduce the distribution of political power based on sectarian affiliation in the often difficult to subdue region of Mount Lebanon. Yet, as Makdisi (2000) points out, it was in the aftermath of the violence in 1860, and evident through the geographical and geopolitical partition of Mount Lebanon, that a social culture of sectarianism developed, inasmuch as "all sectors of society, public and private, recognised that the war and the massacres marked the beginning of a new age—an age defined by the raw intrusion of sectarian consciousness into modern life." In what had been for centuries a multiconfessional society structured by elite hierarchies, the establishment of the *mutasarrifiyya* marked the public space by a "discourse of sectarianism" which "permeated all facets of administration, law, education, and, finally, with the establishment of the Lebanese republic, the state." The impact of the Ottoman and European reform language that took root at the time is still being felt today insofar as it provoked fundamental perceptional changes, making religion in particular

> the site of a colonial encounter between a self-styled "Christian" West and what it saw as its perennial adversary, an "Islamic" Ottoman Empire. This encounter profoundly altered the meaning of religion in the multiconfessional society of Mount Lebanon because it

emphasized sectarian identity as the only viable marker of political reform and the only authentic basis for political claims.

(Makdisi, 2000)

The transforming social identities, in short, shaped the emerging political reality and would become manifest in the formulation of the young state's national policies.

The state of Greater Lebanon, within its current international borders was established by the French in 1920 after World War I determined the destruction of the Ottoman Empire. Nevertheless, when France took over as the mandatory power, it retained much of the political system initially set up by the Ottomans, particularly the distribution of authority among the various sects.

In geographical terms, the *mutasarrifiyya* served as the "territorial nucleus" (Salibi, 1988) for the construction of the new Lebanese state while all around it Britain and France redrew the political map of the eastern Arab world. The Sykes-Picot Agreement of 1916 established the French mandate and divided the Arab provinces of the Ottoman Empire into zones of French and English domination. The French mandate lasted from 1920 until the granting of Lebanese independence in 1943.

Delineating the territorial boundaries of the nation was much easier to do, however, than determining the nature of national identity. Against an increasingly sectarian landscape with complex geopolitical interests played out on Lebanon's 10,452 square kilometres of national territory, Salibi aptly draws our attention to the fact that

> the conviction persisted for a long time that there were in fact alternatives to Lebanon as a state—viewed as being essentially a Christian political achievement—which could serve the interests of the Islamic communities better. It was only as these alternatives began to vanish under changing regional and international circumstances that the worth of the Lebanese political achievement to all the parties concerned started to attract increasing recognition, until all began to demand their rightful shares in it, as is the situation today.

Pluralistic or divided society?

With the violence and partition that characterised Lebanese society during the mid-nineteenth century came a concerted effort on the part of the infighting elites, the Ottoman authorities, and foreign missionaries to face the dilemma of how to construct a modern society. Thus, politics and education, which had traditionally reinforced a nonsectarian social order, became a means for sectarian division.

The confessional political system inherited from the period of the Ottoman reform of 1845 and reinforced by the French mandate in Lebanon (1920–43) defined the distribution of power between the various communities based on their respective demographic weight. This arrangement was laid out in the 1943 National Pact, which "marked the start of a new phase of inter-sect political relationships which had evolved over the centuries" (Tannous, 1997). The pact stipulated that the Parliament would have a six-to-five ratio of Christians to Muslims, and that the position of president would go to a Maronite Christian, that of prime minister to a Sunni Muslim, and that of speaker of the house to a Shiite Muslim. Problematically, however, this distribution of political power, which continues to be applied today (with the exception of an equal ratio of Muslim and Christian representation for parliamentary seats, cabinet posts, and high-ranking civil service positions as agreed in the 1989 Taef peace accords), is based on 1932 census results (themselves widely viewed as suspect by scholars). The fact that the current demographic weight of each community is unclear and that no official census has been carried out since 1932 reflects the sensitivity of this key political issue. Even granting that Christians originally formed a majority of the population as late as 1943, there is little doubt that "the balance of numbers in the country [has] long been tipping increasingly in favour of the Muslims" (Salibi, 1988/1989).

With the power of national decisionmaking at stake, it comes as no surprise that Lebanon has, to date, been unable to reach a consensus on census taking. This has been compounded by the additional controversy about who is to be officially considered Lebanese, particularly with regard to the substantial population of citizens abroad, considered to be predominantly Christian, who are denied voting rights. The implications on development planning, constrained by this climate of sectarian classification, have proved burdensome. Moreover, when mandatory France created the state of Greater Lebanon in 1920, it faced the difficult union of urban and rural communities. As has often been the case elsewhere, there was an initial influx of the rural population to the cities as agriculture declined. As Corm (1988) describes,

> two historical events made this meeting between the Mountain and the City even more difficult. First, the closing of the country's southern border with Palestine which became the Israeli state in 1948. This accelerated the decline of the economy of Lebanon's southern areas which had been structured on the basis of intensive trade with Palestine. Second, the end of the economic union between Lebanon and Syria, a legacy from the French mandate, in 1950.

It was predominantly the rural Shiite community who bore the brunt of these new trade barriers, even as they remained more isolated from the social and cultural changes, largely the provenance of Western influence, that were impacting the cities. As the traditional world of Ottoman Syria declined, the Christian communities were more receptive to Western influences—influences that had become more and more institutionalised in education, trade, and the political landscape. The rural character of Lebanon began to give way in the 1950s when "the urbanization of Lebanon assumed explosive proportions, which were difficult if not impossible to manage." Furthermore, the violent confrontations that erupted between Muslims and Christians in 1958 "had resulted in a general political collapse, which shook Lebanon to its foundations, opening the way for social changes on a more rapid and radical scale" (Salibi, 1976). In short, the end of the nineteenth and first half of the twentieth centuries, with their shifting economic and political realities, "marked a rupture, a birth of a new culture that singled out religious affiliation as the defining public and political characteristic of a modern subject and citizen" (Makdisi, 2000).

Contributing factors to the 1975–89 civil war

April 1975 marked the beginning of what was to become Lebanon's long civil war. The outbreak of conflict in this small territory began as the internal and regional situation grew more and more explosive, particularly in the wake of the 1967 and 1973 Arab-Israeli wars. The national, regional, and international conditions that contributed to the destabilisation of Lebanon are numerous and nuanced, and we will not be able to treat them here in their entirety. Neither is it our purpose to explain the causes of the civil war but, rather, to provide a quick overview of the main contextual factors and accompanying ideological influences in order to better understand the evolution of educational policies over the course of the twentieth century.

The principal contextual factors at work in the region, prior to the outbreak of the Lebanese civil war in 1975, were linked in large part to the geopolitical redistribution of power following the two world wars, in particular such factors as

- The creation of Israel in 1948 on its southern borders.
- The influx of Palestinian refugees (estimated to represent between 10 and 15 percent of the population residing in Lebanon) following the Arab-Israeli wars of 1948 and 1967.
- The creation of the Palestine Liberation Organization (PLO) in 1964.
- The establishment of the PLO's political and military infrastructure in Lebanon following the suppression of their activities in Jordan during Black September in 1970. The presence of the PLO became intertwined with domestic Lebanese politics and contributed to deepening ideological divisions along sectarian lines.
- The rise of Arab nationalism in the region. Led by President Nasser of Egypt, pan-Arabism, or the Arab national unity movement, had as a principal tenet the idea of recovering the territory of Palestine and "appeared for a moment during the 1960s to have the authority to inherit naturally the succession of the Ottoman Empire" (Corm, 1988). During the height of this unitarian, secular Arab nationalist movement, Syria and Egypt "politically merged" as the United Arab Republic (1958–61).
- The ideological divisions of the bipolar cold war geopolitical configuration. The Soviet Union supported the Palestinian resistance and the Arab nationalist movement, while the United States supported Israel and conservative Arab governments. The Palestinian commando movement was seen as the "spearhead of Soviet-backed radicalism in the Arab world" (Salibi, 1976).

Against this contextual framework, the Lebanese were divided ideologically and, typically, along sectarian lines, over the following internal and regional factors:

Internally

- The need for political modernisation of the Lebanese state and the reform of the sectarian system based on changing demographic and social realities, particularly as a result of the rapid urbanisation of the 1960s.
- The need for social reform and the redistribution of economic opportunities.

Regionally

- Pan-Arab nationalism. While most Lebanese Muslims welcomed the establishment of the United Arab Republic, and supported the idea that Lebanon join the unification, most Christians, along with the ruling government at the time, preferred to stay out of any Arab union.
- The role of President Nasser in influencing, and, for some, instigating the 1958 Muslim and Druze revolt against President Chamoun.
- The Palestinian issue, which became the heart of the Arab nationalist cause. In Lebanon, various Palestinian organisations were "able to strike firm roots by taking advantage of the deep cleavage in opinion between the Christian and Muslim Lebanese, the conservatives and the radicals, over the sensitive Palestinian issue" (Salibi, 1976). The fragile configuration of the Lebanese social mosaic was affected, in other words, as the

Muslim-dominated leftist and pan-Arab parties supported the Palestinian resistance from Lebanese soil, while most Christians, and particularly the Maronites, opposed this support.

- The role of the Lebanese army in supporting or containing Palestinian resistance activity against Israel from Lebanese soil, particularly in the face of Israeli retaliation of Palestinian commando attacks and the real threat of Israeli invasion and occupation of southern Lebanon.[2]

In sum, the Lebanese had conflicting views, which had become interwoven with the larger political and ideological struggles in the region, regarding the activities of the PLO. Furthermore, the contentious redistribution of political power between Christians and Muslims, and deepening ideological divisions, made the outbreak of violent conflict all but inevitable.

The Taef peace accords of 1989

The fifteen-year period of armed conflict (1975–89) came to an end with the signing of the National Reconciliation Agreement or "Taef Agreement," in Taef, Saudi Arabia, as a result of efforts at mediation by, among others, Saudi Arabia, Kuwait, and Morocco. Based on the agreement, the Constitution was amended on August 21, 1990. One article of the Taef accords stipulates that "abolishing political sectarianism is a fundamental national objective."[3] Conceived of in accordance with a "phased plan," the article concretely outlines the need to establish equal representation of Muslims and Christians in government positions and public agencies and immediately calls to "abolish the mention of sect and denomination on the identity card." The Taef Agreement further articulates significant principles on social unity, stating that:

- Culturally, socially, and economically, balanced development is a mainstay of the state's unity and of the system's stability.
- Efforts would be made to achieve comprehensive social justice through fiscal, economic, and social reform.
- Lebanon's soil is united and belongs to all the Lebanese. Every Lebanese is entitled to live in and enjoy any part of the country under the supremacy of the law. The people may not be categorised on the basis of any affiliation whatsoever, and there shall be no fragmentation, no partition, and no repatriation (of Palestinians in Lebanon).
- No authority violating the common coexistence charter shall be legitimate.

The above principles relative to the "balanced development," "unity of the state," "social justice," "supremacy of law," and emphasis on the "common coexistence" of citizens also constituted the underlying vision inspiring the special section of the Taef Agreement on education. While education was not a main topic on the Taef meeting agenda, legislators addressed this issue, along with other issues that were thought to have played at least an indirect role in the outbreak of the war, as it was also believed to be important to the process of the social reconstruction of the Lebanese nation. Concern about the role of schooling in moulding the new generation of Lebanese into one nation translated into questioning aspects of educational planning and the development of curricula, textbooks, and learning materials.[4] The most important point appeared to be the perceived need to unify the history and civics textbooks.

This was largely inspired by the recognition of Lebanese deputies that education was not playing its role of promoting national cohesion among the youth. During the Taef conference, there was no specific meeting for education per se, but the deputies were convinced that curricula should be revised and that history and civics textbooks should be unified in order to be used by all Lebanese students at public and private schools. [5]

As a result of the agreement, all the main communities are now involved in decisionmaking processes, which, in turn, necessitates a greater degree of compromise in order to reach consensus on many national issues, including education. However, before turning to these issues, and in order to fully understand the educational reform orientation, it is necessary to outline the historical development of the school system in Lebanon, characterised as it is by a fragmented structure and management system, compounded by weak public control on curriculum content and textbook development in learning areas such as history, civics, and religious education which are most explicitly related to identity formation.

SCHOOLING, CURRICULUM, AND NATIONAL COHESION

Missionary schooling and the transformation of "communities of knowledge"

As mentioned in the previous section, the partition of Mount Lebanon in the mid-1800s laid the framework for a divided and sectarian social development. The introduction of modern forms of schooling, which preexisted any form of central state control, also allowed for the beginnings of an increasingly sectarian institutionalisation of knowledge. Previously, in contrast, an elite community (which included notables, those who chronicled their histories, Ottoman government officials, and religious leaders) had "regarded its control over religious and secular knowledge as essential to a hierarchical ordering of society" (Makdisi, 2000). Indeed, in many ways, the Ottoman borders of Mount Lebanon determined the boundaries of accepted domains of knowledge.

> Whereas both commoners and notables accepted inherited norms that organized political space and determined the composition of hierarchy . . . only members of the community of knowledge, which included secular notables, their advisors (the mudabbirs), the upper Christian clergy, and the Druze mashayikh 'aql, had the power to explain, legitimate, alter, or otherwise mediate such boundaries. Religious and secular knowledge were deployed in the service of stability and hierarchy. Although personal law and education lay within the purview of each religious community, the realms of education, law, and politics reinforced one another; each was an element in maintaining the domain of secular obedience to the Sultan.

The spread of European and American mission schools considerably altered this more traditional control over the landscape of knowledge and, with it, the societal order. To cite one example, the nineteenth-century ambitions of the Jesuits "aimed to 'regenerate' an entire population primarily through the medium of local education." Thus, "authoritative" versions of history vied with each other in competitive circulation, either legitimated by the type of schooling through which they were narrated (each religious community tended to have a missionary sponsor with their own established schools) or marked by a lack of educational representation (as was the case with the predominantly Shiite community, "the only confessional community which took no central part in the educational movement of the time") (Abouchedid and Nasser, 2000).

The capitulation treaties between France and the Ottoman Empire enabled the former to send missionaries into Lebanon who felt that one of the best ways to protect Catholics was by converting adherents of other rites. In carrying out their tasks, Jesuits, Capuchins, Lazarists, and later Protestants upgraded traditional local Christian schools and established new ones. At first, and in line with a conversionary zeal, the education provided in these schools was heavily ecclesiastical in nature and form. However, with an increasing elite demand for a secular "education for the world," the missionaries were compelled to adapt their teachings. Nevertheless, "modern education did not stem from, and hence reinforce, a religiously integrative social order but reflected, and gave credence to, a religiously segregated landscape." The Druze elites, for example, sent their children to Protestant schools and "accepted an implicit orientation toward Britain, whereas Maronites embraced the Jesuit schools and thereby committed themselves to an explicit orientation toward France" (Makdisi, 2000).

While it is never easy to determine to what extent the specific socialisation processes embedded in schooling impact on the general social identity of individuals and communities, scholars insist on the importance of these early missionary schools as a means to understanding the overall social and political development of Lebanon.

In general, the Catholic missionaries advanced Maronite and French interests and language through schooling, while the British and Americans emphasised Arabic language and culture in the curricula of their schools—an orientation that would be more in line with nationalist Arab sentiment in the twentieth century. In addition to founding the Syrian Protestant College—later the American University of Beirut—in 1866, and printing books, American missionaries established roughly 132 schools around the turn of the century, while the British-Syrian mission opened forty schools prior to World War I. The French Jesuit and lay missionaries were similarly industrious. The Moslem Charitable Purpose Association also started organising schools of their own, but in far inferior numbers to the Christians. As Ghait and Shabaan (1996) note, "on the eve of World War I, there were 100 private Christian but only 3 private Islamic schools" (citing Jabbour, 1992). This was of further significance in terms of the varying mediums of instruction inasmuch as

> prior to World War I foreign languages spread mainly along sectarian lines with the Catholics and Maronites learning French, the Moslems Arabic, and the Moslem and Greek Orthodox elites English. This linked religion to education and planted the seeds of educational and socio-economic inequalities among the various sects of the Lebanese society.

Nevertheless, Arabic was and has remained the lingua franca of ceremonial, societal, and everyday communicative functions. In sum, through these networks of schools, foreign missionaries in the region became indirectly involved in the internally divisive and controversial issues relating to national identity at the critical time of the birth of Turkish and Arab nationalisms in the nineteenth century.

Challenges in developing a unified national school curriculum

During the period of the French mandate(1920–43), the French government played a direct role in Lebanon's educational legislation and practices. Beginning in 1923, the Haut Commissariat published an educational periodical, *Bulletin de l'Enseignement*, which covered curricula, statistics, legislation, and so on, while throughout the 1920s Lebanese and French scholars developed the curricula. In 1924 the French established the Division de l'Instruction, which later became the Ministère de l'Instruction Publique in 1926. French was made an official language alongside Arabic, and every school was required to include a certain minimum number of hours of French-language instruction in its curriculum. Such policy reflected an imbalance of power between the French and Lebanese authorities regarding the status and place of the Arabic language. Additionally, first the French authorities and later the Lebanese officials introduced and maintained a system of official examinations on the basis of which certificates and diplomas were awarded, which in turn qualified their holders for entry into certain professions (Frayha, 1985).

> Despite the efforts made by the mandatory authority to centralise the educational system, many factors (internal and external; religious and political) defeated this intention. Legislation relative to education tended to reinforce confessional autonomy.
>
> With the establishment of the Lebanese Republic in 1926, confessional communities gained further constitutional prerogatives, which allowed them to maintain their own schools. Article 10 of the Lebanese Constitution of May 23, 1926, which is the only Article in the Constitution that deals with education, echoed Article 8 of the French Mandate by acknowledging freedom of education to confessional communities. Hence, Christians, Muslims, and Druzes were able to organise their own schools. The perfunctory inspection of private schools by the Ministry of Education allowed private schools to shape and execute their own educational programmes.
>
> (Abouchedid and Nasser, 2000)

Since that time the existence of parallel systems and diversified curricula has characterised school education in Lebanon. The government of independence in 1943 was faced with the urgent task of unifying coexisting communities into a nation and looked upon education as the best means to achieve this goal. Therefore, a number of legislative measures were enacted after 1943 to reorganise the Ministry of Education, to centralise the educational system, to control or supervise the private schools, to revive and encourage the public schools, and to introduce new curricula emphasising the place of Arabic language (Frayha, 1985).

Nevertheless, the new government tended to maintain the freedom of religious groups to open and run their schools rather than do away with the religious constraints binding the whole educational system. A case in point was the new government's 1943 amendment of the abovementioned 1926 Constitution, which left Article 10 untouched. Article 10 states that

> Education is free in so far as it is not contrary to public order and good morals and does not affect the dignity of the several faiths. There shall be no violation of the rights of the religious sects to have their schools, subject to the general prescription concerning public education which are decreed by the state.

This article was also retained during post–civil war amendments to the Constitution in 1991, reinforcing the language of the 1989 Taef Agreement. Currently, there is general scholarly consensus that education policies continue to reflect confessional cleavages. What was described in 1949 about parents' choice of school type for their children being a reflection of their religious affiliation is still applicable today: "a Catholic parent is likely to place his child in a Catholic school. Greek or other Orthodox children, when they do not go to their schools, usually prefer a lay school. . . . Most Protestant children go to Protestant schools. . . . A Muslim parent would usually prefer to send his child to a Muslim school."[6] Nevertheless, Muslims do frequently send their children to Christian schools, though the opposite is very rare.

The first national government of 1946 in the post-independence period, believing schooling to be an effective means for unifying coexisting communities, enacted a number of legislative measures with a view to

- centralise the educational system;
- supervise/control the private sector;
- supervise textbook design and production;
- design and administer official examinations; and
- renew school curricula.

The curricula of 1946—developed by educators at the Ministry of Education, discussed and approved by the cabinet, and issued by legislative decree—were based on three main policy orientations:

1. the use of Arabic as the language of instruction;
2. an emphasis on citizenship education; and
3. an attempt to introduce/impose the new national curricula to/on the private sector.

The curriculum objectives reflected the government intention to impose the above revised policy orientations on all schools in order to bring the new generation together by teaching them about a common national identity and shared values. Yet, as the studies discussed below will demonstrate,[7] these new policies made little or no impact on students' political orientation. This is not surprising, since only the public schools followed the government policy while private schools followed their own, with no discernable government supervision or interference.

The 1946 curricula were not, in their turn, revised until 1968, when the Ministry of Education followed the same procedure in order to introduce new curricula. It formed a central committee through a presidential decree nominating the director general of the Ministry of Education as its head. The members were to be presidents of the universities functioning in Lebanon, directors and department heads of the Ministry of Education, and four members representing the private sector. Traditional academics, rather than curriculum specialists, were considered when forming the curriculum committee.

While there was no explicit statement of rationale for revising curricula in 1968–71, the reform of school curricula was largely influenced by the movement toward the Arabisation of education popular at the time. Claiming the use of French and English to be expressions of "cultural colonisation," Arabisation maintained that Arabic should be used as the main language of instruction. We thus argue that Arabisation, combined with the general political atmosphere that was influenced by Arabism and that implicitly refused the emphasis on "Lebanism" present in the 1946 curriculum, led the education decisionmakers to introduce new curricula.

We argue that the revised curricula was clearly influenced by the ideological rationales of the pan-Arab and predominantly Muslim and leftist groups. What had been emphasised in 1946 curricula regarding the "Lebanese nation" and "Lebanese identity" was eliminated in the 1968–71 curricula. Schools, especially private ones, felt freer in the 1960s and early 1970s to promote their own divergent views of national identity and sense of civic loyalty. Thus, these curricula clearly constituted a basic but negative divergence in their role and nature regarding the promotion of social solidarity and common national identity.

A few years later, in 1975, the war broke out, and violent civil strife lasted for fifteen years. During the civil war period, the number of private schools increased and their control by the Ministry of Education was understandably limited. Yet even confronted with the difficult circumstances, some ministry initiatives were introduced. For instance, the former minister of education, Mr. Boutros Harb, initiated National Flag Day in 1979 as a national occasion to be celebrated by the Lebanese directly prior to "Independence Day." In an interview, in reference to the background and consequences of that initiative, Harb stated:

> I found out that there was no strong relation between the youth and their country. Also, we used to see many flags raised everywhere in Beirut, all except our national one. I launched the idea to be a practical application of what students learn theoretically at school. A large number of people supported it, but they were afraid to end up with another religious division. Actually the opposite happened where all the Lebanese (almost) raised flags on their houses, cars, and workplaces. Students came from both sides of Beirut to meet at the Museum square which formed the border line between East and West Beirut during the war, to show their solidarity and common identity.[8]

This initiative was not taken by the cabinet, but by the minister himself, and Flag Day is celebrated by all schools and students even today.

Minister Harb had also tried to revise the 1968–71 curricula for two main reasons: first, to change the focus from rote memorisation of facts or mere "filling of students' heads" to developing skills, values, and attitudes; and second, to impart civics education.[9] Both civil society and politicians, concerned as they were about the tense and explosive internal situation at the time, seemed relatively uninterested in education, and, because any plan for educational reform in Lebanon is not accepted unless it is supported by the whole government and other leaders in the country, this attempt to revise the curriculum failed.

Education as a vehicle for social and civic reconstruction (1990–2003)

The Taef Agreement of 1989, which included a special section on education concerns, is largely credited with forming the basis for renewed critical attention to the curriculum in postwar Lebanon. The agreement emphasised the following:

- Education shall be provided to all and shall be made obligatory, for the elementary stage at least.
- Freedom of education shall be emphasised in accordance with general laws and regulations.
- Private education shall be protected, and state control over private schools and textbooks shall be strengthened.
- Public vocational and technical education shall be reformed and shall be reinforced and developed in a way that meets the nation's developmental needs.
- Educational programmes (curricula) shall be reexamined and redesigned to reinforce national identification and integration, to ensure spiritual and cultural openness, and to unify history and civic education textbooks.

Yet a review of the central or centralising role of the Ministry of Education in general and of curriculum in particular was also necessarily in competition with and dependent on concerns for a national economic restructuring. The Lebanese government, responding to fiscal and other concerns following the implementation of the Taef Agreement, developed a plan for economic reform in 1992 that included a component relative to education. In turn, the Ministry of Education requested the Educational Centre for Research and Development (ECRD) to develop and propose a similar reform plan for the education sector.

The first step in drafting the proposal for reform was to define general aims and goals of the educational process by posing the question, What citizen does Lebanon need in post-conflict reconstruction? The issue was to reach an appropriate balance between the social, economic, and civic dimensions of school education. These dimensions were reflected in the definition of a citizen who is educated, productive, tolerant, and who believes in coexistence with others and is proud of his or her Arab identity. Based on the common conviction that Lebanese society expects the school system to shape such a citizen, the ECRD started drafting the first version of the educational plan.

The government approved the third amended version of the plan in 1994. It included general principles regarding internal peace, social unity, and citizenship such as

- strengthening the sense of belonging to a common Lebanese national identity, in addition to spiritual and educational openness, by reviewing and developing curriculum; and
- providing the new generation with basic knowledge, skills, and expertise, with an emphasis on national identity and authentic Lebanese values such as liberty, democracy, tolerance, and rejection of violence.

Regarding the intellectual and humanistic dimensions, the plan states that:

- There is a belief in the humanistic values and principles that respect the human being, recognise the importance of reason, and encourage the pursuit of learning, hard work, and ethics.
- The Lebanese understanding of the meaning of coexistence is based fundamentally on the divinely inspired religions, which inspire the spiritual culture in Lebanon—a very precious culture, which should be safeguarded and cherished. Thus, Lebanon is a model state of the interaction of civilisations and spiritual and intellectual freedom— values that contrast with the doctrines, beliefs, and regimes based on discrimination and religious fanaticism.

On the educational and social levels, the following objectives are included:

- The supremacy of the law over all citizens is the only means of achieving justice and equality among them.
- The respect of individual and social freedoms, as guaranteed by the Constitution and elaborated by the Charter of Human Rights, is of vital necessity for the continued existence of Lebanon.
- Participation in social and political activities within the framework of the Lebanese democratic parliamentary system is a right for every citizen and represents a responsibility toward his or her society and country.
- Education is a national priority and a social necessity.[10]

The plan lays down the guidelines of the sociopolitical framework for any future educational activity. This framework must be based on promoting democratic values by emphasising the supremacy of law, equality among citizens, human rights, and participation in social and political activities. The plan also considers education a priority and necessity. The implicit message here is that Lebanon has the elements necessary for making it a model of religious and cultural interaction in the Middle East.

The New Framework for Education in Lebanon followed the plan, which includes some changes at the levels of pre-primary, elementary, intermediate, and secondary education. The new framework kept the official examinations at the end of the last two cycles, but it did not include religious education among the curriculum subjects. New subjects were introduced such as computer science, technology, sociology, economics, and a second foreign language. The framework that was approved by the government in 1995 also featured other subjects, especially arts and civics.

Most of the new subjects reflected some concern about globalisation. Computer, technology, economics, and a second foreign language (mainly English) were seen as necessary for an "international citizen" living in the twenty-first century. However, Dr. A. El-Amine, who was a member of the committee that formulated this new framework, observed that, "The 'Framework' was not based on social or national concerns. Rather, it was a purely academic exercise. Two members of the committee introduced some suggestions based on socio-economic concerns, but we did not adopt these suggestions." When asked about the lack of elective courses at the secondary level, Dr. El-Amine responded that, "the administrators at the Ministry of Education stood against that suggestion for fear that such a step would create a mess in the high schools."[11]

The Plan for Educational Reform and the New Framework for Education in Lebanon established the social, national, and academic principles for the new curricula, which formed the third step in the process of educational reform. These principles included

- child/student-centred learning;
- subject-based curriculum;
- the Arab identity of Lebanon;
- the acceptance of others; and
- the national unity of all Lebanese people.

The principles underlying the structure and content of the new national curriculum frameworks were therefore clearly based on a mix of both pedagogical/educational principles advocating new methods of teaching and learning and political/national principles aiming to strengthen national cohesion.

Parochial schooling and civic socialisation

Religious and sectarian (political) differences among the Lebanese are mirrored in the composition of the student bodies of the private schools. Although enrolment in community schools is overwhelmingly determined in terms of religious and sectarian identity, demand for an education that is perceived to be of better academic quality, in addition to the ability to cover tuition fees, helps to explain the fact that a small percentage of students attend denominational schools that differ from their religious origin. It is generally accepted that public schools, on average, represent lower academic standards than do private schools.

However, from the point of view of civic and political socialisation, recent research appears to suggest that public schooling promotes more open-minded and tolerant attitudes toward members of other religious communities than does private schooling (Frayha, 2002). But when it comes to political attitudes regarding national and regional issues, students' religion proves to be a significant factor, while their socioeconomic background does not. The research supporting this view was undertaken in an effort to begin to measure the extent to which civic socialisation, which has as its aim the reconstruction of a unified social mosaic, can be promoted through the civics curriculum. Based on a survey of more than twelve hundred twelfth-grade students (aged 17–20) from both public and private schools, the findings also suggest that the religious and sectarian affiliation of public school students neither determines their perceptions of the "other" nor their general attitude of respect for coexistence.

Clearly, however, the outstanding question remains that of the relative weight of schooling on civic socialisation, particularly in comparison with the impact of other agents of socialisation (e.g., family, community, religious organisations). We would like to offer that the detailed research that exists in Lebanon, which assesses the impact of various social actors on *political* socialisation, is highly relevant to our discussion of *civic* socialisation. To this end, it is important to note that extensive research done in the area of political socialisation indicates that religious affiliation is a predictor of political orientation, confirming earlier observations among university students (Jabra, 1970; El-Amine, 1975). Research conducted in the late 1970s on freshman students in four Lebanese universities in order to study the effect of schooling on their political beliefs and orientations indicated that religious affiliation was indeed shaping students' political orientation, while factors such as their socioeconomic background and type of school they attended (Jesuit, Muslim, Protestant, or public) were not similarly significant (Wehbe and El-Amine, 1980). In clearly identifying the impact of sectarian identity on the political orientation of university students, the findings demonstrate the significant impact of the family and the community in political socialisation.

More recently, a similar study confirmed the observation that political attitudes and beliefs are shaped by sectarian affiliation and that most university students surveyed defined their political orientations far more in terms of religious-sectarian political movements and far less in terms of secular ideologies (El-Amine and Faour, 1998). Analysing the strong presence of religious movements on campus, the study suggests that "the Islamic movements represent to the poor group a political 'ideology' opposing economic manipulation and Western domination much like what socialist and communist movements represented to them in pre-war (1975) time."[12] The study therefore seems to indicate that young Lebanese today are tending more toward religious fundamentalism in their political ideologies than the previous generation. Such findings have important implications for the shaping of civic identity through schooling and official curriculum.

The results of the studies referred to above also suggest that political socialisation is essentially a result of family and community affiliation and a realm on which schooling appears to have very little influence. Despite these important limitations, our research suggests an important role for public schooling in the formation of more tolerant attitudes toward different religious groups and to the reinforcement of a shared sense of national identity. It will be important to continue focused research on pupils' attitudes and follow their evolution, from new recipients of the new civics curriculum in basic education all the way through to university. The challenge of assessment given the parallel sectors in education, however, will remain. Although the share of enrolment in the public sector has risen from under 15 percent in 1930 to almost 40 percent in 2001 (see Table 1), the fact remains that the majority of children continue to be schooled in a private sector that is overwhelmingly of a confessional nature.

Table 1: Distribution (%) of Students in Public and Private Sectors in 1930 and 2001

Sector	1930	2001
Public	15	39
Private	85	61

Source: Data reported in Ministry of Education, 2001, *Statistical Bulletin* and *Bulletin de l'Enseignement*, vols. 8 and 9 (1930, 1931).

In sum, this section has outlined how, as part of the modernising reform landscape of the nineteenth century, private confessional schools—backed by religious communities who considered education to be a means of preserving and reproducing group identity—arguably perpetuated denominational cleavages in Lebanese society. When education was first institutionalised, social and religious divisions were reflected in the variety of educational institutions, the fragmented structure of the educational system, and the diversified curricula. The private sector preceded public schooling, and both sectors have operated in a parallel fashion both in terms of management and orientation. The freedom to establish private schools following either the French or Anglo-American pattern led to the "superiority of the confessional-controlled private sector of education over the public one . . . ma[king] it difficult for the state to employ the schools as an agent of national integration" (Abouchedid and Nasser, 2000).

POLICY DIALOGUE AND CONSENSUS BUIDLING

The process of curriculum development

The official request for developing new curricula was made by the Ministry of Education to the ECRD as part of the reform process. The ECRD is in charge of educational planning, the revising/developing of school curricula, the writing of textbooks, and the in-service training of teachers. The president of the ECRD is its highest figure of authority and also the president of all committees. This institution enjoys autonomy in its financial and administrative activities, although the minister of education has tutelage authority over it. To carry out the Ministry's request, the ECRD formed the Consultative Committee, comprised of the head of the ECRD, the general director of the Ministry of Education, a General Education inspector, a UNESCO representative, representatives of both Lebanese public and private universities, representatives of private schools, and two or three education specialists. The composition of this committee was meant to reflect the educational, political, and religious structure of Lebanese society while also including some international expertise. The committee defined the aims and objectives of the curricula and made decisions while taking into consideration the views of educational institutions and integrating research findings where possible, as well as weighing the recommendations of non-governmental organisations (NGOs). Following approval of these decisions by the ECRD Council of Specialists, the Ministry of Education, the Council of *Shawra*, and the cabinet, the curricula were then issued by presidential decree.

The ECRD also formed subject-matter committees, who reported to the central committee. These groups were charged with developing subject curricula based on the main aims and objectives. All committees and subcommittees included members from both the public and private sectors and from universities and schools (including representatives from Islamic, Christian, and secular schools). The specialised subcommittees drafted the detailed learning content and structure of each subject. The Consultative Committee then revised and approved the detailed curricula, which were published as an appendix to the presidential decree. When finalised, the new curricula went to the director general at the Ministry of Education, who instructed the six Educational Regions to implement them at the school level with the support of the Educational Inspectorate. Figure 1 represents the process of developing and implementing school curricula. The feedback relation between these institutions is represented by ( ).

Figure 1: Organisational Framework for Developing the New Curricula

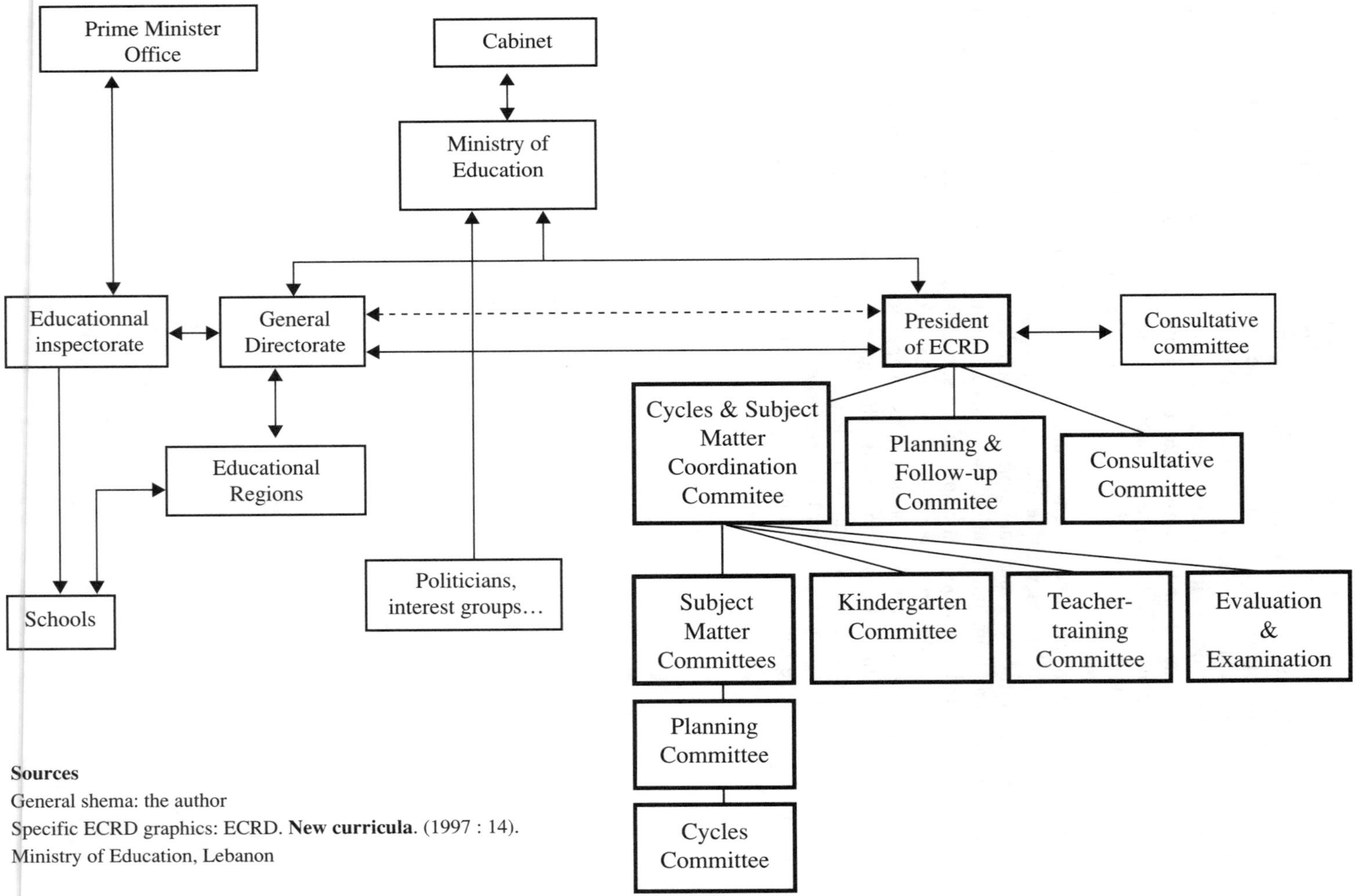

Sources

General shema: the author

Specific ECRD graphics: ECRD. **New curricula.** (1997 : 14).

Ministry of Education, Lebanon

Modalities of consultation and participation in policy reform

The postwar educational challenge was to mould a new generation of Lebanese youth with a common national identity based on a set of shared social and civic values and an acceptance of the pluralistic and unified nature of Lebanese society. While curriculum planners considered social studies to be an appropriate vehicle for the inculcation of such principles and values, the process of translating these ideas into the development of common history and civics curriculum and textbooks and relevant religious education was problematic. Central to the problems faced by the Consultative Committee was reaching consensus about the extent to which Lebanese identity is distinct from or embedded in a wider Arab national identity. In order to better understand the complexity of this issue, it is worth citing the historian Kamal Salibi (1976), as he defined the key problematic elements behind the question of what constituted prewar Lebanese identity:

> Among the Lebanese themselves, the Christians and the Muslims differed radically from one another in the interpretation of the country's Arab role. Among the Christians, and more particularly among the Maronites who were the leading Christian Lebanese community, the Arabism of Lebanon was poorly appreciated. To many of them, Lebanon was essentially a sovereign national homeland of basically Christian character which, in the final analysis, had more in common with the Christian West than with the Muslim Arab world. In this perspective, the Arabism of Lebanon could only be seen as a formality which the Christians conceded out of necessity, because their Muslim compatriots insisted that they should do so. Christians who saw the Arabism of Lebanon in this light failed to realize that the international significance of Lebanon, and the glamour and prosperity that went with it, were the natural by-products of the fact that the country, while being a sovereign democracy with a special character, was also an integral part of the Arab world.

Understanding that some of these cleavages only deepened during the protracted conflict, the Consultative Committee felt that the most critical issue it faced was that of defining the nature of Lebanon's identity and belonging. The committee discussed three points of view: the Lebanese Arab identity, the Arab identity, and the Lebanese and Arab identity. These three views ranged from those who wished to place greater or lesser emphasis on the primary relevance their national (Lebanese) or regional (Arab) identity. They ended up with a compromise: Lebanese identity and Arab identity.[13]

Another sociopolitical issue that created controversy in the committee was that of pluralism in Lebanon. Even though Lebanon can be considered a plural society from a sociological point of view, the term "pluralism" is politically charged and was interpreted by pan-Arab and predominantly Muslim groups as implying deep cultural differences among the Lebanese. Thus, the committee members agreed to use the term "diversified society" instead of "plural society."[14] Commenting on such an incident, Awit said, "Sometimes we gave up insisting on certain terminology if it was likely to lead to controversy. That happened many times but we were able to overcome such as problems." This view was echoed by Daw:

> We had many conflicting views within the committee, but we decided to move out of everyone's zone to a national zone. In this way we were able to communicate better and compromise on many issues.[15]

Once these fundamental issues cleared, a consultative process, representing a wide range of stakeholders, was essential for drafting, assessing, revising, and approving civics and later history curricula. The former general educational inspector, Dr. Kazem Makki, described the atmosphere of discussion within the civics committee by saying, "we used to study and discuss each point until we reached consensus, at least most of the time. Discussion used to pave the way for agreement."[16] Developing such social studies curricula in other contexts might not be as problematic as it was in Lebanon. It took all parties much effort and courage to put aside their interests for the sake of the national and social interests. "Compromise" marked the mechanism of the committees' work and was typically necessary in order to overcome serious disagreement over substance.

The stakeholders involved in educational reform are from both the public and private sectors and include professionals from various religious groups. Representatives of both sectors have participated in all activities concerning educational changes. Regarding the role of interest groups, it was an achievement to have them agree at all on the aims and objectives of the new curricula in general, and on those for the history and civics curricula in particular.

According to Dr. Assad Youness, the main figure of the inner committee that developed the plan, the aims and objectives were also based on a review of studies carried out by Lebanese scholars and NGOs. Regarding the structure of the drafting committee, Dr. Youness stated:

> The members were from various religious groups. It is known how people would not accept such a plan if those who drew it up were from the same religion. Also when we wanted to get feedback on the first draft, we held meetings with religious and political leaders as well as educators from AUB (American University of Beirut) and Kaslik (University of the Holy Spirit).[17] After that we revised the first draft.

Meanwhile, a cabinet committee was formed of ten ministers representing all factions to follow up the development of the plan, and ten meetings were held between the two committees. It is possible to critique the above modalities of consultation along the following lines. First, the structure adopted to support curricular reform was based on a centralisation of authority. Nevertheless, according to the 1971 law that established the ECRD, there should be a council for coordination, headed by the minister, and bringing together all of the heads of directorates reporting to the minister, including the ECRD president. This council, however, does not exist, and the general directors were included instead as committee members or coordinators—that is, as subordinates to the ECRD president (El-Amine, 2003). Furthermore, the consolidation of power at the top meant that the committee work at the bottom tended to be fragmented and inconsistent. This is reflected, in turn, in the lack of uniformity of the final curriculum documents.

The scope of postwar education and curriculum reform

Curriculum is defined in Lebanon as a plan for school and students' activities that organises areas of knowledge, skills, and attitudes to be acquired by students through certain teaching strategies. The new curricula took its final form in an 832-page document including

1. general curricular objectives;

2. weekly distribution plans;

3. per-subject general objectives, scope, and sequence, specific objectives for each cycle, and content coverage for each class; and

4.   Arabic, French, and English translations for subjects taught in those three languages.

An evaluation of this document undertaken by the Lebanese Association for Educational Studies (LAES) for UNESCO (2003) showed that

- The Curriculum Document did not include any clarifications on the nature of the "General Objectives," the "Specific Objectives," and the "Scope and Sequence Charts." Neither was there a separate guiding document on how this material should be composed. This led to a great confusion between the general and specific objectives, as well as to the formulation of the objectives by frequent additions of a number of verbs at the beginning (recognize, identify, etc. . . .) to the content themes.
- The document was an incoherently structured one suffering from clear discrepancies in presentation of the subject matters (content sequence, objectives distribution and nature, weekly distribution plan, scope and sequence tables, etc.). The same observation applies to teaching (or curricular) objectives which were set later to help textbooks writers.
- The Assessment Scheme was issued very late: three years after the New Curricula were made public; a fact which confused teachers on how to conciliate teaching by objectives and evaluating by competencies. (El-Amine, 2003)

Even though the expectation that the education sector could contribute to consolidating national unity was explicitly rooted in the Taef Agreement of 1989, it took a further five years after the end of the conflict for a clear Plan for Educational Revival (PER) to be introduced. Table 2 is an illustration of the components laid out in the Taef accords and the PER, and the degree to which they have been acted upon. It will allow us to briefly compare both how the stated aims and objectives have evolved, and to what degree those intentions have been realised to date (El-Amine, 2003).

Table 2: Aims and Objectives of Postwar Educational Reform:
   Intended Versus Implemented

As Cited in Taef Agreement (1989)	As Covered by PER (1994)	As Implemented
1. Reform of technical education	—	—
2. Reform of the Lebanese University	—	—
3. Reform of public education	**1a.** Educational administration	—
	1b. School administration	—
	2. School buildings	(Maintenance of existing buildings)
	3. Special education	—
	4. Activities and sports	—
	5. Educational services—guidance and educational information	—
4a. Curricular development	**6.** Curricula	**1.** Curricular development
4b. Unification of civics education textbook	**7.** School textbooks	**2a.** Delivery of new textbooks
		2b. Unification of civics education textbook
4c. Unification of history textbook	—	—
	8. Teachers	**3.** Teacher training
	9. Learning tools	—

Source: El-Amine, 2003.

This comparative table shows that of the nine components covered by the PER, only three have been acted upon, namely, curricula, textbooks, and teacher training. Such a limited application of intended aims allows us to surmise that the educational context has remained largely unchanged since the end of the civil war (three of the four components relative to the Taef Agreement and six of the nine from the PER). Indeed, a certain inertia has long hampered the education sector, with the structure of the Ministry of Education, for example, remaining largely stagnant over the past thirty-two years (1971–2003). Undoubtedly, the fact that the general educational context has not been reformed has negative repercussions on the effectiveness of the executed reforms.

The education system continues to accommodate two parallel sectors, the public and the private, and the curriculum reform has had to be executed through an old public machinery. The centralisation of the educational system with its strict hierarchy has continued since the French mandate. However, its effect over the private sector is limited to:

1. Checking and approving the textbooks that have not been written by the ECRD. Public schools are required to use ECRD textbooks, while private schools are free to choose from either these textbooks or others that have been written and published by private institutions and then approved by a special committee at the ECRD. Two conditions need to be met for approval. First, the textbook content and orientation should be in harmony with the official curriculum. Second, there should be no implicit or explicit offence demonstrated toward any religious belief. These measures notwithstanding, a large number of private schools do get language, mathematics, and science textbooks from France, Britain, or the United States without their having been evaluated or approved by any governmental institution.

2. Recommending principles for evaluation and assessment based on officially prescribed curricula in all subject matters. However, private schools can generally avoid a strict adherence to the official curricula except at the ninth- and twelfth-grade levels, when students of both sectors have to take the same official examinations.

CHALLENGES POSED BY SENSITIVE LEARNING AREAS

The development of new school curriculum in postwar Lebanon did not go smoothly, since a number of controversial issues emerged in the process of negotiation that involved a range of social, political, and religious groups. Some of the committee members referred to their respective educational, political, and religious authorities to clarify positions in view of reaching agreement on certain critical and sensitive issues, especially concerning social studies and language policies, and particularly concerning the position of the Arabic language. Some interviews were carried out with certain participants who helped in developing the 1997 curricula in order to shed light on difficulties, negotiations, conflicts, compromises, and the mechanisms of their work.

The reform process concerning the two delicate subjects of civics and history was to go through complicated steps and stages, and the constitution of the committees required for developing curricula, writing textbooks, and supervising the whole work reflected this complexity. It was agreed from the outset that the committee members were to be chosen from all religious communities for two reasons:

- The religious groups would object to being excluded from the committees that were to write the two most important textbooks.
- If a textbook, especially history, were to have on its cover the names of authors all belonging to the same religion, a large number of schools and leaders would not recommend its use.

A specific committee was formed in 1995 to develop general objectives for civics curriculum.

The government approved the proposed objectives in 1995, and this became the first adopted part of the new curricula. Another committee for the same subject was formed to lay down the objectives and curriculum details for each teaching cycle and grade. Its work was published along with the general education curricula in 1997.[18]

The work of curriculum and textbook committees was to be revised and approved by the Council of *Shawra*, which was formed of six scholars: three Christians (Maronite, Greek Orthodox, and Greek Catholic) and three Muslims (Sunni, Shiite, and Druze). These six members also represented varying political views of Lebanese groups. The approved curriculum document was sent to the ECRD Specialists Council for its additional approval and also to the Ministry of Education in order to be studied and approved by the cabinet after the Council of *Shawra* had given its view. Finally, the curricula were issued by presidential decree.

In addition to the formal procedures outlined above, the ECRD sent a draft of the new curricula to certain organisations and institutions in order to get their feedback on the proposed aims, objectives, and content. However, students, as the key parties concerned, were not consulted regarding their needs and expectations.

Drafting and approving new history curricula

During the civil war, it was said by a prominent Druze leader that, "the continuing civil war in Lebanon was, in a fundamental way, a war to determine the correct history of the country." He further maintained that "the rewriting of the Lebanese history textbook was a necessary precondition for any lasting political settlement in Lebanon, if not the primary one" (Salibi, 1988/1989). The fact that the development of history curricula and textbooks took three years longer than those developed for other subjects, thereby proving to be the most difficult task of the education reform process, lends credence to these statements. Two consecutive committees needed to be formed in order to lay down the subject objectives. Yet one important reason why the process was so drawn out was because the members of these committees were chosen to reflect the Lebanese social structure, representing all groups and persons specialised in the subject of history and its teaching.

As a result of the committee participants' divergent views, developing the history curricula required much discussion and compromise. Joseph Abi Rached, the committee secretary, describes the work of the two committees that developed the curricula: "At the beginning, each member brought with him his own ideology, trying to make his view prevail over others. Some wanted to consider the Lebanese as Arabs since 4000 BC but were opposed by others."[19] Essentially, the difficulty stemmed from how to balance this view against the social transformation of the region following the Arab conquest in AD 636 and the adoption of the Arabic language. The question then was how to combine and balance divergent historical narratives, which place a greater emphasis either on the Phoenician or the Arab legacy of Lebanon, and on what sets Lebanon apart from the rest of the Arab world as opposed to what embeds it within that tradition. It was a question for which an answer proved difficult given the political and sectarian space that the discourse of history has occupied in society.

When the first committee was not able to finish its task, another one was formed whose members shared some common views. This committee's way of working was impressive, examining all details with much discussion and compromise. Again, compromise did not mean sacrificing agreed-upon facts for the sake of political or social gain, but achieving a common understanding on certain sensitive issues, such as the character of Prince Fakher al-Din, Prince

Bachir Shihab II, the Palestinian involvement in Lebanon, the causes of the 1975 civil war, and Lebanon's national identity. Awit and Daw gave an example of how compromise was reached by considering both the internal and external factors behind the breakout of the civil war. Significantly, when it came to internal (national) parties involvement, all sides were seen to be blamed.

The term "political sectarianism" was also problematic. The committee members disagreed among themselves on the correct way of using it. Some said it revealed fanaticism while others said it described the real situation. In the end, they opted to remove it from the curricula and textbooks since the term was deemed to have negative political implications. When controversial issues were discussed but not approved within the committee, some of the members would rely on a reference group to determine what to do with these issues. Thus, stakeholders at various levels were informed and involved in formulating the final version of history objectives and the few written (but not yet published) textbooks.

Once the history curricula had been developed and approved by various committees and the specialist council at the ECRD, and approved by the Council of *Shawra* and the government, they were published, on June 22, 2000, by Presidential Decree No. 3175. Eleven writing committees were subsequently formed by the ECRD (representing the equivalent of one committee for each textbook) to write the textbooks for grades two through twelve. An educational committee accompanied each writing committee in order to deliver the historical information in an appropriate pedagogical manner. When the drafting of a textbook was finished, the Consultative Committee studied it word for word and kept signed minutes of their specific discussions, suggestions, and recommendations. Reaching consensus on the content of the history textbooks was vital to ensure that they would be adopted by schools and would not cause problems.

After history textbooks had been written for grades two through six, and in spite of their approval by their respective committees, the minister of education suspended their distribution. He objected to a lesson title in the third-grade textbook about the nature of the AD 636 Arab conquest of what is now Lebanon. The title read, "They had all gone and Lebanon remained: independence of a country." Some interpreted the mention of the Arab conquest as an attempt to put the Arabs on a par with other conquerors. The minister formed a new committee to revise these textbooks. As of this writing, nothing has been initiated. The suspension of the textbooks is a particularly strong example of the difficulties that persist in reaching consensus on Lebanon's history, and caused one leading Lebanese historian to note that:

> We can say that after more than 12 years since the Taif Accord, teaching of history in the country remains as it has always been: subject to the interests and shifts of different groups, and that agreement to unify curricula and textbooks as a means to unify the people and the country have produced nothing new, except more of the same debate and casuistry that goes as far back in the history of the country as the framing of the Lebanese Constitution in 1926.
>
> (Bashshur, cited in El-Amine, 2003)

The eventual evaluation criteria for the final review of the textbooks, once they are available, will assess the degree to which their content

- complies with the curriculum objectives defined;
- helps create social unity;

- contains ideological and sectarian biases; and
- is appropriate for specific academic levels.

There is an additional dimension to add to the controversy around the history textbooks. Prior to undertaking an evaluation of the new history curricula (see below), Dr. Abd al-Massih accompanied the development of the history textbooks. In an interview, he proposed that at least some of the difficulties facing the history textbooks resulted from the fact that the standardisation of these books was controversial. In particular, some groups did not like to see another textbook taking the place of the one they had, or they were wary of its content. Thus, they did their best to either eliminate or postpone the textbook's publication.[20] Religious groups, who advocated the teaching of history from their own perspective, were the main opponents to the new textbooks. Arguably, their opposition was not only rooted in ideological but also economic interests, since at present, especially in the private schools, more than six history textbook series are used. One unified history text would have clear market (loss) implications for traditional publishers.

In sum, from an ideological perspective, the curriculum committed to was one that had been stipulated by the Taef Agreement even though the modifications to it reflected additions rather than any fundamental change in approach. More seriously, as this writer has noted elsewhere, the postponed distribution of the unified history textbooks, prescribed by the Taef Agreement, to more than 400,000 students can be seen as going directly against the agreement (Frayha, 2003). Arguably, as El-Amine (2003) points out, "the Lebanese people still differ over the past, or over the past dimensions of their identity, as if what was mentioned in the Taif Agreement was merely a very general statement whose meanings did not extend to details, or was a political text that did not reflect the political culture prevailing in the society."

Religious education

Religious education has not traditionally been included in official public school curricula in Lebanon. However, in the very recent past, Christian and Muslim clergymen have begun to put pressure on the government to integrate "religious instruction." The view of the ECRD was that it would be most appropriate to introduce "culture of religions" as a common subject for all students, allowing them to learn about other religions and thus develop a better understanding of people with whom they did not share the same faith. In the discussion that follows we will outline the terms of this debate and the nature of the process of consultation among the diverse stakeholders.

The three documents of educational reform in Lebanon (the Plan for Educational Reform, the New Framework for Education, and the General Education Curricula and Their Objectives) did not provide any guidelines or indications about the integration of religious education in the intended official school curriculum. In a rare demonstration of solidarity, the religious leaders of both Muslim and Christian communities lobbied together to integrate religious instruction into the curricula. In 1998, the cabinet adopted Decision No. 73, requesting the ECRD to study the possibility of adding religion to the curricula. In 1999, a committee at the ECRD presented the rationale for reconsidering a comparative approach to religious education, rather than religious instruction, and based their view on the following arguments:

- enhancing national unity;
- emphasising the common values among monotheistic religions;

- showing students how these religions value the human being; and
- demonstrating interconfessional cohesion among the Lebanese in every aspect of life.

Based on the ECRD recommendations, the cabinet adopted another decision to include religious education in the curricula, using textbooks that were to be written by the ECRD. In order to develop the curricula for religious education, a special committee was formed by the ECRD, which was headed by the ECRD president and included clergymen nominated by their superiors to represent the major religious sects, four specialists in the field of theology or philosophy chosen by the ECRD, and two curriculum development specialists from the ECRD.

The first meeting of the committee was not auspicious; differences in views emerged immediately between the ECRD and the clergymen. The latter objected to what the ECRD was tasked to do, namely, the writing of common textbooks for Christian and Muslim students based on common spiritual values. In contrast, the clergymen wanted separate textbooks for each religious group at school, and they ultimately pushed the issue again at the government level. The government decision (2000) demonstrated the cabinet's acceptance of most of their demands:

- the development of two sets of textbooks for the separate religious instruction of Muslims and of Christian learners in grades one to nine;
- the inclusion of a section introducing the other religion in each textbook;
- the development of a unified textbook for both Christian and Muslim students at grades ten and eleven; this textbook should include specific issues from both religions in one part, and material showing the common values of the two religions in another part; and
- the entrustment to the ECRD for the preparation of these textbooks.

As was to appear later, the religious leaders would prove unsatisfied with the new government decision, despite the fact that it demonstrated a clear compromise between the previous official decision and their own demands.

When the Curriculum Committee resumed its meetings at the ECRD in order to begin laying out the general objectives of this subject, the representatives of the religious communities again expressed their objection, this time to the new decision. They wanted to have two textbooks for each grade with no information about the other religion. The reason for this was ostensibly related to the difficulty of finding a suitable person to teach the sections in which reference was made to the other religion. If the teacher was Christian and teaching about the Christian religion, for example, would he or she be able to teach accurately the part about Islam, or vice versa? A Druze sheikh on the committee voiced his objection to this concern, advocating common textbooks to promote common understanding and points of view. The other clergymen, however, did not accept his view, and they asked the government to modify its latest decision and allow for the development of separate and independent textbooks for each religion. As yet, no further steps have been initiated.

While this debate was playing out, a group of "secularists" declared their objection to religious teaching in school and, especially, in the public schools. A Lebanese NGO, the People's Rights Movement, conducted a survey among school students asking them for their opinions about religious teaching in their schools. The students' responses indicated the following:

- The majority of students refused to have their classes divided during this session as in the past, when students of the same religion used to remain in the classroom for religious instruction while those of other confessions undertook other activities.

- Some students from the same religion, but belonging to different sects, expressed their dissatisfaction with the person who would teach them if he or she were not from their particular sect.

- The majority of students believed that parents should teach about their particular religion at home (religious instruction), and social studies teachers should teach about religion in general at school (comparative religious studies).

- Some students believed that the teaching of religion at school would reinforce fanaticism.

- Other students expressed a preference for a unified textbook on religion for Christian and Muslim students.[21]

Many scholars and intellectuals also opposed religious education in Lebanese schools. A teacher and activist said, "Religious sects in Lebanon enjoy constitutional rights and freedom to express their views and preach their faith. Why should school become an additional platform for their activities?"[22] Dr. Marwan Fares, a member of Parliament, commented on this issue by saying, "It seems that the function of religious education in Lebanon is a social matter but, unfortunately, it has a political objective." Abdallah Zakhia, vice president of the Lebanese Human Rights Association, expressed concern about the "contradiction between a democratic state and compulsory religious teaching in school. Religious teaching is a proselytising activity which the state cannot control."

As mentioned previously, the dominant school type in the Lebanese education system is the private one, and these schools, typically parochial in nature, have a long history of using textbooks for religious teaching. Charbel Antoun carried out a study on seventy-seven textbooks used for religious teaching in private Lebanese schools. The resulting findings were interesting, and a few are quoted here:

- The language used in these textbooks was discriminatory based on distinctions between "us and them," "our faith and their faith," "Christian and Muslim."

- When mention was made of the other religion, it was not done in the service of studying more about it but to show superiority over it.

- There was a strong emphasis on morals.

- Emphasis on teaching religious dogma led the textbook authors and teachers to discriminate between different sects of the same religions.

- Indoctrination was prevalent in the textbook materials.[23]

It became clear from these findings that emphasising religious teaching as it was practiced in the private sector was not going to serve social unity among the Lebanese youth. The concern was that students, who might never have thought in a discriminatory way about others, would be led to do so if the school emphasised their particular religious identity. The findings also revealed the potential danger of religious education if it is abused in a fragmented society. Moreover, short-term political interests have been shown to occasionally prevail over the concern about the future of the state. Politicians in Lebanon are often accused of supporting the views of religious leaders and of going along with their demands at the expense of national interests.

What do other stakeholders say about introducing religious education to schools? A study conducted by the Lebanese Association for Educational Studies indicated that 47.3 percent of principals, 59 percent of coordinators, 51.1 percent of teachers, 54.2 percent of students, and 65 percent of parents supported the government position about a common curriculum on the two religions.[24]

In sum, religious education will remain a controversial issue whether it is implemented or not. The issue is very sensitive and requires various Lebanese groups and institutions to deal with it seriously. With its potential to promote social divisions if abused, it will be vital for educators to take the religious factor into consideration if they are working on all fronts to reconstruct the society. The main preoccupation at present concerns the possible consequences of applying the old policy of dividing learners into two groups according to their religious affiliations during the religious education session. Such a practice is, in effect, teaching children of the same school class that they are different from each other and hence, implicitly, that they should not be with each other in certain situations.

Evaluating new civics education curricula and textbooks

Dealing with the issue of national unity is a key concern in the introduction to the new civics education curriculum. The implicit assumption is that education can positively address the sectarianism, clannishness, and regionalism entrenched during the war, and thereby contribute to national unity (El-Amine, 2003). The subject distribution plan stipulates that the subject be taught for one hour each week, in all grades (one through twelve). It is worth noting that the introduction makes no mention of the political system.

The many efforts relative to the process of developing and approving the new civics curricula and textbooks were accompanied by difficulties, controversies, and compromises. A summative evaluation of the curricula can give us a clear idea of their effectiveness. The question to be answered is whether curricula and textbooks have met the stakeholders' expectations.

Dr. Adonis Acra carried out an evaluative study of the civics curricula, and his findings indicate both the presence of positive points as well as certain shortcomings. Regarding the positive aspects, Acra states the following:

- The curricula are based on global and modernised values of freedom, justice, tolerance, human rights, and dialogue among civilisations.
- The curricula aim to change the individual's mentality as a social being and his civil education as a citizen of a state. Consequently, change should effect the large group that the individual belongs to.
- The curriculum objectives try to deal with the society members' relations with each other in order to strengthen a new Lebanese social structure based on the principles of unity and belonging.
- These objectives tend to form a citizen able to participate in social and political life, capable of producing national and renewable culture (as opposed to the prevailing one).
- The curricula aim at enhancing citizenship based on clear relations between the citizen and the state.[25]

The shortcomings of the civics curricula are summarised as follows:

- The premise of the curricula refers to the Taef Agreement more than to the Constitution. Since the former is incorporated into the latter, it would be less controversial to refer directly to the Constitution.

- The curricula content, as a whole, is more idealistic than realistic. What students learn theoretically at school contradicts practice in real life. This might lead students to consider civics like any other subject, one to be studied for examination only.

- The curricula include objectives about "civil security" (*silm ahli*) instead of "civil peace" (*salam ahli*). Peace, not security, should be emphasised as a value for national-social life and the international situation.[26]

- The curriculum does not cover a number of basic concepts such as plural societies, democracy and its requirements (freedom of expression, freedom of press, and independence of justice), meritocracy, the independence of institutions, and sovereignty.[27]

In general, the civics curricula are seen to have made some progress in telling teachers, students, parents, and concerned citizens that civics is there to contribute in forming a new citizen who is able to interact with his compatriots, participate in his community's affairs, and value freedom, democracy, and human rights. The curricula reflect, up to a certain point, the will to promote social unity, as the Plan for Educational Reform requires. The shortcomings found by Acra and other researchers could be avoided when revising these curricula.

Regarding the content of civics textbooks, two studies were carried out, one by Dr. Aisha Zoreika and another by the Lebanese Association for Educational Studies (LAES). Zoreika studied the first-, second-, and third-grade textbooks. She looked at the scope and sequence of the subject content, the objectives, the teaching methods, and their evaluation.[28] She also interviewed students and surveyed hundred teachers in Beirut. Some of this study's findings can be summarised as follows:

- The selection of topics is suitable to children's ages and is based on a universal methodology.

- The writers successfully produced texts that allow students to participate in some activities in order to gain various skills for socialisation.[29]

- The subject content was not well designed. Lecturing dominates the teaching activities and does not promote social interaction and participation.[30]

- Some suggested activities do not match the stated objectives.

- The negative aspects of some chapters outweighed the (expected) positive ones.[31]

- Most of the teachers are not specialised in social studies.

These conclusions are relevant, since the challenge of civics currently lies in the teaching and learning methods used. If the teaching and learning process fails to attain the stated objectives, there are questions to raise about teachers' performance.

The second study, which also assessed civics textbooks, along with other textbooks, was undertaken by the Lebanese Association for Educational Studies. The Textbook Content and Students' Needs evaluation study included teacher, student, and parent questionnaires on the existence of pedagogical approaches for the development of skills and attitudes, the relationship between the subject curriculum and the textbook, and the function of the textbook. The findings indicated that the content was ranked as average (the ranking scale included good, average, and weak) in the areas of skills and attitudes and of responding to students' needs, while the content was ranked as good in the area of matching with curriculum objectives and the function of the textbook. A noted negative aspect was the excessive amount of information included in the textbook, particularly definitions of concepts, technical terms, and political and social principles and theories. The study recommended that

> the concept of the school textbook be radically reviewed so as to make it, in addition to be a reference, a tool among others to teach students specific skills related to the subject matter, as well as thinking and social skills. The study also recommended that the content be reduced to allow the teaching of these skills and the integration of assessment activities into the school textbooks.

> (UNESCO-LAES, 2003)

A further aspect of the analysis of civics textbooks dealt with the depiction or treatment of gender, professional and political personal personalities, and language. Researchers found that females were given only a limited place as story heroes or in lesson titles. Further, when it came to sociopolitical and economic relations and jobs, males were the main figures while females usually had secondary roles. Professionals were considered to be less important than political leaders. The textbooks, for example, dealt in detail with recognised skills for the former while ignoring those for the latter, implying that leaders do not need professional skills. Personality characteristics were noted as being divided and/or associated with the following categories:

- The political leader is strong, responsible, and authoritarian.
- The scientist is professional, powerless, and tempered.
- The soldier is loyal to the country.
- The creative person is ambitious, hardworking, and usually a foreigner.[32]

Textbook content is often understood to have more of an impact than curriculum objectives at school, since students and teachers deal with textbooks on a daily basis. The findings of these two studies serve to caution Lebanese educators about the shortcomings found in the civics textbook content, which, in turn, might negatively affect the expected outcomes of teaching civics.

Finally, some mention needs to be made concerning the implications that implementing the new social studies curricula will have for teacher training. The essential role to be played by well-trained teachers in the successful implementation of these curricula cannot be overemphasised, and in supporting these teachers the education system has had to face a number of serious challenges. Statistics on the Lebanese teaching body show that 60 percent of the teachers currently in service did not graduate from a teacher institute. A plan for in-service training had to be developed to make up for the lack of skills these teachers required in order to carry out their school duties competently. When the new curricula were launched in 1998, a small number of teachers were trained during a short summer session. Such training was repeated with better conditions during the following two summers. In addition, the ECRD and a team from the World Bank developed a new project for long-term training activities. The aim of the project was to produce a long-term training process at each proposed training centre in each subject matter, especially social studies. Emphasis was put on teaching civics and history as the core courses that help form Lebanese citizens. Social studies teacher training programs were planned, and some outlines for new teaching methods were drafted at the ECRD for prospective trainers in order to help teachers to promote teamwork, tolerance, and respect among their students and foster their active classroom participation.

Comparing 1968–71 and 1997–2000 social studies curricula[33]

The 1968–71 social studies curricula did not include any objectives at the intermediate (sixth to ninth grades) and secondary (tenth to twelfth grades) levels. The only mention at the elementary level was that

> The social studies courses are intended to mold the student into a good citizen through moral and social education as well as geographical and historical knowledge. The teacher should always demonstrate the importance of social collectivity and good ethics and should help to develop patriotism among the students. Both Arabic and social studies curricula are strongly connected together in the first three grades. It is recommended to study the two subjects together.[34]

Thus, the Arabic course of study for the first, second, and third grades included topics relating to the child's social environment, historic figures from Lebanese and Arab history, and Arab national holidays. In addition to these course objectives the curriculum stated that the Arabic textbooks containing stories about Lebanese and Arab heroes and the other texts were intended to refine the morals and manners of the children, to implant in them a love of the country, and to enhance the socialisation process.[35] It is curious that the curriculum developers ignored the social studies objectives as such, emphasising them instead in the Arabic-language curriculum.

Objectives of civics education

Civics and history curricula (1997 and 2000) included many objectives concerning social coexistence, social unity, national identity, democratic behaviour, and human values. Civics curricula specifically included

- preparing students morally to fit in with their society's human values;
- educating them to accept others and solve their problems with peers peacefully and fairly;
- developing their social understanding of being members of the whole society, which is enriched by its diversity;
- enhancing their participation in public life;
- enhancing their attachment to their Lebanese identity, territory, and country within a democratic political framework; and
- enhancing awareness of their Arabic identity and belonging.[36]

Objectives of history curriculum

History objectives were based on national, educational, and cultural principles as stated in the Constitution, such as:

- Lebanon is a sovereign and independent country, united by its people and land.
- Lebanon is Arabic in its identity and belonging.
- No power contradicting the common coexistence pact has any legitimacy.

Based on these constitutional principles, the curriculum makers emphasised the following objectives in teaching history:

- enhancing student pride in a national Lebanese identity, strengthening loyalty to Lebanon, and emphasising Lebanese unity through a common cultural, geographic, and historical heritage;

- developing national and Arabic feelings in students;

- building a common national memory showing the importance of Lebanese achievement and destiny despite suffering during civil conflicts;

- providing an awareness of the distinctiveness of Lebanese culture and its belonging to a larger Arab culture;

- building an awareness of the negative consequences of fighting among the Lebanese; students should realise that the current needs and future ambitions are to be satisfied by applying democratic values, equality, justice, and equal opportunities (for Lebanese citizens); and

- demonstrating Lebanese and Arab resistance to Israeli occupation.[37]

A study carried out by Dr. S. Abd al-Massih on the new history curricula presents the following findings:

- The objectives decisively solved the issue of Lebanon's identity and its Arab belonging. This achievement brought together the prevailing and conflicting ideologies over Lebanon's national identity.

- The objectives highlight the importance of religious values.

- The objectives included the study of the history of other areas, i.e., the areas that were stripped from the Lebanese princedom in 1845 and reannexed to Greater Lebanon in 1920. The idea was to have students studying a continuous history of present-day Lebanon.

- The general history objectives (as stated earlier) have been developed under the contextual influence reflecting the situation of the end of the internal war. It is obvious that a compromise was made on some issues.

- The history of Lebanon after independence in 1943 was given the right place in the new curricula, which responded to students' interests. The old curricula did not include anything about the contemporary history of Lebanon that was of interest to students.

- The curriculum structure in some grades is based on the chronology of presidential terms, which could have been avoided.

- This curriculum could be seen as serving a transfer period (between war and peace). Thus, it tried to establish a vision of Lebanon between what used to be offered to students and what is going to be offered to them in the future.

- Ideology, in some objectives and contents, prevails over scientific approach.[38]

In many ways it is difficult to make a comparison between the previous history curriculum (regarding its objectives) and the new one. The former did not include any declared objectives, while some implicit ones could be extrapolated inasmuch as it overlooked the ideas of a "Lebanese nation," a "Lebanese entity," and a "Lebanese identity." This was done in deference to the prevalent pan-Arabist question at the time. Conversely, the new curricula clearly included objectives regarding Lebanese identity and Arab identity. Daw points to this change by saying, "the old curricula were based on the National Pact of 1943, while the new ones are based on the Taef Agreement. Thus, the significant place of Pan-Arabism was to be defended and well considered." Dr. Makki further noted that when the Consultative Committee members had difficulties agreeing among themselves on some points, the former minister of education intervened, by calling the committee for a meeting and helping to bridge the gap.[39]

In terms of content, the 1968–71 civics curricula emphasised, as did the 1946 curricula, moral education, family relations, the role of security authorities, city councils, taxes, a citizen's duties and rights, and the role of government institutions, international organisations, and so on. These subjects were part of the official examinations until Decree No. 4202, Article 1, declared that, "civics education will be suspended in the Baccalaureate examination in 1973." Since examinations, not curricula, were the most important element in Lebanese schools, civics was virtually suspended from the entire secondary program. Although the government did not justify the action, the motivating factors could arguably be found in students' ideological orientations, the contrast between the textbook content and reality, and the controversies caused by some topics. It is important to note that when civics was taken out of the school programs, religious education was reinforced. A special memorandum in 1973 (No. 262/7173) issued by the minister of education instructed all schools to devote one hour per week to religious education.

The 1997 civics curricula included similar topics to the 1968–71 curricula, but new topics were added, such as the issue of Palestine, the Lebanese resistance to Israeli occupation, the value of liberation, the importance of social coexistence and unity, patriotism, and so on. Scholars agree that the content of the civics curricula of 1997 seems more related to the actual situation through its consideration of the current issues in Lebanon and the region, and through its focus on patriotism and social cohesion after a long and destructive civil war. The 1968–71 history curricula provided an overloaded content for the three schooling levels and covered Lebanon's history, the old civilisations, Arab history, and world history. The content was arranged using a chronological approach and was not consonant with the stages of children's development. For instance, introducing a second-grade child to prehistory is not necessarily the right educational approach, since children have not yet developed a sense of historic time at this stage.

The content of the history curricula developed in 2000 covers various periods of Lebanon, the Arabs, and world history, but with a different approach. The second- and third-grade students, for example, are to study the "current history" of their family, school, community, and region. The upper-grade students deal with ancient and contemporary history, ranging from Lebanon in Phoenician times (3000 BC) up to the Taef Agreement (AD 1989).

A comparison of previous and new curricula reveals clear differences in terms of approach to the periods covered. The former did not include the major sensitive events that faced Lebanon after its independence in 1943, while the latter included all of those events. The reason given was the need to study history as it is, in order to understand what is happening now, on the one hand, and to learn from past experience in order to appreciate peace and tolerance on the other.

The dominant methodological paradigm underlying the 1968–71 social studies curricula was subject based, designating learning content to be taught by teachers, understood by students, and tested by the Ministry of Education. Curriculum developers conceived of social studies education as consisting of various topics to be covered in daily textbook assignments. Although some democratic values were included in the curriculum objectives, no specific suggestions were given about their attainment. In addition, no extracurricular activities that could allow for the development of civic attitudes through social action, such as community service, were encouraged or mentioned. Also, social unity was not given due attention, even though Lebanon was in the midst of a difficult political situation and facing social disintegration. Thus, the social studies curricula seemed to aim at producing students competent in the repetition of facts without their critical integration into sensitive questions relating to diverse composition of Lebanese society and the nature of responsible citizenship.

The content of the 2000 history curricula is more relevant to students' interests and level of ability, since it deals with contemporary issues and events that affect a student's life. At the first elementary cycle, for instance, learning about the child's family and community is now considered to be a new approach in Lebanese curriculum development. Also, studying what happened during the period between Lebanon's independence and the Taef Agreement has become recognised as a necessity for young students.

CONCLUSION

We have seen throughout this chapter how the social development of Lebanon could be otherwise described as the development of a social culture of sectarianism, with sectarianism representing a new historical imagination and, furthermore, an idea that "draws meaning only within a nationalist paradigm and hence that it belongs to our modern world" (Makdisi, 2000). The various reform discourses introduced in 1860, following a series of particularly violent clashes between Maronites and Druze, provoked fundamental changes in the perception and governance of the public space. Sectarian identity became institutionalised and broadly understood as both an authentic and legitimate organisation of social identity and knowledge.

The role of education likewise shifted through time and could be described, for our purposes, as encompassing three key epochs reflecting changing political interpretations of national cohesion:

1. *Missionary schools*: Initially attempting to fulfil a function of conversion, the missionary schools quickly adapted to respond to the changing needs of social elites as power relationships shifted in relation to competing Ottoman and European reform initiatives. Ironically, the control of secular modern knowledge in the hands of missionaries merely served to institutionalise its distribution along sectarian lines. Nor did parochial education have a negligible effect on students' eventual economic opportunities due to differing mediums of instruction (namely, French or English). This tradition of private schooling not only contributed to the sectarian institutionalisation of knowledge, but also to the formal division of Lebanese societies' learning communities. Sectarianism was a precursor to a form of national identity that insisted on religious affiliation as its main criteria.

2. *The French mandate, independence, and the years leading up to the civil war*: Public schooling was not established in Lebanon until the 1920s under the French mandate. A variety of factors contributed to the perpetuation of social cleavages during this time, namely,

   a.   that religious communities saw education as a means of preserving and reproducing group identity;
   b.   that the private sector continued to enjoy a dominant position in Lebanese schooling with little or no successful state control over it; and
   c.   that the removal of civics from the social studies curriculum in 1973, for example, was replaced by an increased number of hours for religious education.

The concept of national cohesion, from the late 1950s on, was extended to fall under an Arab nationalist paradigm, which, in the eyes of some, threatened to overwhelm the particular aspect of Lebanon's Christian identity. National identity, now that there was a nation-state to refer to, was confronted not only with its rootedness in the question of religious identification, but extended to the point of collapse in insisting on a regional positioning as well.

3. *Post–civil war years*: The educational vision of Lebanon following the civil war is grounded in an understanding of the meaning of coexistence as reflected in the inherent value of its diverse spiritual culture. Education for social and civic reconciliation is grounded in the premise that reforming the history and civics curricula, in particular, serves as a mechanism for reinforcing national cohesion. A common text for the public and private sectors—in which major sensitive historical content has been included (where it was previously excluded) for discussion and consideration along with a methodology that aims to be more immediately relevant to students—has, interestingly, shifted the role of schooling from one of institutionalised divisions to one endeavouring to construct national unity.

An underlying premise of curriculum development in postwar Lebanese society is that elements for social cohesion and the promotion of citizenship among the country's youth are to be developed in curricula in order to help schools play their role in social reconstruction. As a result, the new curricula emphasise the role of social studies in general, and of history and civics in particular. Common civics textbooks for all Lebanese students have already been developed, and the writing of common history textbooks is underway.

Lebanese educators and legislators believe that the previous practice of choosing from among many history textbooks, which differed in their interpretation of events, did not help in creating a common national memory among students. Thus, the current reform is underpinned by the hope that developing unified curricula and textbooks for all Lebanese students will help bring them together around the same sense of national and civic identity. The curriculum revisions were initiated with the development of civics curricula in 1997 and of history curricula in 2000. Such work was considered a national achievement in and of itself, since committee members represented all Lebanese groups.

While the current education reform process holds promise in its efforts to reconstruct national cohesion as opposed to reinforcing sectarian divisions, there are still a number of key challenges to the envisioned change:

1. Constitutionally protected freedom allows the private sector to continue to create its own priorities when it comes to social unity and national citizenship. Each group of private schools promotes its own views regarding the major national issues. Moreover, the constitutional protection of private schools could arguably be seen as functioning at the expense of public schooling.

2. Schooling, and particularly public schooling, remains highly politicised, and it is still possible for well-placed individuals to derail decisions arrived at through broad-based stakeholder consensus.

3. Recent studies tend to demonstrate that public school students show greater tolerance toward sectarian differences, and it has been encouraging to note a rise in public school enrolment since 1930. Nevertheless, the private sector persists in being the majority provider of education in Lebanese society, and the continued lack of state control over this sector remains problematic.

4. Political leaders and civil society don't consider education reform a high priority. The impetus for reform was strong immediately following the civil war, but its centrality relative to other social, political, and economic issues has since lost ground. Follow-up and continued accountability of education officials remains crucial if the reform plan is to be successfully implemented.

5. There is still no declared national educational policy and strategy, particularly with regard to a vision for the role of general, vocational, and higher education.

Finally, the curriculum development that accompanies the education reform cannot be expected to resolve outstanding issues of national cohesion on its own. As has been evident throughout this chapter, the broader contextual social, political (national, regional, and international), and economic realities will continue to contribute to the social ideals that inform and determine the role of schooling in Lebanon.

Endnotes

[1] Editorial note: Some scholars date this initial settlement to the tenth and eleventh centuries (Makdisi, 2000).

[2] Israel invaded Lebanon in 1978, three years after the outbreak of the Lebanese civil war, and occupied the territory until their withdrawal in 2000.

[3] Available at http://www.monde-diplomatique.fr/cahier/proche-orient/region-liban-taef-en.

[4] Interestingly enough, some of these ideas were contained in an address delivered by the Lebanese President Suleiman Frangié to the Lebanese people in February 1976, during the first year of the civil war. The address entitled "The New Lebanese Covenant" began by reiterating that

> Lebanon is an Arab country, sovereign, free and independent. . . . The traditional practice (*urf*) in the allocation of the three highest offices of state (*al-ri asat al-thalath*), whereby the President of the Republic shall be a Maronite, the President of the Chamber of Deputies a Shi ite Muslim, and the Prime Minister a Sunni Muslim, is reaffirmed; each of the three shall be regarded as a representative of all the Lebanese. Parliamentary seats shall be divided equally among Muslims and Christians, and proportionally (among the sects) within each group; accordingly, the Electoral Law shall be amended to secure a fairer popular representation. . . . The confessional distribution of the Civil Service offices shall be abolished, and the principle of competence applied instead. . . . Effort shall be made to secure general social justice through fiscal, economic and social reform. . . . Public instruction shall be enhanced, with a view to make free instruction general and compulsory, and educational curricula shall be developed to promote national unity. (Salibi, 1976)

[5] Interview with Deputy Boutros Harb (February 2003), who participated in the Taef Agreement.

[6] Mathews, R., and Akrawi, M., 1949, *Education in Arab Countries of the Near East*, Washington: American Council of Education, p. 416.

[7] Please see section below on "Parochial schooling and civic socialisatión."

[8] Harb interview.

[9] Ibid.

[10] Ministry of Education—ECRD, 1994, *Plan for Educational Reform*, Beirut: ECRD, pp. 8–12.

[11] Interview with Dr. Adnan El-Amine (December 2002).

[12] El-Amine, A., and Faour, M., 1998, *University Students in Lebanon: Background and Attitudes*, Beirut: Lebanon Association for Educational Studies, p. 349.

[13] Interview with Dr. Henry Awit, member of the Consultative Committee, and general secretary of St. Joseph University, Beirut.

[14] Ibid.

[15] Interview with Mr. Anwar Daw (February 20, 2003), member of the Consultative Committee and former head of Nabatieh Educational Region in the South. He is currently the director general of the Public Employees Coop.

[16] Interview with Dr. Kazem Makki (February 2003), member of the Consultative Committee and general coordinator of writing the civics textbooks.

[17] This university is considered as having represented the Christian view during the civil war, especially in what relates to educational issues.

[18] Ministry of Education—ECRD, 1997, *General Education Curricula and Their Objectives*, Beirut: ECRD, pp. 714–33.

[19] Interview with Joseph Abi Rached (February 2003).

[20] Interview with Dr. Abd al-Massih (January 2003).

[21] See People s Rights Movement, 2000, *Compulsory Religious Education in Lebanon* (in Arabic), Beirut, pp. 13-22.

[22] Ibid, p. 28.

[23] See People s Rights Movement, 2000.

[24] LAES, 2001, *Evaluation of New Subjects in the Curricula*, p. 30.

[25] See Acra, Adonis, 2003, *Evaluating Civics Curricula*, report in Arabic.

[26] Ibid.

[27] This final shortcoming is introduced from the following additional report: UNESCO-LAES, 2003, "Assessment of Goals, Educational Ladder, and Subject Distribution Plan," in *The Evaluation of the New Lebanese Curricula* (report), Lebanese Association for Educational Studies.

[28] Zoreik, A., 2002, *Civics Education: How Do We Deal With It*, Beirut: Arab Scientific.

[29] Ibid., p. 21.

[30] Ibid., p. 39.

[31] Ibid., pp. 56, 67.

[32] UNESCO-LAES, 2003, pp. 1–11.

[33] The Ministry of Education revised the 1946 curricula in three stages: the secondary level in 1968, the complementary level in 1970, and the elementary and kindergarten levels in 1971. Regarding the new curricula, all subject matter curricula were developed by 1997 except history, which was not done until 2000.

[34] Ministry of Education, 1971, *Educational Curricula*, Beirut, p. 29.

[35] Ibid., pp. 17–25.

[36] Ministry of Education—ECRD, 1997, p. 714.

[37] *Lebanese Gazette*, June 22, 2000, pp. 2115–18.

[38] Abd al-Massih, Simon, 2002, *Evaluation of the New History Curricula*, unpublished study in Arabic.

[39] Makki interview.

References

Abd al-Massih, S. (2002.) *Evaluation of the New History Curricula*. Unpublished study in Arabic.

Abouchedid, K., and Nasser, R. (2000.) "The State of History Teaching in Private-Run Confessional Schools in Lebanon: Implications for National Integration," *Mediterranean Journal of Educational Studies* 1(2).

Acra, A. (2003.) *Evaluating Civics Curricula*. Report in Arabic submitted to the Lebanese Association for Educational Studies, Beirut.

Corm, G. (2003/1991.) *Le Proche-Orient éclaté: 1956-2003*. Paris: Collection folio/histoire, Gallimard.

———. (1988.) "Myths and Realities of the Lebanese Conflict," pp. 258–74 in Nadim Shehadi and Dana Haffar Mills, eds., *Lebanon: A History of Conflict and Consensus*. London: Centre for Lebanese Studies, I. B. Tauris.

Education Centre for Research and Development (ECRD). (1997.) *New Curricula*. Lebanon: Ministry of Education.

El-Amine, A. (2003.) *Curricular Reform in the Context of Conflict: Case Study— Lebanon*. Unpublished paper presented for UNESCO: International Bureau of Education (IBE) training seminar for curriculum developers in Bosnia and Herzegovina, Geneva.

El-Amine, A., and Faour, M. (1998.) *University Students in Lebanon: Background and Attitudes*. Beirut: Lebanon Association for Educational Studies.

Frayha, N. (2003.) *ECRD in 1,017 Days*. Beirut.

———. (2002.) *School Effect on Citizenship Education*. Beirut: Sharikat al-Matbouat.

———. (1985.) *Religious Conflict and the Role of Social Studies for Citizenship Education in the Lebanese Schools Between 1920 and 1983*. Dissertation, Stanford University, California.

Ghait, G. M., and Shabaan, K. A. (1996.) "Language-in-Education Policy and Planning: The Case of Lebanon," *Mediterranean Journal of Educational Studies* 1(2).

Haut Commissariat. (1923–31.) *Bulletin de l'Enseignement*. Beyrouth: Publication du Service de l'Instruction Publique.

Lebanese Association for Educational Studies (LAES). (2001.) *Evaluation of New Subject Matters in the Curricula*.

Lebanese Gazette, June 22, 2000.

Makdisi, U. (2000.) *The Culture of Sectarianism: Community, History, and Violence in Nineteenth-Century Ottoman Lebanon*. Berkeley and Los Angeles: University of California Press.

Mathews, R., and Akrawi, M. (1949.) *Education in Arab Countries of the Near East*. Washington: American Council of Education.

Meo, L. (1965.) *Lebanon: Improbable Nation*. Bloomington: Indiana University Press.

Ministry of Education. (2001.) *Statistical Bulletin*. Beirut: Educational Center for Research and Development.

People's Rights Movement. (2000.) *Compulsory Religious Education in Lebanon* (in Arabic). Beirut.

Salibi, K. (1989/1988.) *A House of Many Mansions: The History of Lebanon Reconsidered*. London: I. B. Tauris.

———. (1988.) "Introduction: The Historical Perspective," pp. 3–13 in Nadim Shehadi and Dana Haffar Mills, eds., *Lebanon: A History of Conflict and Consensus*. London: Centre for Lebanese Studies, I. B. Tauris.

———. (1976.) *Crossroads to Civil War: Lebanon 1958–1976*. Beirut: Caravan Books.

Shehadi, N., and Haffar M., D., eds. (1988.) *Lebanon: A History of Conflict and Consensus*. London: Centre for Lebanese Studies, I. B. Tauris.

Tannous, H. (1997.) "Religious Diversity and the Future of Education in Lebanon," *Mediterranean Journal of Educational Studies* 1(2).

UNESCO-LAES. (2003.) "Evaluation of Subject Curricula," in *The Evaluation of the New Lebanese Curricula*. A Report of the Lebanese Association for Educational Studies.

Wehbe, N. and El-Amine, A., (1980.) *Système d'enseignement et division sociales au Liban*. Paris: Le Sycomore.

Zoreik, A. (2002.) *Civics Education: How Do We Deal With It*. Beirut: Arab Scientific Publishers.

Appendix 1: Resources

(1) Resource Persons Interviewed

Abd el-Massih, Simon
Professor at the Lebanese University

Abi Rachid, Joseph.
Ex-Secretary of Civics and History Curriculum Committees at ECRD

Awit, Henry
Secretary General of Université Saint-Joseph—Beirut

Daw, Anwar
Head of the Government Employees Cooperation

El-Amine, Adnan
Professor at the Lebanese University
President of the Lebanese Association for Educational Studies

Harb, Boutros
Deputy and former Minister of Education

Makki, Kazem
Former General Inspector of Education

Youness, Assad
Specialist in planning at ECRD

(2) Curriculum Policy Documents Reviewed

Ministry of Education. (1997.) *General Education Curricula and Their Objectives*. Beirut: ECRD.

———. (1995.) *New Framework for Education in Lebanon*. Beirut: ECRD.

———. (1994.) *Plan for Educational Reform*. Beirut: ECRD.

———. (1971.) *Educational Curricula*. Beirut: ECRD.

Appendix 2: Fact Sheet - Lebanon

Total population:	3.5 million
Population under 15 years of age:	30.2%
Life expectancy at birth:	73.3 years
Gross national income per capita:	US$ 3,811
Purchasing Power Parity GDP per capita:	US$ 4,170
Public expenditure on education (as % of GDP) (1998–2000):	3.0
Adult literacy rate (age 15 and above):	86.5%
Youth literacy rate (age 15-24):	92.1%
Net primary enrolment ratio:	74%
Net secondary enrolment ratio:	70%
Children reaching grade 5:	97%
Structure of education system:	5 + 4 + 3

Compulsory education: Act No. 686, promulgated on March 16, 1998, includes an article amending a previous provision. The new provision now reads as follows: "Education shall be free and compulsory in the initial primary stage and is a right of every Lebanese person of primary school age. The conditions for such free compulsory education shall be determined by a decree adopted by the Council of Ministers, as shall its regulation." The prescribed age for the primary stage ends at eleven years in accordance with the system now in force and will be increased to twelve years under the new structure. (Information available at http://www.right-to-education.org/content/age/lebanon.html.)

Language of instruction: Arabic is the major language of instruction. French and English are also major languages of instruction in private schools, although foreign languages are also taught in public schools.

School types: Parallel public and private systems (an estimated 60 percent of school enrolment is in the private sector).

Official and recognised languages: Arabic (official), French (official), and English.

Religion(s): Islam and Christianity (Maronite, Druze, Sunni, Shiite, Greek Catholic, and Greek Orthodox are the main religious groups).

Cultural groups: The two culturally distinct groups that exist today in Lebanon, representing some 8 to 10 percent of the population, are the Armenians (7–8 percent) and the Kurds (2–3 percent).

Sources: The author and UNDP Human Development Report (2003)

Chapter 5

Curriculum Reform, Political Change, and Reinforcement of National Identity in Mozambique

Juvenal Balegamire Bazilashe

Adelaide Dhorsan

Cristina Tembe

About the Authors

Juvenal Balegamire Bazilashe is a professor in the Faculty of Education at the Eduardo Mondlane University in Maputo. Previously, he lectured in the Teachers' Training College of Bukavu, Democratic Republic of the Congo, for eight years, and in the Education Institute of the University of Neuchâtel, Switzerland, for three years. He has prepared critical analyses of African educational systems for the UNESCO International Bureau of Education in Geneva and for NGOs such as Christian Aid and ActionAid. He has written a text on the educational system of Mozambique, proposing a bridge between education, literacy, and vocational training, where leaders freely chosen or coopted by the peasants would use an integrated management of the different resources and initiatives (such as training, health, sources of energy, and water management) in sustainable villages aimed at self-reliance.

Adelaide Dhorsan is an educational officer at the National Institute for the Development of Education (INDE) in Maputo and is in charge of designing the new curriculum and overseeing its implementation. The institute was created in 1978 as a specialised institution, under the authority of the Ministry of Education, but with academic and administrative autonomy. The institute is responsible for translating policy decisions through the development of curricula, syllabi, textbooks, and other teaching and learning materials. Adelaide Dhorsan is actively involved in projects related to the Bilingual Education program involving teacher training, the selection of experimental primary schools, and the implementation and monitoring of bilingual education. She also teaches general linguistics and applied linguistics with a focus on education in the French Department, Faculty of Languages, at the Pedagogical University in Maputo. Adelaide Dhorsan holds a master's degree awarded by the University Paul Valérie–Montpellier III in sociolinguistics and is working on her PhD thesis relative to Diglossic Bilingualism in Southern Mozambique.

Cristina Augusto Tembe lectures in the Curriculum Development Department of the Faculty of Education at the Eduardo Mondlane University in Maputo. Previously she lectured on reading and writing techniques in the Faculty of Education at the Pedagogical University in Maputo for two years. She has also worked on curriculum planning at the National Institute for Development of Education, participating in the writing of Portuguese-language textbooks and teachers' guides for thirteen years. She has authored an article entitled "The Acquisition of Portuguese as a Second Language." In addition, she has been involved in planning and training at the teacher training colleges for three years. She is a former member of the Technical Committee for Basic Education at the SADC level (serving for two years) and for two years was national director for basic education in Mozambique.

List of Acronyms

ANC	African National Congress
CPLP	Community of Portuguese Speaking Countries
DANIDA	Danish International Development Agency
EP	Ensino Primario (Primary Education)
FRELIMO	Frente de Libertação de Mozambique (Mozambican Liberation Front)
IMF	International Monetary Fund
INDE	Instituto Nacional de Desenvolvimento de Educação (National Institute for the Development of Education)
INE	Instituto Nacional de Estatísticas (National Institute of Statistics)
MINED	Ministério da Educação (Ministry of Education)
PCEB	Plano Curricular do Ensino Básico (Basic Education Curriculum Plan)
PIDE	Polícia de Intervenção e Defesa do Estado (Portuguese Secret Police under Salazar regime)
RENAMO	Resistência Nacional Moçambicana (Mozambican National Resistance)
SADC	Southern African Development Community
SNE	Sistema Nacional de Educação (National Education System)
UNDP	United Nations Development Program
UNESCO	United Nations Educational, Scientific and Cultural Organization

INTRODUCTION

Like so many countries in the world, Mozambique has artificial borders and a multiethnic and multicultural population. It was not immune to internal and international ideological tensions, and suffered through two major violent conflicts during the latter half of the twentieth century. The first, lasting a decade, was a struggle for independence against Portugal, which was finally won in 1975. The second, lasting sixteen years, began in 1976 within the context of the cold war, and pitted the Mozambican government, supported by communist countries, against RENAMO, the rebel Mozambican National Resistance movement backed by Rhodesia and South Africa.

During the colonial period, the Portuguese language was introduced in civil administration, commerce, and schooling, although the Catholic missionaries translated the Bible into local languages both for religious aims and so they could teach in some of the same languages spoken in the areas around rural schools. After independence in 1976 the Mozambican government chose Portuguese as the national language and extended its use across all schools and literacy programmes. The purpose was to consolidate national unity and create a bridge between the country, its population, and the rest of the world. After more than twenty years, it has become obvious that even if national unity has been consolidated politically, the gap between the Portuguese-speaking urban inhabitants and the rural communities speaking local languages has widened. The local cultural and ethnic specificities have been neglected, and the number of out-of-school children is still very significant, due mainly to the difficulties of mastering the Portuguese language both as a second language (different from the mother tongue) and as a medium of instruction.

What were the rationales behind curriculum change in Mozambique? What did Mozambicans decide to change in their school curricula? Were the changes related to the consequences of the struggle for independence and the armed conflict that followed? If so, how? Was curriculum reform initiated on the basis of a need for reconciliation and the strengthening of social cohesion? How was curriculum reform related to the social and cultural development needs of Mozambican society? What other national and international factors informed the need for change in school curricula? What consultation strategies have been adopted to ensure broad participation in the process of curriculum change? How is the government preparing for the implementation of the New Basic Education Curriculum in January 2004? What is the role of donors in supporting the government concerning the implementation of this new curriculum? These are the questions that this chapter attempts to answer, exploring the possible links between the experience of armed conflict, recent political change in Mozambique, and the reinforcement of national identity through curriculum reform.

We argue that education in Mozambique has undergone two clearly identifiable paradigm shifts and is currently engaged in a third. Despite limited scientific data, the first shift arguably accompanied Mozambique's colonisation, as the idea of education shifted from elders' inclusive sharing of traditional knowledge with children to the idea of school education as a vehicle of domination and social exclusion. Considerable evidence indicates that the colonial authorities employed a deliberate policy of exclusion with respect to the education of native Mozambicans. Not surprisingly, the second shift coincided with and resulted from independence. In newly independent Mozambique, education was promoted as the basis for the people to take power. It was essential to and accompanied a homogenising nationalism that rejected tribalism (which it saw as archaic) and focused on cultural and linguistic unity. The third conceptual shift concerning the role of education in Mozambique, even if it fails to be explicitly articulated, is clearly reflected in the efforts to introduce new language policies and locally developed curricula. It points to an education system less concerned with establishing uniformity and more concerned with understanding how the nation's cultural diversity can contribute essentially to its unity.[1]

Note on methodology

This study was prepared by a team of three persons based in Maputo. Two members of the team have been closely involved in the current process of curriculum reform. While one has been working at the National Institute for the Development of Education (INDE), the second had worked at the Ministry of Education and is now a lecturer in curriculum development at the Masters' Programme at University Eduardo Mondlane. The third member of the team was able to provide critical insight as someone who was not directly involved in the process of curriculum reform. Research involved a review of official documents produced by the Ministry of Education and the INDE, including documentation on the development of the National Education System (SNE) and a review of reports resulting from national consultations. Interviews were also conducted with representatives of a range of stakeholders involved in educational and curricular reform (see Appendix 1). Furthermore, a limited number of observations and interviews with pupils were conducted in a pilot school in Maputo. The team met once a week over a ten-month period (September 2002 to June 2003) in order to analyse the official documents collected and the results of conducted interviews and observations. The drafting of the study was based on the collectively developed framework in the final version that resulted from the international colloquium "Curriculum Change and Social Cohesion in Conflict-Affected Societies," organised by the UNESCO International Bureau of Education (Geneva, April 3–4, 2003). The discussion at the Geneva colloquium allowed for an exchange between two members of the Mozambican team and authors and researchers from the six other contexts participating in the collaborative project. This opportunity for exchange highlighted the multiple ways in which the process of curriculum reform in Mozambique has been shaped and determined by a national and regional context of armed conflict.

Organisation of text

This text begins with an overview of the armed conflicts that affected Mozambique before and after independence in 1975, outlining the context and root causes of these conflicts and the social issues resulting from them. The second section focuses on the new government's struggle against the colonial legacy and illiteracy, the introduction and construction of a National Educational System, and the devastation caused by the "civil war" in terms of the destruction of school infrastructure and equipment as well as the enrolment of both pupils and teachers as combatants. It concludes with a focus on the new hopes for strengthening national unity and identity which have been pinned onto the current process of educational reform. The third section analyses the consequences of the colonial and national education systems in terms of racial segregation and social exclusion, and the proposals of the new curriculum that aim to transform the school into a place where the local cultural and social diversities are taken into account.

The fourth section underlines the significant challenges that Mozambique faces in terms of socioeconomic development and poverty reduction in a context of high dependency on donors. The central fifth section presents the New Basic Education Curriculum within the wider context of the legacy of exclusion. The argument is made that the rationales that underlie the New Basic Education Curriculum are not directly related to the post–civil war process of reconciliation, but rather are linked to changes in the international context and in national economic policy, and to the need for the Mozambican people to recognise and reinforce shared national identity while recognising cultural diversity. Some of the new curriculum's innovative aspects are outlined, and space is devoted in particular to the introduction of Mozambican languages in primary education. The sixth section deals with the modalities and processes of consultation and participation, highlighting the challenging and sensitive areas encountered in developing the new curriculum. The seventh section is a brief analysis of the processes and results to date that are associated with monitoring the pilot implementation of the new curriculum in some schools, in anticipation of its national implementation in January 2004. The chapter concludes with some final remarks and recommendations concerning the focal points of this reform, namely, language policy, the introduction of local content during the lessons, teacher training, and the role of donors.

BACKGROUND TO CONFLICT AND PEACE

It is important to emphasise the fact that, while contemporary struggles in African countries are referred to as "ethnic conflicts," the armed conflicts experienced in Mozambique in the second half of the twentieth century (1964–75 and 1976–92) may more appropriately be defined as anticolonial and ideological conflicts. The first of these was the armed liberation struggle against Portuguese colonisation. Although the Portuguese presence in Mozambique started as early as the fifteenth century with the establishment of some coastal settlements, the process of colonisation was initiated in the nineteenth century. Confronted with stiff resistance from many different indigenous groups, Portugal succeeded in completing the process of pacification and consolidation of military domination as late as 1920. Despite this, active opposition to colonisation and its segregationist policy continued until the initiation of the liberation struggle in 1964.

Segregation and colonial domination

During the colonial period, all languages and cultural systems other than the colonial language and the official Catholic religion were marginalised. The twenty local Bantu languages and their various dialects were referred to as "dog's languages." Exclusion of the local population was the norm. Speaking Portuguese and belonging to the Catholic religion were essential preconditions for some degree of social and economic integration, although this remained an exception for a small minority of nonwhites. Deep social divisions were thus created during the colonial period, when the overwhelming majority of the people of Mozambique were excluded and denied basic cultural, political, and social rights, with the exception of the small minority of mulattoes, who were tolerated. The three racial designations of white, assimilated ("assimilado"), and black, and even mulatto, were official forms of social segregation.

The assimilation policy was introduced after World War II in response to anticolonial opposition and the new demand for semiskilled labour created by colonial economic development (Gomez, 1999). The economic development model adopted by the colonial authority implied a significant demand for manual and unskilled labourers more than for trained workers, and resulted in the limited development of more primary and technical schools in the colony. The assimilation process adopted by the central government was greeted with some opposition from poorly educated and untrained white settlers, particularly those living to the north of the Limpopo River. Allowing native Mozambicans to access even minimal levels of basic education and training was perceived as a threat and as potential competition with white settlers for access to limited employment opportunities. Their fears were proved groundless, however, since the policy of assimilation did not represent any significant channel for social, economic, and political integration for the overwhelming black majority. In the end, only a very small share of the population ever came to be considered "assimilated." Moreover, assimilated black individuals continued to be subject to discrimination and were disadvantaged compared to white settlers, even when the latter were less educated or illiterate.

From armed struggle for liberation to "civil war"

Mozambique's armed struggle for independence began in 1964, when more than half of the other African countries were already free from French and British colonisation. Maintaining that the African national independence movements sweeping the continent were not relevant to the situation of their colonies, Portugal attempted to prevent political upheaval in Mozambique. In addition to the surveillance of political activity by the state security police (PIDE) set up in 1956, Portugal tried to isolate Mozambicans from the changes taking place in the rest of Africa. Educational segregation and deprivation were essential tools in this strategy of isolation and domination. The initial sources of inspiration for Mozambican nationalism were imported from abroad, either via the forced or migrant workers in neighbouring countries, or by way of the small privileged minority that lived and studied abroad. The exposure of Mozambicans to African national thought and to the ideology of liberation outside their country led to the establishment of the Mozambican Liberation Front (FRELIMO) in Dar es Salaam in 1962.

The white minority that dominated society in Mozambique and other southern African countries could no longer ignore the political changes taking place in the region around them. Yet as a means to dampen the struggle for Mozambican independence, begun in 1964, the colonial power reactivated old conflicts between different indigenous groups. Colonial authorities revived and exploited, for example, the remote tensions and rivalries between the Macuas and the Macondes in the Cabo Delgado Province at the start of the FRELIMO armed struggle. Despite these obstacles, the struggle for independence ended in 1975, forcing the majority of the Portuguese to leave Mozambique for Portugal and South Africa. FRELIMO installed a socialist government in Maputo.

Independence, however, did not mark an end of hostilities. Arguably, Mozambique's "civil war" (1976–92), begun barely a year after independence and fought between FRELIMO and the Mozambican National Resistance (RENAMO), was the complex national and regional reflection of the international cold war. That this intricate dynamic remained unacknowledged at the time (with the armed conflict itself not publicly acknowledged until 1983) is seen by some as one of the major reasons for the later confusion and disorder.[2] At the international level, communist parties and governments supported FRELIMO both in its struggle for Mozambique's independence and in its war against RENAMO, while South Africa and renegade Rhodesians supported RENAMO. Meanwhile, FRELIM O supported the African National Congress (ANC) and the Zimbabwean guerrilla movements, which were combating the apartheid policies of the governments of South Africa and Rhodesia. To fight these guerrilla groups, RENAMO was created in Rhodesia, trained and armed at first by the Rhodesian government and later by the South African regime. Its principal backers were South Africa, Portuguese military intelligence, and some of the Portuguese who had had to leave the country in 1975. At the national level, both protagonists recruited their members from among the different indigenous groups throughout Mozambique. RENAMO also welcomed former FRELIMO soldiers. Among the social forces against the government policy and the Marxist revolution were the Catholic Church and other religious groups, traditional chiefs, potential entrepreneurs, and small farmers.

Today, some political parties try to increase social tensions between the Mozambican populations in the north, centre, and south, citing disparities between the three regions of the country concerning the level of economic development and the distribution of public infrastructure, such as schools, hospitals, and roads. Regional development gaps are used by some political parties, for example, in an attempt to mobilise popular indignation in the north and centre over how the south is more developed in terms of its schools (primary, secondary, and tertiary), hospitals, roads, and opportunities. Having learned from the divisive recruiting techniques of FRELIMO and RENAMO, and as a mean(s) of avoiding further manipulation of ideological, indigenous, and socioeconomic domains, the state and NGOs working in social services are continuously developing activities and sensitisation tools to promote the culture of peace throughout the country.

Toward the peace agreement of 1992

The peace agreement between the FRELIMO government and the RENAMO insurgency was negotiated with the facilitation of the Sant'Egidio Community and signed in 1992 in Rome. A ceasefire was immediately established, and the two parties started transforming their armed struggle into a political one. The first democratic elections, organised in 1994 with the presence of international delegates, were followed by a second round of elections in 1999.

Several years before the 1992 peace agreement, the political situation and social climate were slowly changing in Mozambique. In 1987, Mozambique committed itself to the structural adjustment policy of the World Bank and the International Monetary Fund (IMF), accepting the principles of a market economy and beginning a progressive transition from a socialist, planned economy to a capitalist, free market economy. In 1990, the Parliament adopted a new constitution admitting and encouraging a multiparty political system and the opening of private schools. These measures were a reflection of a changing international environment emerging from the collapse of the Soviet system in 1989, and the end of the bipolar cold war world order and its logic of confrontation by proxy in the developing world.

Perhaps more directly, the changing regional context and the beginning of the end of the apartheid regime in South Africa in 1990 were to have a significant impact on Mozambique, as on other countries in the southern Africa region:

> The beginning of change in South Africa, even before the demise of apartheid, helped to bring peace and independence to Namibia. It also helped the peace efforts in Angola and Mozambique, where insurgent forces could no longer depend on the support of South Africa's apartheid regime. In Mozambique, the October 1992 peace agreement ended 16 years of vicious warfare and led to elections in 1994. The government won, despite receiving less than half the votes, and the former armed insurgents accepted the result.
>
> (Smith, 1997)

Despite certain tensions between the two main protagonists of the national Mozambican political landscape, the country has benefited from stability, and the people from security, during the decade since the peace agreement was signed. Much like the processes of political, social, and economic change, the education system has also been undergoing a process of reform. Indeed, the context of peace and political stability resulting from the end of the war, the government's demonstrated political will to undertake policy reform, and the readiness of both a less divided civil society and international cooperation partners were essential ingredients for the initiation of a process of policy dialogue aimed at defining national development orientations for the country as it attempted to address the legacy of decades of internal armed conflict.

EDUCATION REFORM AND CONFLICT

The process of curriculum change in basic education currently underway in Mozambique is to be understood against the backdrop of this long process of political and social upheaval, although it may be argued that economic factors were the main catalyst for current reform. Current alteration of the Mozambican education system follows a first attempt immediately after independence in 1975, and a second in 1983 when the National Education System (SNE) was introduced under Law 4/83 on March 23 and subsequently revised by Law 6/92 on May 6. Both reforms were initiated within a national and regional context of conflict, during the war for independence from Portugal and the subsequent civil war.

The education system under the Portuguese aimed primarily at the reproduction of colonial domination and was conducive neither to national unity and the building of a national culture nor to the respect for human rights and the promotion of peace and stability. Indeed, domination dating back to the end of the fifteenth century and culminating in the authoritarian and fascist regime in place in Portugal until 1974 was based on the denial of basic social, cultural, and political rights for the Mozambican people. With the exception of the "assimilados," the legally categorised "indigenous population" was seen as having to be civilised and Christianised. Mozambican culture and indigenous languages were completely neglected by the Portuguese colonial school system, which was based solely on Western scientific conceptions of knowledge and Christian values and beliefs. In short,

> "civilization" meant that indigenous children had access to the first two grades of elementary school, if at all locally existing. Occasionally, particularly in the urban zones, they might find possibilities to pursue education at as high a level as grade four. Beyond that no schooling was available to them, with the exception of the few who were recognized as assimilados, those who had assimilated, i.e. rejected their own culture. For the children of the Portuguese settlers, the situation was entirely different. For this relatively small number there was a variety of schools—primary and secondary schools for general education, vocational schools, teacher training colleges, and even a university—all providing curricula exactly as in Portugal.
>
> (Pereira and Visser, 1990)

After independence, the Mozambican government reinforced the ideas of national unity and identity as defined by a Marxist revolutionary culture that was developed over more than a decade of anticolonial liberation struggle during the Luta de Libertação (1964–75). The Marxist-Leninist ideology of the Mozambican Liberation Front which marked the history of the struggle for national liberation and independence shaped social, cultural, and educational policies based on the premise that African traditions and languages were an expression of obscurantism and possible sources of tribal division.

> The Frelimo Party personifies the highest patriotic traditions and the conquests of the people won by the revolutionary fighters in the course of the national liberation struggle, the people's war of liberation, the defence of the country and the fight against old and new exploiters. The Party, forged and tempered in the process of national and social liberation, raises national unity and patriotic values to their highest level. It is the concrete expression of the most noble patriotic sentiments of our people. It is the guarantee of national

independence. For this reason, the Party fights intransigently against tribalism, racism and divisiveness as fundamental enemies of our people's unity, of independence and of our national consciousness.[3]

Such ideology inspired from a socialist development model translated into policies based on the perceived need to build a new person who would be open to scientific and technological progress and to positive values. The aim was the creation of a unified socialist nation that would not revert to local values systems and loyalties that might create division and give Western imperialist states the opportunity to dominate Africa.

Map 1: Mozambique in the Southern Africa Region

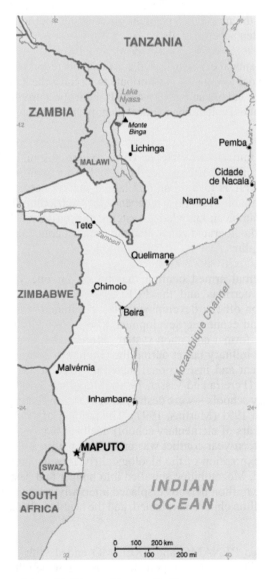

Source: http://www.lib.utexas.edu/maps/cia03/mozambique_sm03.gif.

217

With independence came the opportunity for national political control of education. The education sector was nationalised and became the sole responsibility of the Ministry of Education, taking responsibility away from the Roman Catholic Church, which had been the main provider of "rudimentary education for the indigenous" during the colonial era (Pereira and Visser, 1990). Education was defined as a constitutional right and was rendered obligatory for all citizens. Although a low-income country characterised by low levels of socioeconomic development, Mozambique managed to achieve high levels of literacy and to significantly expand access to basic education during the first decade of independence. Ambitious school construction programmes were launched, and popular and voluntary literacy campaigns in 1975 and 1976 provided some one million individuals with access to basic literacy skills. In the first five years after independence (1975-80), illiteracy was reduced from a dramatic 93 percent to 72 percent, with primary enrolments increasing threefold during the same time period. The education projects of the newly independent government did not, however, only look to improve literacy and broaden access but also

> to expand the educational experience of the national liberation struggle. [According to the policymakers,] school for all should contribute to rescuing the dignity of the Mozambican people, valuing their culture and their history. It should be a privileged social space for the formation of the nation, cultivating national identity and national unity.
>
> (UNDP, 2000)

Curriculum revision was initiated in 1975 in Beira, where colonial school curricula were reviewed from the angle of their irrelevance both to Mozambican culture and new social and political realities, as well as to training and labour-market needs. The three educational models, which were available for post-independence curriculum reform, included the informal endogenous Mozambican knowledge systems, the ten-year FRELIMO revolutionary educational experience in the liberated zones, and the socialist educational model of the Soviet Union and its eastern bloc allies.

However, the violent internal armed conflict that broke out one year after independence between the RENAMO guerrillas and the FRELIMO government took a heavy toll on Mozambican society and on official development efforts initiated at that time. The impact of armed conflict on social and economic development efforts was disastrous, as was the effect on the development of the formal education system. Moreover, education—much like health services—was a deliberate military target during the conflict; school infrastructure was under systematic attack, equipment and instructional materials were destroyed, and teachers were mutilated and assassinated (Pereira and Visser, 1990). More than 3,400 schools—an estimated 58 percent of all elementary schools—were destroyed or closed, affecting more than 1.3 million students between 1983 and 1991 (Martins, 1997). The number of primary schools of the first level (EP1, the first five years of elementary school) declined from 5,730 in 1980 to 3,381 in 1992. This devastating sixteen-year conflict was embedded within a wider regional conflict in southern Africa, itself an expression of the ideological rivalries and confrontation of the cold war era. During this period, Mozambique spiralled into hunger and destruction, with over one million people killed, three million persons displaced internally or as refugees in neighbouring countries, a quarter of a million children orphaned, and the health and educational infrastructure devastated.

The armed conflict between RENAMO and FRELIMO ended with the peace agreement of 1992, which was welcomed by the civilian population, as it signalled the return of security and allowed the government to resume development efforts and social, economic, and educational reform. The main challenge of these reforms was to rebuild confidence and reinforce national unity and identity in a population that had been a victim of Western ideological rivalries and was harshly affected by an extremely violent conflict in which civilians and social groups from all parts of the country were affected regardless of their regional, cultural, linguistic, or religious origin.

At the level of social, cultural, and educational policy, the protracted conflict of the 1970s and 1980s halted the attempts to define the Mozambican national identity and sense of citizenship that had characterised the early years of independence. Although the revolutionary ideology of the FRELIMO managed to define certain traits of the Mozambican national identity in terms of opposition to tribalism, regionalism, and individualism, for example, attempts to fully define Mozambican African identity were thwarted as a result of armed conflict, political instability, and social division. The challenge was to learn to live together, respecting ideological differences, transforming formerly hostile belligerent parties into political parties, creating a climate of unthreatening political dialogue and exchange in view of redefining the nature of national identity and citizenship. Such changes required an accompanying process of change of the formal education system through which a new generation of Mozambican citizens were to be shaped for the new emerging social, civic, political, and economic realities.

Foremost among these realities was the new national political climate that resulted from transformed ideological configurations at the international level and characterised the geopolitical landscape at the end of the cold war in the late 1980s and early 1990s. One of the effects of these changing political ideologies was a shift in perception that allowed Mozambican languages and local cultural systems to be seen as positive constituent elements of a new conceptualisation of Mozambican identity as multicultural and multilingual, rather than as possible sources of division that might weaken national cohesion. However, political and cultural development cannot be dissociated from social and economic dimensions, and the new curriculum to be implemented in 2004 cannot hope to significantly contribute to a more cohesive national society without reinforcing social and political stability, promoting equitable socioeconomic development, reducing economic dependency, combating the HIV/AIDS pandemic, and taking an active role in regional integration.

In sum, the reform initiated at independence in 1975 was a response to both a colonial heritage of division, discrimination, and denial of African identity and dignity as well as to the needs and realities of post-conflict social and political reconstruction following more than a decade of a liberation struggle against the Portuguese. Likewise, the reform of 1983[4] was initiated in the midst of the internal conflict. The reform currently underway, following the 1992 peace agreement, is a challenging undertaking from the angle of social cohesion. The challenge is threefold in that it attempts to

1. respond to the long heritage of violence, destruction, and division;

2. resume efforts aimed at defining and consolidating an official national Mozambican African culture and identity; and

3. respond to the much more recent regional and international changes associated with the end of the cold war and the resulting reconceptualisation of Mozambican identity as multicultural and multilingual.

The changes introduced in this new curriculum are presented by the government as a continuation of official efforts at preserving Mozambican culture and strengthening national identity as defined in national policy frameworks. According to the Plano Curricular do Ensino Básico (PCEB) or the Basic Education Curriculum Plan (INDE/MINED, 1999):

> the main challenge of this curriculum is to transform the teaching so that it becomes more relevant, that is, to train citizens so that they can contribute to enhance his/her life, his/her family, community and country life, preserving national unity, maintaining peace and national stability, further developing democracy and human rights, and preserving Mozambican culture.

The new curriculum nevertheless introduces important changes as it redefines Mozambican national identity in terms of a multilingual and multicultural society. The continuing effort to "preserve national unity," in other words, is not in doubt. It is the definition of what constitutes national unity that is undergoing a transformation.

FROM RACIALLY SEGREGATED SCHOOLING TO SOCIAL EXCLUSION

The history of the Mozambican schooling system may be characterised by diverse forms of segregation ranging from the cultural and political segregation of the colonial era to the socioeconomic exclusion reflected in the regional development gaps. The main issue for the colonial government in Mozambique, reflected through the education sector in particular, had been to ensure policies and rules to perpetuate the colonial system. Under the colonial assimilationist policy, education was intended to provide minimal education and training for a restricted workforce that could directly serve the colonial interests (Duffy, 1962, cited in Gomez, 1999). While the colonial education system was theoretically under government control, two types of school systems coexisted: public schooling for white and assimilated people that provided basic literacy and numeracy skills in Portuguese as well as basic environmental education; and the missionary-run "rudimentary school" system for the black people supported mainly by the Roman Catholic Church. The main aim of the rudimentary schools was to guide and "civilise" the indigenous people and to render the black communities more servile as a consequence of the religious component in their education. Gomez (1999) wrote that, "according to Mondlane, this education, separated and handed over to the Catholic Church, intended to indoctrinate the children of the native black Mozambican, providing the Government with a docile population loyal to Portugal." A further characteristic difference between the public schools and the missionary schools was that the former tended to be established in urban areas and the latter in rural and suburban areas.

It may be argued that all colonial education was essentially planned to produce a small Europeanised person who was to serve the colonial government and preserve the same values (Mondlane, 1977, cited in Gomez, 1999). Gomez notes that education and training were given great importance throughout the history of the FRELIMO liberation movement and government primarily because of their weak colonial heritage. The FRELIMO education system, both during and after the liberation struggle, was geared to train people for political and military roles, and focussed on production-type activities for national rebuilding.

The left-wing military coup of April 25, 1975, in Portugal led to a new era of independence in Mozambique and strongly marked the education system. Many Portuguese teachers left the country, and new syllabi were developed for primary education. The main changes in curricula were related to history, geography, language, and natural sciences. In 1976, the National Commission for Textbook Writing was created to present new proposals to teachers. The fastest pace of reform was effected through the establishment of the INDE, which was created to deal with curricular issues. Under INDE guidance the first National System of Education was produced in 1983.

Despite the context of civil war, the Constitution of the Republic of Mozambique, approved and enacted in November 1990, established in Article 92, Chapter III, on Economic and Social Rights and Duties, that:

1. In the Republic of Mozambique education shall be a right and duty of all citizens.

2. The State shall promote greater and equal access to the enjoyment of this right by all citizens.

This allowed for the design of the National Policy of Education and the Education Sector Strategic Plan. To introduce curriculum reforms, it was deemed necessary to undertake a large consultation of stakeholders from different areas throughout the country. Those consultations determined that 80 percent of the core curriculum content would be applicable for the whole country, and 20 percent of the content would be locally adapted. Each school would define the local content, guided by the geographic, historical, and cultural particularities of the pupils and the location of the school community. The invitation to design locally relevant curriculum was to be done according to two principles:

*   A more in-depth understanding of a subject that is only treated generally in the core curriculum: for example, in a school situated in an area where the cotton plant is agriculturally and economically important, instructors would be invited to delve into greater detail about cotton when it was touched upon in the core curriculum.

*   The introduction of new subjects that are otherwise not studied in the core curriculum: for example, the school may consider that the pupils should learn more about something very specific to the area, such as a particular local event, situation, plant, animal, or artistic technique.

Just as the core contents were decided through a broad consultation of stakeholders throughout the country, local contents were decided by each school: members of different institutions—in public, private, and civil society—were invited to join the school staff, the teachers, and the parents to assist in defining the content of each course to coincide with the interests of the local community. The idea was that in this way pupils would be prepared to become active members of their individual communities as well as their country.

Although access to basic education was significantly expanded following independence, the National System of Education was created in 1983, and education was proclaimed to be a constitutional right in 1990, public educational efforts were still unable to respond to students' needs. Unable to integrate all school-age children in the public system, the government had to open education to other stakeholders. The first type of educational provision was the community school in 1990–91, in Gaza Province, and later the first private school was opened.

Community schools are those that do not have profit as an objective; the communities—religious or social groups—build the schools and "manage" the administrative issues. These schools belong to specific communities and aim to educate their children. For the most part, the communities are responsible for teachers' salaries; in select situations, however, the government pays salaries or has a formal link with the teachers. When first begun, religious groups also had the opportunity to provide an education with a religiously oriented curriculum that could differ from the national curriculum.

Private education is expensive, and private schools are mainly located in urban areas. Children from rural areas, and/or whose parents are poor, do not benefit from private schooling. There are, however, new stakeholders responsible for private and community schools who help to reduce this gulf in educational opportunity and thus the numbers of illiterate and out-of-school children.

Unlike during the colonial era, there is no official segregation in schooling today. However, great economic, regional, and social disparities do exist and continue to be reflected in patterns of school enrolment. Despite government efforts to ensure basic schooling for all, enrolment figures remain low, with an average net enrolment ratio for seven-year-olds of 66 percent (MINED, 2001). Moreover, distribution of school enrolment is overwhelmingly concentrated in EP1, grades one through five, with very low enrolment ratios at the level of grades six and seven (EP2) reflecting low average levels of educational attainment (see Figure 1):

> the system has a broad base in EP1, but is then abruptly narrowed in EP2, which is the second level of primary education. This is because of the organisational form of EP2, which functions by independent subjects, similar to secondary education. This makes it very expensive and difficult to expand throughout the vast national territory, because of the number of teachers needed for EP2 to function fully.
>
> (UNDP, 2000)

Figure 1: Distribution of School Enrolment by Learning Cycle

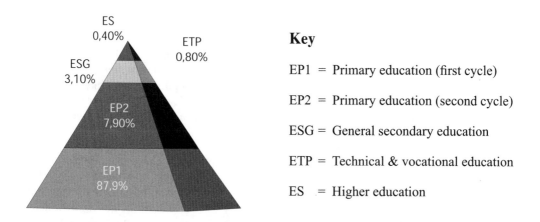

Key

EP1 = Primary education (first cycle)

EP2 = Primary education (second cycle)

ESG = General secondary education

ETP = Technical & vocational education

ES = Higher education

Furthermore, an analysis of promotion, repetition, and dropout rates (see Appendix 2) indicates the low internal efficiency of the National Educational System during the years 1992–93, 1994–95, and 1998–99. The average rate of promotion is low, and repetition and dropout rates are consistently high. Despite the decrease observed in dropout rates between 1992 and 1999, the primary school system still has a very high wastage (with repetition at 25 percent and the dropout rate at 18.3 percent). Moreover, the gender situation did not improve, because females continued to fail and drop out more frequently than males (Guz, 2000).

The persistent high level of repetition is catastrophic for Mozambique, a poor country with a very high rate of children who cannot go to school because the places are too limited.

> When a pupil repeats a year or abandons the school, the average number of years per pupil needed to complete EP1 surpasses the stipulated five. Under these conditions, the pupil who needs more than one year to finish the grade, is using space, teaching time, books and other resources that could be used by other pupils. For example, in 1999 there was a repetition rate of 24% in EP1—in absolute terms, that was 495,000 pupils. By way of illustration, one should note that, to find room for these repeating pupils the system had to mobilize 4,950 additional classrooms (1 room for 100 pupils in two shifts), and the same number of teachers.
>
> (UNDP, 2000)

Furthermore, the troubling number of out-of-school children is linked to the social and economic consequences of protracted armed conflict that has resulted in low family incomes. Widespread household poverty, in turn, serves as a constraint on national economic and social initiatives. To reduce these difficulties, the government considers that the measures to be adopted should be those of training more teachers, building more schools, and reinforcing the support given to communities in terms of textbook provision.

Many argue that it is the medium of instruction those new teachers will use, and the language in which those textbooks are written, however, that institutionalises another form of exclusion. Many children do not learn in their mother tongue, or even use one of the languages they master, due to the fact that Portuguese has been, until very recently, used as the sole medium of instruction in Mozambique.

> Of the 17 million inhabitants, more than 95% have a Bantu language as their mother tongue. Only the minority (25%) who have been to school speak Portuguese, which is the official language, and probably far fewer can write it. Furthermore, the language mainly exists in the urban centres where 17% of the population live. The minority are privileged in regard to education, access to better paid jobs, and also the possibility of relating to the political and social processes of the country. The elite masters speak Portuguese; the majority who live in the rural areas do not.
>
> (Rønning, 1997)

This situation creates a disadvantage for Mozambican children, and especially for those in rural areas where very few people speak Portuguese. They have to learn the Portuguese language as both a medium of communication and a medium of instruction. According to Joseph Poth, who was in charge of UNESCO's LINGUAPAX Project, "an education that separates the child from the language spoken in his family is one of the main causes of repeating years and dropping out of school" (UNDP, 2000).

The complexity of the linguistic situation is significant and renders more inclusive policymaking problematic. Mozambican society is composed of several indigenous groups and religious communities, with approximately twenty languages belonging to the Bantu language group, each with up to four to five dialects (INE, 1997). Mozambican languages are characterised by an oral tradition, and many have only recently acquired written forms. Recent census data indicate that while 39 percent of the total population of approximately twelve million inhabitants above the age of five speak Portuguese as a second language, only a small fraction, in urban areas, speak Portuguese as a mother tongue (6.4 percent). In rural areas, the share of the population that speaks Portuguese as a first language is just over 1 percent. The vast majority of the Mozambican people—an estimated 94 percent—speak one of the Bantu languages (INE, 1997).

In a country in which 70 percent of the inhabitants reside in rural areas, 90 percent of EP1 and 73 percent of EP2 schools are rural. The distribution of admission rates and enrolment ratios across provinces reflects significant regional disparities (see Table 1).

Table 1: Disparities in the First Cycle of Primary Education: Distribution by province and gender

Ministério da Educação - Direcção de Planificação
Indicadores de Cobertura Escolar, Ensino Primário do 1º Grau, 2001
Indicators of school school, Primary Education 1st Level, 2001

Província Province	Taxa bruta de admissão Gross admission rate			Taxa bruta de escolarização Gross enrollment rate			Taxa líquida de escolarização Net enrollment rate		
	HM	H	M	HM	H	M	HM	H	M
01 C. Delgado	137,2	148,9	125,6	91,2	106,9	75,7	54,1	59,6	48,7
02 Gaza	135,0	136,5	133,5	134,1	138,6	129,6	71,7	72,0	71,5
03 Inhambane	126,1	124,9	127,3	129,7	136,2	123,3	71,0	71,4	70,6
04 Manica	125,3	137,3	113,6	100,6	117,3	84,5	58,1	64,3	52,2
05 Maputo	140,8	140,8	140,8	142,8	146,1	139,5	80,6	80,1	81,0
06 Nampula	107,9	114,2	101,6	81,8	95,6	67,8	47,3	51,1	43,4
07 Niassa	125,7	136,5	115,1	88,5	101,7	75,4	58,3	63,5	53,1
08 Sofala	110,2	124,5	95,8	86,3	102,2	70,4	54,3	60,8	47,8
09 Tete	120,8	128,9	112,6	83,8	94,2	73,4	55,9	59,9	51,9
10 Zambézia	134,9	143,8	125,9	95,6	111,0	80,2	61,7	68,3	55,0
11 C. Maputo	107,5	106,2	108,7	134,8	135,6	134,1	86,2	84,8	87,6
Total do País	123,8	131,1	116,5	99,3	111,5	87,2	59,9	64,0	55,8

HM - Homens e Muheres / *Male and Female* ; H - Homens / *Male* ;

Given the constitutionally declared commitment to promote greater and equal access to basic education, the high illiteracy rates that continue to be observed (estimated in 1998 at over 40 percent for males and almost 60 percent for females), as well as the high attrition rates mentioned above, demonstrate the degree to which education continues to exclude a sizeable portion of the population. While it must be acknowledged that significant progress has been made in expanding access to basic schooling, dropout patterns continue to be of serious concern and the equitable provision of quality education in a predominantly rural and multilingual setting remains challenging. Nonetheless, opening up the curriculum reform process to broad stakeholder input has given voice to the crucial issue of linguistic inclusion. The aim of designing a curriculum with core and local contents discussed above intended to develop the principle of equitable access to the same knowledge and skills and, additionally, to reinforce the principle of recognising the differences and particularities of each region, province, district, and village in the country.

ECONOMIC CONTEXT OF REFORM

In order to fully understand the new curriculum reform in its capacity to reinforce national unity, it is important to outline the economic context in which it was taking shape. For the past ten years, many foreign companies and donors have considered Mozambique to be one of the best-qualified countries in Africa for investment in macroeconomic terms. Attracted by the climate of political stability, they have decided to sustain the economy of this country, which has a continuous positive real growth rate. But the country has been so impoverished that it has very serious problems of unemployment, a lack of educated people for specialised jobs, and a lack of dynamism and creativity in the creation and management of new companies.

Nature of donor involvement

Mozambique is one of the most aid-dependent countries in the world despite the fact that after independence it adopted an autonomous and fairly sceptical approach to aid. A decade later, however, the country had little choice but to accept aid on a large scale as a result of drought and a foreign-backed war conducive to economic destabilisation. When relief and rehabilitation efforts were at their peak, particularly in the early 1990s, there was a large influx of aid and aid agencies. In recent years, as the country has moved out of an emergency phase into long-term development, there has been an accompanying decline in the level of aid, the number of donors, and the number of NGOs involved. However, the country is still heavily dependent on foreign aid and is likely to remain so for the foreseeable future.

The Ministry of Planning and Finance (MPF) reported that aid makes up between 55 and 60 percent of the government budget. Other aid, especially that which is managed by NGOs and Churches, does not enter Mozambique through the government. It is also evident that aid has contributed to a brain drain away from government as many civil servants have either stopped working for government services and joined NGOs, or spend more time doing consulting for NGOs than working for the government institutions where they hold full-time employment.

Mozambique has also become heavily indebted, largely as a result of the same reasons that led to its dependence on aid. The large debt burden is a serious obstacle to the country's efforts to reduce poverty. Although the country is benefiting from debt cancellation under the Heavily Indebted Poor Countries initiative (HIPC initiative), the extra resources freed up for development by the initiative are negligible and there is a growing coalition calling for total and unconditional debt relief for Mozambique. However, even if all debt is cancelled, Mozambique will still need large sums of aid to address its developmental challenges.

Implications for education reform

Aid dependence and indebtedness have undermined Mozambique's sovereignty inasmuch as the conditions attached to aid have forced the country to accept some controversial policy changes. The fragmented coordination of aid has further undermined the government's capacity to set priorities and design its own programmes. For example, the Ministry of Education, guided by the Government Programme, which has both the quality and expansion of education as its main aims, was able to define the National Educational Policy. However, the Ministry of Education has not been able to carry out all of the planned activities, because of a lack of human and financial resources.

In the case of the national project for the reform of curriculum, the government was not able to dedicate money to it, even though the macroeconomic situation of Mozambique was satisfactory, and the project was mainly financed by the Netherlands with management of the funds under UNESCO's responsibility. Consequently, the INDE, defined as the institution in charge of executing the decisions concerning the new curriculum, does not have direct access to funds. Thus, while some decisions could be executed, others had to wait because they were either not considered to be priorities by the donors or because they were simply bogged down in the lengthy (up to a year long) processes of getting access to the funds.

As an example of the former, it is currently possible to visit pilot schools that are experimenting with monolingual programmes because UNESCO frees funds very quickly for them. However, no pilot schools are experimenting with the bilingual programme with the exception of those whose funds come from NGOs interested in supporting the experience. As an example of the latter, all of the technical work of preparing schoolbooks in different languages has been done, but bureaucratic processes have contributed considerably to the amount of time it has taken to get money from the World Bank for the reproduction and distribution of the schoolbooks and related teaching and learning materials for use in the schools. Teachers' initial and in-service training—programmes whose implementation is essential to the overall success of the curriculum change initiative—face the same funding difficulties. Finally, discussions are currently ongoing with donors with a view to reducing the unit costs of the school building programme, in the hope that more schools can be built with the same amount of money.

THE NEW BASIC EDUCATION CURRICULUM

Confronting a legacy of exclusion

In Mozambique, the National Institute for Development of Education is a central institution of the Ministry of Education whose main objectives are to deal with curriculum and curricular material for primary and secondary education, and primary school teacher training. It was created in 1978 as a specialised institution, under the authority of the Ministry of Education but with academic and administrative autonomy. It is responsible for translating policy decisions through the development of curriculum, syllabi, textbooks, and other teaching and learning materials. At the beginning of 1980, the INDE had such diverse partners as UNESCO/UNDP, the Democratic Republic of Germany, and other countries.

Since 1997, the Netherlands, DANIDA, the World Bank, and UNESCO have supported the INDE as the implementing agency in the designing and developing of the Basic Education Curriculum Change Project under the supervision of the Ministry of Education. The objectives of this project are

- to build consensus about the curriculum changes;
- to develop a curriculum framework for basic education;
- to develop syllabi for basic schooling (grades one to seven);
- to develop a framework and curriculum for teacher training and to design modules for teacher training;
- to develop the management capacity for the curriculum change; and
- to facilitate research and studies on curriculum development.

In order to carry out these activities, the INDE held consultation forums, which involved parents and teachers, community leaders, members of Parliament, and educational officers at central, provincial, and district levels in order to try to build consensus about the content and to approve the curriculum. Following the different decisions concerning the new curriculum, the INDE had to guide their technical realisation, and facilitate and monitor trials in the pilot schools.

The conception and preparation of the new curriculum took into account considerations outlined in various technical studies carried out by the Ministry of Education and, more particularly, by the INDE, as well as by other individuals and collective entities. For example, in 1989, the Swedish International Development Cooperation Agency (SIDA) financed a project conducted by the INDE, which aimed at assessing textbooks and their use. The results of this assessment provided additional support for the necessity of undertaking curriculum reform.[5]

The considerations and recommendations, along with the experiences of the countries in the region and the Paises Africanos de Língua Oficial Portuguesa (the African countries with Portuguese as the official language), provided the foundations for the development of the new curriculum, though it should be noted that this was quite a long and drawn-out process. The Stockholm Educational Institute and SIDA helped the INDE carry out a project of capacity building in order for its educational officers to develop research skills related to curriculum development.

In 1995, the government approved a National Educational Policy whose priorities were defined according to three axes: increasing equitable access, enhancing the quality and relevance of the teaching, and reinforcing the institutional capacity building of the Ministry of Education (MINED, 1998a). Improving the relevance of the teaching would help augment the capacity to improve one's life by using knowledge and skills acquired in school. Families and communities raised the issue of the relevance of what was taught because the curriculum for primary school was mainly designed to prepare the individual to enter secondary school. Taking into account that most of the primary school leavers do not go on to secondary school, it was important to prepare them with life skills so that they could more ably support their families and be more useful to society as a whole.

The New Basic Education Curriculum, which will be implemented in 2004 throughout the country, will endeavour to offer pupils better opportunities to succeed by introducing local languages as the medium of instruction (mainly at the first- and second-grade levels in rural areas). The new curriculum refers to a constructivist methodological perspective, with the learner at the centre of the teaching-learning process, focusing on the teacher-learner, learner-learner, and learner-community interactions. At this time, the INDE has prepared schoolbooks and teacher's guides for the first languages that will be introduced. It is now a matter of reproducing and distributing them to different schools and training the teachers about the strategies of teaching in the local languages. School libraries will also play an important complementary role.

Prioritising basic education was absolutely necessary because Mozambique's development aspirations were not thought possible without renewed primary education that would work to eliminate illiteracy and exclusion. The three axes of priorities chosen by the government are of a technical nature and could be selected in any country to combat illiteracy and exclusion. They were responding to principles like Education for All (EFA), and the specific problems of a country at the end of a dramatic conflict were not taken into account. The largely unacknowledged particularity of the post-conflict situation in developing education reform will be the subject of the next section.

Rationales for curriculum change

Framed against the context of a recent and protracted "civil war," one might imagine that the prevention of violent conflicts would constitute one of the fundamental principles for the development of the new curriculum. However, it does not clearly appear that, before designing the new curriculum, there was a deepened debate on the causes and consequences of the conflict. Nor was there any assessment of the contributing or catalytic role of education at the level of the Mozambican collective consciousness. It is worth noting, in this respect, that the peace agreements did not contribute to a formulation of such a debate, as they do not make any explicit mention of education reform. Indeed, the idea of reforming the curriculum emerged before the end of the war. When it did, at least two factors helped dampen any serious questioning of the role of education in promoting social exclusion or social inclusion: (1) the same educational officers who had conceived of the first curriculum after independence were put in charge of the development of the new curriculum, and (2) the Mozambican elites held the same views as these traditional education officers and wished to continue with the main principles espoused in the Portuguese system of education.

Moreover, as RENAMO did not design an educational project that might have stimulated a public debate, the rationales of education reform remained rather more implicit than explicit. Implicitly, objectives of the new curriculum—which, for example, aim to make education more relevant with a view to preserving national unity and Mozambican culture, strengthening democracy, and increasing respect for human rights—do reveal both an awareness of the profound crisis within Mozambican society following sixteen years of war and the need to respond to the new challenges of modern society. We would like to make the case that a more profound, explicit reflection on the potential contribution of education to the conflict may have allowed for a more considered approach to such thematic areas as the role of schooling in the prevention of violent conflict, the consolidation of national unity, and the building and reinforcement of democracy and respect for human rights.

That this did not occur is probably due to the fact that the internal economic crisis and the collapse of the supporting Marxist European regimes forced the government to adopt swift political and economic reforms. Those changes meant a transition toward an increasingly democratic regime supported by a market-oriented economy, whose aim was to eliminate the basis upon which RENAMO continued its justification of the war. While the peace accord negotiations were long, the reconciliation process was so rapid that the government could continue to integrate the processes of curriculum change begun previously when the government made its democratic and economic transition.

Many analysts agree that the curriculum reform project became necessary after Mozambique decided to accept the Structural Adjustment Policy in 1987–88, committing, thus, to the transition from a Marxist to a market economy. The reform was seen as necessary, because Mozambique had to create a synergy with all other southern African countries and members of the Southern African Development Community (SADC) concerning education policy. The introduction of English, Mozambican languages, and civic education to the new curriculum is at least in part a result of that desired synergy.

Shifting language policies

As mentioned previously, during the colonial period, Portuguese was a language spoken by few people, namely, the Portuguese settlers and some assimilados. Very few indigenous people could learn the new language because they did not have access to schooling and contact was limited between Portuguese, assimilados, and the majority of the native Mozambicans, who spoke a variety of Bantu languages. At independence, the priority of the government and the FRELIMO Party was to build national unity by ending social and political oppression. For FRELIMO, chief among the forms of oppression was ignorance, because

> not only did illiterate people lack political consciousness, but they were at the mercy of traditional knowledge and practices which condemned them to poverty, made them superstitious and perpetuated the tyranny of customs like lobola, polygamy and initiation. Frelimo's programme of social reform was to cover all these issues, and its prime purpose was to create the social integration which colonial rule had failed to achieve. Its foundation was to be universal literacy.
>
> (Newitt, 1995)

Thus, one of the elements reinforced was the dominant place of the Portuguese language in the construction and management of the nation. Portuguese became the only language of schooling and administration, and the government began a concerted literacy campaign. Local languages were considered to be possible sources of division among the Mozambican people. Local cultures were considered elements of obscurantism, and their development had to be avoided. As expressed by Helge Rønning (1997), "there existed, and still exists, an attitude in political circles of equating the development of African languages with tribalism, and that raising the question of a different language policy is tantamount to questioning the project of national unity."

The sixteen years of internal conflict, however, destroyed these efforts at unification through schooling not least by the destruction of many schools and the displacement of the population both within and beyond the country. Schooling and literacy programmes declined, while the national economy was deeply affected. Meanwhile, Mozambique was an active member of the frontline countries combating apartheid in South Rhodesia and South Africa. Only after the end of the war could these countries, along with other southern African countries, try to create a synergy between their educational policies, particularly concerning the introduction of English and local languages in their curriculum. They even expressed the wish of "progressively achieving the equivalence, harmonisation and standardisation of the education and training systems in the Region, which is the ultimate objective of the Protocol on Education and Training (SADC, 1997).

The policy of using Portuguese alone as the official medium of instruction after independence also introduced a permanent conflict between the parents and their children. The children were educated in Portuguese at school while, at the same time, their parents were participating in a literacy programme taught in local languages. The parents had the feeling that their children were losing their local culture and customs because they were learning more about foreign cultures in a foreign language. Many children dropped out of school very early because they could not achieve proficiency in the Portuguese language, which was in effect a barrier to their understanding of all other subject areas. The parents, meanwhile, could not help their children at home because they also lacked proficiency in Portuguese.

In retrospect, it appeared to many educationists that introducing the Portuguese language as the unique language of education had increased the barrier between the Portuguese-speaking people living in cities and the rural people speaking Mozambican languages. In the end, the imposition of the Portuguese language, rather than having served to support the unity of the country as intended in 1975, was seen to have reinforced social, cultural, and economic divisions instead. This stimulated the introduction of local languages in the new curriculum, featuring the consideration of the introduction of a bilingual programme as one of the main changes. Introducing education in local languages was proposed for the first years of elementary school, in addition to the introduction of more local cultural elements in the curriculum and, finally, the gradual introduction of the Portuguese language in the elementary school programme. Members and delegates of civil society from rural areas proposed the bilingual programme during the national forums on the curriculum change process.[6] Yet it must be stated that even now, the bilingual programme is not really the priority of some actors, especially the elite of the nation who were educated as assimilados or children of assimilados. Given the complexity of the issue and the persistent linguistic tensions,

> [i]t is imperative to define a policy that establishes, among other things, the principle of equality of all national languages. But this should not be understood as denying, or relativising, the importance of Portuguese which, in many cases, is a point where the various cosmic visions and cultures that shape Mozambican society meet, communicate and enter into dialogue. For many people, Portuguese has become endogenous and expresses the construction of a Mozambican identity. It is also through this language that Mozambicans have access to the scientific and technological knowledge accumulated by humanity. It is in Portuguese that Mozambique expresses itself and is heard in the concert of nations.
>
> (UNDP, 2000, citing Juvane and Buendia)

With this perspective, we can analyse the curriculum change of the National Education System as a paradoxical process: continuity at the level of political discourse and rupture regarding the approach taken toward establishing the content of the various subjects. The political discourse continues to speak of curriculum change in order to reinforce national unity and to celebrate the Mozambican culture. Yet the main point of departure from the past is that elements considered previously as possible causes of division (local languages) and elements of obscurantism (local cultures) are introduced in the new curriculum as focal points aimed at reinforcing the national identity.

The direction of curriculum change

Compared to the current curriculum, in addition to being more relevant and of more practical use, the new curriculum is less rigid and prescriptive, leaving room for local, cultural, and linguistic aspects to be addressed, while simultaneously reinforcing national unity and the integration Mozambique into the southern African region. The New Curriculum seeks to introduce the following innovations:

1. *Learning cycles*: Learning units aimed at developing specific skills and competences in the pupil. The curriculum has seven grades organised into two levels. The first level is divided into two learning cycles, the first corresponding to grades one and two and the second corresponding to grades three, four, and five. The second level corresponds to grades six and seven and comprises the third learning cycle. In the current curriculum, learning units correspond to each grade.

2. *Integrated learning in basic education*: Developing students' skills, knowledge, and values in learning areas in an articulated and integrated manner. Learning content is organised on the basis of an integrated approach to the various thematic units and subjects.

3. *Localised curriculum*: Twenty percent of each subject's total teaching time is allocated to school-based local curriculum, taking into account the local knowledge of communities.

4. *Introduction of Mozambican languages into the teaching/learning*: There will be three modalities: a bilingual education programme, and two modalities of a monolingual education programme.

    a. *Bilingual Education Programme*: Simultaneous teaching in both Portuguese and in Mozambican languages. During the first three years the number of courses taught in Mozambican languages is dominant. After the third year this begins to shift to an increasing number of courses taught in Portuguese, and by the sixth year instruction in Portuguese is dominant (to the same degree that instruction in Mozambican languages was dominant in the first year).

    b. *Monolingual Education Programme(s) in two modalities*:

        (1) Portuguese is the language of instruction. Mozambican languages are used as a resource (to explain difficult concepts not first grasped in the language of instruction). The Mozambican languages are not taught as a subject (or second language) (unless they are chosen optionally in the sixth and seventh years).

        (2) Portuguese is the language of instruction. Mozambican languages are taught (separately) as a subject.

5. *Introduction of English*: Begun in the third learning cycle (grades six and seven) to enable the pupil to develop a basic vocabulary.

6. *Introduction of crafts as a subject*: Applied to all of the learning cycles to develop the practical activities necessary for the pupil's integration into his/her community.

7. *Introduction of moral and civic education as a subject*: Aims to develop students' respect for moral, patriotic, civic, and religious values.

Mozambican languages in the new curriculum

Perhaps the most important change introduced as part of the new curriculum is the introduction of Mozambican languages. For the introduction of Mozambican languages in the National Educational System, the new curriculum adopted the process discussed below.

Bilingual Education Programme:
Mozambican languages as media of instruction and Portuguese as a subject

The bilingual model adopted has taken into account the structure of primary education organised into three learning cycles. Of the several existing models, Mozambique has opted for a transitional model with some maintenance characteristics, in order to guarantee the development of progressive bilingualism in the pupils; the model will be developed as shown in Figure 2.

For the first learning cycle (grades one and two), the pupil's mother tongue is the only medium of instruction, with both the mother tongue and Portuguese taught as subjects. Portuguese will help to develop oral skills in order to prepare for the acquisition of reading and writing skills in the Portuguese language later in the second cycle.

During the second learning cycle (grades three to five), the process of gradual transition of the medium of instruction from the first language (L1) to the second language (L2) will be initiated. At the beginning of grade three, pupils will start acquiring reading and writing skills in Portuguese through a process of transfer of skills acquired in L1. In grade three, the medium of instruction is still L1, while L2 is the medium of instruction from grade four onward. L1 and L2 are taught as subjects in the second cycle, much like they are in the first cycle. L1 continues to be auxiliary of the teaching-learning process in order to explain and clarify difficult concepts, particularly in subjects such as mathematics, natural sciences, and social sciences. In the fifth grade, pupils of the bilingual curriculum will be subject to a national examination together with pupils who have followed the monolingual Portuguese curriculum. It is expected that these pupils already possess the necessary competences to successfully pass this examination and explains why the linguistic transition occurs relatively early in the process, starting from grade three. The examination at the end of the second cycle (grade five) is a transitory measure, because it is foreseen that when complete primary education (grades one to seven) is implemented throughout the country, there will be only one national examination at the end of grade seven. During this period, transition of media of instruction will occur from fourth grade, but a more important role for L1 will be maintained in order to provide for the development of a more balanced bilingualism.

Figure 2: Transitional Model of Bilingualism in Primary Education: Time allocation for L1 and L2 as media and subjects of instruction

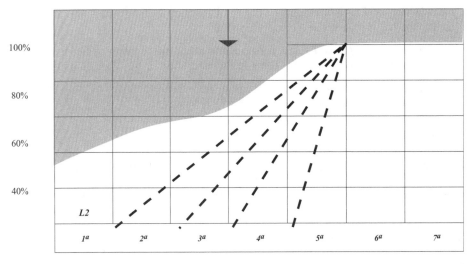

During the third learning cycle (grades six and seven), the Portuguese language will be the only medium of instruction, and it is expected that the pupils will already possess a sound mastery of both Portuguese and L1. L1 will continue to be taught as a subject only and should eventually serve, as in previous learning cycles, as an auxiliary in the teaching-learning process. At the end of this third cycle, the pupils will have to take a national examination that provides certification for the completion of basic schooling. It is expected that students will have acquired the necessary fluency in Portuguese to undertake the subsequent post-obligatory education and training. As the official language, Portuguese is the only medium of instruction at subsequent levels of education. Moreover, it is also the language that allows entry into the job market, as well as access to other national institutions. Given the dominant position of Portuguese in social, economic, and political life, it is crucial for the pupils to fully master this language by the end of the basic education. Alongside competency and fluency in Portuguese, it is expected that the pupils who completed the basic schooling cycle should possess sound linguistic skills in their mother tongue—skills in L1 that would serve as pedagogical supports for a positive transfer of linguistic skills so as to acquire literacy in L2.

Monolingual programme:
Mozambican languages as resources and Portuguese as second language

Another modality for the introduction of Mozambican mother tongues is to consider them as auxiliaries of the teaching-learning process in the monolingual programme in Portuguese (L2). There are two main rationales for the adoption of such a strategy: First, the adoption of the bilingual education model foresees the use of L1 as an auxiliary for the teaching-learning process, mainly from grade four, where the main medium of instruction becomes the Portuguese language. Second, from the pedagogical point of view, the ideal situation would be to ensure that initial literacy skill acquisition is in the mother tongue. However, economic and logistic constraints are such that programmes of bilingual education will not be able to cover the whole country in the short or medium term. We should therefore conceive a strategy in which local languages are used as auxiliaries of the teaching-learning process, especially in rural areas where Portuguese is almost not used at all. This is why it is advocated to use these languages as a resource, with appropriate methodologies.

Monolingual programme:
Mozambican languages as the subjects and Portuguese taught as the second language

Mozambique is a country that possesses, like many other African countries, linguistically homogeneous areas (mostly rural) and heterogeneous ones (urban and peri-urban areas). Several cultures and, consequently, several languages converge in these areas, and the pupils there speak Portuguese as the mother tongue or the L2. In linguistic contexts of this nature it is not possible to apply the proposed model of bilingual education, because its application presupposes that the pupils and the teacher share the same language.

However, it is equally assumed that the students can gain access to the local languages, as a way of establishing or maintaining contact with the Mozambican culture. Another reason that justifies this option is that it increases the effectiveness of the communication in a multilingual context, and contributes to the reinforcement of national unity on the basis of respect for cultural diversities and identities. It is in this context that the third modality of use of these languages is introduced in the teaching-learning process, as a curricular subject. In this case, the language will be chosen by the school itself; it can be a local language (of the area) or not.

Pedagogical innovations

Innovations in the approach to the structure and content of the new curriculum also reflect the effort to promote a culture of peace even if they have not been explicitly formulated as a response to the conflict. In large part, this is reflected through a pedagogical shift. To date, the main characteristic of the national pedagogical tradition in Mozambique has been the recognised authority of the teacher in the classroom: teaching dominates, and the pupils are not seen as being at the centre of the learning process. The students have to listen while the teacher is teaching, and they have to do the homework the teacher assigns. There is no possibility for them to take initiative during lessons. Nor do the teachers have any margin for freedom and creativity, as they strictly follow a very detailed and prescriptive curriculum and are assessed on their students' achievement of it. Mirroring this relationship is the Ministry of Education, used to sending instructions to school directors who, in turn, tell the teachers to implement them.

The new curriculum, on the other hand, promotes a different pedagogy that places the pupils at the centre of the entire teaching-learning process. For this to be possible, the teacher cannot continue to dominate, but must instead facilitate a learning process based on communication in which the learner is actively involved. The main challenge is to (re)train teachers to perform their new tasks as facilitators with active methods. The teachers will have the opportunity to be more creative and to take more initiative, although this does imply a corresponding change in attitude. Teacher training centres have to review and revise their curriculum in order to bring teachers up to date in the spirit of the new challenges. They have to organise workshops aimed at improving the competencies of the teachers who are working in elementary schools, because the majority of those teachers are not qualified and many have only the equivalent of a primary school certificate. Without improving their capacity to master the content of their courses and the strategies of the teaching-learning process, Mozambique cannot succeed in enhancing the quality of education.

Some issues are considered to be priorities, and the new curriculum has introduced new elements into schooling in Mozambique. Girls' education is one of those priorities. By building up a maximum of schools in rural areas and by recruiting and training as many female teachers as possible, the government hopes that parents will be more receptive to the idea of sending their daughters to school. Other decisions were also made, such as allowing pregnant girls to continue their education in public schools, increasing the sanctions against teachers who commit sexual abuses on their pupils, and developing gender-sensitive content across different curriculum disciplines.[7]

The approach of the contents on sexual and reproductive health and the prevention of STD/HIV/AIDS was discussed too, especially as a subject of sex education in the schools, taking into account the curricula of Portugal, Brazil, and Nigeria. A workshop was organised in September 2002 aimed at adjusting the curriculum to a new approach toward sexual and reproductive health, STD/HIV/AIDS, in all the disciplines from grades one to seven. Contents were defined for each level of the primary school, in order to get a general view at the level of the basic education curriculum. The work developed by INDE/MINED in this area is part of the global strategy of prevention and combating of STD/HIV/AIDS.

POLICY DIALOGUE AND CONSENSUS BUILDING

Modalities of consultation and participation in policy reform

We would like to outline the two dominant modalities of consultation for policymaking discussions. The first is characterised by meetings with experts and the staff of the Ministry of Education in order to study problems, produce very technical reports, and adopt political decisions according to the conclusions and recommendations of the experts and educational officers. The second possibility is that of a large consultation of the population through their representatives at different levels (villages, districts, provinces, government) and from different areas of the country. Both modalities have been developed and used in the process of designing the new curriculum. The following stakeholders have been implicated through the process, and each group or council had its members, tasks, and levels of intervention well defined.

Directive Council
(Conselho Directivo do Ministério da Educação)

Participants: The political-administrative leadership composed of the minister, vice minister, secretary general, national directors, and provincial directors of the Ministry of Education.

Role: Internal MINED ownership, decisionmaking, and validation
- to define the educational policy instructions to which the Basic Education Curriculum Change has to refer;
- to assure the articulation of the Curriculum Change Project with the other issues of the Educational Strategic Plan;
- to select the participants to the National Forum for Curriculum Change; and
- to approve the Basic Curriculum Plans, textbooks, and materials and ensure their wide publication and distribution to all the national educational institutions.

National Forum
(Fórum Nacional de Consulta para a Transformação Curricular)

Participants: MINED, civil society, and wider expert opinionmakers: members of the Ministry of Education, Educational Commission, Parliament, vice chancellors of universities, delegates of main religious congregations, political and social personalities from provinces, delegates of main national NGOs, and delegates of Mozambican factories and trade unions.

Role: Wider social consultation for consensus and approval

- to elaborate proposals related to the Learning Basic Needs for the Mozambican population;
- to elaborate proposals related to the enhancement of the drafts of the different curricular materials already developed;
- to create a consensus about the sensitive curriculum contents; and
- to contribute to the validation of different produced curricular materials.

Curriculum Change Co-ordination Commission
(Comissão Coordenadora da Transformação Curricular)

Participants: MINED, INDE: project director (INDE director), vice director, coordinator of the Pedagogical Area (INDE member), coordinator of the Teaching Area (INDE member), researcher specialised in Education Area (INDE member), and donors: (Netherlands), UNESCO.

Role: Technical decisionmaking and technical consensus assurance

- to propose and execute the process of selection of the INDE personnel and others coming from other places in order to elaborate the issues and necessary written products;
- to ensure the designing and quality of the written products and their realisation within the allotted time;
- to coordinate INDE technical teams in the process of the production of the curriculum material, and of the research issues directly linked to the project;
- to plan and organise the meetings of the National Forum, the meetings of the Coordinator Commission, and the training of the National Group for Curriculum Change; and
- to present quarterly Reports on the Project Process.

Project steering committee
(Comité de Acompanhamento do Projecto)

Participants: The government representative, donor countries, the INDE, CTA (chief technical advisers), and UNESCO.

Role: To assess project activities

- to determine the reasons for adjustments at the project level;
- to suggest necessary measures in order to solve the problems and promote the project enhancement;
- to prepare the semestral project reports; and
- to plan detailed semestral activities.

National Curriculum Management Team
(Comité Directivo da Transformação Curricular)

Participants: the INDE, CTAs (chief technical advisers), and key implementers: project director (INDE), project vice director, coordinator of the Pedagogical Area, coordinator of the Teaching Area, experienced researcher, Basic Education national director, Planning national director, director of the Institute for Teachers' Skills Improvement, and chiefs of the Provincial Pedagogical Departments.

Role: Technical decisionmaking and technical consensus assurance

- to select the national groups in charge of promoting the area of curriculum change;
- to ensure the collection of the contributions and suggestions of the national groups in charge of promoting the area of curriculum change;
- to elaborate textbooks and all the necessary materials in relation to the training-participation-action activities; and
- to ensure the execution of workshops and capacity-building activities on curriculum management at the level of the provinces.

Technical groups
(Grupos técnicos)

Participants: INDE personnel coached by consultants specialised in different areas.

Role: Technical materials production

- to elaborate curriculum materials of the curriculum change process, incorporating experienced teachers;
- to produce methodologies, instruments of data collection, reports, and other issues of research (national and international) for the curriculum change process; and
- to integrate into the curriculum the consensus realised through the consultation structures.

Provincial Curriculum Transformation Groups
(Grupos Provinciais Para a Transformação Curricular)

Participants: Thirty provincial "consultants" plus approximately 363 people at a national level whose composition was of twenty-two technicians from the Provincial Pedagogical Directions; forty-one inspectors from the Ministry of Education; 130 educational officers of the Ministry of Education, more or less one per district; twenty-two pilot school directors; and 150 teachers selected according to their experience and recognised by their colleagues (one per district).

Role: Design and implementation feedback and feed-forward at the provincial level

- to promote the curriculum change in the provinces using appropriate strategies for each of the stages and activities;
- to ensure the consultation of ideas in the process of curriculum change; and
- to give support to INDE technicians regarding the actual experiences of using the drafts of the curriculum materials.

There has been consultation at a provincial level, where the thirty different provincial "consultants" were representative of different categories of stakeholders from the village to the level of each province. Forums were organised at the national level with delegates from each province, reflecting political, economic, social, cultural, religious, and academic interests. Forum participants had to give their opinions in working documents at the beginning of the process of consultations in each province separately, and then again at the national level. Those working documents were prepared by groups of experts from the INDE or independent educational officers. The experts had and still have a technical role of producing working documents or other technical material, or supervising the implementation of pilot experimentations of the curriculum in some schools. The third group, the decisionmaking group—mainly composed of representatives from the Ministry of Education (and the Directive Council), the INDE, donors, and international organisations such as UNESCO (Steering Committee)—makes decisions concerning political and financial decisions, which are the most important in the curriculum change process.

Figure 3: Executive Structure of the Curriculum Project Management

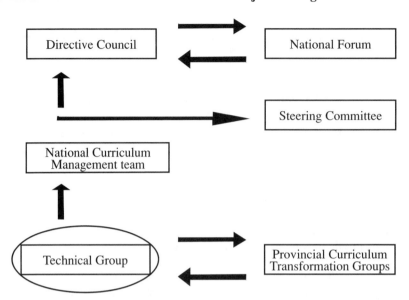

The consensus building was presented as a strategy of the process of the basic education curriculum change. That strategy aimed at identifying the needs and demands of the civil society at the level of basic education. Consensus was reached at the level of three National Consultative Forums organised during the process of the basic education curriculum change, establishing representative criteria for its political, economic, social, religious, academic, and cultural participants. The functions of those forums were to channel the aspirations of civil society as they related to Basic Education and to create a consensus about the basic aspects of the curriculum reform that could ensure national unity defined by cultural and linguistic diversity in a multiparty regime.

However, according to external assessments undertaken during the process, the consensus building was relatively weak at the provincial and local level, because the teachers neither concretely nor actively participated in the process and the implication of the communities was reduced to the bare minimum. There was no systematic recording of discordant voices at different levels, nor of the alternative proposals related to the approach to sensitive questions (with regard to the sixteen-year war, the official holidays and commemorative days, and national heroes, for example) or to recent history (including the struggle for national liberation, the introduction of the Mozambican languages in the schooling process, and sex education, among other issues).

To some, participation in the national forums was aimed at just confirming the predetermined questions, validating the materials already approved at a central level, and receiving clarification about some specific questions. For these critics, the complex structure built up around the consultative process was essentially window dressing. However, as this strategy was used for the first time in the history of curriculum development in Mozambique, perhaps it would be fairer to point out that the Ministry of Education and the INDE were unused to public consultation in building a consensual curriculum that reflects national realities, and that they undertook the effort to the best of their ability and with good intentions.

Introducing Mozambican languages

Mozambique is a multicultural and multilingual country with some twenty Mozambican languages, all of Bantu origin and all with their respective variations in dialects (each language has about four or five dialects). These languages coexist with Portuguese, the official language and until now the only officially recognised language of instruction. All the Mozambican Bantu languages have recently adopted a written form, and eighteen have a standardised spelling.

Portuguese was the only language of instruction in official schools since the time of colonisation, and at independence FRELIMO chose to extend this to all the schools, for which there was only one admitted curriculum. The first debate was about the possibility of introducing Mozambican languages into the new curriculum. The elite and the educational officers who had participated in designing the post-independence curriculum were opposed to this idea and wanted to maintain the status quo, that is, to have Portuguese as the only language of instruction. Members of civil society and representatives of the rural areas wanted the Mozambican languages to be introduced into the new curriculum. They were sensitive to the fact that Portuguese was becoming an element of division between rural and urban Mozambican people instead of reinforcing national unity, as it had been intended to at the end of the liberation war.

To select a medium of instruction in urban or rural areas was the second subject of debate, and it was not an easy task. The diversity of languages and the ways in which people are dispersed throughout the country complicated the process of decisionmaking, especially given the principle that decisions should be a matter of consensus. It was seen to be important that the curriculum be negotiated with the main interested parties in appropriate forums. In the end, it was decided to introduce sixteen languages in the initial phase according to the main criteria of national coverage. In other words, the languages cover virtually the whole country so no province is excluded in this phase. Ultimately, however, it is the rural areas that are more concerned by this shift in policy. In urban areas, the Portuguese language will continue to be taught and will dominate because the mixture of populations coming from different rural areas, who speak different Mozambican languages, make it difficult to choose one indigenous language over another.

> The sixteen chosen languages already have written materials, including textbooks, and some already have standardised spelling. Civil society is demanding additional languages in the initial phase, and other Mozambican languages will also be gradually introduced once the appropriate conditions have been created. As Juvane and Buendia point out, however, there is still no social consensus on how to manage the relationship between the various languages that exist in Mozambique. In practice, the country faces a dilemma of an unbalanced and competitive co-existence between the ex-colonial language and the indigenous African languages.
> (UNDP, 2000)

Nevertheless, we must insist that the adoption of Mozambican languages as teaching tools in the Basic Education Curriculum Change reflects an unprecedented shift of perspective in linguistic and cultural policy and planning in Mozambique. This important decision is seen as having an additional, secondary impact, in that it may affect the high dropout rate, which in many instances is seen as related to linguistic-cultural factors that influence learning at school.

Restructuring curriculum content

Social sciences

The introduction of social sciences represents a new concept in the curriculum. It includes history, moral and civic education, and geography. At the primary level, all of these subjects are to be taught in an integrated manner. The concepts of the different subjects, in other words, are not to be handled in an isolated manner, but in a specific context based on the thematic unit. The role of the social sciences in the context of basic education, according to the social science curriculum, is to contribute to the civic education of the citizens, so they can live well integrated into the environment, and participate actively in the social and economic development of the country.

In the first learning cycle, the contents of the social sciences (including the cross-curricular approach of the moral and civic education) are integrated in all the disciplines. In the second learning cycle, in the third grade, some contents of geography are approached in the discipline of natural science, while the others are taught by the remaining disciplines. Starting from grade four, the social sciences are treated as a separate discipline. Mozambique as a whole is studied in grade six. In the third learning cycle, grades six and seven, the African continent is approached in its physical, economic, social, and historical aspects.

Moral and civic education

Although moral and civic education does not appear as a subject in the first and second cycles, it is a crosscutting issue in all subjects and grades. In the third cycle of the basic education, while maintaining their crosscutting character, it is also a specific subject with its own place in the timetable. This subject aims at developing values, attitudes, and skills for good relationships based on democratic principles and respect for human rights. From a historical perspective, the introduction of this subject in the new curriculum responds to the demands of the recent changes in the political, social, and economic system in Mozambican society and in a context of globalisation. However, it would be important to analyse the selection and organisation of the subject matter, and the integration of local sociocultural aspects. According to the teaching programme, this discipline aims at

- recognising the importance of good behaviour in the family, at school, and in the community;
- recognising the school as the place that completes and enlarges capacities and life skills;
- understanding that human relations are determined through rights and duties;
- developing love and the patriotic spirit of being proud of national unity; and
- assuming the importance of solidarity between Mozambique and other countries.

In the current curriculum, the issue of religion is handled in a similarly integrated manner in the social sciences. Religion does not have special treatment as a separate content, but is addressed from the viewpoint of respect for freedom of religious expression and identification of the various religions present in Mozambique.

History

Regarding the subject of history, it was difficult to reach a consensus on the interpretation of some historical events in order to define contents for the different levels. Among the sensitive events were, for instance, the civil war, some festivals and commemorative dates, and the definition of national heroes. These subjects have been seriously discussed among the different consultation organs. Despite considered deliberations, it was clear that it was still much too early to open deepened debates and interpretations on such subjects; as long as that remains the case, an approach of omission has been proposed. Analysing the curricula of the second and third cycles, we verified that the previously foreseen approach of the contents of those subjects was simply eliminated. This is probably a sign that things were discussed and continue to be discussed in very specialised circles of academics and politicians. However, there is no publicity around these discussions, because no consensus even among these smaller consultative groups has yet been reached.

After independence all Mozambican schools followed the same curriculum, but the changes in the socialist world affected the contents in Mozambican schools, mainly in the subjects of geography and history. The peace agreement of 1992 and the climate of democracy caused some disparities on approaches to the contents related to history, language, and the unified policy of the country. For instance, a small number of teachers refused to talk about FRELIMO history or heroes and its role in the independence process, or to sing the former national hymn.

PILOTING AND MONITORING IMPLEMENTATION OF NEW CURRICULUM

Pilot programmes

On the whole, teaching programmes using the new curriculum are well structured, have relevant content, and have clear pedagogical guidelines. Whereas the pedagogical tradition focussed on the teacher as the centre of the teaching-learning process and did not give methodological suggestions but only prescriptions, that tradition no longer corresponds to the spirit of the new curriculum, which is centred on the pupils and open to teacher-pupil creativity and cooperation.

Regarding the pilot projects, two groups were involved in different but complementary activities. The implementation group was responsible for training and pedagogically supporting the involved teachers, through training sessions, seminars, the elaboration of didactic materials, and participative support to the teaching-learning process. The monitoring group, composed of trainers from teacher training centres, was in charge of accompanying and monitoring the trials. Using ethnographic and not participative observation techniques, it had to describe and analyse the teaching-learning process in these schools.

In October 2002, the monitoring group presented the following results of their observations recorded from May to September 2002 to the implementation group.[8] These observations could be grouped around the general categories of student achievement, teachers' capacity to deal with new pedagogical approaches and organisation of learning content, and lack of adequate teacher support.

- Student achievement:

  o first-grade pupils' results are better compared to those of the third- and sixth-grade pupils;

  o first-grade pupils already know how to read and to write simple sentences; and

  o results of the rural schools are better than those of the urban districts.

- Teachers' capacities:

  o in some cases, teachers have difficulties using the local languages as a resource;

  o teachers are very dependent on the textbooks, and they do not adapt the existent materials to the draft/trial curriculum;

  o teachers do not motivate the pupils to develop mental arithmetic;

  o lessons of visual education and occupations are usually theoretical;

  o teacher-pupil and pupil-teacher interaction does not exist;

  o answers to the teacher's questions are given in chorus much of the time; and

  o work in groups doesn't constitute practice in the classrooms.

- Lack of adequate training and support:

  o there are no libraries in the schools for teachers' consultation;

  o no training was developed for the teachers of music and English;

  o teachers have difficulties accomplishing the integration of different disciplines in their classes;

  o teachers have difficulties integrating the local curriculum into the planning of their lessons; and

  o implementation teams do not regularly attend the classes, and there is no support from the District and Provincial Education Directions.

The monitoring group considered that these field observations correspond to the expectations from the implementation group. They reinforce the need for an increased presence and greater support to the teachers from the INDE and the Ministry of Education in general, but also from the District and Provincial Education Directions.

The problem of teacher training has exacerbated many other identified problems, such as multidisciplinary integration issues, the development of local curriculum, visual education and skills, and the application of the participative learning techniques. The results mentioned above indicate that the in-service teacher training offered by the INDE and the Ministry of Education in the pilot schools was not successful in making up the knowledge deficit, the methodological gaps, and the resistance to the active and participative pedagogical practices. The new programmes, while necessary, are not sufficient in themselves for the overall transformation of the basic education curriculum. Aspects such as teacher training, better working conditions in schools and better living conditions for teachers, and the creation of small school libraries, among others, are essential for the success of the new curriculum.

A key question, therefore, remains: Will the government's budget be able to afford to address these problems without neglecting others such as education for all children (especially for girls), the building of elementary schools in every village, the building of secondary and professional schools in many districts according to their needs, the extension of literacy programmes wherever necessary, and the creation of connections between formal and nonformal education?

Monitoring policy and practice: Identifying indicators of change

The new curriculum has not yet been implemented. The nationwide implementation of the newly developed curriculum is scheduled for January 2004. The monitoring group is currently divided into two subgroups in charge of monitoring the pilot schools. The first is composed of the INDE educational officers, who monitor all pilot schools and provide some training and support to the pilot schools' teachers in order to allow them to deal with the new curricular approach both through team teaching in the classrooms and through workshops. The second monitoring subgroup, supervised by the Faculty of Education of University Eduardo Mondlane, is composed of classroom observers coming from the teacher training colleges for primary schools. These trainers have to observe classes and to inform the university supervisors as follow-up.

Probing perspectives of youth

Piloting of the newly designed Basic Education Curriculum was initiated in January 2002 in the first, third, and sixth grades and extended to the second, fourth, and seventh grades in January 2003. Pilot trials will begin in the fifth grade in 2004 and will be extended to all grade levels nationwide.

Bearing in mind that this only constitutes the initial phases of pilot implementation, it is important to document the way in which pupils perceive the relevance of the new curriculum. We have therefore investigated the opinions expressed by seventh-grade students[9] in pilot schools as to the changes they have experienced in the curriculum since the previous school year. The students identified a number of changes, indicating a significant shift toward more active teaching and learning processes, including

- increased group work;
- field trips and study visits;
- practical activities related to local curriculum content involving members of the local community;
- increased teacher emphasis on local culture and knowledge; and
- development of practical and vocational skills training.

In addition to the above, students were very interested in the introduction of the English language in their cycle. They consider English to be very important to their futures in terms of potential integration into the labour market. As far as social sciences are concerned, students consider the introduction of "moral and civic education" to be positive because they believe it is important to develop such values as respect, peace, culture, democracy, and human rights. However, because teachers continue to deal with history and geography as distinct subject areas rather than one integrated area of learning, students have not responded well to the changes. This is consistent with the general observation that aspects related to the thematic and multidisciplinary integration were not mentioned by the students interviewed. This appears to suggest that teachers do not yet succeed at integrating one particular thematic content into a variety of different disciplines or, conversely, that the pupils do not yet understand the way in which this is being done. Finally, students' observations reveal that some teachers do their best to put the pupils at the centre of the teaching-learning process and that the more practical and active aspects are welcomed by the pupils.

It is necessary to say that the trial of the New Basic Education Curriculum has been undertaken without updating the didactic material used by the pupils and the teachers, who are still using the textbooks and guides for the old curriculum. This situation creates clashes with some introduced innovations and methodologies. For example, in social studies—a fusion of geography and history, and an innovation of the new curriculum—the two different textbooks of the old curriculum, geography and history, are used. Neither the students' Portuguese textbooks nor those of any other courses have integrated subjects. To try to resolve this situation, the INDE sent schools some complementary teachers' materials. But those materials need research efforts in order to achieve their thematic and multidisciplinary integration.

Students' perspectives on the relevance of the content and pedagogy of the new curriculum will be an important source of ongoing assessment of the curriculum implementation starting in 2004.

CONCLUSION

The recent history of Mozambique is dominated by two armed conflicts that were not ethnic but, instead, anticolonial and ideological. The first one was a national struggle for freedom from Portuguese colonialism and the attendant educational system, and for the construction of new citizens liberated from the obscurantism of African traditions. The second conflict had more to do with the international context of the cold war and had dramatic consequences for education in terms of the destruction of school infrastructure and equipment and the voluntary or forced enrolment of young pupils, students, and teachers in the fighting.

The local economic crisis and the international and regional political changes forced the two belligerents to sign a peace agreement and to start a new era. As peace was reestablished, the transformation of the Basic Education Curriculum that had already begun was finally able to receive the sustained support it needed. It was important to strengthen the national identity through the introduction of Mozambican languages and local issues in the new curriculum. It was similarly crucial to open the country to the regional contacts through the introduction of English in primary school and to prepare young Mozambicans for successful lives in the event that they do not continue their studies after primary school.

The interpretation and introduction of the issue of Mozambique's recent history in the new curriculum remain controversial. However, as the country is reinforcing the climate of peace and strengthening the structures and processes of democracy, there is hope that the former combatants, with the support of the wider society, will continue to be peace builders, and that they will be able to reach a consensus concerning a legitimate interpretation of recent history. Currently, the new curriculum is seen to represent an opportunity for Mozambicans to go deeper in finding and reinforcing ways toward national unity.

The process of curriculum change has involved many stakeholders in various meetings and forums. They have participated, as representatives of many different categories of the

Mozambican population, in dialogues and debates in order to get a significant consensus about the necessary innovations to be introduced in primary schools. Those representatives, as well as the teachers, the pupils, and the parents, are now waiting for the implementation of the new curriculum in January 2004.

We would like to offer that the following are the incipient challenges facing the Mozambican government:

- How do we consolidate the acquired place for local languages, cultures, and realities in the national curriculum?
- Where can we find enough resources to train teachers and enhance their social conditions so that they can quickly replace unqualified teachers and those who are dying from HIV/AIDS?
- How do we increase the number of new well-equipped schools and achieve the capacity to freely implement the national education policy, without depending too much on donors?

Recommendations

The goal of the new curriculum is that it be both dynamic and open to changes, in order to improve the preparation of the pupils for real life. The new approach is meant to give confidence, particularly as related to local curriculum and crafts. These aspects would allow pupils to learn issues for immediate use, and school leavers could find ways to participate in community life.

Language policy

The instructional language and the local curriculum remain complex points. It is not clear why it is so hard to get funding for the project related to bilingual pilot programmes. It seems that the donors and members of the elite do not appreciate the integration of the local language and culture into the official curriculum. Educational policies about local languages as mediums of instruction or subject should be gradually introduced, due to issues of pedagogical and organisational difficulties.

Teacher training

Another critical component should be the teachers' training level, mainly concerning qualifications, because of the deep changes being introduced. The difficulty of addressing this situation is caused by the great disparity between the number of students that teacher training colleges should admit and the low number of tenth-grade leavers qualified to apply. One group of students could be enrolled in order to prepare to become teachers while another group—the large number of teachers who are already teaching in schools and are not yet appropriately qualified to implement the new curriculum, either in terms of newly introduced content or methodologies—could be in a special programme. We cannot, furthermore, speak of teachers and not mention the fact that many of them are victims of HIV/AIDS and that the recruitment and training of new teachers should take into account the very important number of those teachers who are dying very young.

Ensuring relevance of curriculum content at both national and local levels

The current curriculum of Basic Education is seen as theoretical because it is not very well linked to current realities and local life. It is necessary to change society's view of the relevance of schooling. The new curriculum hopes to achieve this by having adopted a design that gives more attention to both national *and* local issues. Moreover, there will be regular revisions to update the curriculum. This means that all of the stakeholders should be interested by what is happening in the school, the place where the future of the village and the nation is continuously and progressively designed.

The role of donors

Finally, Mozambique has to deal with its large dependency on foreign donors. Perhaps donor dependency is not reflected as much in terms of policymaking because the Ministry of Education is supposed to be guided by the Government Programme where both quality and the expansion of education are the main aims. Donors are not supposed to define the policy options available to the Ministry of Education. However, it is important to note that the ministry cannot follow through with all of its planned activities, because of the lack of human and financial resources. As an example, the bilingual education programme and the related teaching learning materials suffer from a lack of funding.

Endnotes

[1] Please see UNDP National Human Development Report on Mozambique, 2000, as an additional reference on this issue. The report is available at http://www.sardc.net/HDev/MHDR2000/Eng/Chapter3/index.html. See, in particular, chapter 3 and its special contributions.

[2] Communication with Roy Carr-Hill, October 2003.

[3] Article 2 of Frelimo Party Programme and Statutes.

[4] "Assessing the limitations of the impact of the 1983 educational reform is to recognise the pertinence of the critical positions and arguments which at the time advised against introducing a new educational system. These positions were based on findings on the ground which showed that the appropriate organisational and institutional conditions to guarantee a successful education reform did not yet exist. Here, as in other areas, the political will overrode the technical rationale." UNDP, 2000, National Human Development Report on Mozambique.

[5] See, for example, the following references of studies carried out by the INDE such as Martins, Z., 1993, analysing regional and gender disparities through promotion rates in primary education; Palme, M., 1993, evaluating teaching materials in general issues for lower primary education; Hyltenstam and Stroud, C., 1993, evaluating teaching materials in language issues for lower primary education; and Kilborn, W., 1993, evaluating teaching materials in mathematics for lower primary education.

[6] Please see section on *Modalities of consultation and participation in policy reform* for a more in depth discussion.

[7] Gender-sensitive content development includes promotion of the girl s statute, prevention of pregnancies and sexual diseases including HIV/AIDS, and girls participation in political, economic, and social life.

[8] Antuia Soverano, 2002, "Síntese da avaliação nas escolas de experimentação," Grupo de avaliação.

[9] Data collected in an urban pilot school.

References

Benson, C. (2000.) "The Primary Bilingual Education Experiment in Mozambique, 1993–1997," *International Journal of Bilingual Education and Bilingualism, Multilingual Matters*.

Buletin da Republica nº 19, série. (1992.) *Lei 6/92 de 6 de Maio: Sistema Nacional de Educação*. Maputo: Imprensa Nacional.

Capece, J. A. (2001.) *O resgate do saber das comunidades locais para a melhoria da qualidade od ensino de Ciências Naturais do primeiro grau do nível primário, em Moçambique*. Pontifícia Universidade Católica de São Paulo, Tese de Douturamento.

Dias, H. N. (2002.) *As desigualidades sociolinguísticas e o fracasso escolar em direcção a uma prática linguístico-escolar libertadora*. Maputo: Promédia.

Gomez, M. B. (1999.) *Educação Moçambicana—História de um Processo: 1984–1992*. Maputo: Livraria universitária.

Governo de Moçambique—*Plano quinquenal do Governo, 2000–2004*.

Guro, M. Z. (1999.) *Os estudantes dos Centros de Formação de Professores Primários em Mozambique*. Maputo: INDE, Cadernos de Pesquisa nº 29.

Guz, A. da. (2000.) *Education for All: The Year 2000 Assessment Report of Mozambique*. Report prepared for the World Education Forum of Dakar, Senegal, April 26–28, 2000. Available at http://www2.unesco.org/wef/countryreports/mozambique/contents.html.

INDE. (2001a.) *Relatório do Seminário sobre a produção do livro escolar do Ensino Básico*.

———. (2001b.) *Relatório do Workshop Regional sobre a Reforma do Ensino Secundário em África*.

———. (1999a.) *Programas do Ensino Básico. 1º, 2º e 3º ciclos*.

———. (1999b.) *Relatório do II Fórum Nacional de Consulta à Sociedade Civil sobre a Transformação Curricular*.

———. (1998.) *Melhoria da Eficácia da Reforma e Desenvolvimento Curricular*.

———. (1997a.) *Relatório do Debate sobre "Estratégias de Introdução e Expansão do Ensino em línguas moçambicanas."*

———. (1997b.) *Síntese dos Principais Problemas e Recomendações Apresentados em Estudos de Diagnósticos sobre o Ensino Básico em Moçambique*.

———. (1996.) *Relatório do Seminário—consulta à Sociedade Civil "Construindo o Currículo para a Escola Primária Moçambicana."*

INDE/MINED. (1999.) *Plano Curricular do Ensino Básico*. Maputo.

INDE, PEBIMO. (1996.) *Ensino Bilingue: Uma alternativa para a escolarização Inicial (EP1) nas Zonas Rurais.*

INE. (1998.) *II Recenseamento Geral da População e Habitação 1997: Resultados preliminares.*

———. (1997). *Anuário Estatístico—1997.* Maputo: INE.

Ivala, A. Z. (2002.) *O ensino de História e as relações entres os poderes autóctone e moderno em Moçambique, 1975–2000.* PUC I São Paulo, Tese de Doutoramento.

Kilborn, W. (1996.) *Final Reports and Recommendations from the Evaluation of Teaching Materials for Lower Primary Education in Mozambique.* Maputo.

Martins, Z. (1997.) "Mozambique: Considération sur la recherche en Sciences de l'éducation, formulation des politiques et prise de décisions," *Perspectives* 27(4): pp. 671–80.

MINED. (1998a.) *Plano Estratégico da Educação—1999–2003.*

———. (1998b.) *Plano Estratégico da Educação: Projecto de Promoção da Transformação Curricular do Ensino Básico.*

———. (1996a.) *Educação Básica em Moçambique: Situação actual e Perspectivas.*

———. (1996b.) *Programa do Ensino Primário do Primeiro Grau.*

MINED—Direcção de Planificação. (2002.) *Estatística da Educação. Levantamento Escolar 2002.*

———. (2001.) *Estatística da Educação. Levantamento Escolar 2001.*

Ministério do Plano e Finanças. (2001.) *Plano de Acção para a Redução da pobreza e promoção do crescimento económico.* Versão final aprovada pelo conselho de Ministros em Abril de 2001.

Minter, W. (1994.) *Apartheid's Contras: An Inquiry into the Roots of War in Angola and Mozambique.* London: Zed Books.

Newitt, M. (1995.) *A History of Mozambique.* London: Hurst.

Patel, S. (2001.) *Introdução das línguas moçambicanas no ensino.* INDE (unpublished).

Pereira, L. F., and J. Visser. (1990.) *The Role of Education in the Process of Cultural and Socio-economic Reintegration of Children and Teachers in the War Zones of Mozambique.* The Hague: Centre for the Study of Education in Developing Countries.

Rønning, H. (1997.) *Language, Cultural Myths, Media and 'Realpolitik': The Case of Mozambique, Media Development 44(1).* Available at www.wacc.org.uk/media/ronning.html.

SADC. (1997.) *Protocol on Education and Training.*

Smith, D. (1997.) *The State of War and Peace Atlas. O*slo: International Peace Research Institute.
UNDP. (2000.) *Mozambique: National Human Development Report.* Education and Human Development: Trajectory, Lessons and Challenges for the Twenty first Century, Maputo.

UNESCO/MINED. (1998.) *Plan of Operations of the Curriculum Transformation Project.*

Appendix 1: Resource Persons Consulted

Ministry of Education

- Telmira Pereira, Vice Minister
- Armando Nhavoto, Former Minister
- Zefanias Muhate, Permanent Secretary

National Institute for Educational Development

- Simão Mucavele, Director
- Miguel Gomez, Former Director
- Constancio Xerinda, Former Chief of the Curriculum Development Department
- Albertina Moreno, Chief of the Curriculum
- Narcisso Hofisso, Coordinator of the Social Sciences Technical Group
- Samina Patel, Former Coordinator of the Bilingual Education Group

Pedagogical University

- Carlos Machili, Vice Chancellor

UNESCO

- Noel Chicucue, National Programme Officer in Education and Focal Point for Non Formal Education at UNESCO/Mozambique

Appendix 2: Promotion, Repetition, and Dropout Rates, 1992–93, 1994–95, 1998–99

Grades	Rates	1992–93			1994–5			1998–9		
		Total	M	F	Total	M	F	Total	M	F
1	Promotion	60,2	64,0	55,4	61,3	65,3	56,3	61,8	64,4	58,6
	Repetition	28,0	27,4	28,6	27,3	26,6	28,2	27,3	26,9	27,7
	Dropout	11,8	8,6	15,9	11,4	8,1	15,5	10,9	8,7	13,6
2	Promotion	60,9	62,1	59,3	64,2	66,0	61,5	63,5	65,1	61,3
	Repetition	26,7	26,6	27,0	25,4	24,9	26,2	25,3	24,8	25,9
	Dropout	12,4	11,4	13,7	10,4	9,1	12,2	11,2	10,1	12,8
3	Promotion	57,3	58,7	55,4	57,3	59,2	54,6	59,6	60,9	57,8
	Repetition	25,4	24,4	26,8	27,1	25,8	28,9	25,5	24,5	27,1
	Dropout	17,3	16,9	17,8	15,6	15,0	16,6	14,8	14,6	15,2
4	Promotion	60,1	61,7	57,9	63,5	65,7	60,4	63,4	64,7	61,2
	Repetition	20,4	19,7	21,3	23,0	22,1	24,3	21,2	20,1	23,0
	Dropout	19,5	18,6	20,8	13,5	12,2	15,3	15,4	15,2	15,7
5	Promotion	59,6	59,8	59,3	58,1	58,8	57,1	63,3	63,8	62,5
	Repetition	20,4	19,7	21,2	20,3	19,5	21,5	20,0	19,4	21,1
	Dropout	20,0	20,4	19,4	21,6	21,8	21,3	16,7	16,8	16,4
1–5	Promotion	53,7	55,4	51,4	55,6	57,8	52,6	56,6	57,9	54,9
	Repetition	25,3	24,7	26,2	25,6	24,7	26,7	25,0	24,3	26,1
	Dropout	21,0	19,9	22,6	18,8	17,5	20,7	18,3	17,8	19,1

Appendix 3: Fact Sheet - Mozambique

Total population:	18.2 million
Population under age 15:	44% of total

Health
Infant mortality rate: 139.2 deaths/1,000 live births
Life expectancy at birth: Total population: 36.45 years

HIV/AIDS (1999)
Adult prevalence rate: 13.22%
People living with HIV/AIDS: 1,200,000
Deaths: 98,000 persons

Social and cultural groups
Indigenous tribal groups: 99.66%
(Shangan, Sena, Makua, etc.)
Euro-Africans: 0.2%
Indians: 0.08%
Europeans: 0.06%

Religions: indigenous beliefs 50%, Christian 30%,
Muslim 20%

Languages: Portuguese (official), more than twenty indigenous languages

Adult (15+) literacy rate (1998): 42.3% (total)
58.4% (male)
27% (female)

Net primary enrolment ratio (2000–01): 54%
Net secondary enrolment ration (2000–01): 9%

Public expenditure on education (as % of GDP) (1990): 3.9
Public expenditure on education (as % of GDP) (1998–2000):2.4

Gross domestic product (in billions): US$ 3.6
Purchasing Power Parity GDP per capita: US$ 200

Population below poverty line (2000): 70%
Unemployment rate (1997): 21%

Sources: The authors and the UNDP Human Development Report 2003
Note: All figures for 2001 except if otherwise stated.

Chapter 6

Citizenship Education in a Divided Society: The Case of Northern Ireland

Michael Arlow

About the Author

Michael Arlow holds a teaching and research post in the Graduate School of Education at Queen's University, Belfast. Until recently, he was the principal officer for Citizenship Education at the Northern Ireland Council for the Curriculum, Examinations and Assessment. He was formerly the director of the Social, Civic and Political Education Project at Ulster University. He has been consulting with four to five people with expertise in educational responses to conflict in Northern Ireland (acting as a key reference group).

List of Acronyms

AERA	American Educational Research Association
CASS	Curriculum Advisory and Support Services
CCEA	Northern Ireland Council for the Curriculum, Examinations and Assessment
CCMS	Council for Catholic Maintained Schools
DE	Department of Education (since January 2001)
DEL	Department for Education and Learning
DENI	Department of Education Northern Ireland (until December 2000)
DHFETE	Department of Higher and Further Education, Training and Employment
DCAL	Department of Culture, Arts and Leisure
ELB	Education and Library Boards
EMU	Education for Mutual Understanding
ERO	Education Reform (Northern Ireland) Order 1989
ETI	Education and Training Inspectorate
GBA	Governing Bodies Association
GCE	General Certificate of Education
GCSE	General Certificate of Secondary Education
GNVQ	General National Vocational Qualification
HMSO	Her/His Majesty's Stationery Office
ICT	Information and Communication Technology
IFI	International Fund for Ireland
INCORE	International Conflict Research (Northern Ireland)
IRA	Irish Republican Army
NFER	National Foundation for Educational Research
NICED	Northern Ireland Council for Educational Development
NICIE	Northern Ireland Council for Integrated Education
NUU	New University of Ulster
PGCE	Post Graduate Certificate in Education
PSE	Personal and Social Education
SCPE	Social, Civic and Political Education (Project)
SCRP	Schools Community Relations Programme
TRC	Transferor Representatives' Council
UNESCO	United Nations Educational, Scientific and Cultural Organization

INTRODUCTION

The main focus of this chapter will be on the development of proposals for the introduction of the subject Local and Global Citizenship as a statutory part of the Northern Ireland curriculum through the activities of the Social, Civic and Political Education Project (SCPE). The centrality of the SCPE pilot and of the perspectives of youth to the reform impetus in Northern Ireland has led to a particularity in the structure of the Northern Ireland study, in that these themes will be addressed in the sections that deal with the assessment of schooling as a factor of conflict and reconceptualising curriculum as a result of conflict, rather than in the section on research, monitoring, and evaluation as indicated in the general case study framework.

This study is informed by an understanding of curriculum at two levels. First, with regard to curriculum as structured learning experiences that are supported and informed by curricular documents, resources, training, assessment, and evaluation. These experiences may or may not be prescribed by statute; may or may not take place in the classroom; and may derive from the informal socialising impact of school life and human interaction. The SCPE curriculum defined in this sense may be seen as adopting a "peace-building approach."

Second, the study is informed by the idea of curriculum as a legal framework for learning that takes place in schools. A major challenge relates the extent to which SCPE can carry over elements of the first definition of curriculum into the second. In other words, how far can statutory curricula be used to influence the way in which members of school communities relate to each other and to wider society? It is too early to even attempt to answer this question definitively, but if the question is not asked the intentions of SCPE will not be fully understood.

While SCPE developed a curriculum in the first sense, it now seeks to influence the statutory curriculum. A process of reform of the statutory Northern Ireland curriculum is underway, but as the education system attempts to evolve better ways of legislating for learning, consensus has not been reached about how it will be achieved. The process of curriculum policy change is far from complete and must struggle with broader policy issues that are only comprehensible in the wider social, political, and educational context of Northern Ireland.

Central to that context is the identity-based and often violent conflict that inevitably has had a profound impact on the education system. Northern Ireland is a deeply divided society with strongly held and often conflicting values. Policy formation in such a context has the potential to be highly problematic and runs the risk of reinforcing existing divisions.

The SCPE pilot represents an attempt to develop a curricular response to the conflict which is effective in promoting social cohesion. It is not an isolated intervention but builds on earlier policy and practice. The education system has been responding to both conflict and violence in a wide variety of ways, with varying degrees of success, for a considerable period of time. The rationale and approaches adopted by SCPE become more comprehensible when set against that background.

The publication of *A Shared Future* (Community Relations Unit, 2003), a consultation document on the future of community relations policy, reflects the difficulty of reaching an agreed definition of the meaning of social cohesion in Northern Ireland. The consultation document was based on a review of current community relations policy submitted to the Northern Ireland Executive in January 2002. It is likely that the delay in issuing the consultation paper was a reflection of the difficulty in reaching agreement on the precise nature of the community relations problem and on the general direction of community relations policy. *A Shared Future* proposed the aims of fostering

- "a shared society in which people are encouraged to make choices in their lives that are not bound by historical divisions and are free to do so; and
- a pluralist society with respect and tolerance for cultural diversity, where people are free to assert their identity."

The aims are qualified by the statement that

> no one is arguing for an artificially homogeneous Northern Ireland, and no one will be asked to give up or suppress their chosen identity. We recognise the views of those who do not wish to have closer integration of communities.

In the document there is clearly a tension between a desire to create shared spaces or to integrate communities and the desire to maintain separate and segregated communities. It is also interesting to note that the document implicitly assumes that most individuals identify themselves with either the Protestant/Unionist community or the Catholic/Nationalist community. The reality is somewhat more complex.

Within the agreed analytical framework there are four key issues for investigation:

Informing policy change: SCPE has used a range of strategies in its attempt to influence the statutory curriculum. Significant themes include collaborative curriculum development with teachers, piloting, evaluation, and liaison with education authorities and other civil society partners.

Reaching consensus: A major challenge in the design of Local and Global Citizenship has been to ensure that the curriculum is not perceived as partisan. Success in addressing this challenge will have implications for the ability of the education system to implement the curriculum. Here it will be important to consider the composition of the project advisory group, the selection of pilot schools, information-sharing strategies, and discussions with education authorities.

Implementation: Transition from pilot to mainstream is a complex and problematic process that involves securing finance, developing effective partnerships, and finding robust models for expansion and training.

Broader education policy: As SCPE has evolved into Local and Global Citizenship and moved toward implementation, a range of broader policy developments have impacted progress, some positively, some negatively. Constraints imposed by future developments are likely to continue to impact progress. It will be useful to reflect on these as part of ongoing strategic planning.

This chapter documents the development of an important and potentially controversial strand of education policy through a process of "bottom-up" curriculum development into mainstream education practice. While at an advanced stage, the process is not yet complete and the final outcome is not yet clear. The preparation of the study has offered opportunities to reflect critically on developments to date, current approaches, and possible future directions.

This study may prove a useful resource for those seeking to evaluate the Social, Civic and Political Education Project as a model for curriculum development. It may also be useful for any assessment of the conceptual and curriculum frameworks of Local and Global Citizenship and their mediation from curriculum document to classroom practice. It is hoped that the exploration of these themes may offer opportunities for more effective dialogue in our own context and a record of our experience that may be useful in other contexts.

Methodology

At a two-day meeting in Geneva in August 2002, participants agreed on a work plan and, despite diverse working contexts, an analytical framework for the case studies. A review of the literature relating to each of the main elements of the Northern Ireland study was undertaken during September and October 2002. The review included an analysis of curriculum and policy documents, project and evaluation reports, consultation documents, and analyses of the Northern Ireland conflict and education system. Some key texts are listed in the References.

As part of ongoing project evaluation work, interviews had already been conducted with key stakeholders, school principals, and teachers. These existing data were supplemented by interviews with individuals from a range of organisations with both policy and academic orientations who have been involved in shaping or implementing education policy in relation to the conflict. Interviews were conducted through meetings with individuals, by telephone and e-mail.

Additionally, the case study drew on existing research that sought the views of young people on a range of related issues, for example:

- *their experience of education and of the Northern Ireland curriculum* (the Cohort Study—commissioned by the Northern Ireland Council for the Curriculum, Examinations and Assessment [CCEA] and the department and carried out by the National Foundation for Educational Research [NFER]);
- *education and the conflict* (e.g., Democratic Dialogue, Youthquest 2000, NI Life and Times Surveys, etc.); and
- *participation in the Social, Civic and Political Education Project* (including research conducted for two internal evaluations).

Drafts of the case study were circulated to a number of policymakers and academics for comment and feedback. I am particularly grateful for the help of:

- Alistair Bradley, Department of Education;
- Carmel Gallagher, Council for the Curriculum, Examinations and Assessment;
- Professor Tony Gallagher, Queen's University, Belfast;
- Christine Jendoubi, Department of Education;
- Bernie Kells, Council for the Curriculum, Examinations and Assessment;
- Alan McCully, School of Education, University of Ulster;
- Norman Richardson, Stranmillis University College; and
- Professor Alan Smith, UNESCO Centre, University of Ulster.

BACKGROUND TO CONFLICT

The nature of social composition

As Alan Smith (1999) has argued, the geographical proximity of Britain and Ireland and their strategic relationship on Europe's northwestern edge ensured that the history of the two islands would be closely interconnected. Over the course of centuries, that relationship has encompassed conquest and resistance, and exchanges of peoples, religion, culture, trade, technology, ideas, and language.

It is possible to trace the origins of the conflict to the arrival of Norman settlers from England in 1170. Initially, British control of Ireland was limited to a small area around Dublin known as the "Pale." It was not until the fifteenth century that this situation changed significantly and the conquest of the rest of the island was completed.

Following the English Reformation, the Protestant Episcopal Church was established by law. The vast majority of the Irish population remained faithful to the now proscribed Catholic Church. Protestantism in Ireland came to be seen as the faith of the foreign English invaders. Links began to grow between the Irish and the cause of Catholicism in Europe. The English came to see Ireland as a potential route for a Spanish attack on England.

Ulster, the northernmost of Ireland's four provinces, and the most Gaelic in culture, was particularly resistant to English control. By 1607, organised Irish Catholic resistance in Ulster had been effectively destroyed by Elizabeth I, and the English were ready to embark on the comprehensive colonisation known as the Plantation of Ulster. The Protestant, English-speaking colonists from Scotland and England were culturally distinct from the indigenous Catholic, Irish-speaking population who remained after the Plantation in greatly reduced circumstances. Within a hundred years only 5 percent of land in Ulster remained in Irish Catholic possession.

New towns and villages were established, and others were renamed. Most notable of these is the city of Londonderry, formerly known as Derry. In January 2003, the city council announced plans to restore the official name to Derry. David Trimble, leader of the Ulster Unionist Party and former first minister of Northern Ireland, described this initiative as "purely sectarian triumphalism … [that] will do enormous damage to community relations throughout Northern Ireland" (reported on BBC News, at www.bbc.co.uk/news, on January 31, 2003).

Incidents like this lend weight to John Darby's (1997) observation that "within 50 years of the Plantation, the broad outlines of the current conflict in Northern Ireland had been sketched out." One territory was now occupied by two groups hostile to each other, one believing that the other had stolen its land, the other fearing the threat of rebellion. The history of the following centuries was to be one of sporadic rebellion and repression. Ulster became increasingly distinct from the rest of Ireland as the industrial revolution brought wealth to Belfast and the surrounding areas.

The pattern of rebellion and repression looked set to continue into the twentieth century. World War I presented Irish Republicans with an opportunity as England's energies were focused elsewhere. They rose in violent rebellion against British rule on the streets of Dublin in 1916. The chain of events that followed, including the execution of the leaders of the rebellion and, subsequently, a bitter war of independence, led to a treaty that partitioned Ireland in 1921. The Irish Free State was comprised of twenty-six of Ireland's thirty-two counties, and is now the

Republic of Ireland.

In the north of the island, six of the nine counties of Ulster were to constitute Northern Ireland. Under the provisions of the Government of Ireland Act (1920), each state was to have its own parliament with jurisdiction over domestic matters. Each state would send representatives to Parliament in London, and a Council of Ireland would deal with matters of common interest. Both new states were born in violence. Civil war immediately broke out in the Free State, and many of the act's provisions never came into operation.

In Northern Ireland, a two-thirds majority (Protestant, Unionist) wished to remain under British rule; the remaining third (Roman Catholic, Nationalist) supported the reunification of Ireland. Initially many Catholics refused to cooperate with the new structures. Catholic teachers submitted their students for examinations in Dublin, and even refused to accept salaries from the new Northern Ireland government. Gradually and reluctantly, many accepted the need to accept new realities even if only for an interim period. The Northern Ireland state was deeply concerned with security, and saw the Catholic minority as a threat, often excluding them from areas of public life and discriminating against them in housing employment and voting.

During the 1960s, a civil rights movement, partly inspired by similar movements elsewhere, began to address issues relating to discrimination against the Catholic community in terms of access to political power, social provision, and cultural recognition. Civil rights protests and the responses to them led to violence that rapidly spiralled out of control. The Royal Ulster Constabulary, the predominantly Protestant police force, failed to deal appropriately with the emerging situation. In support, the British army was deployed, and was initially welcomed by the Catholic community as a peacekeeping force. Soon, however, perceptions changed, and the army came to be seen as bolstering British rule. Initially casting themselves as the defenders of the Catholic community, the Irish Republican Army began to orchestrate a campaign of violence which increasingly was aimed at the removal of the British from Ireland. In 1971 the British government suspended the Northern Ireland Parliament and instituted direct rule from London.

The issues underlying the conflict are complex and open to multiple and conflicting interpretations. It is hardly surprising, then, that analyses of the origins and nature of the conflict have never been in short supply, nor that the debate can be a heated one.

Darby (1997) observes that there is a popular view, held by only a few academics—not including himself—that "the Northern Ireland Conflict is a religious conflict." The majority are willing to identify themselves as either "Protestant" or "Catholic." In the 2001 census (data available at www.nisra.gov.uk/census), 43.8 percent described their community background as Catholic, 53.1 percent as Protestant, 0.4 percent as other, and 2.7 percent as having none. Clerics take a prominent role in public and political life, and the Churches exercise considerable influence. Often the "other side" is described in religious terms. Sectarianism is commonplace. (See Appendix 3, Map: *Catholics and Protestants as a Percentage of the Population. District Council Areas. 1991*).

The labels Protestant and Catholic match very closely to the terms Unionist and Nationalist, and opposing political and constitutional aspirations are, without doubt, a potent element of the mix. Unionists aim to preserve the constitutional link with Britain and to resist any attempt to move toward a united Ireland. The conflict is likely to be seen in terms of constitutional and security issues. Some Nationalists aim to address issues of discrimination and injustice within Northern

Ireland to create a context in which Protestants and Catholics may live together peacefully. Others aspire to the removal of British influence from Ireland and the reestablishment of a united Ireland.

Some have espoused explanations based on race and ethnic identity. Others have identified economic or ideological factors and saw the conflict as disguised class warfare. As Darby (1997) reminds us, at one time Marx and Engels regarded Ireland's social inequalities as a "[l]ikely trigger for general social revolution."

Whatever analysis is preferred, it is clear that the Northern Ireland conflict is the result of the complex interaction of historical, political, religious, economic, and cultural issues. The conflict has often been placed alongside the most intractable of ethnic conflicts, such as South Africa or the Middle East. The term "ethnic conflict" is useful where ethnicity is defined as "the subjective, symbolic, or emblematic use by a group of people of any aspect of culture in order to create internal cohesion and differentiate themselves from other groups" (Paul Brass, quoted in Bush and Saltarelli, 2000). This understanding is particularly useful in the context of this study in that it offers a framework for comparison with other conflicts.

The nature of the conflict

The "Troubles" erupted on the streets of Northern Ireland in 1968, and despite changes in style and intensity, violence has been a consistent feature of life there ever since. The intercommunal rioting that had characterised the violence of the late 1960s gradually gave way to "low intensity conflict" (Darby, 2003), with three sets of protagonists, represented by the British state, Irish Republican paramilitaries (Catholic), and Loyalist paramilitaries (Protestant). While some of the paramilitary organisations became increasingly sophisticated in terms of strategy and in the deployment of technology, violence often continued to have explicit sectarian expression.

Since 1968 there have been more than 3,600 deaths and forty thousand casualties. The figures represent many individual and family tragedies compounded by the fact that police investigations into more than eighteen hundred of the killings remain unsolved. In a small population of 1.7 million there are few communities or families that have not been directly affected. Violence has deepened divisions between the communities, reinforcing old hatreds and fostering new ones. There has also been a significant impact on the economy.

Yet when assessed against comparable conflicts elsewhere, the level of violence has been relatively low. Darby (1986) has suggested that a number of factors have contributed to prevent the escalation of violence. He describes the conflict as being "waged by proxity," in that only a relatively small number of people are directly involved in violence.

Another factor is the existence of a narrow middle ground sustained in part by cross-community groups that facilitate contact and communication. At the same time, there is a high level of functional integration. Most Catholics and Protestants mix with members of the other community, at work or even in social settings, in full awareness of their differences, and find it possible to "suspend animosities" (Darby, 1991). Functional integration has been facilitated by the development of a sophisticated "social grammar" of avoidance (Gallagher, 1989); people tend not to talk about religious and political issues in contexts where members of both communities are present.

Such functional integration is not always comfortable or welcome. Recent findings by the Northern Ireland Life and Times Survey suggest that the desire for the two communities to live apart is, if anything, growing stronger (Northern Ireland Social and Political Archive, 1998–2001).

Young people and the conflict

Young people have been significant participants in the conflict through active involvement in street disturbances and as members of paramilitary groups. They have also been victims. In the under-twenty-four age group, 1,276 young people—90 percent of them male—were killed in the conflict up to March 1998. This accounts for slightly more than a third of the total number of fatalities. The total number of children aged eighteen and under killed in the same period was 391, of which 74 percent came from the Catholic/Nationalist community (Smyth, 1998).

Children have been injured, been victims of punishment beatings and shootings carried out by paramilitary organisations, been bereaved, had members of their families imprisoned, and been witnesses of violence. Research (McGrath and Wilson, 1985) indicates that almost 20 percent of children aged ten to eleven surveyed had been in or close to bomb explosions. In Ballymurphy, an area of West Belfast, McAuley and Kremer (quoted in Leitch and Kirkpatrick, 1999) found that among nine- to eleven-year-old children, 90 percent had seen a hijacked vehicle burning, more than 50 percent had seen shooting incidents, and 37 percent had witnessed a bomb explosion.

In less tangible ways young people have experienced the effects of prolonged exercise of emergency powers and segregation in housing and education. For example, the 1991 census estimated that more than 50 percent of the population lived in areas that were more than 90 percent Protestant or Catholic. The impact of a segregated education system will be discussed below.

While it is clear that all children in Northern Ireland have suffered to some extent as a result of the conflict, it is also the case that children from some areas had very little direct experience of violence, while children from other areas had much more direct experience. In some areas the death rate is more than ten times the average rate for Northern Ireland as a whole. The areas with the highest rates are also those with the highest levels of deprivation.

The nature of the peace

From the early 1970s various attempts at political settlement driven by the British government and including elements of power sharing between the two communities failed in the face of opposition from within Northern Ireland. The British government was increasingly frustrated by the inability to reach a settlement and was also concerned that ongoing attempts to deal with the conflict as a security issue and to contain violence were not sustainable. While the British often saw themselves as neutral parties in the conflict, they were regarded as part of the problem by the Nationalist community. It became apparent to many that Britain could not bring about a lasting settlement on its own.

The Anglo-Irish Agreement of 1985 was negotiated with the Irish government without reference to the people or politicians of Northern Ireland. The Irish government for the first time recognised the "principle of consent" that Northern Ireland should remain part of the United Kingdom unless a majority within Northern Ireland decided otherwise. The 1985 agreement secured a consultative role for the Irish government in the affairs of Northern Ireland, allowing it to act as an advocate for and guarantor of the Nationalist community.

The British government effectively recognised what is now commonly known as "parity of esteem," or the equal validity of both Nationalist and Unionist positions. In this spirit, new efforts were made to deal with inequalities between the two communities. The agreement also opened the way for enhanced security cooperation between the two governments.

The Irish Republican Army and its political wing, Sinn Féin, began to realise the potential for electoral success and the limitations of a strategy of violence in this emerging new context. Relationships with Nationalists, the Irish government, and Irish Americans were strengthened to enable the exploration of alternative political strategies. The Clinton administration became increasingly open to involvement in Northern Ireland. Similar moves were also taking place within Loyalist (extreme Protestant/Unionist) paramilitary organisations. Mainstream Unionist parties began to look more and more intransigent by comparison.

As well as promoting dialogue between the main Northern Ireland political parties, both the British and Irish governments established secret contacts with the Republican movement. On August 31, 1994, the IRA declared "a complete cessation of military operations." The Combined Loyalist Military Command followed suit on October 13. The British government and the Unionists were suspicious of the commitment of the IRA to the ceasefire and demanded decommissioning of weapons before face-to face negotiations could take place.

Amidst growing frustration, the IRA cessation broke down at 7:01 p.m. on February 9, 1996, when a massive car bomb was detonated near Canary Wharf in London, killing two, injuring one hundred, and causing £85 million worth of damage. Talks continued, but little progress was made until the election of Tony Blair as Labour prime minister in May 1997. By July the IRA had reinstated their cessation of violence, and talks recommenced with renewed vigour.

Despite rumours of splits and dissention within both Sinn Féin and the Unionist Party a settlement was reached. The "Good Friday" or "Belfast" Agreement (generally, Nationalists prefer "Good Friday," Unionists prefer "Belfast") was signed on April 10, 1998. Julia Langdon (2000), the biographer of Mo Mowlam, secretary of state for Northern Ireland at the time, has commented that "it may not have been perfect in anyone's book, but that was partly the point: everyone was a little dissatisfied."

Nevertheless, in the referendum that followed on May 22 simultaneously in Northern Ireland and the Republic of Ireland, 71.2 percent of voters in Northern Ireland and 94.39 percent in the Republic voted in favour of the agreement. Since then the Northern Ireland Assembly and the power-sharing Executive, set up under the agreement, has had a precarious existence. Violence has continued, though at greatly reduced levels.

The 1998 agreement created a new political context in which issues like the constitutional status of Northern Ireland, policing, and the role of human rights suddenly became open to debate. Society was challenged to define what democracy means or could mean in Northern Ireland. A second and related challenge was to question the values that had driven our society, transcend the sectarian, religious, cultural, and even legal values of the past, and evolve a set of shared values capable of underpinning a sustainable peace.

A number of issues have remained unresolved, including policing and the decommissioning of weapons. Crises relating to these issues have led to the Assembly and the Executive being suspended on a number of occasions. Following the discovery of an alleged IRA spying operation, both governing bodies were again suspended by the secretary of state for Northern Ireland, to be in effect from midnight on October 14, 2002. Elections were due to be held on May 29, 2003, and it seemed likely that the centre parties would lose ground. An atmosphere of mistrust and a lack of progress in negotiations, however, led to the suspension of the Assembly on April 28, 2003, and the postponement of the anticipated elections until the autumn. Once again the British and Irish governments and local politicians are engaged in negotiations aimed at the reestablishment of the devolved administration. As of this writing, in November 2003, elections have still not taken place.

As Darby (2003) comments, "[t]he peace process has delivered changes unimaginable in 1994, but in 2003 the strength of the underlying sectarian suspicions and fears seemed as stark as ever." Northern Ireland society still seems to be characterised by a lack of consensus around issues of central importance in any democratic society. Continuing paramilitary activity and low-level violence after the 1998 agreement suggests that there is not yet consensus that democratic politics rather than violence is the way forward. Historically, civic life and the law enforcement and legal system had been experienced, by some, as sectarian. A sense of shared ownership of these crucial areas of public life is, at best, only beginning to emerge.

In the 1998 referendum 71.2 percent of the whole population and an estimated 53 percent of the Protestant community voted in favour of the agreement. It was sufficient to allow the agreement to proceed, but a significant minority refused to give its assent. According to research conducted by Queen's University published in the Belfast Telegraph on February 19, 2003, only 36 percent of Protestants said that they would still vote for the 1998 agreement, although 60 percent said that they did still want it to work.

In recent research conducted with fourteen- to eighteen-year-olds (Smyth et al., 2000), 42 percent of young people questioned described their citizenship as Irish, 23 percent as British, and 18 percent as Northern Irish. It may be argued that in Northern Ireland, there is not yet consensus on democratic values, nationality, or, even after the agreement, the legitimacy of the state.

Education and the agreement

The 1998 agreement made only two direct references to education (see Appendix 1). This may indicate the level of priority that local politicians gave to education, but it also reflects the hurried and pressurised context in which the agreement was finalised. One reference was a commitment to the development of integrated education, the second to the development of Irish-language education. In the context of Northern Ireland as a whole, mention was made of the need to encourage a "culture of tolerance."

The devolved administration established as a result of the agreement has led to greatly increased local control. This has been seized as an opportunity to develop local solutions to local problems across a wide spectrum of policy issues, not least in education. Martin McGuinness became the first education minister in the new Executive. He is a member of Sinn Féin, and for many years, leading Unionists have alleged that he is a member of the Army Council of the Irish Republican Army. His controversial appointment has led to tensions within the education system and with the Assembly Education Committee.

The 1998 agreement gave a strong impetus for all government departments to reflect on ways in which they could contribute to a sustainable peace. The two references to education in the agreement encouraged the Department of Education (DE) to establish related working groups on Integrating Education and a Culture of Tolerance. Both made recommendations before the end of 1999. This initiative was only a small part of a much wider agenda for change which continues to develop within and beyond the education system. Other initiatives include:

- The **Post-Primary Review**, which explored alternatives to academic selection at age eleven and possible changes to the structure of post-primary education. On October 11, 2002, just days before the collapse of the Northern Ireland Executive, Martin McGuinness announced that the last selection procedure in its present form would take place in 2004. A working group was established in May 2003 to bring forward specific options for the future organisation of schools, and it will report to the education minister by October.

- The **Curriculum Review** began in 1998 and is being conducted by the Northern Ireland Council for the Curriculum, Examinations and Assessment. It involves a comprehensive and radical review of the curriculum with the intention of moving toward a more skills-based approach and has specific provision for Personal Development, Citizenship, Employability, and ICT. Phased implementation will begin in September 2005.

- The **Schools Community Relations Programme (SCRP) Review** was conducted by the University of Ulster. The programme has existed since 1987, initially as the Cross-Community Contact Scheme, to provide funding for schools to facilitate cross-community programmes for their pupils.

- The **Review of Public Administration** is underway and may have far-reaching consequences for all the bodies involved in the administration of education.

- A **Review of Community Relations Policy** was launched in January 2003.

These and other initiatives give the feeling that there are no longer any fixed points in the Northern Ireland education system. It seems that everything is currently under review. In this context of change, it is hardly surprising that serious thought is being given to the way in which the curriculum prepares our young people for participation in the social, civic, and political dimensions of local and global society.

CHARACTERISTICS OF THE PRESENT-DAY EDUCATION SYSTEM

Management system

The education system in Northern Ireland is relatively small, with just over 350,000 pupils in full-time education and twenty thousand teachers.

When the devolved Northern Ireland Assembly has been in operation, the minister of education, Martin McGuinness, was answerable to it. His work is scrutinised by the Assembly Education Committee. Currently, with direct rule in operation, the minister, Jane Kennedy, is answerable to the UK Parliament at Westminster. Before the agreement, the Department of Education Northern Ireland (DENI) was responsible for all aspects of education. After the agreement, responsibilities were divided between the DE and the Department of Higher and Further Education, Training and Employment (DHFETE), which was later renamed the Department for

Education and Learning (DEL). In addition, some of DENI's responsibilities relating to culture, museums, and arts were transferred to the Department of Culture, Arts and Leisure (DCAL).

The DE has responsibility for all aspects of preschool, primary, and secondary education, the youth service, teacher education, and the promotion of community relations within and between schools. The DEL has responsibility for further and higher education and training.

Three branches of the DE are of particular note in the context of this case study:

- The **Standards and Improvement Division** is responsible for policy on curriculum and assessment in schools, teacher education, and resource allocation to the CCEA.

- The **Education and Training Inspectorate** (ETI) is charged with the provision of inspection services, including evaluation and reporting on the quality of education in schools, colleges, and other educational and training organisations. They monitor the effectiveness of the advisory and support services provided by the Education and Library Boards (ELBs), advise the minister, and assist in the formulation and evaluation of policy;

- The **Equality, Rights and Youth Service Division** is responsible for the promotion of community relations between young people and for policy on informal youth service provision.

(A complete overview of the DE organisational structure may be found at http://www.deni.gov.uk/about/.)

The Department of Education works with nine statutory bodies and a range of voluntary bodies involved in the management of education. Many of the statutory functions of the department are devolved to a variety of agencies.

- The five **Education and Library Boards** are geographically defined education authorities fully funded by the DE and are responsible for the administration of public education at a local level. They advise the DE on a range of issues, including the needs of their particular area and more general policy issues. They are responsible for the management of education and library and youth services, and provide curriculum advisory and support services. Elected members of local district councils constitute 40 percent of the membership of the boards. Other members include representatives of the Churches and those with a specific interest in educational services. Protestant Churches are included as Transferors' representatives (see below); the Catholic Church is represented on all of the ELBs. The five ELBs employ more than seven thousand full-time and twenty-two thousand part-time staff.

- The **Northern Ireland Council for Curriculum, Examinations and Assessment** advises the minister of education on issues relating to curriculum, and has a responsibility to monitor the curriculum, engage in research, and develop guidance materials. The CCEA administers assessment procedures including a range of examinations and the Transfer Procedure, a process of academic selection at age eleven. The CCEA also has a regulatory function relating to the GCSE, GCE, and GNVQ examinations offered in Northern Ireland. Wide and ongoing consultation with the education system is conducted through advisory and working groups.

- The **Council for Catholic Maintained Schools** (CCMS) came into being in 1988 and was constituted as a statutory body in 1990. It is the employing authority for the Catholic maintained sector. It advises the DE on matters relating to the sector.

- The **Youth Council for Northern Ireland** encourages the development of youth provision, the efficient use of resources in the sector, and mutual understanding and respect through the activities of the youth service.

- The **Staff Commission for the Education and Library Boards** advises the ELBs and the DE on training and employment issues in the ELBs.

- The **General Teaching Council for Northern Ireland** was recently established as a professional body for teachers.

Voluntary bodies include

- The **Northern Ireland Council for Integrated Education** (NICIE). The DE has a statutory duty to promote integrated education and meets this by funding the NICIE. The council provides advice to the department and to those who wish to establish a new integrated school or to transform an existing school to integrated status. The NICIE also offers an advisory service to integrated schools.

- **Comhairle Na Gaelscolaíochta** (Council for Irish-Medium Schools). The DE has a statutory duty to promote Irish medium schools. Comhairle Na Gaelscolaíochta has a similar function to the NICIE in relation to the Irish medium sector.

- The **Transferor Representatives' Council** (TRC) represents the Protestant Churches, which, at the foundation of Northern Ireland, transferred control of their schools to the state in return for full funding and an ongoing role in the management of these schools. Churches represented are the Church of Ireland, the Presbyterian Church, and the Methodist Church.

- The **Governing Bodies Association** (GBA) represents voluntary grammar schools.

The TRC and the GBA are not statutory organisations, and they receive no public funds from the DE.

There are a number of teachers' unions active in Northern Ireland. There has not been a strong tradition of parental organisation except in relation to single issues such as the Transfer Procedure or Integrated Education.

There is a significant degree of decentralisation, especially for such a small system. This leads some to argue that is heavily overadministered; indeed, the Review of Local Government aims to address this issue, among other things (although following the suspension of the Northern Ireland Assembly, the Review of Local Government also went into abeyance). But the management structure has gradually evolved since the foundation of the state and has been shaped by the nature of the divisions in Northern Ireland. More recently the equality and human rights agendas have begun to appear on the horizon. How much of an impact they will have remains to be seen.

While the system is complex and unwieldy, some argue that it does seem to encourage or even necessitate partnerships and democratic styles of working in many, though not all, areas. However, others claim, with more justification, that the system encourages sectionalism, provides limited scope for common action, and encourages neither partnerships nor democratic styles of practice. Evidence for this view lies in the fact that the system as a whole remains largely characterised by divisions, between religion and class mainly, but also, to some extent, by gender. The complexity of the system can give rise to dynamics that lead to rivalry and competition, sometimes, though not always, along sectarian lines. This is particularly so in the current context of change, where the long-term existence of some agencies may be in question. In the context of the curriculum review, tensions have been evident between the CCEA and ETI in regard to policy development, and between the CCEA and the ELBs in terms of policy implementation.

The school system

In 1831, Ireland became the first country in Europe to introduce a National School system, which aimed to provide mixed education for children of different denominations. However, by the end of the nineteenth century the National Schools had in effect become denominational schools, and were often in the control of local clergy.

Following the creation of Northern Ireland in 1921, another unsuccessful attempt was made to establish a nondenominational school system. The Protestant Churches transferred their schools to the state but retained a role in their management. The schools were fully funded by government and offered nondenominational religious instruction. In 1968 the management role was extended to all state schools, creating a de facto Protestant school sector.

The Catholic Church initially refused to engage with the new institutions in Belfast and declined to transfer its schools, even at one point appealing to the government in Dublin to continue funding them. The Catholic Church retained control of their schools and received 100 percent government funding for recurrent costs and 65 percent for capital expenditure. This was later raised to 85 percent and more recently to 100 percent in light of research that indicated that graduates from Catholic schools tended to have lower qualifications than graduates from Protestant schools and that the attainment deficit was linked to the funding differential (Gallagher et al., 1994). All voluntary schools have the option of accepting 100 percent funding, although the non-Catholic voluntary grammar schools have, by and large, not opted for this.

The 1947 Education Act introduced a selective system of grammar and secondary schools which is still largely in place. Currently, the Transfer Procedure involves tests that are taken in the final year of primary education, at age eleven. They determine whether pupils go on to the more academic grammar schools or to secondary schools. Approximately 35 percent gain admission to grammar schools. A review of this controversial system is currently underway.

The structure of the education system is complex and reflects the divisions in Northern Ireland society. A distinguishing characteristic is segregation. There are parallel systems of Protestant and Catholic schools. Most pupils attend mainly Protestant or mainly Catholic schools. At the post-primary level, schools are in general segregated on the basis of ability and often by gender.

There are four distinct school management types. Most pupils attend mainly Protestant controlled secondary or mainly Catholic maintained secondary schools. The more academically able, as identified through the Transfer Procedure, attend voluntary grammar schools. Voluntary grammar schools are, de facto, segregated by religion, most being either predominantly Protestant or predominantly Catholic. There are also a number of controlled grammar schools.

Since the early 1980s, Protestant and Catholic parents have been the main driving force behind the development of both primary and post-primary integrated schools where equal numbers of Protestant and Catholic pupils are educated together. Grant-maintained integrated schools are new schools established to provide an integrated alternative to existing schools at both the primary and post-primary level. Additionally, there are a small number of schools within the Controlled Sector which have transformed to become integrated schools. Integrated schools cater to approximately 4 percent of the school population.

Some schools are not in receipt of public funds: these include a number of Irish medium schools and integrated schools that do not meet viability criteria, but which are seeking to gain public funding in due course; a small number of independent Christian schools (most associated with the Free Presbyterian Church) that do not seek public funds, in order to provide a distinctive Bible-based curriculum; and one or two wholly independent schools that rely on fee income from parents.

The complex nature of the system undoubtedly incurs additional expense to the public purse. During the 2000–01 school year there were 35,800 surplus places in schools, and the many divisions in the system mean that the average enrolment of schools is smaller than in, for example, other parts of the United Kingdom. Other costs to society are more difficult to analyse.

Initial teacher training

In the division of responsibilities between the DE and the DEL after the 1998 agreement, the DE was given control of policy relating to initial teacher training, while funding is the responsibility of the DEL.

Most primary teacher education is provided by Stranmillis University College, which is predominantly Protestant, and St. Mary's University College, a Catholic teacher training college, through a four-year bachelor of education degree programme. Most post-primary teacher education is provided by the University of Ulster and Queen's University, Belfast, through a one-year Post Graduate Certificate in Education (PGCE) course. All of the institutions are oversubscribed, with up to five times more applications than places; consequently, the calibre of students is high.

Institutional setting for curriculum development

The CCEA is funded by the DE and has a statutory obligation to keep all aspects of the curriculum, examinations, and assessment under review and to advise the minister of education. The CCEA operates a number of standing committees with relevant broad-based representation. Of particular significance in this context is the Curriculum and Assessment Committee. These committees report to the CCEA Council.

The council is the policymaking body within the CCEA and has a membership of seventeen, including representatives from education, industry, and commerce as well as government assessors (one each from the DE, DEL, and ETI). Once the council has offered advice to the minister, policy decisions are made based on that advice, the advice of DE officials, and a range of other statutory and nonstatutory bodies.

The DE frames and sponsors legislation that will follow the normal legislative process through either the Northern Ireland Assembly or through the UK Parliament, depending on whether the devolved administration or direct rule is in operation. Within the Northern Ireland Assembly, the Education Committee exercises a central role in scrutinising the work of statutory bodies, the policies adopted by the minister, and proposed legislation.

The CCEA works both formally and informally with a wide range of education partners in the development of their advice. As we have seen with the SCPE, research, curriculum, or resource development work may be commissioned from external individuals or agencies like universities. In qualifications or curriculum development, official CCEA working groups are established with representation from the ELBs, ETI, teachers, and other interested parties. The chief executive and other officers within the CCEA hold regular informal meetings with stakeholders.

The CCEA has a duty to produce guidance materials to support the curriculum and when appropriate will itself, or with others, produce teaching and learning materials. The ELBs, through their Curriculum Advisory and Support Services (CASS), also have a role in producing support materials and supporting teachers directly through in-service training.

As the new curriculum moves toward implementation, the CCEA and ELBs with Department of Education support will need to work in close partnership. Inevitably, tensions occasionally arise between the partners. Arguably, such tensions may be exacerbated by the Review of Local Government, which is likely to have a significant impact on the administration of education. The pressures generated by the demands of the Curriculum Review are also likely to require careful handling at a strategic level.

Educational/curricular traditions and implications for reform

Since the 1989 Education Reform (Northern Ireland) Order (ERO), which introduced the current Northern Ireland curriculum (see Appendix 2), there has been a perception that curriculum change was driven by the central government and that consultation exercises were purely cosmetic. John Elliott argues in the English context that the result of education reform in the 1990s has been to "de-professionalize teachers and reduce their role to the status of technicians" (Elliott, 1998).

Many teachers have felt that the content, methods, and philosophy of teaching have been dictated by the heavily prescribed nature of the curriculum itself and the associated assessment arrangements. Fuelled by school league tables,

> the accountability dynamic . . . placed an emphasis on the necessity for schools and teachers to prove rather than improve [and] generated within schools an environment which was not conducive to experimentation nor the development of pedagogic approaches which liberate learning.
>
> (Hesketh, T., and Bowring-Carr, C., in Gardner and Leitch, 2001)

The impact on students is reflected in Friere's challenge to his own time and context:

> The tradition however has not been to exchange ideas, but to dictate them; not to debate or discuss themes, but to give lectures; not to work with the student, but to work on him, imposing an order to which he has to accommodate. By giving the student formulas to receive and store, we have not offered him the means for authentic thought.
>
> (Freire, 1974)

Effective practice in citizenship education in Northern Ireland requires teachers to be curriculum developers. They need the confidence to let students ask questions, and to allow them to pursue the answers. As I will indicate below, effective teachers often have no other choice than to become facilitators in the learning process rather than the repositories of knowledge they sometimes feel professionally bound to be.

In the pilot, some teachers became very enthusiastic about the active participatory methodologies. Often teachers simply need to be supported and empowered to embrace flexibility and be responsive to student needs. In the Northern Ireland context this will mean gaining the confidence to take risks and to deal with uncomfortable issues. A senior official has commented in an interview for this study that "Flags and Emblems, marching, punishment beatings, all the hard stuff, the local stuff needs to be on the agenda . . . in every school." This in turn means learning the skills to deal with emotional reactions in themselves and pupils.

The challenges outlined here have been recognised by policymakers. The same official continued that the pedagogy that allows this type of learning to take place is as important as the content of the citizenship curriculum, and wanted to promote the possibility that this "style of participative pedagogy spreads . . . to the rest of the school." The official did not underestimate the reality that this would "be a big culture change for teachers. They are not used to being questioned."

The importance of this type of pedagogy in citizenship clearly contributed to the commitment of some policymakers to support the expansion of the pilot and also goes some way to account for the scale of the in-service training programme. It is to be hoped that the same commitment will encourage policymakers to address the issue of initial teacher training with the same vigour.

Teacher training

The initial teacher training institutions are already responding to the introduction of citizenship. The University of Ulster and Queen's University, Belfast, offer optional and subsidiary courses in citizenship as part of their PGCE programmes. Stranmillis and St. Mary's have made some provision within existing programmes and are considering how to enhance provision.

Some research (McCully and Montgomery, 2000) has suggested that the beginning of a teacher's career may not be the most appropriate stage to offer teacher training. It may be argued that student teachers are more concerned about establishing their own professionalism through effective classroom control and mastery of their own subject area. Inviting them to engage in more progressive methods may undermine their confidence and ability to function effectively in the classroom. It can also be argued that when teachers have had a few years of experience and gained a measure of established professional confidence and control, they are much better placed to begin to engage in what one teacher described as the "selective suspension of authority" (in McCully, 2000) that is required by citizenship teaching.

I suspect that in this, a balance must be struck. Many of the skills that are desirable for citizenship teaching are also desirable in other subject areas, and indeed may become increasingly required across most subjects. While some of the skills may not be common or indeed valued in some schools, a case can be made that while students are being equipped for the current job market, they must also be prepared for the future in a rapidly changing education system.

The Speak Your Piece project, based at the University of Ulster in partnership with Channel Four and Ulster Television, sought to develop innovative approaches to teaching controversial issues. It was an influential project, not least on the SCPE. One interesting feature was that it brought teachers together with youth workers for training and developmental work. Particularly interesting in this context was the finding that bringing the two professional groups together proved to be

> a mutually rewarding experience and an important catalyst for professional development. Teachers benefit from the active learning approaches of the youth workers; youth workers benefit from the conceptual planning framework adopted by teachers.
>
> (McCully, 2000)

Some in both sectors argue that there are important lessons for training in each sector and perhaps a challenge to offer some level of joint training.

Initial teacher training in the United Kingdom is driven by a competency model based on an extensive list of competencies which teachers require at various stages of their professional development. It is open to question whether the existing list of competencies includes requirements for these types of skills. It is also open to question whether the competency model is capable of delivering the type of teachers that are needed.

The issue of provision of full citizenship courses at the initial teacher training level is currently being addressed, but it is unlikely that the competency model will be reconsidered or amended. There are those seriously advocating both courses of action.

ECONOMIC CONTEXT OF REFORM

Resource assessment

Funding of £132,000 (US$ 224,400) for the original two-year SCPE pilot was secured by the University of Ulster. A small percentage was provided by the CCEA as seed money, and the remainder came through the Citizenship Foundation from the Nuffield Foundation and another donor. This approach mirrored earlier initiatives where organisations used a small amount of official funding as leverage to secure more substantial charitable funding.

The second phase of the project was originally intended to run from 2000 to 2003. The CCEA increased its contribution to just over £241,000 (US$ 410,000) over the three-year period, while the International Fund for Ireland (IFI) agreed to contribute an additional £164,000 (US$ 279,000). It was anticipated that the DE would contribute additional funding at a later date to allow the appointment of ELB citizenship officers and an expansion of the pilot.

Originally, the new reviewed Northern Ireland curriculum was due to be implemented in September 2001. The DE had duly allocated funding to cover the anticipated in-service training needs. As the timescale of the review lengthened, the DE became aware that this allocation was unlikely to be spent within the funding period. Enquiries were made about possible alternative uses. Since the SCPE pilot had been in operation since 1998, it was ahead of the rest of the review process. Alan Smith's longstanding record of commitment and expertise in the area and the positive evaluations of the project were significant factors in persuading the DE to use the funding to support a major expansion of the pilot.

Plans were drawn up, and in September 2001, the DE secured ministerial approval for an expansion of the pilot accompanied by a major in-service training programme to be conducted by the ELBs in collaboration with the CCEA.

During 2002, the five ELBs each nominated an officer with responsibility for citizenship. The DE provided additional funding to support all five posts, roughly equivalent to half of each salary. The CCEA has been working closely with up to three officers from each ELB to prepare and support the in-service training programme, which began in November 2002.

In May 2002, the DE wrote to all post-primary schools, inviting them to join the pilot in one of four phased expansions (see Table 1) involving cohorts of approximately seventy schools beginning in 2002–03. Each school will be offered in-service training for up to five teachers: three at key stage 3, and two at key stage 4. Each teacher will receive seven days of training over a three-year period, including one residential. Schools will introduce Local and Global Citizenship in years eight and eleven in September following their initial training year.

It is anticipated that by 2007 all post-primary schools will have had an opportunity to participate in training and will have provision for Local and Global Citizenship. The training programme will have required expenditure of approximately £1.4 million (US$2.4 million), making it one of the largest in-service training programmes to take place in Northern Ireland. It is anticipated that Local and Global Citizenship will become a statutory requirement once all schools have had an opportunity to participate in the pilot. It may be argued that this mainstreaming process provides evidence that the SCPE pilot has significantly influenced the methods of change management adopted by the education authorities more generally. Extensive piloting is also to be used in other areas before statutory obligations are placed on schools where, formerly, change was introduced primarily by legislation.

Table 1: Local and Global Citizenship Pilot Expansion

	Cohort 1	Cohort 2	Cohort 3	Cohort 4
2002–03	Training			
2003–04	Years 8&11	Training		
2004–05	Years 9&12	Years 8&11	Training	
2005–06	Year 10	Years 9&12	Years 8&11	Training
2006–07		Year 10	Years 9&12	Years 8&11
2007–08			Year 10	Years 9&12
2008–09				Year 10

The implementation of Local and Global Citizenship through the expansion at this juncture has raised a number of difficult issues. The final shape of statutory provision for citizenship has not yet been defined. While there is a clear understanding of the core conceptual areas of the programme and of the pedagogies that are deemed to be appropriate, there are still major questions that cannot be definitively answered. Ultimately, the statutory curriculum may offer schools the freedom to decide whether citizenship is infused across the curriculum or whether discrete time will be required. Some ELB officers, teachers, and principals are uneasy, and reluctant to move too quickly.

Citizenship is also ahead of the field in the sense that through it, the CCEA is developing ways in which to work with other organisations in the education system to effect implementation. This is a sensitive process; mistakes have been made, and are perhaps inevitable. There remains a risk that the citizenship agenda could be damaged because of broader issues of policy as these partnerships are forged.

Nature of donor involvement

Significant funding opportunities are offered in Northern Ireland by a number of donors, including the European Union Programme for Peace and Reconciliation in Northern Ireland and the Border Region of Ireland and the IFI. Donors like these have been essential in funding programmes at an early stage of development. In the case of SCPE, the Citizenship Foundation, the Nuffield Foundation, the IFI, and another donor played an important funding role. While SCPE funders worked with the project in a number of ways and evaluated the project, there was little or no interference in the policy choices the project made.

Once the pilot entered the mainstream of the Curriculum Review, it was agreed that unspent IFI funds could be used to allow the University of Ulster to shift the focus of its work to consider the implications for initial teacher education and the development of a framework for an evaluation of the introduction of Citizenship Education. Funding for the expansion of the pilot itself came from the DE to the CCEA and the ELBs. In general, policy implementation is funded directly from government sources.

ASSESSMENT OF SCHOOLING AS A FACTOR OF CONFLICT

Following the outbreak of violence in 1969, a debate emerged about the extent to which the causes of sectarian violence could be attributed to the segregated school system. Some participants in the debate focused on the right of parents to choose schools that provide an education based on religious principles and moral values. Adherents of this position tend to see segregation as an issue peripheral to the conflict.

Others—Frazer (1974), for example, in a chapter entitled "Education for Aggro"—have claimed that segregated education perpetuates the conflict and that while it continues, so will the conflict. As Gallagher (1995) has observed, those who have suggested a significant causal relationship between segregation and the conflict have generally followed one of two main approaches to this question.

The "cultural hypothesis" argues that segregated schools offer differing and potentially opposing cultural environments that mirror the divisions in wider society. Young people are effectively schooled in two divergent cultural systems. Consequently, they come to perceive the other community as different and alien, in part because they have been educated to be different and alien. The evidence however, is inconclusive; there are many commonalities, especially in relation to the formal curriculum.

The "social hypothesis" argues that regardless of curriculum, school ethos, or indeed anything else that happens in the schools, it is the mere *fact* of segregation that matters. The existence of segregated schools is supported and endorsed by society, the Churches, and the government. Divisions are thereby validated and emphasised. The effect on pupils is to foster mutual ignorance and fear.

There is not as yet a clear consensus about the relationship between segregation and the conflict, nor is the evidence unambiguous. This continues to be an area of contention that is likely to remain unresolved. A variety of approaches have been taken to moderate any negative impact of segregation or to promote integration; these are discussed below.

The curriculum and educational responses to the conflict

Violence and the divisions in Northern Ireland society have had a significant impact on some schools and very little impact on others. Initially, the reaction was often to develop schools as safe havens that attempted to exclude engagement with issues related to the divisions and conflict in wider society. However, there were many who felt that schools ought to be making a significant contribution to stability and peace building.

Early initiatives were often driven by committed individuals, by voluntary organisations, and by the universities. One pioneer, a school principal (Malone, 1973) with government, academic, and charitable support, was instrumental in establishing a curriculum development project that included cross-community contact.

In 1974, Malcolm Skilbeck, director of the School of Education at the then New University of Ulster, established the Schools Cultural Studies Project (SCSP) with charitable and government funding. His situational analysis of Northern Ireland culture found it to be "thin, translucent and aggressive . . . encapsulated and fixed." He found that teachers were often "the naïve bearers of [sectarian] culture" (Skilbeck, 1976). The SCSP aimed to develop creative, experimental approaches in schooling and curriculum and to encourage mutual understanding in social relationships among young people.

Work focused on the development of teaching resources. The process was often difficult, but an issues-based curriculum emerged adopting humanities and social science teaching methods for what are now described as years eight to twelve in post-primary schools. More than fifty teachers and fifteen hundred students participated in the course.

Many other initiatives and projects developed within both the academic and voluntary sectors. They were often on a small scale and did not have an immediate effect on educational policy, but they did begin to form a pool of individuals with expertise and to create a context in which policy change became possible.

The education system was as much entangled with the issues that gave rise to the conflict as was the rest of society. Issues involving the administration of schools and the curriculum could easily be presented in ways that made any intervention appear to have sectarian motivation. It may be argued that the violence was seen as a temporary aberration, a passing emergency that did not require a policy response in areas like health and education. Schools often responded by conceiving of themselves as " 'oases of peace,' providing children with an environment relatively protected from the violence but also insulated them from the social issues around them" (Smith, 1999).

By the 1980s the Department of Education began to address community relations issues directly. It is possible to identify three strands of educational intervention, each of which had been pioneered in the activities mentioned above. The earliest strand to emerge fostered curriculum initiatives in the existing segregated school system. The Department of Education Northern Ireland formally expressed support for this approach in Circular 1982/21, where it recognised that "Our educational system has clearly a vital role to play in the task of fostering improved relationships between the two communities in Northern Ireland." The circular went on to state that

> The Department wishes to emphasise that it is not questioning the right to insist on forms of education in schools which amount to segregation. It considers, however, that this right is coupled with an inescapable duty to ensure that effective measures are taken to ensure that children do not grow up in ignorance, fear or even hatred of those from whom they are educationally segregated.

> (DENI, 1982)

In 1987, DENI formed a group based in the Northern Ireland Council for Educational Development to encourage curriculum development "related to education for reconciliation." This work of this group provided the basis for legislation in 1989.

By the late 1980s, official guidance material had been issued and the Education and Library Boards were appointing officers with responsibility for Education for Mutual Understanding

(EMU). Initially, EMU did not enjoy universal support, and there were those on both sides of the divide who saw it as social engineering driven by a desire to dilute cultural identity.

The second strand encouraged contact between pupils attending predominantly Protestant and predominantly Catholic schools. Early attempts were often ad hoc and unsystematic, but later ones like the Inter School Links project based at the University of Ulster began to move the agenda forward. In 1987, DENI established the Cross-Community Contact Scheme to provide funding for schools engaging in contact programmes.

The third strand encouraged the development of cross-community integrated schools. Following an initiative by parents, Lagan College, the first planned integrated school, opened in 1981. It attempted to maintain a religious balance within both staff and pupil populations. A deliberate attempt was also made to reflect both cultural traditions in the curriculum.

The ERO attempted to strengthen each of the three strands of intervention described above. While it was recognised that for the foreseeable future most pupils would continue to be educated in segregated schools, the government took responsibility to encourage the development of integrated education.

Education for Mutual Understanding and Cultural Heritage were made compulsory cross-curricular themes that sought to encourage respect for self and others, the building of relationships, an understanding of conflict, an appreciation of interdependence, and cultural understanding. The themes became operational in 1992 as one conjoined theme. It was anticipated that through them, schools would also be encouraged to engage in cross-community contact schemes.

Under the same legislation, common history (1990) and religious education (1993) curricula were also introduced. History at key stage 3 included studies on the Normans in Ireland, Ireland 1600–1700, and Ireland 1801–1921. At key stage 4, a choice was offered between studying Northern Ireland 1939–65 or 1960–90. In general, predominantly Protestant schools favoured the less controversial, earlier period.

Religious education at key stage 4 required a study of two Christian denominations. In practice, many Protestant schools studied two Protestant denominations while many Catholic schools studied the Catholic and Orthodox denominations. These examples suggest that taking the line of least resistance by offering choice may lead to absurdity rather than promote approaches that encourage more community understanding and tolerance.

Following a ministerial directive, the CCEA developed a new modular GCSE in social and environmental studies which aims to prepare students for citizenship and address issues of local significance. The programme came into operation in 1996, and students were able to choose four modules from a selection that includes Cultural Identity and Heritage, Rights and Responsibilities in the Law, and Communication and the Media.

In post-sixteen education, an advanced-level GCE is offered in Government and Politics. It includes a study of political ideas and institutions in Britain, Northern Ireland, and either the Republic of Ireland or the United States.

Strong criticisms, especially in relation to the manageability of the new Northern Ireland curriculum, soon emerged. A review took place in 1994–95, and modifications went into effect after September 1996. A five-year moratorium on curriculum change was imposed in an attempt to build confidence and promote stability in the education system. During that period, there was a perception among many teachers that while the curriculum itself remained unchanged, they continued to be inundated by change in related areas particularly in assessment arrangements and the post-sixteen curriculum.

Rationales for curriculum change

As I have already indicated, the 1998 agreement and the establishment of the institutions that arose out of it have given an enormous impetus for change right across the full spectrum of public policy. The moratorium on curriculum change was due to end in September 2001. On both sides of the Irish Sea there have been increasing frustrations with our varieties of the national curricula. The impending turn of the millennium also provided a focus on the need for a curriculum better fitted to the "changing needs of pupils, society and the economy" (CCEA, 1999).

The CCEA identified the main pressures for change as coming from the imperative to prepare young people to respond to changes in communications technology; modes of employment and leisure; economic migration and globalisation; shifting moral values; and population growth, global warming, and depletion of natural resources.

During the period of the moratorium on curriculum change, the CCEA had engaged in a range of evidence-gathering activities in preparation for the next round of curriculum change. A curriculum monitoring programme involved significant numbers of teachers in face-to-face and questionnaire feedback. The longitudinal Cohort Study monitored the perceptions of nearly three thousand pupils and their teachers of the curriculum at key stage 3 over a three-year period.

The research conducted by the CCEA indicated that teachers understood the existing curriculum aims but felt that they were not sufficiently carried through to the component parts of the curriculum. Research relating to values education (Montgomery and Smith, 1997) suggested that nowhere in the Northern Ireland curriculum was the values dimension sufficiently clearly articulated.

The Cohort Study (Harland, Moore et al., 2002) revealed that the curriculum at key stage 3 lacked perceived relevance, resulting in diminishing enjoyment and progressive disengagement for many pupils, including the most able. It also found that most pupils make only slow progress in the first two years.

A series of ten "Curriculum 21" conferences that focused on key curriculum issues were held and their recommendations published. A range of research and development projects examined issues relating to skills and values in the curriculum. Liaison with educational bodies in the United Kingdom, Europe, and North America was ongoing. The evidence provided by this work combined with the political opportunity presented by devolution offered a strong case for change.

Rationale for the reformulation of EMU

As Gallagher (1998) has pointed out, government support and funding for community relations initiatives in education, especially after the ERO, enabled the development of a substantial pool of expertise and experience in the voluntary, statutory, and academic sectors. Considerable reflection had taken place on the effectiveness of practice.

Smith and Robinson's evaluation of EMU (1996) was particularly influential in setting an agenda for change in the area of curriculum. They found that there was an insufficiently developed conceptual framework; many found EMU to be an elusive bird. There had often been an assumption that prejudice and hatred was based on ignorance and misunderstanding, yet increased contact and improved understanding did not necessarily improve relations. For some, it was a means of obtaining money for an occasional school outing with a school from the other community that did little to promote genuine mutual understanding. Whole school dimensions could be neglected, and contact between the communities was often emphasised over and above a curricular approach.

The underpinning values of EMU were seen as "vague and aspirational" and lacking in clarity. This led some to see EMU as being "contaminated" by political motivation that sought to "bring the two communities together." It was further weakened by a lack of focus on human rights. Teachers rarely progressed toward more controversial aspects of EMU, or toward political education, in part because they felt ill equipped to deal with controversial issues and were afraid of doing more harm than good. They also identified a lack of cooperation between statutory bodies with responsibility for EMU.

Yet it must also be recognised that EMU was in many ways a bold initiative that helped to change the nature of discourse in Northern Ireland by introducing a language that "allows people to express their support for cultural pluralism and political dialogue rather than sectarianism and political violence" (Smith and Robinson, 1996). The recent report *Towards a Culture of Tolerance: Education For Diversity* recognised that EMU and other initiatives

> have had considerable success in breaking down barriers, opening people's minds and establishing new networks of contacts. However, it is not surprising that, in the face of centuries-long social divisions, they must be seen as merely the beginning of social transformation.
>
> (DENI, 1999)

Smith and Robinson indicated that EMU had to move on:

> The challenge now is whether such initiatives can help young people move beyond the "polite exchange" so that they can engage with each other in meaningful discussion of controversial social, cultural, religious and political issues.
>
> (Smith and Robinson, 1996)

Evidence was emerging that young people themselves perceived the need to move in this direction. A survey of thirteen hundred young people in Northern Ireland between the ages of sixteen and twenty, carried out for Democratic Dialogue, a Northern Ireland think tank (Fearon et al., 1997), showed that they felt "alienated from political parties and politicians, but not from politics." They wanted to explore controversial issues but recognised that they needed the knowledge and skills to do so. Seventy-nine percent expressed the desire to learn about politics in school. *Inside the Gates: Schools and the Troubles* (Leitch and Kilpatrick, 1999) later reinforced this message, recommending that the curriculum should respond to young people's "expressed desire to address controversial issues related to this society, the recent history of Northern Ireland and contemporary events as they happen."

The 1998 agreement itself sharpened the challenge by creating a new political context and urging the larger society to create dynamics that would contribute to sustainable peace:

> The tragedies of the past have left a deep and profoundly regrettable legacy of suffering. We must never forget those who have died or been injured, and their families. But we can best honour them through a fresh start, in which we firmly dedicate ourselves to the achievement of reconciliation, tolerance, and mutual trust, and to the protection and vindication of the human rights of all.
>
> (Governments of the United Kingdom and Ireland, 1998)

One senior civil servant described a sense of opportunity and responsibility to effect change: "Education is the major lever for social change. One of the first questions that subsequent generations will ask is . . . when you had power locally, what did you do with it? What did you do to try to move society on?" Political developments had created a new context where new priorities could be developed which addressed and expressed local needs in fresh ways.

In April 1998, shortly after the agreement was signed, the CCEA hosted the "Society 21" conference, where it was strongly argued that the existing curriculum did not provide "sufficient opportunity for educating young people about democracy and constructive civic and political participation" (CCEA, 1999). It was proposed that recommendations for this area should be developed building on the work of EMU and the experience of our neighbours in developing citizenship curricula. The proposal to introduce citizenship reflected a desire "to contribute towards the maintenance of peace" (CCEA, 1999) in the post-agreement context.

In 1999 the ETI conducted a survey of provision for EMU involving twenty-five schools in the post-primary sector (DE, 2000). The report illustrated good provision and effective teaching, but also found significant shortcomings. In a majority of schools there were "significant weaknesses, or weaknesses outweighed strengths in policy and planning arrangements for EMU."

A minority of teachers were comfortable or confident in dealing with issues related to conflict, and in a majority of schools there was insufficient professional development for teachers, particularly on handling controversial issues. Only about a third of schools involved their pupils in projects dealing with "aspects of citizenship and the workings of democracy and which involve the pupils and teachers in examining potentially sensitive issues." The Youthquest 2000 survey (Smyth et al., 2000) supported this finding, showing that only one-third of young people surveyed had specific classes in school which addressed such issues as sectarianism.

The Cohort Study (Harland et al., 2002) later gave similar messages. It indicated that pupils found EMU-related work valuable. However,

> in Year 9 and especially in Year 10 . . . in particular high attainers, began to express how this work was common "sense" and that they did not learn anything from it.
>
> (Harland et al., 2002)

Pupils reported that they would like more help understanding the problems of Northern Ireland, and that this might have a direct benefit to wider society. The study also found that in many schools, only a minority of pupils were involved in EMU activities; in effect, there was no common entitlement in relation to EMU.

Issues around citizenship education were becoming increasingly important around the world, with new programmes emerging in the United Kingdom and Ireland. Research at home and the example of other contexts made a compelling case for curriculum change in this area. The 1998 agreement and the Curriculum Review offered an opportunity, and the political will to change had been clearly expressed from a number of quarters.

RECONCEPTUALISING CURRICULUM:
CHANGING CURRICULUM PARADIGMS AS A RESULT OF CONFLICT

Changes in curricular paradigms

Local and Global Citizenship

Local and Global Citizenship is defined by a conceptual framework, a values base, and associated teaching and learning approaches or programme characteristics. The conceptual framework that emerged from the SCPE pilot is at the heart of Local and Global Citizenship and will form the basis of the statutory entitlement. It is based on four closely interrelated thematic areas:

- Diversity and Inclusion
- Equality and Social Justice
- Democracy and Active Participation
- Human Rights and Social Responsibility

Each thematic area is investigated in local, national/European, and global contexts through issues, some of which will relate to the divisions in Northern Ireland. It has always been easy to avoid the difficult local issues by focussing on global issues. Conversely, a parochial curriculum based solely on local community relations issues fails to give a sense of our place in the world, or of the breadth and magnitude of issues that confront humanity.

It is not accidental that concepts contained in the thematic areas are difficult. The difficulty of the language reflects the nature of citizenship education and the complexity of the issues we are asking young people to engage with. In Northern Ireland, the very concept of citizenship is problematic; it is therefore important that the conceptual areas be seen as problematic as well, in that they give rise to issues that are open to multiple, conflicting, and changing interpretations.

The recognition of the problematic nature of the core concepts has far-reaching consequences. A transmissional approach to teaching and learning will be open to accusations of indoctrination. Where practice is best, the teacher will have a distinct role in the classroom, but it will not be that of the expert imparting a predefined body of knowledge. The teacher's role becomes more one of facilitating enquiry. This in itself may pose significant challenges for teachers who have not been trained to adopt such a role.

It is not uncommon for citizenship education to be promoted in response to a perceived deficit in young people. After all, declining rates of participation in elections and in traditional civic institutions are common to much of the Western world. A curriculum conceived with the intention of making good that deficit will aim to induct young people into civil and political life. It is, however, likely to be transmissional in character and to implicitly value uncritical compliance.

Northern Ireland remains a deeply flawed society, and any deficit does not lie with young people alone. Local and Global Citizenship seeks to develop the capacity of young people to reflect upon and shape society by engaging their interest, enthusiasm, and idealism through a range of active and participatory experiences that extend their skills and knowledge as citizens.

The notion of societal deficit implies that a citizenship curriculum will have a future orientation. It will encourage young people to reflect on society as it is, to identify strengths and weaknesses, and then to envisage a better society or a "community of the future." The student's community of the future will be shaped as much by the identification of elements to be preserved and fostered as by identification of elements requiring change. The task is to imagine a society that is more inclusive, more just, and more democratic.

The invitation to respond creatively to issues through imagining reflects an attempt to engage students both rationally and emotionally. Young people are more likely to engage with issues if the issues are felt to be relevant. If we do not engage their idealism and concern, their learning is likely to be superficial. Playfulness and even a degree of naivete are integral parts of imagining and are important to teaching and learning, but imagining is not the end of the process. The exploration of issues arising from the core concepts of Local and Global Citizenship encourages students to engage in critical reflection and discussion based on the values expressed through human rights principles.

Students are encouraged to find practical and realistic ways in which they can narrow the gap between the world as it is and their future community, by developing the skills necessary to engage in democratic processes. In doing so they are also exposed to alternatives to violence and to avoidance of contentious issues.

In a democratic society, skills, vision, and determination are no guarantee of a successful outcome. Young people will discover for themselves the disappointments of democracy. If, as they deserve, they are prepared and guided appropriately, they may learn much that is positive from their encounter with democratic disappointment.

It is now widely recognised that the capacity of young people for active and participatory citizenship is best developed through active and participatory teaching and learning approaches (for example, Hahn, 1999). For example, students learn most about effective ways to participate in democratic processes by engaging in these processes in the safe forum of the classroom or school. These approaches are much more likely to secure the involvement of young people if they are also challenging and enjoyable.

Local and Global Citizenship is intended to be open ended; it is not about teaching students *what* to think and do, but *how* to think and do. It does not attempt to promote political correctness in the classroom. On the contrary, it seeks to promote open and frank discussion. The classroom becomes a community of enquiry in which contemporary, relevant issues and students' personal views on them are discussed, clarified, and challenged.

Through the investigation of the concepts of diversity and inclusion young people explore the breadth and depth of diversity in their own community, in national/European and global contexts. When young people reflect on feelings engendered by the sight of an Orange Hall, an

Asian on the street, a Roman Catholic Church, or two men holding hands in public, they are challenged to confront their own emotional reactions and to consider strategies for dealing with difference.

As with many citizenship issues, those presented by diversity and inclusion may involve conflict. Any conflict will have both rational and emotional dimensions. When exploring ways to manage conflict, students will also learn about the management of their own emotions and sensitivity to the emotions of others. This has important consequences for the nature of teacher education for Local and Global Citizenship, especially regarding the skills and approaches required when exploring controversial or sensitive issues.

As students reflect on the concepts of diversity and inclusion, the challenge emerges of how to ensure that our diverse society can also be a just and equitable one. Investigation of the concepts of equality and social justice provides opportunities for young people to explore society's need for rules and laws to safeguard individual and collective rights, and ensure that everyone is treated equally and fairly.

Since rules and laws are not always just, it will be important to discover how rule and law making and changing processes may be influenced. Similarly, rights and values will clash in any society. Young people consider how to handle these conflicts democratically without resort to violence or avoidance.

Through the investigation of the concepts of democracy and active participation, young people will investigate ways to participate in, and to influence, democratic processes. They will develop an awareness of some key democratic institutions and their potential role in promoting inclusion, justice, and democracy.

Underlying each thematic area are the concepts of human rights and social responsibility. It is recognised that rights often conflict and, consequently, are not absolute. Human rights instruments such as the Universal Declaration of Human Rights, the UN Convention on the Rights of the Child, and, perhaps in time, the proposed Bill of Rights for Northern Ireland will provide a context within which young people can clarify and critique their own views, and evaluate alternatives.

Exploration of the conceptual framework, underpinned by human rights principles and accompanied by active and participatory teaching and learning approaches, aims to assist in the development of young people as responsible and active individuals and contributors to society, the economy, and the environment in Northern Ireland and beyond.

Direction of curriculum change

In 1999, the CCEA sent advice to the minister of education and secured his approval for a review of the Northern Ireland curriculum to proceed in 1999 for phased implementation from 2001. The review process would aim to

> provide a curriculum and assessment framework which meets the changing needs of pupils, society and the economy; has the confidence of teachers, pupils, parents, employers and the wider public; and widens educational opportunity and improves learner motivation and achievement.
>
> (CCEA, 1999)

The first objective of the CCEA Curriculum Review was to "clarify the aims and values of the school curriculum" and to articulate them in such a way as to "influence and shape the curriculum and the nature of teaching and learning" (CCEA, 1999). In phase one, the review would include a reexamination of the purposes of education, and the cross-curricular themes. Phase two would review the individual subject areas in order to make explicit their contribution to the aim.

The Cohort Study revealed that there was almost no awareness of the aim among students, and that it was rarely referred to in curriculum planning. Intellectual development was perceived to be well provided for, but the other elements were seen, in reality, to be at the periphery of the curriculum. Social and emotional development were not specified in the aim but were felt to be important component parts of a rounded education.

The phase one consultation document proposed

- a new aim—"to enable young people to achieve their potential and to make informed and responsible choices and decisions throughout their lives"
- three overlapping and interdependent curriculum objectives—"The Northern Ireland Curriculum should provide learning opportunities for each person to develop as:

  o an individual;
  o a contributor to society; and
  o a contributor to the economy and the environment"

- underpinning values—"It is proposed that the following values are clearly stated as underpinning each of the Curriculum Objectives:

  1. We value each individual's unique capacity for spiritual, moral, emotional, physical and intellectual growth;

  2. We value equality, justice and human rights within our society and our capacity as citizens to resolve conflict by democratic means;

  3. We value the environment as the basis of life and the need to sustain it for future generations; and

  4. We value each individual's right to work and to earn a living in accordance with personal preference and attributes" (CCEA, 2000)

- generic skills, defined under the headings of

  o ICT skills
  o Interpersonal skills
  o Learning skills
  o Personal skills
  o Physical skills
  o Thinking skills

- the introduction of new areas

    o Citizenship
    o Education
    o Personal Development and
    o Employability

In consultation, approval ratings for the new aim (91.4 percent), objectives (91.4 percent), values (89.9 percent), and skills (86.7 percent) were overwhelming. Of the small number of respondents who disagreed with the new aim (5.7 percent), some were concerned that there was no explicit reference to spiritual or moral values, and some felt that there needed to be a stronger recognition of the community relations dimension. Support for the new areas was less enthusiastic.

The CCEA recommended to the DE that the proposals should be accepted with minor adjustments to wording to reflect views expressed in the consultation. The review has proceeded broadly on that basis, although both values and skills have been further developed.

Social, Civic and Political Education

Through research and from evaluations of EMU, an agenda for change was beginning to emerge. It included aspirations to develop a more clearly defined values dimension in the Northern Ireland curriculum, a more robust conceptual framework for EMU with a clearer definition of underpinning values, and a stronger focus on human rights and political education. To achieve this, designated, discrete time in the curriculum, better support for teachers to address controversial and sensitive issues, and greater institutional commitment in schools were required. However, such an agenda poses significant conceptual and practical challenges in the context of a divided society struggling to emerge from conflict. Even if the CCEA or the DE had the capacity to address these challenges in a "top-down" curriculum development exercise, they would have left themselves open to accusations of social engineering.

Earlier initiatives had shown that voluntary projects outside the formal system, not led centrally by statutory organisations, were more likely to engage enthusiasm and commitment and perhaps lead to more sustainable process of development. To some it seemed that the time was right to create a context within which commitment and the emerging agenda could be developed. It was important to such a process that detailed proposals were not defined in advance but would emerge from within a group.

The University of Ulster School of Education has played an important role in the research, development, training, and evaluation of initiatives related to pluralism, social justice, democracy, human rights, and the teaching of controversial issues. Alan Smith in particular had an established record of involvement, through, for example, the integrated education movement, the evaluation of EMU (Smith and Robinson, 1996), and the Speak Your Piece project (McCully, 2000). Building on this work Smith sought support from the CCEA, and through the London-based Citizenship Foundation secured funding to establish the Social, Civic and Political Education project.

The SCPE project was conceived as a two-year endeavour operating from September 1998. Through a process of curriculum development involving direct engagement and consultation with teachers the project aimed to produce

- a curriculum proposal for key stage 3;
- a group of trained, committed, and knowledgeable teachers;
- a citizenship programme operating in more than twenty post-primary schools;
- guidance material;
- a directory of relevant resources available in print and on the Internet; and
- experience to inform the Curriculum Review.

The SCPE pilot worked with twenty-five schools with a good geographical and social spread and representing each of the main educational sectors. Each school nominated a teacher with responsibility for SCPE and a senior management team link to advise on management issues. Training and consultation days were used to develop the curriculum framework, to train the teachers, to plan and reflect on piloting, and to review the needs of the group.

From September 2000, SCPE received further funding from the CCEA and the International Fund for Ireland. It became an official CCEA pilot operated by the University of Ulster. This was to enable it to

- complete the development and piloting of the citizenship curriculum;
- develop exemplar teaching and learning resources;
- develop models of cooperation between NGOs, schools, and curriculum developers;
- develop in-service and preservice training programmes; and
- develop a model of implementation.

Plans emerged for an expansion of the pilot, and in January 2002 the project was absorbed into the CCEA. At this point, the area adopted the name "Local and Global Citizenship."

The university retained a role in evaluating the expanding pilot. By this time, the pilot had drafted a suggested programme of study for Local and Global Citizenship and had evolved a series of recommendations about pedagogy and management issues, including timetabling, in the "Guide to Effective Practice and Implementation," summarised below.

Effective practice in SCPE happens when

- there is a strong focus on active and experiential learning approaches;
- there is discrete provision of approximately 5 percent of curriculum time allocated to SCPE;
- classes last at least one hour:

  o to facilitate active and participative pedagogies and
  o because of the sensitive nature of some SCPE issues;

- teachers and coordinators are given time for specialist SCPE in-service training;
- the teachers and coordinators are volunteers who have a personal commitment to the area;

- teachers already have open relationships with pupils and are confident, trained, and willing to engage in the discussion of controversial issues;
- SCPE is seen as a whole-school and a whole-curriculum issue, and the subjects of history, geography, RE, PSE, and English, and so on are recognised as providing a context for the exploration of contemporary issues;
- consideration is given to the formation of school councils, or the effectiveness of an existing council is reviewed;
- staff and pupils are aware of human rights principles; and
- the senior management team:

  - is aware and supportive of the active pedagogies used and sensitive nature of issues dealt with in SCPE and
  - is aware and supportive when adverse parental or community reactions occur.

POLICY DIALOGUE, CONSENSUS BUILDING, AND RESISTANCE: CHALLENGES POSED BY SENSITIVE LEARNING AREAS

Modalities of consultation and participation in policy reform

I have already described a number of research projects that sought the views of a variety of stakeholders prior to the formal beginning of Curriculum Review. In this section I propose to focus on the methods used by the initial SCPE pilot project to include a range of stakeholders in the process of deciding on the changes required to the curriculum to enhance the provision Citizenship Education.

Initially, informal discussions were held with a wide range of stakeholders in the education system. This principally involved conversations with ELB and EMU officers, school principals, and teachers who had been involved in earlier initiatives. The main intentions of these discussions were to explain what the project hoped to achieve and to identify schools that might be willing to participate.

To ensure involvement beyond existing networks, information and an invitation to join the pilot were circulated to all post-primary schools. Project staff followed up these contacts with visits to schools when requested and were often made aware of the existing pressures on schools in terms of workload, financial constraints, and the already overloaded curriculum. High levels of enthusiasm were also encountered in some schools.

The schools recruited to the pilot were spread across Northern Ireland and were representative of the main school sectors. Some schools were located in areas deeply affected and others in areas barely touched by violence. This was important, since the pilot was envisaged not only as a curriculum development project but also as a vehicle for detailed and ongoing consultation with a representative selection of teachers and schools. It must be recognised, however, that as the participants were (we hoped) volunteers, they were more likely to be predisposed to this type of work than the wider school and teacher population.

As the pilot progressed, the most detailed consultations took place with the pilot teachers. Time was spent during training days reflecting on the conceptual framework, the resource materials, and the practicalities of making SCPE operational in schools. Teachers were encouraged to keep their principal and senior management link informed of developments and feedback views and thoughts on these days. This reflected a strong commitment by the project team to "ground the developments in the experiences of teachers and the needs of schools" (Watling, 2001).

From an early stage the project sought to engage with a wide range of stakeholders in an attempt to build strong and effective partnerships. This was also a means of carrying on continuous and informal consultation and of building consensus.

In February 1999 the project team met with the education spokesmen of the major political parties, who expressed general support for the SCPE initiative. Regular meetings were held with officials from the DE, the CCEA, the ELBs, and other educational bodies.

The project was launched in Parliament Buildings on May 5, 1999. More than 110 organisations were invited to attend and offered opportunities to work with the pilot in the development of the programme. A number of these organisations contributed significantly to the development of the SCPE framework and resources.

The SCPE pilot consulted formally with stakeholders through the advisory group, which met approximately twice per year. The group included representation from

- the Department of Education, including

  - the Inspectorate,
  - the Community Relations Branch, and
  - the Curriculum Branch;

- the Education and Library Boards (all five ELBs represented);
- the CCEA;
- the CCMS;
- the National Council for Curriculum and Assessment (the Curriculum Council for the Republic of Ireland);
- the Focus Group (representing the EMU community);
- the Youth Council for Northern Ireland;
- the Citizenship Foundation;
- the University of Ulster School of Education;
- the Politics Association (a professional body for politics teachers);
- Co-Operation Ireland (an NGO with significant involvement in community relations activities); and
- members of the media, including

  - BBC Northern Ireland Education and
  - Channel Four Schools.

The advisory group was regularly attended by influential policymakers, individuals with considerable experience in the area, and other interested parties. It was a very useful channel for the dissemination of the work of the pilot, discussion of areas of difficulty or controversy, and general advice.

Three evaluations of SCPE were undertaken, each with the intention of soliciting the opinions of different constituencies on different aspects of the project. The first evaluation was an internal evaluation conducted by a teacher, Vera Heaslip (Heaslip, 2000). It aimed to

- collate experiences of the pilot from both pupil and teacher perspectives;
- gather examples of effective practice in teaching structural provision within schools; and
- identify gaps in project provision.

Heaslip interviewed teachers in five of the pilot schools and pupils in two. Teachers were asked about the year eight framework, resources, the recommended teaching approaches, assessment, and the strengths and weaknesses of the pilot. Pupils were asked about their enjoyment of the programme, the degree to which it provided challenges, and strengths and weaknesses.

Dr. Rob Watling, from the University of Leicester, conducted the second evaluation for the Citizenship Foundation. It included twelve semistructured interviews with key stakeholders ranging from teachers to policymakers. There were also field visits to pilot schools and three postal surveys of pilot teachers and their managers.

After consultation with the Citizenship Foundation and the project team, the evaluation was designed to investigate the following research questions:

- How does SCPE fit into (and impact on) the wider educational context of Northern Ireland?
- How do teachers and the wider educational community perceive and respond to the SCPE initiative at various points in its development?
- What are the most significant strengths and weaknesses of the project for the various stakeholders? Do these change during the course of the project?
- How can the experiences of the project inform the development of new forms of social, civic, and political education in Northern Ireland and elsewhere?

The final evaluation (Birthistle, 2001) again sought the views of pilot teachers, school managers, and pupils on a range of issues. Again there was little indication of opposition to the introduction of SCPE so long as this was facilitated by appropriate changes brought about through the curriculum review and resourced adequately by the DE especially in terms of training.

In this phase of the SCPE pilot, it is striking and indeed surprising that there was so little opposition to a potentially controversial area. Watling identified some resistance in the EMU community, some of whom saw SCPE as undermining EMU. Better communication and collaborative working has helped to address such concerns. Contrary to expectations, in three years of piloting in twenty-five schools there were no reported parental complaints or formal complaints from other quarters.

One official interviewed for this case study commented that, "Northern Ireland is a very funny place. . . . Things that you think are going to create the most fuss, create the least . . . [for example] the common Programmes of Study for History and RE—miracles, individual separate miracles in their own right, no fuss at all."

It is important to state that in the consultations that took place, project staff and the evaluators genuinely gave opportunities for all views to be expressed. Negative views were expressed and valued, as they helped to direct the development of the SCPE project.

As the pilot was increasingly absorbed into the Curriculum Review, the processes for consultation were absorbed in the formal CCEA processes for consultation on the review as a whole. Modes and outcomes of those consultations will be discussed below.

Identifying and dealing with difficult issues with regard to sensitive learning areas

In general, difficult issues can be identified at a relatively early stage because of the way in which the CCEA works in close partnership with key stakeholders in the education system. Difficulties often emerge through research, or in working groups convened to focus on a specific area. If missed at this stage, issues may be identified through standard consultation processes.

However, there are those in the education system who feel that final decisions are made by the CCEA project without a serious attempt to engage with some natural, and indeed essential, partners. There is a perception in some quarters that this consultation was at times token and superficial. There have been tensions between the pilot and other parts of the system, and questions have been raised about the overall strategy for managing change. This problem is exacerbated by the general climate of change, in which many consultations are being conducted simultaneously and schools and teachers can find it difficult to engage with, and respond effectively to, every proposal.

When advice is sent to the minister of education by the CCEA, the minister will review it and take other advice before acting. The final check in the system is at the level of parliamentary scrutiny. These processes often help to build consensus, indicating lines of development which are inadvisable or sensitive, or enabling a process of negotiation to take place where necessary.

As we have seen, the CCEA reports on consultations to date indicate that a high degree of support has emerged around the central aims of the Curriculum Review, although there continue to be a number of unresolved and difficult issues at key stage 3 in particular. Debates have focussed on assessment and on how to deal with the addition of new elements (Citizenship, Employability, and Personal Development) to an already overcrowded curriculum.

The issue of a crowded curriculum at key stage 4 seems to have been resolved by proposing that the only statutory areas will be Citizenship, Employability, Personal Development, and Key Skills. The main driving force for the key stage 4 curriculum is assessment through GCSE examinations. This in itself is likely to ensure a balance of provision in the existing subject areas.

At key stage 3 a number of possibilities have been explored, including the reduction of content in individual subject areas and a more minimal specification of the statutory curriculum through curricular areas rather than subjects. While schools are keen to have more flexibility, they are fearful of diluting the identity or downgrading the status of individual subject areas. No resolution to this debate has yet been reached, but perhaps the most important issue is the question of where to draw the dividing line between what is statutory and what is advisory. The mechanisms for deciding the issue are likely to be further consultation and piloting of different models. Although it does seem certain that citizenship will become a part of the statutory curriculum, how the question of the crowded curriculum is resolved has the potential to have a significant impact on the final shape of this provision.

Languages

According to the 2001 census (data available at www.nisra.gov.uk/census), 4.6 percent of the population of Northern Ireland speak, read, write, and understand Irish, while 89.6 percent have no knowledge of Irish. In the main, Irish is identified with the Roman Catholic/Nationalist community. The 1998 agreement promoted parity of esteem for the Irish language; while some may object to the promotion of Irish, the role of languages in the curriculum in relation to social cohesion is not currently a matter of controversy in the context of Curriculum Review. Most education is conducted in English, although Irish is widely taught in predominantly Catholic schools. A growing number of parents are sending their children to Irish medium (IM) schools.

Where appropriate, the DE provides documents and press releases in Irish as well as English (and Cantonese upon request). Similarly, the CCEA provides documentation in Irish if appropriate.

Civics/citizenship

There was always a possibility that a proposal to introduce Citizenship Education could provoke significant controversy. That risk has not been realised, nor is it now likely to be realised. Some strategies for addressing this risk were built into the initial SCPE pilot project and are described above. Once the SCPE project was absorbed into the CCEA Curriculum Review process, the issue was taken forward by the CCEA through the formal processes of consultation. Consultation on phase one of Curriculum Review mirrors subsequent consultations and will be considered, since it is the most directly relevant to Local and Global Citizenship.

Following the publication of proposals to introduce citizenship education, the Northern Ireland Assembly Education Committee invited the CCEA to present the proposals and responded to them in a memorandum. The committee supported the introduction of specific programmes for Personal Education, Citizenship, and Employability but expressed the concern about how these programmes would be fitted into an already full curriculum (CCEA, 2001).

By the end of the consultation period, in June 2000, some 426 written replies were received from schools, colleges, and others. At twenty consultation seminars, approximately seven hundred teachers had opportunities to voice their opinions. Fifty meetings were held with other stakeholders.

In the phase one consultation report (CCEA, 2001), the overall approval rating for the introduction of a programme of citizenship at key stage 3 was only 55.7 percent; 30 percent were opposed, and 14.3 percent were undecided. However, it is particularly interesting that significantly more secondary schools were in favour (65 percent) than grammar schools (48.8 percent), a majority of whom were either against or undecided.

Of the 30 percent of respondents who were opposed to the introduction of citizenship, many expressed their opposition in terms of one or more of the following areas:

- **time allocation**: some were concerned about extra time required for citizenship;
- **cross-curricularity**: some argued that it should be integrated into existing areas;
- **content appropriateness**: some argued that the concepts were too abstract and too difficult to deliver;
- **sensitivity**: some saw it to be too controversial; some were supportive but felt "it would be difficult to implement given the political climate"; and
- **political appropriateness**: some felt that the programme was based on an underlying political agenda and that this was not a legitimate role for schools.

The view of the DE and of the CCEA seemed to be that the approval ratings in the consultation, while not overwhelmingly supportive, were sufficient to progress the citizenship agenda through further piloting.

History

In 1990 a statutory history programme of study was implemented under the provisions of the Education Reform (Northern Ireland) Order of 1989. Prior to this, there had been no common history curriculum. The new programme specified that an investigative approach that allowed for the incorporation of different views was to be used. For the first time history teachers had to tackle controversial issues related to the conflict.

The CCEA advocated a "shift in the emphasis of school history teaching towards education about the development and experience of democratic processes and the threats to them, with young people being encouraged to apply their thinking to . . . the gradual development of the concept of universal human rights and responsibilities."

It seems that history is currently faced with two challenges: first, to respond to the citizenship agenda; and second, to become more relevant to the needs of young people. Carmel Gallagher argues that young people must be allowed to construct meanings for themselves through history rather than have meanings imposed on them. She continues that this must of necessity bring with it a stronger values dimension to history:

> there are those who feel comfortable with teaching history so long as it stays in the past—a kind of purism which views as politics and considers attempts at developing values and attitudes through history as social engineering.
>
> (Gallagher, C., 1998)

Work carried out by the CCEA to illustrate how history can more directly address the conceptual themes of citizenship has been welcomed by history officers in the ELBs. It is, as yet, unclear how much of this work will be part of any statutory requirement. The issue will be resolved through the processes of consultation operating across the breadth of the Curriculum Review.

Religion

In Northern Ireland, religious education (RE) has historically provided a focus for controversy. In the late 1980s the Churches objected to proposals for the ERO which they felt would undermine their role in education and the status of RE. The government revised its proposals and agreed to the development of a statutory programme of study. The four main Churches (Roman Catholic, Church of Ireland, Presbyterian, and Methodist) were invited to draw up the programme. A working group was appointed and a core syllabus produced.

This undoubtedly raised the status of RE, but it also proved controversial. Barnes (1997) observes that the Churches considered the syllabus to be "a model of Christian cooperation and unity." However, most media attention was drawn to the fact that all religions other than Christianity were excluded. A number of commentators—for example, Barnes (1997), Richardson (1990), and Green (quoted in Barnes, 1997)—saw it as deeply conservative. Green argued that "the taxpayer will be financing what amounts to fundamentalist church schools." Barnes has written that "it does not encourage pupils to think for themselves about religion, and its narrow focus prohibits the development of the necessary skill of assessing religious beliefs, experiences and commitments—a skill much needed in our increasingly pluralist world."

The CCEA (1999) proposed that there "should be a shift in Religious Education towards understanding world religions, in particular Islam, as well as other Christian denominations in Northern Ireland." RE, however, is the direct responsibility of the DE, and as provided for in law, the Churches were invited to reestablish the working group to review the core syllabus. The group intends to include a World Religions dimension, but the fundamentally Christian approach is unlikely to change. Opposition to this continues to emanate from some academics, the Northern Ireland Inter-Faith Forum, and others.

In the first instance, the responsibility for seeking consensus lies with the review group. Section 75(1) of the Northern Ireland Act of 1998 requires that public authorities have due regard of the need to promote equality of opportunity between certain different individuals and groups. Consequently, the proposals will be subject to an equality impact assessment. This may yet have a significant impact on the proposals. Once the proposals are finalised they are submitted to the DE and may be accepted or rejected in their entirety. If the DE has concerns with elements of the proposals, it may be possible to ask the Churches to reconsider those elements. Final decisions are then made through normal legislative processes either in the Northern Ireland Assembly or at Westminster, depending on what constitutional arrangements are in place.

Curriculum balance

The 1989 Northern Ireland curriculum had been criticised for being unmanageable and overloaded. A limited review in 1994–95 reduced statutory requirements within programmes of study. The Cohort Study had found that only 4 percent of schools were meeting the minimum recommended time allocation for all subjects. In some schools, up to 25 percent of time was allocated to modern languages, and time allocated to RE varied by a factor of five. Teachers frequently expressed a need for more time.

The CCEA initially aimed to respond to these and other issues by:

- creating specific statutory provision for Personal Development, Citizenship, and Employability;
- showing how each subject can help to develop transferable skills; and
- slimming down the content of other subjects to a minimum core to create space for these additional elements and to increase flexibility for teachers to devise curricula appropriate to their students while maintaining a common entitlement.

In phase one of the review process an attempt was made to address the curriculum by suggesting time allocations for each subject by percentage.

However, in consultation, 59.7 percent of respondents disapproved of the proposal, feeling that it would discourage flexibility and encourage fragmented learning, and pupils would be less well prepared for GCSE examinations at key stage 4. Some felt that it could provide a useful tool for challenging the dominance of some subjects, while others argued that it did not go far enough in challenging that dominance. In light of the consultation findings, the CCEA decided to explore alternative mechanisms for ensuring balance at key stage 3.

Phase two of the review at key stage 3 focused on the development of detailed but slimmed down programmes of study for all subjects and new programmes of study for Personal Development, Citizenship, and Employability. In January 2001, as the CCEA prepared to commence consultation on these new proposals, it became clear to CCEA council members that the key stage 3 curriculum remained overcrowded and that it would become a "restrictive strait-jacket" (CCEA, 2002).

Table 2: Suggested Time Allocations

Subject	%
English	10
Mathematics	10
Science	10
Technology and Design	5
History	5
Geography	5
Art and Design	5
Music	5
Physical Education	7½
Modern Languages (1)	5
Modern Languages (2)	5
Religious Education	5
Home Economics	5
Personal Development	5
Citizenship	5
Employability	2½
Information and Communications Technology	2½
Drama	2½

The council made a number of decisions that changed the direction of the review process in significant ways and proposed that the statutory curriculum at key stage 3 should be

- specified in terms of curriculum areas rather than subjects;

- limited to a minimum common entitlement for every pupil, irrespective of future intentions; and
- such that a significant proportion of children (but not all) will be able to complete it in two years.

This would have the effect of allowing much greater flexibility in schools and was designed to encourage curriculum "integration through an issues or theme-based style of teaching." The third proposal would have the effect of creating an additional year of time which could be used in a number of ways.

In consultation (report available on the CCEA Web site, at www.ccea.org.uk), however, respondents were divided on the first proposal to specify the curriculum in areas rather than subjects, with 45 percent for and 55 percent against. More than 70 percent supported the second proposal for a more minimal statutory curriculum. There was strong opposition to the third proposal.

At the time of writing, new proposals influenced by these findings will soon be issued for consultation. It is anticipated that final advice will be given to the minister for education by the end of 2003.

SCPE/Local and Global Citizenship

The SCPE pilot recommended that any future provision for citizenship should involve discrete time of approximately 5 percent as well as cross-curricular dimensions. One principal expressed a view, not widely shared, that he would be willing to provide 10 percent of curriculum time to SCPE because

> Schools will sink if they can't sort out the relationship problems with kids, with parents, with teachers. Without a doubt they will become disaffected places of learning. If [SCPE] can provide some kind of facility for that enhancement of pupil motivation, I think that certainly would give it justification for bigger time in the curriculum.
>
> (Birthistle, 2001)

Throughout the review the place and mode of delivery for Local and Global Citizenship has been an issue. In the early stages it seemed clear that citizenship would emerge as a subject in its own right with its own programme of study. As the direction of the review moved toward a more integrated curriculum, citizenship was placed within the area of Environment and Society, which also included history and geography. Extensive and at times controversial mapping work was undertaken to explore the extent to which citizenship could be delivered through history and geography and the extent to which it required discrete time. More recently, attempts have been made to reassure teachers by making existing subjects more visible in the new curriculum. A new curriculum core has also emerged at both key stages 3 and 4; this is currently known as Learning for Life and Work and is comprised of

- Local and Global Citizenship;
- Personal, Social and Health Education; and
- Education for Employability.

It is likely that this new core will be the foundation of new statutory requirements.

In the current context of uncertainty within the CCEA, there are those who argue that citizenship should be infused through all subjects (history and geography in particular) with the citizenship dimensions clearly identified in statutory provision. There are also those who argue that in addition to infusion through other subjects, citizenship also requires discrete time. I suspect that ultimately schools will be given the freedom to decide on their own preferred mode of delivery.

RESEARCH, MONITORING, AND EVALUATION

Pilot programmes

Citizenship education is being gradually introduced to schools through an expansion of the existing small-scale pilot. This is a deliberate strategy designed to be responsive to the needs of teachers, schools, and the wider society. Teachers in the original pilot warmly welcomed the bottom-up approach and expressed hope that it would be maintained as the process of implementation proceeded. This is a significant challenge, and one that may or may not be met. Already there has been a degree of unease as the bottom-up process begins to encounter the more top-down approach of policymakers. However, the attempt is being made so that teachers and schools will feel able to contribute to the final shape of citizenship education.

Local and Global Citizenship will operate in a pilot mode until at least 2006; by then, more than one thousand teachers and all post-primary schools in Northern Ireland will have had opportunities to participate. Some will be reluctant to embrace citizenship because they see it to have very little relevance to their school or the community in which it is set. Others will be wary because some individuals in their context will be particularly resistant to raising issues related to the conflict. They may fear the breakdown of relationships and exposure to uncomfortable situations for which they feel ill prepared. Many of these challenges mirror the challenges that faced EMU. If implementation is attempted through phased piloting, it is more likely to be responsive to a changing political and educational context.

If this approach is to be successful, it requires that policymakers and those who support teachers adopt many of the characteristics of an effective citizenship teacher. All involved must regard themselves as learners engaging in action research and sharing what experience they have already gained. They must be as ready to listen as to advise. Any attempt to retreat into the production of "teacher-proof" or indeed "trainer-proof" resources and training programmes will be rewarded by a failure of trust and will tend to mitigate against the kind of professional and even personal development that characterises the most effective teachers. The culture of accountability has its place and can be a valuable asset, but as noted above, it can also dampen the impetus toward creativity, risk taking, and genuine human interaction.

Local and Global Citizenship will probably not be subject to inspection by ETI until after 2006. On the one hand this gives schools a little leeway, and time to build capacity. On the other hand it means that some other form of monitoring will be needed. The UNESCO Centre at the University of Ulster is developing an evaluation process that is described in more detail below. This is intended to create a mechanism by which the detailed learning of the expanding pilot may be fed back to policymakers and in turn shape the nature of the citizenship programme. Additionally, the ELBs and the CCEA have their own quality assurance procedures to ensure value for money and to promote effective practice.

Monitoring policy and practice

Local and Global Citizenship will be introduced to schools in Northern Ireland according to the plan described above. The researchers in the UNESCO Centre at the University of Ulster are currently drawing up proposals for an evaluation of the impact of the programme over a four-year period from April 2003 to March 2007.

It is intended to be a rounded evaluation, using a multi-method approach and incorporating a number of relevant levels of impact. The first level relates to pupils and a selected number of schools. A research instrument will be designed and piloted with the intention of evaluating citizenship knowledge, skills, values, and attitudes acquired by approximately three hundred students throughout their key stage 3 experience. A second cohort of year eight students will be surveyed in 2005–06 to provide a comparison over time. In each cohort there will also be a control group of students not involved in citizenship classes. Fourteen case studies will be developed on the basis of interviews with school managers and teachers both involved and not involved in citizenship. Input from students will be solicited through focus groups and the videotaping of citizenship lessons.

The second level relates to the impact of the ELB citizenship training on teachers. It is likely to include descriptive accounts of the training programmes. In 2003–03 and again in 2004–05 teachers' expectations and perceptions of the strengths and weakness of the training will be investigated by means of a questionnaire. Teachers will be surveyed in 2004–05 and again in the following year to establish a profile of teachers recruited to teach citizenship. It will seek to obtain demographic data, and identify previous experience in related areas, sociopolitical attitudes and values. Semistructured interviews will be conducted with citizenship teachers between 2004 and 2006 to explore the understanding of core concepts and the implications for the teacher personally and professionally in the classroom and school settings. Interviews are to be conducted with the five ELB officers in 2004–05 and again in 2006–07 to establish their views on the training provided.

The third level relates to the introduction of citizenship at the initial teacher training level. Student teachers at each of the four training institutions will be surveyed in 2004–05 to establish what knowledge, skills, values, and attitudes have been acquired. A small number of students will be interviewed to explore their understanding of citizenship in greater detail. Interviews and focus groups with lecturers will investigate their assessment of the effectiveness of programmes on offer and of the possibility for the integration of citizenship within existing programmes.

It is intended that the findings of the evaluation will be disseminated at various points during the four-year period. It is also hoped that the research goals and methods will be consistent with research being carried out in England and internationally in order to facilitate useful comparison.

CONCLUSION

As I have observed on a number of occasions throughout this chapter, the context in which it has been written is both fluid in and politically sensitive at a number of levels. Each of these factors has had a significant role in shaping this study.

Perhaps the most obvious outstanding issue is that of devolved government in Northern Ireland. As I indicated earlier, intense negotiations involving the pro–1998 agreement parties and the prime ministers of the United Kingdom and Ireland are in progress as I write. Their aim is to restore the devolved institutions and allow scheduled elections to take place in the autumn. Failure of the negotiations would probably lead to a prolonged period of direct rule and a heightened possibility of violence.

The future of the devolved government may have a direct impact on the education system. If direct rule continues, British ministers may be increasingly reluctant to make major decisions that will result in significant change. This may have consequences for the Curriculum Review and the other reviews currently taking place. Ironically, if ministers are willing to make such decisions, the passage of the relevant legislation is likely to be a much simpler process under direct rule. The potential impact on citizenship is much more difficult to quantify: it could undermine enthusiasm, or it could act as a spur to greater commitment.

Issues of curriculum overload facing the Curriculum Review have a significant impact on Local and Global Citizenship. I have indicated that the Curriculum Review is far from over. Originally, a new curriculum was to be due for implementation by September 2001. Currently the target date is September 2005, and there is the potential for further slippage in timescales, especially in relation to key stage 3. Continuing uncertainty around future statutory requirements might lead to some schools being less willing to join the pilot.

When final decisions about the overall shape of the curriculum are reached, if citizenship is not allocated some discrete time there will be concerns that the coherence and progression of the area will be lost. In that case it will be less likely that the recommended teaching approaches will be used. Local and Global Citizenship might well be divided up between existing subjects and delivered in a superficial way. Evidence from past experience suggests that at best controversial issues would continue to be largely ignored. At worst, teachers would address controversial issues in inappropriate ways and risk doing more harm than good. It becomes less likely that specialist citizenship training would be offered to student teachers, and the sustainability of citizenship after the pilot ends is open to question.

Other reviews of aspects of the education system like the Review of Post-Primary Education have the potential to bring rapid and far-reaching change to the system. The likelihood and impact of such change is difficult to predict, and depends in part on progress in the political sphere.

In the longer term, there are questions about the capacity of Local and Global Citizenship to live up to the expectations of some. Will teachers be able to deliver it effectively? Will young people enjoy it and be challenged by it? Will it have a significant positive influence on the social cohesion of our society? Questions like these must be asked constantly, and answers, provisional though they may be, should be used to inform our current practice and planning. Definitive answers to some of these questions will not be known, perhaps for many years, but those answers will be the ultimate criteria by which to judge the success of the Social, Civic and Political Education Project.

References

Akenson, D. H. (1973.) *Education and Enmity: The Control of Schooling in Northern Ireland, 1920–50*. Newton Abbot: David and Charles.

Arlow, M. (2000.) *Social, Civic and Political Education in Northern Ireland*. Coleraine: University of Ulster.

———. (1999.) "Citizenship Education in a Contested Society," *Development Education Journal* 6(1).

Barnes, P. (1997.) "Reforming Religious Education in Northern Ireland: A Critical Review," *British Journal of Religious Education* 19(2).

Birthistle, U. (2001.) *Citizenship Education—SCPE Internal Evaluation Report*. Coleraine: University of Ulster.

Bush, K. D., and Saltarelli, D. (2000.) *The Two Faces of Education in Ethnic Conflict*. Florence, Italy: UNICEF, Innocenti Research Centre.

Cairns, E. (1987.) *Caught in the Crossfire: Children and the Northern Ireland Conflict*. Belfast and New York: Appletree Press and Syracuse University.

Community Relations Unit, Office of the First and Deputy First Minister. (2003.) *A Shared Future: A Consultation Paper on Improving Community Relations in Northern Ireland*. Belfast: OFMDFM.

Council for the Curriculum, Examinations and Assessment. (2002.) *A New Approach to Curriculum and Assessment 11-16*. Belfast: CCEA.

———. (2001.) *Northern Ireland Curriculum Review: Report of the First Consultation*. Belfast: CCEA.

———. (2000.) *Northern Ireland Curriculum Review: Phase 1 Consultation*. Belfast: CCEA.

———. (1999.) *Developing the Northern Ireland Curriculum to Meet the Needs of Young People Society and the Economy in the 21ˢᵗ Century*. Belfast: CCEA.

———. (1997.) *Mutual Understanding and Cultural Heritage: Cross-Curricular Guidance Materials*. Belfast: CCEA.

Darby, J. (2003.) *Northern Ireland: The Background to the Peace Process*. CAIN Web Service, available at http://cain.ulst.ac.uk.

———. (1997.) *Scorpions in a Bottle: Conflicting Cultures in Northern Ireland*. London: Minority Rights Group.

————. (1991.) *What's Wrong with Conflict? Centre for the Study of Conflict Occasional Paper 3.* University of Ulster, Northern Ireland.

Dunn, S. (1995.) *Facets of the Northern Ireland Conflict.* London/New York: Macmillan/St. Martin's Press.

————. (1990.) "A History of Education in Northern Ireland since 1920," in *The Fifteenth Report of the Standing Advisory Commission on Human Rights Report for 1989–90.* London: HMSO.

————. (1986.) "The Role of Education in the Northern Ireland Conflict," *Oxford Review of Education* 12(3): pp. 233–42.

Elliott, J. (1998.) *The Curriculum Experiment.* Buckingham: Open University Press.

Fearon, K., et al. (1997.) *Politics: The Next Generation.* Belfast: Democratic Dialogue.

Frazer, M. (1974.) *Children in Conflict.* Middlesex: Penguin.

Freire, P. (1974.) *Education as the Practice of Freedom.* London: Sheed & Ward.

Gallagher, C. (1998.) *The Future of History: A Plea for Relevance?* Paper given to the Schools History Project Conference, Leeds.

Gallagher, A. M., et al. (1994.) "Religion, Equity and Education in Northern Ireland," *British Educational Research Journal* 20(5): pp. 507–18.

Gardner, J., and Leitch, R. (2001.) *Education 2020: A Millennium Vision.* Belfast: Blackstaff Press.

Governments of the UK and Ireland. (1998.) *The Agreement.* Belfast: Northern Ireland Office.

Hahn, C. L. (1999.) "Citizenship Education: An Empirical Study of Policy, Practices and Outcomes," *Oxford Review of Education* 25(1&2).

Harland, J., Moor, H., et al. (2002.) *Is the Curriculum Working? The Key Stage 3 Phase of the Northern Ireland Curriculum Cohort Study.* Belfast: CCEA.

Heaslip, V. (2000.) *Social, Civic and Political Education: An Internal Evaluation of Year 8* (unpublished).

Langdon, J. (2000.) *Mo Mowlam.* London: Little, Brown.

Leitch, R., and Kilpatrick, R. (1999.) *Inside the Gates: Schools and the Troubles: A Research Report into How Schools Support Children in Relation to the Political Conflict in Northern Ireland.* Belfast: Save the Children, Belfast.

Malone, J. (1973.) "Schools and Community Relations," *Northern Teacher* 11(1).

McAuley, P., and Kremer, J. (1990.) "On the Fringes of Society: Adults and Children in a West Belfast Community," *New Community* 16 (2): pp. 247–59.

McCully, A . (2000.) *Speak Your Piece: A Development Project for Teachers and Youth Workers, Final Report*. Available at http://www.ulster.ac.uk/unesco.

———. (1999.) *Teaching Controversial Issues as Part of the Peace Process in Northern Ireland*. AERA Conference Paper.

———. (1985.) "The Relevance of the Teaching of Cultural and Social Studies to the Handling of Controversial Issues in the History Classroom," in R. Austin, ed., *Essays on History Teaching in Northern Ireland*. Coleraine: University of Ulster.

McCully, A., and Gallagher, C. (1996.) "The Contribution of Curriculum Enquiry Projects to Educational Policies in Northern Ireland," in P. Lemish, *Education in Societies in Conflict*. Tel Aviv: Ford Foundation.

McCully, A., and O'Doherty, M. (1998.) *Teaching Controversial Issues in a Divided Society*. British Educational Research Association Conference Paper.

McCully, A.W., and Montgomery, A. (2000.) "What Have Values Got to Do With It?" in G. Easdown, ed., *Innovation and Methodology: Opportunities and Constraints in History Teacher Education*. Lancaster: History Teacher Education Network.

Montgomery, A., and Smith, A. (1997.) *Values Education in Northern Ireland*. Coleraine: University of Ulster.

Northern Ireland, Department of Education. (2002a.) *A Review of Post-Primary Education: Report on Responses to Consultation*. Bangor, Co. Down.

———. (2002b.) *A Review of the Schools Community Relations Programme*. Bangor, Co. Down.

———. (2001.) *Education for the 21ˢᵗ Century: Report by the Post Primary Review Body*. Bangor, Co. Down.

———. (2000a.) *The Effects of the Selective System of Secondary Education in Northern Ireland*. Bangor, Co. Down.

———. (2000b.) *Report on a Survey of Provision for Education for Mutual Understanding (EMU) in Post-Primary Schools*. Bangor, Co. Down.

———. (1999.) *Towards a Culture of Tolerance: Education for Diversity*. Bangor, Co. Down.

———. (1996.) *The Northern Ireland Curriculum, Key Stages 3 and 4: Programmes of Study and Attainment Targets*. Bangor, Co. Down.

———. (1987.) *Cross Community Contact Scheme. Circular 1987/47*. Bangor, Co. Down.

———. (1982.) *The Improvement of Community Relations: the Contribution of Schools. Circular 1982/21*. Bangor, Co. Down.

Northern Ireland Council for Educational Development. (1988.) *Education for Mutual Understanding—a Guide*. Belfast: NICED.

Northern Ireland Young Life and Times Questionnaire (1998) (1999) (2000). Available at http://www.ark.ac.uk/nilt/ylt.

O'Connor, S. (1980.) " 'Chocolate Cream Soldiers': Evaluating an Experiment in Non-Sectarian Education in Northern Ireland," *Journal of Curriculum Studies* 12(3): pp. 263–66.

Osborne, R. D., Cormack, R. J., and Gallagher, A., eds. (1993.) *After the Reforms: Education Policy in Northern Ireland*. Belfast: Policy Research Institute.

Richardson, N. (1990.) *Religious Education as if EMU Really Mattered*. Belfast: Christian Education Movement.

Robinson, A. (1983.) *The Schools Cultural Studies Project: A Contribution to Peace in Northern Ireland*. Coleraine: NUU.

Skilbeck, M. (1976.) "Education and Cultural Change," *Compass, Journal of the Irish Association for Curriculum Development* 5(2).

Smith, A. (2003.) "Citizenship Education in Northern Ireland: Beyond National Identity?" *Cambridge Journal of Education* 33(1): pp. 15–31.

———. (2001.) "Religious Segregation and the Emergence of Integrated Schools in Northern Ireland," *Oxford Review of Education* 27(4): pp. 559–75.

———. (1999.) *Education and the Peace Process in Northern Ireland*. Paper presented to the Annual Conference of the American Education Research Association, Montreal, April 1999.

Smith, A., and Robinson, A. (1996.) *Education for Mutual Understanding: The Statutory Years*. Coleraine: University of Ulster.

———. (1992.) *Education for Mutual Understanding, Perceptions and Policy*. Coleraine: University of Ulster.

Smyth, M. (1998.) *Half the Battle: Understanding the Impact of the Troubles on Children and Young People in Northern Ireland*. INCORE, University of Ulster.

Smyth, M., et al. (2000.) *The Youth Quest 2000 Survey*. INCORE, University of Ulster.

Watling, R. (2001.) *Social Civic and Political Education Project: External Evaluation*. Centre for Citizenship Studies in Education, University of Leicester.

Appendix 1: References to Education in the Agreement

RIGHTS, SAFEGUARDS AND EQUALITY OF OPPORTUNITY

Reconciliation and Victims of Violence

13. The participants recognise and value the work being done by many organisations to develop reconciliation and mutual understanding and respect between and within communities and traditions, in Northern Ireland and between North and South, and they see such work as having a vital role in consolidating peace and political agreement. Accordingly, they pledge their continuing support to such organisations and will positively examine the case for enhanced financial assistance for the work of reconciliation. **An essential aspect of the reconciliation process is the promotion of a culture of tolerance at every level of society, including initiatives to facilitate and encourage integrated education and mixed housing.**

RIGHTS, SAFEGUARDS AND EQUALITY OF OPPORTUNITY

Economic, Social and Cultural Issues

4. In the context of active consideration currently being given to the UK signing the Council of Europe Charter for Regional or Minority Languages, the British Government will in particular in relation to the Irish language, where appropriate and where people so desire it:

- take resolute action to promote the language;
- facilitate and encourage the use of the language in speech and writing in public and private life where there is appropriate demand;
- seek to remove, where possible, restrictions which would discourage or work against the maintenance or development of the language;
- make provision for liaising with the Irish language community, representing their views to public authorities and investigating complaints;
- place a statutory duty on the Department of Education to encourage and facilitate Irish medium education in line with current provision for integrated education;
- explore urgently with the relevant British authorities, and in co-operation with the Irish broadcasting authorities, the scope for achieving more widespread availability of Teilifis na Gaeilige in Northern Ireland;
- seek more effective ways to encourage and provide financial support for Irish language film and television production in Northern Ireland; and
- encourage the parties to secure agreement that this commitment will be sustained by a new Assembly in a way which takes account of the desires and sensitivities of the community.

Appendix 2: The Northern Ireland Curriculum

Historically, education policy in Northern Ireland, especially during periods of direct rule from London, has closely followed policy in England and Wales. The 1989 Education Reform (Northern Ireland) Order (ERO) was a Northern Ireland version of the 1988 Education Reform Act for England and Wales. It led in 1990 to the introduction of the statutory Northern Ireland curriculum following a consultation process during the previous year.

The Northern Ireland curriculum aims to

1. promote the spiritual, moral, cultural, intellectual, and physical development of pupils at school and thereby of society; and
2. prepare pupils for the opportunities, responsibilities and experiences of adult life.

> It is intended to constitute between 75 percent and 85 percent of teaching time in both the primary and post-primary sectors. It is specified by:

- **key stages,** which are related to the age of pupils;
- **areas of study** with specified contributory subjects; and
- **cross-curricular themes.**

Table 3: Key Stages in the Northern Ireland Curriculum

	Key Stage	School Year	Average Age
Primary	1	1–4	5–8
	2	5–7	9–11
Post-Primary	3	8–10	12–14
	4	11–12	15–16

The **Primary Curriculum** is comprised of religious education and five areas of study. Subjects indicated in Table 2 have statutory programmes of study. In addition there are four cross curricular themes: Education for Mutual Understanding (EMU), Cultural Heritage (CH), Health Education, and Information Technology. EMU and CH were conjoined in 1992 and are regarded as one theme at both primary and post-primary levels.

Table 4: The Northern Ireland Primary Curriculum

Area of Study	Compulsory Contributory Subjects
Religious Education	Statutory Core Syllabus
English ⎫ Maths ⎬ Science ⎭	English Maths Science Statutory Programmes of Study
Environment and Society	History, Geography
Creative and Expressive Studies	Art and Design, Music, Physical Education
Cross-Curricular Themes	Education for Mutual Understanding, Cultural Heritage, Health Education, Information Technology

The **Post-Primary Curriculum** consists of religious education and six areas of study as indicated in Table 3. Additionally there are six cross-curricular themes: EMU, CH, Health Education, Information Technology, Economic Awareness, and Careers Education. Again, individual subjects have detailed programmes of study which delineate content, skills, and understanding.

Table 5: The Northern Ireland Post-Primary Curriculum

Area of Study	Minimum Requirement
Religious Education	Statutory Core Syllabus
English Maths Science and Technology and Design	Statutory Programmes of Study
Environment and Society	One of: History, Geography, Business Studies, Economics, Home Economics
Creative and Expressive Studies	Statutory Programme for Physical Education
Language Studies	One of: French, German, Italian, Spanish, Irish
Cross-Curricular Themes:	Education for Mutual Understanding, Cultural Heritage, Health Education, Information Technology, Economic Awareness, Careers Education

As with the national curriculum in England and Wales, the Northern Ireland curriculum was criticised for being overly prescriptive and unmanageable. In response, a limited review was undertaken in 1994–95 and a modified curriculum implemented in 1996.

A commitment was given that no changes would be made to the statutory curriculum for a five-year period ending in September 2001. However, significant change continued in other areas, particularly relating to assessment. The DE launched the School Improvement Programme in 1998 and set targets for literacy and numeracy. These and other priorities within the education system and wider society led to a recognition that a comprehensive review of the Northern Ireland curriculum was necessary. The CCEA launched a review in 1998.

Appendix 3: **Catholics and Protestants as a Percentage of the Population District Council Areas 1991**

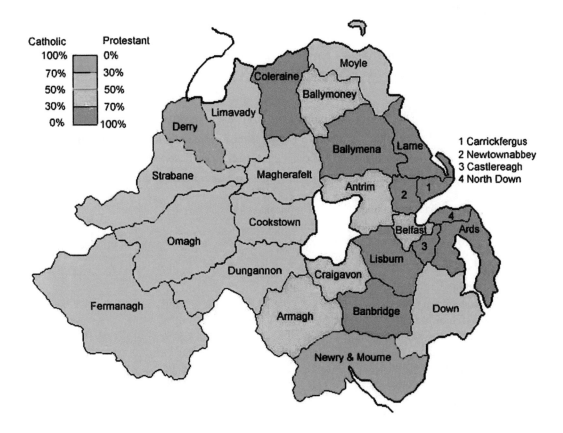

Source: Information based on the Religion Report on the 1991 Census
http://cain.ulst.ac.uk/events/bsunday/pringle002.gif

Appendix 4: Fact sheet - Northern Ireland

Total population: 1,685,267

Unemployment
(persons aged between 16 and 64):   4.14%

The conflict:

- Since 1968, the conflict has caused more than 3,600 deaths and 40,000 casualties.
- In some areas the death rate is more than ten times the average rate for Northern Ireland.
- Almost 20% of children aged 10–11 surveyed had been in or close to bomb explosions.
- In Ballymurphy, an area of West Belfast, among 9- to 11-year-old children:

    - 90% had seen a hijacked vehicle burning
    - more than 50% had seen shooting incidents
    - 37% had witnessed a bomb explosion

Religion:

Catholic	40.26%
Presbyterian Church in Ireland	20.69%
Church of Ireland	3.00%
Methodist Church in Ireland	3.51%
Other Christian (including Christian related)	6.07%
Other religions and philosophies	0.30%
No religion or none stated	13.88%

More than 50% of the population lived in areas that were more than 90% Protestant or Catholic (1991).

Reported religion of pupils in schools in Northern Ireland: 51% Catholic; 42% Protestant; 1% other Christian; 0.3% non-Christian; 6% no religion/not recorded

Education structure: 6 + 3 + 2 (+ 2)

Compulsory education: up to age 16; there are approximately 350,000 pupils in full-time education and approximately 20,000 teachers.

Education system:

- Parallel systems of Protestant and Catholic schools.
- Most pupils attend mainly Protestant or mainly Catholic schools.
- At post-primary level, schools are in general segregated on the basis of ability and often by gender.

Types of schools:

- *Controlled Schools:* Essentially Protestant schools—owned by the Education and Library Boards, although they are mostly controlled by their Boards of Governors. The Protestant churches are represented on the Board of Governors.
- *Catholic Maintained Schools:* Essentially Catholic schools—owned by the Catholic Church but managed by a Board of Governors. The Education and Library Boards provide some financial assistance, by financing recurrent costs and the employment of nonteaching staff.
- *Other Maintained:* Essentially Protestant schools, in that they are owned by the Protestant Church and managed by a Board of Governors. Like the Catholic maintained schools, they receive funding from the Education and Library Boards for the recurrent costs.
- *Voluntary Grammar:* Owned by school trustees and managed by a Board of Governors. For more academically able students, identified through the Transfer Procedure. Segregated by religion, most being either predominantly Protestant or predominantly Catholic.
- *Grant Maintained Integrated Schools:* New schools established to provide an integrated alternative to existing schools at both primary and post-primary level. Partially owned by trustees and managed by a Board of Governors, with their recurrent costs being met by the Department of Education.

Language: English and some Irish (although according to census data from 2001, 89.65% of the population over the age of three has no knowledge of Irish).

Sources: The author; the Northern Ireland Statistics and Research Agency, available at
http://www.nisra.gov.uk/census/Census2001Output/KeyStatistics/keystatrep1.html;
Conflict Archive on the Internet [CAIN], available at http://cain.ulst.ac.uk/;
Department of Education for Northern Ireland [DENI] press release, (March 1999)

Note: All data for 2001 unless otherwise specified.

Chapter 7

Redefining Rwanda's Future:
The Role of Curriculum in Social Reconstruction

John Rutayisire

John Kabano

Jolly Rubagiza

About the Authors

John Rutayisire is the director of the National Curriculum Development Centre (NCDC) in Kigali. Established by the Ministry of Education in 1996, the NCDC is responsible and accountable for curriculum development and endeavours to consult and liaise with other departments and organisations. Its work is closely linked with that of the National Unity and Reconciliation Commission. Within the context of the tremendous effort in policy development in the early 2000s, the NCDC has been the lead institution in the process of development of the textbook policy, curriculum policy, and ongoing language policy in addition to participation in all other MINEDUC policy development processes. John Rutayisire was formerly a senior lecturer in education at the Tonota College of Education in Botswana.

John Kabano, PhD, is a lecturer at the Kigali Institute of Education in the Department of Special Education. His fields of interest include pedagogy, citizenship education and social cohesion, children's rights in education, human rights issues in education, a human rights–based approach to programming, community capacity development, minority issues in education, HIV/AIDS education, and special education.

Jolly Rubagiza, MA, is a lecturer at the Kigali Institute of Education in the Department of Educational Foundations. Her fields of interest include curriculum issues in education, gender and education, and HIV/AIDS education.

List of Acronyms

CDR	Coalition pour la Défense de la République (Coalition for the Defence of the Republic)
CfBT	Centre for British Teachers
CPR	Conseil protestant du Rwanda (Protestant Council of Rwanda)
DfID	Department for International Development
EFA	Education for All
IBE	International Bureau of Education (UNESCO)
ICT	Information and Communication Technologies
IIEP	International Institute for Educational Planning (UNESCO)
MINEDUC	Ministry of Education, Science, Technology, and Scientific Research
MRND	Mouvement révolutionnaire national pour le développement (National Revolutionary Movement for Development)
NCDC	National Curriculum Development Centre
NURC	National Unity and Reconciliation Commission.
PRSP	Poverty Reduction Strategy Programme
SNEC	Secrétariat National de l'Enseignement Catholique (National Secrétariat of Catholic Education)
UNAR	Union Nationale Rwandaise (National Rwandan Union)
UNESCO	United Nations Educational, Scientific and Cultural Organization
UNICEF	United Nations Children's Fund

INTRODUCTION

Context

Rwanda is a small country of 26,338 square kilometres, containing more than eight million inhabitants and located in the heart of Africa (see Map). The country is landlocked, sharing a border with the Democratic Republic of Congo to the west, Uganda to the north, Tanzania to the east, and Burundi to the south.

Map of the Republic of Rwanda

Source: http://www.lib.texas.edu/maps/cia03/rwanda_sm03.gif

In 1994, Rwanda was plunged into one of the genocides that scarred the twentieth century. Following this tragedy, the country found itself faced with an enormous challenge in terms of moral, social, and material reconstruction. This demanded that all human potential be mobilised in an effort at reconciliation and development. Having successfully moved from the emergency to the development phase, the government is presently committed to a number of goals in its development strategy, which include economic growth, national unity and reconciliation, and the reduction of poverty. Education is seen as a major instrument of national development in pursuit of these three goals. Education can provide the human capital necessary for poverty reduction, making available the only kind of negotiable capital to which the majority of the population will have access. It can be the single most powerful instrument to combat prejudice, foster common citizenship, and achieve national reconciliation (Education Sector Review, 2002).

Rationale and purpose

Most Rwandans have come to believe that the political environment that prevailed before 1994 heavily influenced an education system that did not do much in terms of the prevention of conflict. The Rwandan system was characterised by injustice based on ethnicity, regionalism, gender disparity, and religious discrimination, all of which could certainly have contributed to the 1994 genocide. Indeed, there was too much focus on human differences (ethnicity, regionalism) and too little on similarities (issues of common belonging, culture, solidarity). We argue in this chapter that to do away with the historical divisions among the Rwandan people and build a lasting peace, the education system must be reformed to address these concerns. It should emphasise values that can bring Rwandan youth to live peacefully together.

"Concern with the ways in which the content and process of education may actually contribute to precipitate the outbreak and development of violent conflict," the recognition that "weaknesses in educational structure and content may have contributed to civil conflict," and the idea that "an education system that reinforces social fissures can represent a dangerous source of conflict" are all believed to have had a direct bearing on the Rwandan genocide of 1994 (UNESCO: IBE, 2002). We believe that curriculum renewal can make a difference.

It is in view of all this that the curriculum, said to be the heart of any education system, is being given great attention. A number of Rwandans think that a civic education that emphasises the values missing in the former curriculum could bring about unity, reconciliation, and a lasting peace. It is against this backdrop that this study has sought to establish what was taught in schools in the past that could have contributed to social division and conflict and what should be taught today to help prevent future conflicts.

In post-genocide Rwanda, there has been much attention and interest paid to restoring the rule of law, good governance, socioeconomic reconstruction, and security. Nevertheless, in spite of the emphasis on increasing the access to and improving the quality of education for young Rwandans, very little attention has been paid to investing in an assessment of how schools understand and teach about issues related to values that reinforce social cohesion, citizenship, human rights, peace, unity, and reconciliation.

Thus, the challenge for Rwandan schools, and for the education system in general, is to first reach a consensus on how to interpret the events before and after the 1994 genocide, and to then determine how to move forward and look to the future. There is a need to try to situate our understanding of genocide in theories of social identity and collective memory so as to identify the social and psychological issues that may also pertain to the process of building social cohesion and, specifically for Rwanda, reconciliation. From this perspective, the purpose of the present study includes an exploration of the role of the education system and its impact on Rwandan society. Although problems related to history, culture, identity, and collective memory warrant separate investigation, this study seeks to highlight some of the issues in general terms and to raise awareness. The intention is to record some of the historical dimension and document the effort being undertaken in the education reform process, particularly with regard to school curriculum. Our assumption is that it may be possible that both memory and history, as expressed through the school curriculum, might enhance the reconciliation process. However, we must also caution that the influence of the school, as only one aspect of civic socialisation in young people's lives, need not be overemphasised, especially as it is related to the broad national goals of forming a culture of peace, unity, respect for human rights, tolerance, and the instilling of positive values based on democratic principles and good governance.

Nonetheless, it is at school that the essential basic elements of identity formation are promoted for one united Rwandan nation with common citizenship, common goals and ideals, and a spirit of patriotism. Schools should promote the common values that can be formed early in life for the purpose of appreciating cooperation and peaceful coexistence, and of fostering tolerance in groups, communities, and society at large. In sum, the study seeks to record and assess some of the past practices and current reforms, in order to propose the incorporation of a few fundamental aspects of education that are necessary for social cohesion, and essential for the young people growing up today and in the future in Rwanda.

Methodology

This study is part of the whole process of curriculum change and review underway in Rwanda. Indeed, the practice in Rwanda today is that stakeholders in education such as parents, teachers, the community, NGOs, the Churches, and others are consulted on educational policy development from time to time in order to get their input in the building of a curriculum for social cohesion. The methodology used in this case study, therefore, is in line with the current process of educational policy development. The researchers consulted with teachers, head teachers, students, Ministry of Education officials, donors, religious group representatives, and others in order to attempt to find answers to our two research questions:

1. What was taught in schools in the past, and how has that contributed to social divisions and conflict?

2. What values should be taught in Rwandan schools to bring about social cohesion?

The views documented relative to the first question are dealt with in the first two sections, and the essence of the data collected for the second question is developed in detail in the fifth section.

Defining key concepts

For the purposes of clarity we would like to state from the outset how we understand the following terms:

Peace: public quiet, order, and security. It is a state free of war and violence. Peace is not a state free of conflicts, since conflicts are part of human nature. Peace occurs when conflicts are solved through dialogue and communication.

Reconciliation: a settlement of a quarrel or disagreement. It occurs after violence when people agree to recreate harmonious relationships among them. Reconciliation is the cornerstone of social cohesion in conflict-affected societies. Reconciliation allows peace and social cohesion to be brought back. In the case of Rwanda, this is even more important, considering that Rwandans have all lost as a result of the genocide. Apart from the enormous loss of life, the violence brought about social, psychological, economic, and political destruction. In order to rebuild, all Rwandans have to unite. But in order to do this they must first reconcile.

Social cohesion: a state of peace and harmony between different social groups. Social cohesion refers to an image of a society where differing groups live and hold together and try to build their nation. Social cohesion differs from a state of tolerance as people have to communicate and cooperate in their common welfare. In Rwanda this means that the different social groups have to come together to develop the country that they share in common and to which everyone has a feeling of belonging.

"Ethnicity" and "ethnic group": Eriksen (1993) in Haralambos and Holborn (1995) points out that

> *Ethnicity* derives from the Greek word *ethnos* which is itself derived from another Greek word *ethnikos*. This meant pagan or Heathen. The term *ethnic* had this meaning in English until around the middle of the nineteenth century when it started being used as an alternative to race. However, Eriksen argues that in modern anthropology and sociology, an *ethnic group* is usually seen as being culturally rather than physically distinctive.

According to Yinger (1981) in Haralombus and Holbon, an "ethnic group"—or, as he calls it, an *ethnie*—exists in the fullest sense when

> A segment of a large society is seen by others to be different in some combination of the language, religion, race, related culture; the members also perceive themselves in that way; and they participate in shared activities built around their real or mythical common origin or culture.

Richardson (1987; 1990) in Haralombos and Holborn sees "ethnic groups" as a more acceptable term than the available alternatives. He sees "ethnicity" as based on cultural differences between groups, and says:

> This classification approach is attractive in so far as it highlights socio-cultural criteria (unlike the conventional "race " systems) and it accommodates potentially a wide range of groups unlike the two category black and white model.

Nevertheless, Richardson believes that there are serious problems with the idea of ethnicity as well. He argues that in particular, it can be very difficult to distinguish clearly between ethnic groups. He goes on to explain that many groups are themselves subdivided, and they may overlap with other groups. By way of elaboration, he continues by arguing that ethnic groups can be distinguished in different ways, leading to different classifications. Thus, for example:

> Territorial origin could lead to distinctions between Bangladeshis, Pakistanis and Indians whereas *religious affiliation* would lead to distinction between Hindus, Sikhis and Muslims. *Linguistic* criteria could produce a third system.

From the definitions above it is clear that the issue of ethnicity is a complex one. When applied to the Rwandan context by foreigners who may know very little about the situation, it creates a lot of problems.

There has never been any "Hutuland" or "Tutsiland" or "Twaland." Rwandans had the same religion before colonialism and have always had one language—Kinyarwanda. In the absence of clear-cut, distinctive criteria, the colonialists had to find ways and means of applying the divide and rule policy, and they invented theories of origin that have never been supported by any empirical evidence. This explains why many Rwandans attribute their social divisions to colonialists.

In conclusion, Haralombus and Holborn argue that the idea of ethnic group is the least unsatisfactory way of dealing with the problem of classification. According to them, it is more flexible and adaptable than other approaches, and can accommodate changes in people's perceptions about the groups to which they belong. They give the example of the Irish in England as one such group that can be accommodated within the ethnicity framework whereas they do not fit under alternative classifications such as that of "race." The argument concludes by recognising that "[s]ocial divisions between such groups are created, maintained, altered and challenged by humans and . . . are not the inevitable product of supposed biological differences." Finally, it is said that the term "race" remains useful only when ethnic groups either believe themselves, or are so believed by others, to be distinguished by phenotype.

Whatever the case might be, the Rwandan education system, and particularly the curriculum, is faced with the challenge of instilling values that lead to feelings of common belonging and social cohesion, in light of the years of damage caused by the colonial distortion of Rwandan history and culture.

Organisation of the study

In the first section of this study, we present a background to conflict in Rwanda. In the second, we highlight some school practices that reinforced social fissures, creating a dangerous source of conflict. In view of this, we outline in the third section the rationales for curriculum policy change and the framework within which change is to be conceptualised—that is, Vision 2020 and the Poverty Reduction Strategy Programme (PRSP)—as a basis for unity and reconciliation and therefore for national cohesion. The fourth section sets the scene for a new curriculum paradigm in terms of policy and principles upon which new curricula are to be structured and developed. In the last section, we propose an outline of a new curriculum for social cohesion in Rwandan schools based mainly on our research findings.

BACKGROUND TO THE CONFLICT

Perceptions on the causes of conflict in Rwanda

Data analysis from interviews we have conducted indicates that there tend to be two differing views on the evolution of the nature of social divisions in Rwanda. Proponents of the first view maintain that social divisions in Rwanda were created with the establishment of colonisation. However, they admit that while conflict existed in precolonial Rwandan society, it was not of a collective nature, nor was it directed by definition against any particular social group. When the Catholic missionaries arrived in Rwanda, they created social divisions on the basis of socioeconomic status and religious affiliation (e.g., between Hutu, Tutsi, and Twa, and between Christians and non-Christians). They structured political and social relationships based on this differentiation, thus accentuating differences and creating ethnic categories. This view maintains that through the imposition of identity cards, the colonial authorities defined and confined each Rwandan citizen to his or her own ethnic belonging (a practice maintained by post-independence Rwandan governments).

This view further rejects any existence of ethnic groups in precolonial Rwandan society and argues that in the traditional social organisation, Hutu, Tutsi, and Twa referred to social status categories and not to ethnic distinctions. A Hutu was somebody who tilled the land, while a Tutsi owned cattle. *These concepts never referred to a racial content.* This creation of ethnic differentiation became a source of social division, exacerbated by other forms of classification based on religious affiliation, regional residence, and gender. For the advocates of this view, precolonial Rwandan society was characterised as being unified under the reign of one monarch and sharing the same language, culture, and religion. While most proponents of this view deny the existence of social divisions and tensions in precolonial Rwandan society, others will admit to the existence of social divisions, which they attribute to economic differentiations. Generally, however, this first view denies the existence of ethnic distinctions in precolonial Rwanda and attributes both the creation of ethnic identity and ethnicity as a source of social division to the colonial power.

The second view shares the conviction that ethnicity is a creation of colonialism but differs from the first view in that it accepts the idea that ethnic differentiation was a social reality in precolonial Rwanda. In other words, the second view differs from the first inasmuch as it admits that the colonial administration only exacerbated preexisting tensions. The advocates of this thinking accuse proponents of the first view of inadequately analysing the history of Rwanda, and of believing that "every evil" has been a result of colonisation. They promote the idea of studying the history of Rwanda in order to shed light on the facts underlying the origins of ethnic group identity in order to see contemporary understandings of ethnicity more clearly. This second view suggests that, in such discussions, the role Rwandans themselves have played is frequently overlooked, and insists that Rwandans avoid their responsibility in attributing all causes of their misfortune to the classic colonial strategy of divide and rule. In other societies, they maintain, people have overcome the colonial heritage of division, but the people of Rwanda have preferred to amplify it, as stated by one of the respondents: "I do not support the approach of our leaders, always blaming colonialism, we should see the role played by Rwandans in these divisions and conflict." Thus they refute the first view in its attempts to reduce all precolonial differences and divisions solely to issues of economic status.

The position of the authors of the present study is that colonialism fixed the idea of ethnic distinction forever and made it easy for each group to discriminate against the other, culminating in an extreme form of violence in 1994. According to our understanding, the issue of ethnicity in Rwanda is still in a state of hypothesis. As some historians suggest, relevant research needs to be carried out in order to confirm or invalidate the theories on the existence of ethnic distinction in Rwanda. We will explore some of these historical analyses in the paragraphs that follow.

Before the colonialists, there was no known major conflict among Rwandans, who shared a common language and a common culture. Conflict did exist between the kingdom of Rwanda and other kingdoms for purposes of expansion through the process of state formation. There is, however, no record of conflict between the Hutu, Tutsi, and Twa. The different clans, which were shared by all Rwandans, are said to have lived in peaceful coexistence until the advent of the first colonialists. Rwandan people were essentially classified through "clans" and not "tribes," a word that does not rightly apply to the Rwandan context. Precolonial socioeconomic classifications were based on who owned cattle and who tilled the land. Thus those who kept cattle were known as Tutsi, and those who tilled the land were Hutu. The Twa engaged mainly in pottery and related artisanal activities.

In Rwanda, European missionaries who arrived before colonialists deliberately distorted the structure of Rwandan society. Thus the term "tribe" was erroneously but quite deliberately applied to categorise Rwandan people even when the European colonialists were well aware that the Rwandan society did not have any semblance of what should characterise a tribe. As Prunier (1995) observes:

> These are the people who have often and inappropriately been called the "tribes" of Rwanda. They had none of the characteristics of tribes, which are micro-nations. They shared the same Bantu language, lived side by side with each other without any "Hutu land" or "Tutsi land" and often intermarried.

As mentioned earlier, the nineteenth-century Europeans formulated dangerous theories and hypotheses, drawing definitive conclusions based on assumptions. The indubitability of the various hypotheses lay solely in the racist minds of these early Europeans, most of whom were missionaries and explorers, who helped pave the way for colonial rule.

In the case of Rwanda, the famous British explorer John Hanning Speke set this racism in motion. He came to the conclusion that since some kingdoms in the interlacustrine region (the modern Great Lakes region) had a centralised and, in the case of Rwanda, an efficient political and administrative system, they therefore must have had a foreign origin associated with a "superior" civilisation. Prunier (1995) laments that Speke

> Decided without a shred of evidence that these carriers of a superior civilisation were the Galla of southern Ethiopia, an opinion later shared by other 19th century explorers such as Sir Samuel Baker and Gaetano Casati and by 20th century missionaries such as Father Van den Burgt, Father Gorju and John Roscoe. Father Pages, on the other hand, thought that they were descendants of the ancient Egyptians, while De Lacger saw them as coming from either Melanesia or Asia Minor.

Prunier continues to observe that

> Some of these missionaries had become so rhapsodic with this so-called "superior race" that they believed the "Tutsi" had come from a "primordial red race"; others fantasised about India or even as the Dominican Father Etienne Brosse suggested, from the garden of Eden. Some years later the Belgian administrator Count Renaud de Briey coolly speculated that the Tutsi could very well be the last survivors of the lost continent of Atlantis, while as late as 1970 a dignified former French Ambassador to the newly independent Rwanda could pass off as a serious anthropological literature a long poetical rambling about the Tutsi "Magi" who had come from Tibet, with a minor branch making it to Iceland, pushing in front of them the animal steam roller of their giant herd!!

Contemporary Rwandans have to deal with this history, replete with its distortions, unrealistic myths, and hypotheses. That kind of thinking not only influenced but also conditioned the thinking and attitude of Europeans both inside and outside Rwanda. They thought—and many continue to think—that they knew about the social groups in Rwanda. That has had implications on national cohesion of Rwandans, since many of these outsiders with distorted knowledge have had and continue to have a great deal of influence over the population. Missionaries and colonial rulers came to take these distortions as truth—indeed, as a kind of *unquestioned* truth. This in turn directed not only their thinking but also the colonial rulers' day-to-day decisionmaking. This falsification of the nature of Rwandan society was to have a profound effect on the Rwandan population in terms of their self-concept and self-esteem, and this would contribute to the conflict in the 1990s.

Prunier could not put it any better when he concludes:

> If we combine the subjective feelings with the objective political and administrative decisions of the colonial authorities favouring one group over the other, we can begin to see how a very dangerous bomb was almost absent-mindedly manufactured through out the peaceful years of the *abazungu* domination.

We believe that Rwandans should not be slaves to this colonial history of social divisions and divisiveness. Moreover, they must deal with it in a more objective and positive manner. They need to critically assess their problems and the causes of their social divisions and together work to find common solutions. In doing so, they would be taking on the responsibility for their common survival as one nation. They should be proactive and learn from the lessons of history for the purpose of creating a better future, especially for the young. Presently, there are ongoing debates nationwide with various positions adopted on some events in the history of Rwanda, such as those of 1959 during which thousands of Rwandans fled into exile. The answers to the following questions, for example, depend upon the interpretation of those events: Was this a form of genocide? Was it a revolution, as the colonial administration claimed? Who is a citizen of Rwanda? Who can be seen as the rightful owner of disputed land, those who owned it before 1959 or those who occupied it ("illegally") after that? Should those who were forced to flee Rwanda in 1959 be able to reclaim their land and other property, or do the thirty-five years that have elapsed since then invalidate their claims? Should all Rwandans simply share whatever land there is? Who is the judge? Who can decide? These questions and many more need to be addressed. As refugees have been resettled, some progress has been made, though whether or not it has been to their satisfaction is a different question. The challenge for the education system is enormous.

Nature of conflict

Exploring the extent to which conflict seems to have pervaded the Rwandan social fabric is beyond the scope of this study. Nevertheless, the interviews and informal discussions that we have conducted reveal conflicting views and opinions regarding the nature of conflict in Rwanda. In addition to education, other factors have contributed to the recent conflict in Rwanda. Without putting them in any order of importance, interviewees and resource persons consulted have identified the following as possible causes of recent conflict in Rwanda:

- colonial legacy;
- socioeconomic crisis;
- political discontent;
- hatred;
- effects of past violence;
- opportunism;
- breakdown in moral standards and values;
- discrimination;

- oppression;
- favouritism and corruption;
- too many transition periods—from monarchy to colonialism to republicanism to democracy;
- ignorance and backwardness;
- collective behaviour with no individual responsibility;
- unquestioned obedience and submissiveness;
- social powerlessness;
- political powerlessness;
- isolation; and
- absence of external restraints.

The diverse nature of these responses calls for a thorough analysis. A closer look at the list shows that no single factor could account for recent conflict, and that most of these factors affect many societies worldwide and are not specific to Rwanda alone. The remainder of this section examines a selection of the available literature that discuss some of these factors. No single analysis among them seems sufficient to give answer to the question: Why Rwanda?

Unquestioned obedience and submissiveness: A cultural basis for conflict?

It is the Europeans who introduced "indirect rule" in association with the ideology of racial superiority. In the Rwandan context, the missionaries and later the colonialists portrayed the Hutu as obedient and docile and the Tutsi as commandeering and cunning (Prunier, 1995). Such racist arguments have shaped attitudes and mentalities with far-reaching consequences felt to this day.

Prunier observed that there was an unquestioning obedience among the Rwandans and that this was to play a tragic and absolutely central role in the unfolding of the 1994 genocide. Many people have taken advantage of arguments of this nature about the presumed docile nature of Rwandese. Such people tend to downplay the fact that Rwandan culture, like many cultures in Africa, Asia, and Latin America, tend to value the nonexpression of disagreement. This can be extremely misleading to outsiders, and, as Peter Uvin (1998) explains,

> Rwandans are perfectly capable of not following orders. They are capable of protesting authority, as the rapidly growing opposition to the Habyarimana regime by the 1990s indicates. Rwandans are also capable of judging their acts and possess moral systems; they are not devoid of moral values.

In any case, nonexpression of disagreement is not synonymous with obedience, and does not in any way account for the outbreak of the 1994 genocide or any other form of conflict anywhere. To accept such an argument would be tantamount to exempting or absolving the masses that committed genocide of their responsibility, shifting it only to government leaders. Everybody who commits a crime must be held individually accountable. It has now been forty years since we gained independence. We should have learned by now how to overcome the challenges of colonialism and racism. We cannot blame Europeans forever. We must hold ourselves accountable for our actions. It is hoped that education and curriculum reforms might facilitate this process.

Opportunism

During times of upheaval, some people benefit from conflict. They join in to appropriate someone else's property, possessions, or land. Sometimes there is widespread looting of businesses. In the case of Rwanda, similar stories have been told which support the findings of Andre and Platteau (1995) in a study of northern Rwanda that demonstrates how all the Hutu who were killed there during the genocide tended to be either the wealthier ones or social outcasts, suggesting that the 1994 genocide provided a unique opportunity to settle scores for past discrimination and oppression or to reshuffle land properties.

There are also numerous stories to the effect that land grabbing was a reason for participation in the genocide and even a cause of it. However, the authors ask why government ministers, politicians, civil servants, and other officials were not the primary targets, since they had been grabbing land from poor peasants for a long time. As Goldhagen (1996) reiterates, for opportunism to exist, there must be a process of violence into which opportunists can insert themselves and do their dirty work; thus opportunism, by definition, cannot be the primary explanation for the process of violent social disintegration.

Hatred and discrimination

The argument about the breakdown in moral standards and values has its roots in the racism referred to earlier. For decades, through divisive and discriminatory ideology and practices, the Europeans taught the Rwandan people to hate themselves. This racism had penetrated so deeply into the psyche of many Rwandans that even after independence they had come to harbour and believe images of themselves as radically and unchangeably different in their origin and moral character, as well as in their social attributes and roles. This racism lay dormant for a very long time, making it less visible, less of a priority to people, and less needed by both those in power and the masses. But it was abandoned. Thus prejudice toward a group can exist without showing itself in day-to-day behaviour toward all members of that group; it can even exist while allowing exceptions for specific people (Duckitt, 1992; Gamson, 1995).

From the argument above, it follows that racism was reactivated in the 1990s through hate speech and sporadic violence against Tutsi, rendering them socially dead (Goldhagen, 1996). Hence, its rapid reactivation is testimony to its widespread and profoundly ingrained nature, even from the onset of Habyarimana's rule in 1971 to the mid-1980s and early 1990s.

In the 1990s, the ideology radicalised, leading to the genocide that began on April 7, 1994. As Uvin (1998) reminds us:

> This process of radicalisation fed on two basic forces: One emanating from government and the elites and one from the needs of ordinary people. Both these processes were necessary to create genocide. For decades, anti-Tutsi racism had served as a deliberately maintained strategy of legitimisation of the powers that be and was kept alive through a systematic public structure of discrimination and education, in which the different and problematic identity of all Tutsi was constantly being referred to. Under threat by political and economic processes, parts of the elite increased their use of the old strategy and effectively spread it throughout society. This had been done before in 1959 and 1973 and it still worked because so little had changed in Rwanda.

Those who have been following events in Rwanda, particularly during the process of conflict, will be familiar with the phenomenon whereby racist prejudice is used as a means for ordinary people, subject to structural violence and humiliation, to make sense of their predicament, to explain their ever-growing misery through projection and scapegoating.

In Rwanda, the state-supplied racism provided poor Hutu with a sense of value, as well as an "explanation" for the poverty and deprivation they faced daily. As Simpson and Yinger (1953) so clearly put it: "The designation of inferior group comes from those on top—an expression of their right to rule—as well as from frustrated persons often near the bottom, as an expression of their need for security."

The designation of inferior groups and their more or less active exclusion serves an important function of projection and use of scapegoating. Also, the devaluation of others and use of scapegoating are said to be strategies for coping with the stress of persistent life problems, frustration, and lack of self-esteem (Staub, 1990).

Marc Ross (1993) sums it up when he asserts that

> These shared images of the world and plans for a common perception of the differences between one's own group and outsiders; the interpretative processes involved in intense conflict situations emphasize the homogeneity of each party, often using minor objective differences to mark major social distinctions. Outsiders then can serve as objects for externalisation, displacement, and projection of intense negative feelings, which are also present but denied within the group.

Socioeconomic and political factors

The role of socioeconomic and political factors as possible causes of conflict—and, in the Rwandan case, of the genocide of 1994—has been well documented. For that reason, we will only highlight key issues that have an impact on future socioeconomic policy and education as such.

A number of scholars have recently attempted to relate "ethnic conflict" to past discrimination and oppression leading to violence, with the key indicator for the risk of genocide being the existence of systematic differential treatment by the larger society. Others have maintained that ethnic divisions are merely smokescreens, forms of false consciousness kept alive by the elites to mask their economic and political power to divide the forces of resistance. The bottom line, however, is that more or less objective real-world socioeconomic and political differences are ultimately responsible for ethnic conflict, while ethnicity per se is only a symptom of the problem—although a powerful one, for it is so eminently mobilisable (Uvin, 1998). Thus, what are, in essence, class or economic conflicts tend to take ethnic forms because of the salience of these primordial attachments to people and the presence of ready-made institutions, symbols, leaders, and images. However, the core of the conflict is really economic or political imbalance.

Rupesinghe (1988) and Stavenhagen (1990) (cited in Uvin, 1998) support this assertion when they insist that ethnic differences are used consciously or unconsciously to distinguish the opposing actors in a conflict situation, particularly when they become powerful mobilising symbols, as is so often the case when ethnicity does become a determining factor in the nature and dynamic of the conflict. Hence the root cause of the conflict may be economic, but ethnicity can become, over time, an independent factor in itself, taking on independent dynamics and complicating the resolution of the conflict.

Uvin, however, does not feel that the socioeconomic factors adequately explain the Rwandan genocide. He points out that Rwanda was not a case of a small minority exploiting the masses, nor one of an exploited majority rising up to throw off the bonds of exploitation. He adds that, if anything, the violence was committed by the numerically, politically, militarily, and economically dominant group against the minority.

Historians tend to contend that during colonial rule, and probably much earlier, the question of ethnicity in Rwanda was related to socioeconomic differences, and leaders responsible for the genocide evoked reminders of this past inequality and oppression. But this should have ended after independence in 1963. Most agents of the 1994 genocide had not even been born at the time of independence. So why were they so readily willing to kill their neighbours forty years later—neighbours who, in any case, were just as poor and powerless as they were? One can see how ethnicity served as a tool for the political elite to legitimise their dominance and hide from the poor the injustices they were subjected to.

Horowitz (1985) and Moore (1987) raise another theory of ethnic conflict. Violence is likely to happen during periods of rapid change associated with modernisation, socioeconomic development, and political transition. Part of the explanation is that those who benefit from the status quo will be tempted to revert to violence to defend their privileges, while those who seek change will consequently be tempted to do the same.

Another version looks at society-wide processes of unfulfilled expectations that could have led to frustrations and aggression. Dahrendorf (1995) argues that when opportunities are held out for people but are not yet there to grasp, and when economic development accelerates but social and political development lags behind, a mixture of frustration and irresponsibility develops that breeds violence. He adds that such violence can be individual and undirected, but it can also become collective and directed against apparently better-off neighbours, more successful strangers in one's midst, or both. Uvin asks similar questions:

> Why did people not kill those who were much more directly responsible for their poverty-corrupt politicians, and land grabbing civil servants, patronising local party cadres, and corrupt police officials—rather than their equally poor Tutsi neighbours?

A similar argument about economic recession and competition over scarce resources has been raised before, but has not answered the question, mainly because there were many countries that were as poor as Rwanda—or some a great deal poorer—whose societies have remained united and intact. Again: Why Rwanda?

Nature of the peace

The violence was brought to an end when the Rwanda Patriotic Front (RPF) defeated the *genocidaire* regime in 1994. Thereafter, a transitional government was put in place according to the Arusha peace agreement signed in 1993. All parties were included with the exception of two, namely, the Mouvement Révolutionnaire National pour le Développement (MRND) and the Coalition pour la Défense de la République (CDR), which had executed the killings. The power was redistributed by sharing out cabinet and other political posts. For example, the president belonged to one party and the prime minister to another. The Rwandan Parliament was put in place, with members from all political parties.

The inclusion of all parties to form a government of national unity started a process of reconciliation and brought about the beginnings of peace. This was later facilitated by setting up the Unity and Reconciliation Commission and subsequent *Gacaca* system of justice (traditional tribunals) and releasing prisoners, as by the presidential decree of January 3, 2003. All this is in line with fostering unity and reconciliation among Rwandans.

We believe that more research needs to be done to explore the motives of the people who carried out and perpetrated the violence, and to thoroughly understand the social structures that triggered the process that resulted in Rwandan society losing the values, restraints, and ethics which under normal circumstances make these actions impossible and abhorrent to contemplate. The cause of the loosening of Rwandan social and moral fabric should, as we mentioned earlier, give historians, anthropologists, sociologists, psychologists, and philosophers serious questions to explore for many years to come.

ASSESSMENT OF SCHOOLING AS A FACTOR OF CONFLICT

Precolonial education

Before the coming of European missionaries and later colonialists, education in traditional Rwanda was largely informal. There is little documentation describing this system. Moral and social values were transmitted mainly through social interactions between elders and youth through activities such as storytelling (folklore), singing, dancing, and poetry. Boys went hunting, cattle herding, and sporting with mature men and learned the values of honour, courage, honesty, authority, and hard work. Meanwhile, girls stayed home with their mothers and engaged in housekeeping and child rearing. This kind of gender stereotyping was to be reinforced by colonial education, as we shall see below.

Education during the colonial period

Roman Catholic Church missionaries introduced the first form of formal education in Rwanda. The Europeans had no interest in the development of Rwanda as such. Instead, missionaries claimed that their responsibility was to "save the soul" of the Rwandan people from eternal destruction. In the final analysis, however, the authors leave it to the reader to assess this redemptive role in the light of the destructive events that culminated in the genocide of 1994. Rwanda became a predominantly Catholic country with the coming of the Catholic missionaries in 1889. Later, colonial rule under Belgium, and supported by France, reinforced this phenomenon, and the country has long been considered Christian. Since 1994, however, Christians and non-Christians alike have been questioning the Church's moral and spiritual authority over the people it has all along claimed to have saved. Moreover, and given the role of the Church in the education system of Rwanda, it would be interesting to assess the role of education in recent conflict. This warrants further investigation.

Apart from the goal of "saving Rwandans from eternal destruction," the missionaries trained some Rwandans to assist the colonialists as clerks in local administration, the growing of crops, and construction. By 1935, there were 338 primary schools in Rwanda. There was one "special" secondary school in Butare, whose graduates were meant to help expatriate officials of the colonial government. In 1936, some seminaries were established, which taught religion, philosophy, and languages. Most graduates of these seminaries took over leadership of the country after independence. By the 1950s some secondary schools had been founded, including the *écoles menagères* to prepare girls for their future role as housewives. This institutionalisation of gender inequalities reinforced the traditional role of girls and would have a profoundly negative impact on the role of women in the development in modern Rwanda.

In Rwanda, as in other contexts in Africa, colonial education was used as a divisive instrument. The missionaries stressed differences between Hutu and Tutsi pupils, putting them into categories in and out of school. Sowing the seeds of divisions in Rwandan society and of future violence started as early as 1920. Here lies the central question of the role of education in the prevention or as a catalyst of conflicts.

Postcolonial education: The role of schooling

According to interviews conducted for this study, the role of the education system in general, and that of schooling in particular, was highlighted as having contributed to the conflict in Rwanda. Aspects of schooling that are seen as having exacerbated divisions and contributed to violent conflict include practices such as the use of ethnically defined pupil identification files, biased access to national examinations, violent forms of punishment, discriminatory policy, as well as biased content pertaining to the teaching and learning of history and civics.

Pupil identification files (fiches signalétiques)

All Rwandan pupil identification files had to mention the ethnic belonging of each child. In this regard, the child grew up knowing his or her Hutu, Tutsi, or Twa origins as well that of his or her peers. This created divisions and hatred fuelled by the teaching of a history that was divisive. In order to fill in the pupil identification files, teachers would ask pupils to stand up according to their ethnic background. One of our respondents told us that at times many of the children were not aware of their ethnic group identity. In such cases, teachers would rely on stereotypes to help them identify the children correctly. Another respondent said,

> Once, the teacher asked all Hutu to stand up, I also stood up. He observed me and told me, "Sit down. You are not a Hutu but a Tutsi." When I went back home, I asked my parents whether we were Hutu or Tutsi. My parents answered that we were Tutsi.

These practices were prejudicial: "Once a Hutu child knew that you were a Tutsi it was finished. You were no longer friends." In some cases, this practice led children to fight in the classroom or on their way home. It also created a complex of superiority and inferiority within the Hutu and Tutsi children.

According to focus group discussions with secondary school students, in addition to the information contained in the pupils' identification file, the practice of labelling as part of the process of teaching led to further division. As they grew up, "Hutu children did not see their Tutsi peers as friends but as creatures of another nature."

This social division was reinforced by the school system through the teaching of history and civics that emphasised "ethnicity." An example of the institutionalisation of social divisions is exemplified by one of our respondents, who told us that in fact some of the children went to school without an awareness of the existence of "ethnicity" in their society. But the teachers took it as their responsibility to teach children their ethnic groups.

These practices led to conflicts in and out of the classroom, including in the home. This sought to create inferiority and superiority complexes in the relationships among Rwandan children in all areas of their lives. According to our discussions with secondary school students, they think that this phenomenon created and encouraged hatred among themselves.

National examinations

During national examinations, pupils' identification files were used to identify groups of pupils for victimisation. According to our respondents there were three ways through which Tutsi children could access secondary schools:

1. to buy a place in secondary school by paying a bribe;
2. to go to a private school, which required payment of significant tuition fees; or
3. to go abroad.

Violence

Verbal, physical, and psychological violence against individuals and groups of pupils from a particular background was common. According to a group of students and confirmed by some teachers, Tutsi children were sometimes sent back home or beaten and brutalised.[1]

Policy of quotas (iringaniza)

Policies of ethnic, regional, and gender quotas (*iringaniza*) provided a legal framework for discrimination and violence. This policy was introduced during the second republic, 1973–94, and was derived from Article 60 of the law on public education regarding conditions of transition from primary to secondary school. After primary school, students would be admitted to secondary schools following the criteria below:

*   marks, averages, and points achieved in examination;
*   continuous assessment or academic history of a child;
*   regional quotas;
*   ethnic quotas; and
*   gender quotas.

This meant that quotas were defined for the different regions, ethnic groups, and genders. This policy is said to have involved arbitrary criteria, since people were not convinced of the statistics available for the different regions and ethnic groups. It was viewed as a policy introduced to systematically discriminate against certain groups of people within the education system. Indeed, most people acknowledged that those who benefited from it were people from the northern provinces—the home region of the late president Habyarimana. The policy is said to have further discriminated against Tutsi children, and as a result many of them were not able to access secondary education.

Discrimination based on this policy and law sometimes went beyond "ethnicity," regionalism, and gender. This was clearly expressed in the words of one education minister at the time who stated that "I cannot imagine how a peasant child could have access to a secondary school while the child of a *bourgmestre* is left behind."

The teaching of history and civics:
Distortions and amplifications of events in textbooks prior to 1994

Rwanda has experienced stark changes in power elites from colonial times, when Tutsis were favoured, to the post-1959 era, when Hutus were favoured. That is to say, both sides have experienced preference, and both sides have experienced oppression and discrimination. No one has been able to judge which side suffered most in terms of physical, psychological, economic, and other forms of oppression. The oppression of the Hutus was, however, accompanied by a particularly injurious and dangerous message, that of the group's inherent inferiority.[2] In considering the teaching of history and civics, this section reflects on the period of 1959–94, taking into account that prior to 1959 there was no teaching of Rwandan history in formal education. The following discussion will therefore necessarily be more expansive concerning discrimination against Tutsis.

On citizenship

The teaching of history played a major role in social divisions in Rwanda. It portrayed the Tutsi as rich, foreign, and oppressive. The media and political parties reinforced this. It was pointed out that some of the subjects studied emphasised ethnic differences among Hutu, Tutsi, and Twa. Negative aspects about the Tutsi were displayed and amplified. The teaching of history has played a major role in exacerbating social divisions in Rwanda. It was suggested that in the past, the Tutsi were rich although they were foreigners, thus implying that they had become rich through exploiting the "real Rwandans." Children were indoctrinated to believe in the artificial differences. The Tutsi were presented as immigrants from Ethiopia, and negative images of Tutsi were developed that were conveyed by words like "evil," "snake," "cockroach," etc. These were later to be capitalised on by the hate media and ethnic-oriented parties in 1994. In schools, this excited personnel to become adherent to divisionism that inculcated in the children the hatred of Tutsi. This history taught that all Tutsi had been favoured, and all Hutu—who were the "majority" and "native"—had been marginalised.

It can be said that after independence the government in power chose to rewrite the history of Rwanda, dividing it into two periods: (1) before 1959, when, according to them, there was oppression of the Hutu by the Tutsi, and (2) after 1959, when the masses that had been oppressed recovered their lost rights and overthrew the Tutsi domination. Since this history was written under the guidance, direction, and control of missionaries and colonialists, nothing is mentioned about their role in promoting social divisions in Rwanda.

This history does not mention that only a small minority of Tutsi benefited from monarchic rule. It associates all Tutsi with the feudal regime; thus every Hutu feels that every Tutsi has harmed him or her, and all Tutsi feel a historical culpability of what happened to the Hutu—even though many never participated in the colonial administration, or were victims of this administration themselves. In a general way, there has been an excessive generalisation, to the detriment of both Hutu and Tutsi.

The teaching of history about the population of Rwanda also continued to take its inspiration from old theories, such as Hermitic theory. This theory states that "all form of civilisation and evolution known in Africa were the work of a human group named Hermites of Caucasian origin and who crossed into northern Africa." Such an argument tended to deny black Africa the ability to create political and social organisations, techniques, and developed culture. (Mulinda, 2002).

This theory states that the people who first arrived in Rwanda were the Twa, the indigenous people. The second comers were the Hutu, and the last to arrive were the Tutsi, who invaded the Hutu and Twa territories and imposed their domination. Politicians and teachers of history have continued to base their teaching on such theories even though they have long been invalidated by many researchers.

On whips (ibiboko)

The history is based on the accusation that the Tutsi oppressed the Hutu. It teaches pupils that *ibiboko* were introduced and used on a large scale on the Hutu population by Tutsi. In this version, there is a distortion in order to make the facts correspond to the racist ideology of the past. Indeed, during the colonial period, the coloniser compelled the indigenous administrators, who were exclusively Tutsi, to force the population to accept the orders of forced labour from the colonial power. However, all groups—Hutu, Tutsi, and Twa—experienced this oppression. The distortion aims at indicating that only Hutu comprised the oppressed masses, and that only they were beaten. The history presents Tutsi as enemies and justifies the will of revenge. Some of our respondents confirmed that, after having been indoctrinated by these teachings, children fought at school referring to the past "oppression." In other cases, the killing of Tutsi was presented as a strategy for maintaining public order.

On serfdom (ubuhake)

The taught history also incorrectly presented all Hutu as having been subjects of Tutsi all along. This is a distortion of the facts; in the Rwandan monarchical tradition the word "Hutu" referred to a "subject." Poor Hutu, Tutsi, or Twa were referred to as *Bahutu*. Similarly, a Hutu who became prosperous, owned cattle, and acquired subjects, could rise to the rank of Tutsi *kwihutura*. This means that social classes were differentiated more on the basis of wealth, defined essentially in terms of the number of cattle one owned.

Monarchy

The history that was taught indicates that one group dominated the others, and sought to associate all Tutsi to the monarchy. The terms "Tutsi," "foreigners," "oppressors," and "wealthy" became synonymous.

1959, and the transition to independence

This is a point in time that has remained controversial, since people have divergent views and interpretations about what actually happened. The pre-1994 history syllabus presented 1959 as the year when a popular Hutu uprising overthrew Tutsi domination through blood and fire. Most of our respondents, however, indicated that the so-called revolution was not the work of the Hutu but of the colonisers, who wanted to get rid of the Tutsi monarchy because they were starting to demand independence. The colonisers, it is argued, organised and executed the plan to push out the Tutsi with the help of some Hutu. The proponents of this view insist that if it had been a revolution in which people overthrew an oppressive regime, the colonialists should have been targeted, since they, and not the Tutsi, were in charge at that time.

The civic education syllabus was also identified within the school system as having conveyed messages that incited pupils toward ethnic hatred. Again, the controversial year of 1959 was covered, as in the history lessons. Civic education involved teaching and learning about the formation of political parties in Rwanda. The National Rwandan Union (UNAR) Party, which supported the monarchy, for example, was presented (negatively) as having sought to maintain the domination of the majority, whereas the Hutu manifesto was presented only in its positive aspects. In teaching the children about the Constitution, the monarchy was presented as evil (further ascribed to all Tutsi) and associated with colonialism and oppressive rule.

During the study of national symbols, such as the national flag and anthem, children were exposed to messages of hatred and social division. It was also mentioned during the interviews that teachers often deliberately selected examples that indicated the negative aspects of the Tutsi.

We maintain that in contrast to the robust efforts to restore security and infrastructure following the devastation in 1994, not enough critical attention has been focused on analysing and assessing the ways in which schools understand and teach about the Rwandan genocide. This is true with respect both to analysing and to assessing how schools develop this understanding and also to the means that they have at their disposal. Education has clearly been used to divide the Rwandan society. However, the authors are convinced that through restoring memory and reconstructing history as objectively as possible, Rwandans can gradually be helped to draw together as one nation.

Critical analysis of the Rwandan genocide needs to be the subject of an extensive research effort that explores issues and theories of social identity and social categorisation along with issues of stereotyping, collective memory, and community. In adopting that perspective, sociologists, educationalists, anthropologists, and psychologists alike might shed light on the complex and dynamic interplay among the social and psychological factors that underlie the process of social cohesion and reconciliation. This demands resources that are beyond the confines of the current research and reflection, which places an acknowledged limit on the lessons that can be learned from it.

CURRICULUM POLICY DEVELOPMENT

Overview of basic education

Before shifting our focus to curriculum development, we will provide a few indicators on the state of basic education. The education sector in Rwanda is spread over a number of government ministries and departments, among them:

1. the Ministry of Local Government and Social Affairs, which oversees, as one of its functions, nonformal youth programmes including literacy campaigns;

2. the Ministry of Public Service and Labour, which is responsible for youth skills development (vocational education);

3. the Ministry of Gender and Women in Development, which covers gender issues; and

4. the Ministries of Education and Health, which are both responsible for health issues.

In addition, a number of non-governmental organisations (NGOs) are involved in imparting skills to out-of-school youth. Recently, the Ministry of Education embarked on a project called the Catch Up Programme, supported by UNICEF and aimed at out-of-school children. The aim of projects like these is to allow these youth to eventually rejoin the mainstream formal education system.

The formal education system (6+3+3) primary net enrolment ratio (NER) is almost 75 percent for both boys and girls.[3] Both repetition and dropout rates are high. While repetition rates[4] are decreasing at the primary level, the dropout rate is worsening, and the transition rate from primary to secondary is at approximately 37 percent. This is due, in part, to more difficult access to secondary education as a result of both lower supply and the fact that slightly over 50 percent of schools are privately managed.[5]

The Rwandan education system has for a long time been examination oriented, often forcing children to repeat and drop out. Also, due to poverty, many children, and especially girls, have to take care of their families. In addition, most parents lack formal education and provide little follow-up for their children. Schools and classrooms have not been repaired for too long, leaving the whole school environment unattractive to children. Lack of appropriate facilities, textbooks, and pedagogical materials further exacerbates the situation. A more positive trend is seen in the percentage of qualified primary teachers, which has increased dramatically from 63 percent in 1994 to 80 percent in 2001. While the percentage of qualified teachers is also increasing at the level of secondary education, it is still only at 52 percent.

In spite of the tremendous problems and constraints, there has been remarkable progress in the Rwandan education reform process. Improvisation to find cost-effective methods due to limited resources has not hindered the spirit to work harder and more efficiently for change. There is also a fair amount of political stability and economic development, and the education sector should continue to benefit as the donor community continues to respond positively.

The role of the National Curriculum Development Centre in post-1994 reform

In 1996, the Ministry of Education established the National Curriculum Development Centre (NCDC). Although education provision and management has been decentralised in the last couple of years, leaving the ministry to develop policies and monitor standards, curriculum development remains a function of the Central Ministry through the NCDC, whose functions are to

1. conduct research and prepare syllabi for primary, secondary, teacher training, professional technical, and special education;

2. conduct research and prepare teaching and evaluation materials to support any syllabi, including the preparation of teacher's guides, books, mass media programmes, and similar materials;

3. conduct in-service training for teachers who are involved in carrying out experiments and trials of any new syllabi and teaching materials;

4. organise seminars, workshops, and conferences on any syllabus and teaching materials for inspectors of schools and staff of teacher training colleges;

5. organise orientation programmes for provincial directors of education and other stakeholders in education at provincial and district levels to keep them informed of the developments taking place in school curriculum reform;

6. transmit programmes through mass media to support the curriculum reform

developments taking place in education;

7. conduct research through information communication technology to support students and teachers in schools;

8. organise courses, seminars, and orientation programmes for guidance and counselling of teachers and inspectors;

9. ensure that HIV/AIDS-related and other life skills such as peace, unity, and reconciliation, human and children's rights, gender equity, and environmental issues are mainstreamed into the national curriculum; and

10. advise the Ministry of Education on policy issues related to curriculum planning, development, and evaluation.

The NCDC liaises with other departments, including the National Unity and Reconciliation Commission (NURC), the Human Rights Commission, and numerous NGOs.

It should be stressed that while management and delivery of education is decentralised, curriculum development in Rwanda is still centralised. The NCDC endeavours to consult and liaise with other departments and organisations, but is ultimately responsible and accountable for curriculum development. The role of these organisations, other than financial support, may emerge and become clearer as the decentralisation process becomes more pronounced.

It is important to note here that the NCDC works closely with NURC, just as it would with any other organisation in which members have skills, expertise, and experience in their respective areas of specialisation. NURC was established in 1999, and it is involved in

- the promotion of peace, unity, and reconciliation of all Rwandans;
- civic education programmes;
- leadership training;
- youth and community outreach;
- support to community initiatives in promotion of peace, unity, and reconciliation; and
- support to other organisations involved in the reconciliation process (e.g., the Human Rights Commission), the demobilisation of soldiers, the reintegration of returnees from exile or refugee camps, the release of prisoners, and support to survivors.

The working together may take the form of formal or informal consultation and/or workshops or seminars when the NCDC is considering an area that they are involved in.

The early 2000s have seen a tremendous effort channelled through policy development. The NCDC has been the lead institution in the process of development of the textbook policy, curriculum policy, and the ongoing language policy in addition to participation in all other policy development processes of the Ministry of Education, Science, Technology and Scientific Research (MINEDUC).

The Ministry of Education Primary and Secondary School Curriculum Development Policy was formally presented to the Ministry of Education in January 2003 and to a wider audience including donor agencies and other stakeholders during the Joint Review on Education Sector in April 2003.

Between 1996 and 1998, an emergency revision of primary and secondary school curriculum was instituted. These revisions were an essential first step in the urgent process of getting the education system working again after the 1994 war and genocide. The Ministry of Education recognises that a much more thorough-going and systematic revision is now needed, and that the current policy that was ratified at the end of April 2003 will set curriculum development revision parameters. It will provide a detailed basis on which school curriculum and the enhancement of related delivery and evaluation systems will be carried out.

Curriculum may be defined as all learning that takes place in school or in related out-of-school activities, and the systems required to assist and evaluate that learning. It refers to all that is planned to enable learners acquire and develop *desired* knowledge, skills, and attitudes. In the Rwandan context, "desired" refers to in- and out-of-school experiences that enhance the realisation of Vision 2020, the Poverty Reduction Strategy Programme, and other policies and principles aimed at peace, unity, reconciliation, and social cohesion.

Some of the curriculum principles outlined in this policy are directly linked to efforts to strengthen social cohesion and national unity, the most explicit being

- the promotion of peace and reconciliation and a unified and tolerant national identity, in addition to
- the promotion of life skills such as peaceful problem resolution, moral behaviour, and control of emotions;
- respect of linguistic and human rights of children; and
- responsiveness to differing local needs and aspirations.[6]

The delivery mechanisms are conceived according to principles of a democratic and child-centred classroom and evaluation procedures and are designed alongside the principles outlined in the policy. It is important to note that the Ministry of Education policies—both those developed and those still in the process of being developed—have to take into account national goals enshrined in Vision 2020 and the PRSP. As a result, discussion of one without the appreciation of the other would be incomplete. As a matter of fact, it does not make much sense in Rwanda to consider educational reform and social cohesion, and specifically curriculum paradigms, without placing the discussion within the context of broader national goals. Therefore, throughout our discussion, we have continued to make reference to Vision 2020 and the PRSP.

Textbook policy

The textbook policy should be a framework for the provision of attractive and appropriate textbooks, which would serve as the basis for the teaching and learning of skills vital to personal, social, and national development. In 2001, the Ministry of Education, through the National Curriculum Development Centre, initiated a process of policy formulation on pedagogical materials including textbooks, teachers' guides, reference books, and other classroom print materials such as wall charts, maps, and supplementary readers. Thus the textbook policy encompasses not just textbooks but all learning materials. Provision of textbooks and pedagogical materials is seen in the Rwandan context as serving the broader goal of achieving national socioeconomic development.

The government of Rwanda recognises that essential skills can be developed through this kind of media. This will enhance the broader goals of fostering the development of literacy and numeracy skills and creating school leavers who are skilled in science and technology, information and communication technologies (ICT), and entrepreneurship. Perhaps even more important for the focus of this study is that the government of Rwanda, through the development of textbooks and other pedagogical materials, hopes to foster

- national reconciliation, peace, and the unity of all Rwandans;
- nonviolent problem resolution;
- gender awareness;
- respect for others;
- respect for democratic practices; and
- the understanding of health and population issues.

The policy sets criteria for the selection and commissioning of textbooks and other pedagogical materials. Criteria for selection include, among others,

- curriculum-compliant textbooks and other pedagogical materials;
- crosscutting national concerns (e.g., health issues including HIV/AIDS, gender awareness, entrepreneurship, unity, and national reconciliation); and
- emphasising support for a democratic approach and regional and international perspectives.

It should be acknowledged that any effort at curriculum change that does not consider the effective and efficient use of textbooks and other pedagogical materials is unlikely to succeed. This explains the government of Rwanda's emphasis on textbook policy development as a basis for curricula implementation.

Language policy

Before the 1994 genocide, languages in use in Rwanda were Kinyarwanda as a national language, Swahili as a regional lingua franca, and French as the only official language used as a medium of instruction. The conflict in 1959 caused the departure of thousands of Rwandans to neighbouring countries such as Uganda, Kenya, Tanzania, Burundi, and Congo. Others went as far as Europe and North America.

After 1994, the government of National Unity recognised the important role of language education, and saw a need to provide schooling for all Rwandan children in French and English in addition to Kinyarwanda to create a trilingual society capable of maintaining successful political and economic relations with our Francophone and Anglophone neighbours. Given the geographical location of Rwanda with French-speaking countries to the west and English-speaking countries to the east, Rwanda is in a unique position to explore and exploit opportunities in regional trade and business and international communication and labour markets. With no natural resources other than her people, the government recognises the important role to be played by the development of languages in the education system. The "trilingual" education policy is being developed in the context of the Ministry of Education Action Plan for Policy Development and with reference to the two main sources of national policy in education and other sectors, namely, Vision 2020 and the PRSP.

In 2002, the Ministry of Education entrusted the National Curriculum Development Centre with the responsibility to lead a process of developing a national language policy. The drafting committee includes Ministry of Education officials, higher education institutions, representatives of schools, and other stakeholders, and work is in progress.

Currently, Kinyarwanda is used as a medium of instruction from grades one to three (P1–P3), while French and English are taught as subjects. From grades four to six (P4–P6), French and English are supposed to be used as media of instruction and Kinyarwanda taught as a subject. In other words, pupils in upper primary and secondary school will learn in either French or English, but not in both simultaneously. One would be used as medium of instruction and the other taught as a subject. From secondary school to tertiary institutions, students are expected to learn in either French or English without difficulty. Preliminary investigation indicates that there are problems of implementation of this policy, mainly due to a large number of untrained teachers and lack of pedagogical materials. Due to the inherent challenges and contradictions associated with language policy in many developing countries, the drafting committee on language policy has recommended some basic research in order for it to work from a more informed position. Some of the aspects in which basic information is required include:

- investigation into when Kinyarwanda, French, and English should be used as the mediums of instruction or studied as subjects;
- the relative time to be allocated to the learning of Kinyarwanda, French, and English;
- the need for the revision of school curricula in languages;
- the need for supplementary materials and the enrichment of the out-of-school foreign-language environment via radio, television, and such activities as learning through sport;
- the assurance that language skills are effectively examined;
- the availability of textbooks, in what numbers and in which language;
- the training of teachers able to promote trilingual education;
- the linguistic skills expected of children leaving school and for what purpose;
- departmental responsibility for specific aspects of the delivery of the language education policy; and
- planning the activities required to implement the language education policy.

The Ministry of Education is in the process of establishing a reference point in terms of the competencies required of both students and teachers—hence the need for collection of baseline data. Results of the survey should inform the language policy development.

Coordination with the General Inspectorate and the National Examinations Council

As part of qualitative improvements in our education system, the Ministry of Education has been strengthening the General Inspectorate in order to monitor the implementation of new school curricula. In addition to the multiple processes involved, new curricula are a series of products including syllabi, textbooks, teacher manuals, and learning materials of all types (e.g., audio-visual aids, laboratory equipment, etc.).

It should be emphasised that the educational value of officially prescribed curricula will be determined by the degree to which they are properly implemented in the system. In other words, it remains to be seen what the correlation will be between the official intended curriculum and the curriculum that is in fact implemented. Experiences elsewhere indicate that high-quality programmes are quite often stored away in schools, and ongoing classroom activities are considerably different from those suggested by the authors of the new programme. Thus proper implementation requires a strong inspection team. It should be mentioned, however, that proper implementation of these new curricula will require coordinated parallel processes, which include

- preservice and in-service training of teachers in order to bring teachers up to date on the new subject matter, methods, and ideas used in the new curricula;
- adequate and timely supply of all equipment that is needed for implementation of the new curricula; and
- appropriate changes in supervisory staff activities, enriching educational programmes (radio and television), review of university entrance requirements, and, most important, the national examinations system, to which we now turn our attention.

One of the major reform initiatives of the government of Rwanda has been the establishment of the National Examinations Council. Prior to 1994, criteria for selection and entry into post-primary and post-secondary institutions were based on ethnic, religious, and gender lines through the *iringaniza* policy referred to earlier. To ensure fairness and national standards, the National Examinations Council was established in 1997. Since then, tremendous progress has been made in qualitative improvements of the education system; candidates are now selected purely on the basis of merit, resulting in more able graduates. Although national examinations may be used for various purposes, including certification and selection for further education, our concern is with external examinations that are intended to yield a measure of levels of student learning. The point to be emphasised is education rather than certification. This means that the form and content of such examinations exert a profound influence on what is taught in the schools in the year preceding the setting of the examinations. This is known as the "backwash" effect.

The kind of educational thinking where learning rather than certification becomes a guiding principle of pedagogical practice will continue to provide a mechanism through which curriculum will dictate the content and objectives of examinations—and never the other way around. In this way, curriculum relevance will be ensured. Therefore, we insist that it is unsound educational practice to allow an examination to determine what students need to learn and thus what they will be taught. Instead, a set of objectives are used as a guide in devising instructional procedures that lead to the achievement of these objectives, and as a basis for designing the examination to assess the extent of achievement. Hence, the examinations are used to measure what the students have learned.

It is in this context that we stress the importance of teamwork and cooperation between the National Curriculum Development Centre, the General Inspectorate of Education, and the National Examinations Council to ensure that the desired curriculum is monitored and well evaluated. In this respect, the NCDC has started the process of integrating life skills experiences and activities related to HIV/AIDS, gender-sensitive education, peace education, the rights of the child, environmental education, and population education into the curriculum. If the NEC introduces no element of assessment, it is likely that the life skills will be given low priority in the teaching, resulting in the failure to achieve the objectives of educational reform. Thus, some measurement of life skills experiences corresponding to the desired curriculum objectives will have to be included. The two organisations thus have a symbiotic relationship.

As already noted, the primary objective of the establishment of the NEC was to ensure fairness and national standards in summative evaluation. In such a short period of time, the impact of national examinations has been felt across the country, and most Rwandans applaud this initiative. A few examples are given below.

Respect of individual interest

The right of individual candidates to choose and select courses and schools or institutions is now respected. Before 1994, criteria for student placement were arbitrary, with no consideration for individual needs and choice. Today, candidates make a choice based on their interest, motivation, and future employment opportunities.

Clear and fair selection procedures

Before 1994, candidates did not know how or why they were being selected. At present, selection is based solely on merit, thus ensuring transparency and proper accountability. This also implies that the results are published in the print media, which allows both candidates and parents or guardians to question any perceived or alleged irregularities. The NEC is obliged to respond to any queries from the public and ensures that appropriate response and action is taken to meet public concerns. Public accountability has been a great source of legitimacy for continued system reform. This should be a source of reinforcement and a major unifying factor that generates public support for reform.

Disciplinary action

Disciplinary procedures are well laid out. There is provision for sanctions against any form of indiscipline resulting from cheating on examinations by anyone, be it students or teachers. This has ensured greater fairness and maintenance of standards.

Competition

A healthy development in the education system of Rwanda is the competitive nature of schools to produce the best results. This inculcates a sense of excellence. Now that students have a number of options to choose from, they compete openly for admission into the best upper secondary schools (A level) and higher education institutions. This motivates students to work harder. We are convinced that the reforms that have been set in motion will continue to promote the culture of "self-study" in the education system. This phenomenon has been well received by schools and communities that previously could not send children to tertiary institutions. In spite of the numerous achievements we have registered so far, we are mindful of the fact that examinations, like all the other aspects of the education system, need to be constantly improved.

In spite of the progress made thus far in curriculum and in education reform in general, many challenges continue to hinder the process. One of the principal constraints is that of large class size with a teacher-pupil ratio that is sometimes in excess of one to sixty. Nevertheless, Education for All (EFA), a nine-year Basic Education Programme, began with the start of this academic year (2003–04). A further challenge is that the new forms of curriculum delivery demand participatory approaches despite the lack of relevant textbooks and other pedagogical materials to support this innovation. While primary education has benefited a great deal from donor support, the secondary sector has confronted problems in this regard.

A further constraint to the reform process lies in the realisation that in Rwanda, there is an urgent need for a curriculum for teachers that is conceived of in genuine partnership with a curriculum for schools. For example, the NCDC has been making every effort to integrate peace, unity, and reconciliation, human and children's rights, gender equity, and HIV/AIDS education into the national curriculum. If, however, teacher training institutions do not have these themes as a part of their curriculum, then despite successful matriculation, teachers will continue to have a hard time implementing the integrated curriculum developed for schools. Thus, even if more than 75 percent of the teachers at the primary school level are trained, the quality of that training is questionable. Teachers must be equipped to face their new and changing roles.

Admittedly, the improved social cohesion that the new curriculum content hopes to foster is a complex and controversial process. It involves changes in attitude and behaviour that require one to reconcile with oneself before becoming able to do so with one's neighbours. There is a troubling irony that some teachers participated in the genocide but are nonetheless now expected to guide and direct the reconciliation process in their classrooms. This is further expected to reinforce social cohesion at the level of the classroom, the community, and wider society. Thus the following questions beg to be asked: What kind of pre- or in-service training do teachers need? How much of it can post-conflict Rwanda realistically afford?

Finally, it should be noted that any changes in the curriculum will, in the final analysis, be most effective depending on the degree to which a healthy environment is established that allows teachers to flourish. Teachers must

- have information about changes;
- possess values that relate positively to the expected outcomes of qualitative change;
- receive rewards; and
- be encouraged to adopt new changes as part of a larger process of adaptation.

All of this requires a heavy investment in teacher training. Fortunately, as the IIEP: UNESCO 2003 study showed, the will of the post-1994 government translated immediately into new school management practices that constituted new and positive hidden curriculum messages to pupils and teachers. In this way, Rwanda certainly immediately transformed its underlying curriculum, while waiting for overt curriculum change.[7]

RECONCEPTUALISING CURRICULUM IN CONJUNCTION WITH NATIONAL DEVELOPMENT POLICIES

Changes in curricula paradigms and directions

The recent conflict in Rwanda that led to the 1994 genocide took the country to its knees. The economy was shattered, the social and moral fabric loosened, and political institutions weakened (to say the least). Among the priorities of the government of national unity established soon after 1994 were

- security;
- reinforcement of national cohesion and positive values of society;
- promotion of peace, unity, and reconciliation;

- education;
- capacity building and human resource development; and
- poverty reduction.

Rwandan education policy has continued to focus on the promotion of peace and tolerance and on the kind of human resources the country needs for socioeconomic development through the upgrading of skills across all sectors of the economy.

These policy objectives have guided education provision since 1994 and form the basis of curriculum policy change. Some effort has been made in the areas of capacity building and human resource development. A great deal of progress has been registered in the social domain of national unity, peace, and reconciliation. Political stability is being gradually achieved, and the economy has been improving. It should be pointed out, however, that in spite of the progress registered thus far, a lot more still needs to be done. The direction curriculum change should take and the curricula paradigms to be adopted have been widely discussed although not formally documented. It is to this complex process that we devote the next section.

The authors acknowledge the progress made thus far in the Rwandan education system. Nevertheless, a closer look at the education system before the 1994 genocide reveals that the education system—and specifically the *school curriculum*—failed the nation. How else would one explain the criminal activities of teachers, doctors, lawyers, priests, nuns, bishops, and any other profession one could think of? What had gone wrong with the education system?

Between 1997 and 1998, an attempt was made to revise the curriculum. The objective was to attempt to move away from the system that had led to so much suffering, division, and economic declination. These revisions have been hailed as an essential first step in the urgent process of getting the education system working again.

Rwanda is currently in a development phase and no longer needs crisis management. It is acknowledged locally, regionally, and internationally that Rwanda is changing very quickly. This change demands corresponding education reforms to meet the aspirations, needs, and demands of modern society. Therefore, we envision a thorough-going and systematic reform, including curriculum revision. The premise is that the curriculum is the heart of any education system and that the establishment and delivery of effective curricula will contribute significantly to achieving both quantitative and qualitative targets including reconciliation, social cohesion, and national unity. This is the basis for and direction of curriculum change.

The setting of curricula paradigms or patterns is seen in the context of Vision 2020 and guided by efforts at skills development for poverty reduction and socioeconomic development. The Ministry of Education has thus developed a curriculum policy, which sets out principles and criteria for content selection, delivery mechanisms, and evaluation process at the levels of both primary and secondary education. It should emphasise the integration of life skills (e.g., psycho-social aspects, HIV/AIDS, gender sensitivity, peace, unity, and reconciliation, environmental awareness, human and children's rights, and population education), democratic and participatory methods, and fair assessment procedures. It is hoped that the new curricula patterns should reinforce peace, unity, and reconciliation and that Rwandan children should live better lives than their parents.

The mechanisms for achieving social cohesion and national unity through values education are enshrined in a series of national, sectoral, and institutional policies. Therefore, the direction of curriculum change and the curriculum paradigms are set in the context of recent policies by the government of Rwanda, notably, Vision 2020 and the Poverty Reduction Strategy Programme.

These policies have established guidelines upon which the government, and, in this case, MINEDUC, has started a process of policy development of its own, specifically:

- the Education Sector Strategy plan;
- the Education for All plan;
- curriculum development policy;
- textbook policy; and
- language policy.

To understand the direction of curriculum change and the underlying curriculum paradigms, we need to briefly examine each of the policies that will influence education development and curriculum reform and the process of strengthening social cohesion in Rwanda for many years to come.

Vision 2020 and social cohesion

Vision 2020 looks at the current and historical state of Rwandan society and the Rwandan economy, and then provides an implementable programme for effective development to the year 2020. The principal steps in the realisation of this programme are

- an effective state, efficient and transparent public service, with sufficient capacity to formulate and implement enabling and empowering policies leading, in turn, to good governance and popular participation;
- modernisation of agriculture, leading to the transformation of Rwanda's rural economy and a link with other economic sectors;
- development of industry and the service sector, including the attraction and fostering of local and foreign investment, based on a skilled workforce;
- comprehensive human resource development aimed at the public sector, private sector, and civil society;
- development and promotion of entrepreneurship and a business-oriented middle class;
- entry to regional and global trade and economic integration; and
- poverty reduction to improve the quality of lives of all Rwandans.

The transition from the 1994 emergency to the most recent development phase involves a critical change in the planning and management of various sectors, from short-term to medium- and long-term strategic planning.

Each of the steps above for the development of the Rwandan society and economy is crucially dependant on education. The functioning of an effective civil service requires appropriately trained personnel. They need to plan, communicate, evaluate their effectiveness, and, above all, resolve problems and conflicts peacefully. They need to appreciate the overall policies of the government and how they can promote them. Curriculum reform in view of strengthening social cohesion must therefore be seen in this context. We must ensure that such skills are integrated into a cross-curricular programme of teaching life skills, and a bold programme of skills development is essential for the promotion of social cohesion and national development.

Some work has already been completed by the National Curriculum Development Centre in this area, with the development of a life skills–oriented science and technology course for primary schools and the life skills–oriented Primary Teachers Civic Education Programme Resource Book. However, much still remains to be done. In the future, all school subject curricula need to be revised in order to carry forward this initiative in the creation of a dynamic Rwandan economy and society. Teachers will have to ensure that children leaving school have the skills, knowledge, and values that will enable them to take part in the process of social reconciliation and national development. Hence, we need to design teaching strategies and techniques and relevant pedagogical materials to implement these plans. Against this background, education is envisaged to play a key role in the realisation of Vision 2020, which is essential for social cohesion and the subsequent Poverty Reduction Strategy Programme, to which we now turn our attention.

The Poverty Reduction Strategy Programme

A key element in the macroeconomic planning for socioeconomic growth and development programme is the Poverty Reduction Strategy Programme, which forms the basis for national planning efforts over the next decade and guides government expenditures. It underlines the importance of prioritising high-impact programmes and projects in order that they have the greatest effect on poverty reduction. It will also provide a framework within which communities, the private sector, civil society, and external donors can form a partnership to reduce poverty and deprivation among the Rwandese people, providing a basis for social cohesion and national development.

The most recent living standards survey suggests that 64 percent of Rwandan people live below the poverty line. Lifting these people out of poverty remains an important priority of the government of Rwanda. In the Rwandan context, poverty is the outcome of both economic and historical factors. The economic structure reflects a chronic failure to achieve productivity increases given a large and growing population of eight million inhabitants living on a total surface area of only a little over 26,000 square kilometres.[2] This failure became increasingly evident in the late 1980s and early 1990s and led to severe structural problems, most of which have a direct link to the subsequent conflict. The war and genocide of 1994 left a horrific legacy, further impoverishing the country. The immediate need for reconciliation should be seen in a larger context including some of these challenges, and curriculum reform in Rwanda as a catalyst for social cohesion in the service of national development.

For this reason, Rwanda has spent the last eight years developing a national plan for poverty reduction. It details how each sector of the economy will focus its policies and spending on reducing poverty. Through extensive national consultations, the Rwanda PRSP outlines six broad areas for action linked to poverty reduction:

1.   rural development and agricultural transformation;

2.   human resource development;

3.   development of economic infrastructure;

4.   good governance;

5.   private-sector development; and

6.   institution capacity building.

Here again, education is to play an important role. For example, human resource development—which covers all aspects of education as well as health, family planning, water and sanitation, housing, and resettlement—is dependent on the formulation of appropriate education policies and entails a dynamic process of curriculum reform to meet the needs and demands of rapid social change in Rwanda. Education is also included in several other key areas such as good governance (school management) and private-sector development, particularly at secondary and higher education levels, and institutional capacity building across all levels of the education sector.

We shall have to employ multiple interventions in order to reduce poverty through education. For example, we need to adhere to our commitment to the international development targets of achieving Education for All by 2015 and Universal Primary Education (UPE) by 2010. We also need to increase the quality of primary and secondary education. We need to build more schools and classrooms (particularly in rural areas), train more teachers to absorb enrolment growth in pupils, and increase the levels of qualifications for teachers.

We also need to ensure the provision of textbooks and the curriculum materials to schools, a good monitoring system of education through inspection visits and the day-to-day work at provincial and district levels in a decentralised system. We should encourage parental and community participation in schools, curriculum development, and future development in the education system.

Against this backdrop, we are convinced that poverty reduction as a means of reinforcing social cohesion will best be served by developing a curriculum that is relevant to the needs of Rwanda, and that gives our children skills that they can use and values they can adopt to assist personal and national, social and economic development. We are also of the conviction that development of relevant curricula materials on key issues such as life skills in the areas of peace, unity, and reconciliation, gender equity, HIV/AIDS, environment, entrepreneurship, information, communication and technology (ICT), and literacy and numeracy will go a long way to reinforce the process of social cohesion in Rwanda, if we ensure that the curriculum is not merely theoretical but engages children with their subjects, giving them the necessary skills to participate in the labour market and the necessary values to engage as responsible citizens.

Education for All

The global EFA objectives are to

- expand and improve comprehensive early childhood care and education, especially for the most vulnerable and disadvantaged children;

- ensure that by 2015 all children—in particular girls, children in difficult circumstances, and those being cared for by vulnerable people—have access to and complete free and compulsory primary education of good quality;
- ensure that the learning needs of young people and adults are met, through equitable access to appropriate learning and life skills programmes;
- achieve a 5 percent improvement in levels of adult literacy by 2015, especially for women, and equitable access to basic and continuing education for all adults;
- eliminate gender disparities in primary and secondary education by 2015 and achieve gender equality in education by 2015, with a focus on ensuring girls full and equal access and achievement in a basic good-quality education;
- improve all aspects of education quality and ensure excellence, so that recognised and measurable learning outcomes are achieved by all, especially literacy, numeracy, and essential life skills; and
- prevent the propagation and limit the expansion of HIV/AIDS infection within and outside the school environment.

A National Education Forum has already been established to coordinate implementation with representatives from relevant government ministries, NGOs, church organisations, and other international organisation and donor groups.

A secretariat was established in the Ministry of Education and housed in the Division of Primary Education. Thematic groups also have been formed to address each of the seven EFA objectives.[8] In addition, all groups discussed four major crosscutting issues, namely,

- poverty;
- follow-up and evaluation;
- institutional environment and capacities;
- financing and partnerships; and
- school management and the school environment.

It is hoped that an increasingly literate population will be more willing to tolerate and adhere to the national values of social cohesion and less amenable to political manipulation, thus preventing future conflict.

Education sector policy

Policy for the education sector and its objectives reflect the broader policy environment set by the guidelines of Vision 2020, the PRSP, policies on decentralisation and ICT, and the government's commitment to achieve certain international targets—notably meeting UPE and EFA goals by 2015 and narrowing gender disparities by 2005.

To achieve these objectives, we need to address the high dropout and repetition rates that currently exist in our schools. We shall have to review the school curricula and teaching methodology in order to give pupils life skills, entrepreneurial and practical expertise, and psychosocial proficiency with regard to HIV/AIDS and general health and well-being.

The broad goals of the education sector policy are to

- contribute to the promotion of a culture of peace and emphasise Rwandan and universal values of justice, peace, tolerance, respect for human rights, gender equality, solidarity, and democracy;
- develop in the Rwandan citizen an autonomy through patriotic sprit, a sense of civic pride, love of work, and global awareness;
- educate a full citizen who is liberated from all kinds of discrimination, including gender-based bias, exclusion, and favouritism;
- eliminate all causes and obstacles that can lead to disparity in education, be it by gender, disability, or geographical/social group;
- dispense a holistic moral, intellectual, social, physical, and professional education through the promotion of individual competencies and aptitudes in the service of national reconstruction and the sustainable development of the country;
- transform the Rwandan population into human capital for development through acquisition of development skills; and
- promote science and technology, with special attention paid to ICT.

It should be noted that the education sector strategic plan emphasises positive values as a way of reinforcing national cohesion, a prerequisite for social and economic development. Therefore, curriculum-related policies such as textbook, curriculum development, and language policy are directly or indirectly derived from this broad plan, which in turn draws from Vision 2020 and PRSP.

National Unity and Reconciliation Commission

Apart from institutions set up within the Ministry of Education, the government envisages unity and reconciliation as a means through which peace, safety, and the respect of human rights—and, specifically, the right to life—can be restored in Rwanda. The creation of the Commission of Unity and Reconciliation is an important step in the attempt to end a legacy of discrimination based on ethnic origin, religion, gender, and regionalism and to ensure both the transition out of violence and hatred and the consolidation of peace. Established March 12, 1999, the commission has the following objectives:

- to organise and oversee national public debates aimed at promoting national unity and reconciliation in Rwanda;
- to use all possible means that could sensitise Rwandans on unity and to lay it on a firm foundation;
- to conceive and disseminate ideas and initiatives aimed at promoting peace among Rwandans and to inculcate the culture of national unity and reconciliation;
- to denounce any written or declared ideas and actions aimed at or based on disunity;
- to prepare and coordinate the country's programme for promoting national unity and reconciliation;
- to educate Rwandans on their own rights and the rights of others, and to build among them the culture of always respecting those rights;
- to give their views to the commissions charged with the responsibility of drafting laws

that will foster unity and reconciliation among Rwandans and fight against disunity;

- to monitor closely whether government organs respect and observe the policy of national unity and reconciliation among Rwandans; and
- to monitor whether the political parties, leaders, and all the people in general do respect and observe the policy of national unity and reconciliation.

The commission has three departments, one of which is devoted to civic education with the following objectives:

- to prepare the national programme for the promotion of national unity and reconciliation;
- to organise training and prepare training materials on unity and reconciliation;
- to educate Rwandans from all spheres of life on unity and reconciliation, using varied forums such as seminars, workshops, conference, and the media; and
- to follow up and evaluate programmes aimed to promote unity and reconciliation among Rwandans.

Through its Department of Civic Education, the commission works closely with the National Curriculum Development Centre to promote civic values within the school system. In a recently concluded exercise of revision of civic education for primary schools and political education for secondary schools, the commission participated actively to ensure the integration of national values and messages into the curriculum.[9]

POLICY DIALOGUE AND CONSENSUS BUILDING

As we have stated previously with respect to the methodology we used to carry out this study, educational policy development in Rwanda at present is part of a broad process of stakeholder consultation. Our own research, in the course of which we consulted teachers, head teachers, students, Ministry of Education officials, donors, and representatives of religious organisations, reflects the general practice of the NCDC. We feel it may be useful at this point to recall the two key questions around which we structured our research, along with a brief explanation of their original formulation. The questions were:

1. What was taught in schools in the past, and how did that contribute to social divisions and conflict?

2. What values should be taught in Rwandan schools to bring about social cohesion?

The questions were arrived at first and foremost because they were in line with the UNESCO International Bureau of Education's project on curriculum change and social cohesion in conflict-affected societies of which this study is a part. Secondly, we were working on the assumption that the curriculum failed to promote social cohesion in Rwanda. It was, therefore, important to come up with questions that would provoke answers to help us understand the role played by the curriculum in creating social divisions, as well as the role it should play to bring about social cohesion.

Based on the analytical framework that resulted from the colloquium with other members of the project team carrying out respective studies ("Curriculum Change and Social Cohesion in Conflict-Affected Societies," Geneva, August 2002), the authors held a series of meetings to work out methods of the consultation process and consider resources available to implement the plan. It was then decided that we should collect all available information in the form of documents, to create some kind of a "data bank" of our own.

The authors started consultation with teacher educators, teachers, curriculum developers, and other Ministry of Education officials and religious representatives both because they are key people in the education system and because, in the case of teacher educators from the twelve provinces (including the city of Kigali), it was cost-effective to gather them together in one place rather than consult with them in their respective provinces.

The first consultation process was done through a seminar focussing on the twelve national teacher training colleges (TTCs) as our starting point. There are twelve provinces in Rwanda, with a teacher training college in each of them. The target sample included three teacher educators from each of the TTCs. In addition, other participants included representatives from the National Curriculum Development Centre, the Ministry of Education, and religious organisations. (See Tables 1, 2, 3, and 4 in Appendix 2.)

The team decided in favour of this kind of consultation because the use of a general questionnaire had been ruled out (its design, production, administration, and analysis would far outstrip the available resources). The aim of the seminar was to assess the attitudes of teacher educators regarding values that should be integrated into the national curriculum. The seminar consisted of such activities as:

- **Formal presentations**: Presentations of the context, objectives, and expected results.
- **Individual work (brainstorming)**: The sixty participants were divided into nine groups. Each group member had to write down, without consulting the others, all the values he thought should be taught to Rwanda children in order to bring about social cohesion.
- **Group work**: After this individual work, the members discussed the written values, and then select the ten values they considered most relevant and important. Each value had to be discussed and agreed on or rejected by all member groups.
- **Plenary work**: A reporter from each group had to present to the participants the ten selected values, and explain and justify why those values had been selected. This was very important, since one group could have chosen the same value but have given it a different meaning. Thus, all the values were written down in order to make them visible to all participants, and to avoid the selection of two values bearing the same meaning. After this exercise, the plenary discussed all the reported values, and decided on a final ten values that were relevant for social cohesion.

The focus was mainly on the nature and implication of civic/values education on Rwandan society. The team insisted on directing the discussions toward analysing the strengths, weaknesses, opportunities, and threats of our current system. The participants were asked to make recommendations for improvement in relation to past conflicts in Rwandan society.

Following the successful two-day seminar, in which the twelve provinces were represented, the team embarked on individual and group consultations (see Appendix 4). This process was to be reinforced by our own professional and experiential knowledge of the history and culture of our country and society.

We used the same method as we previously applied to teacher educators. There was first a short presentation of the case study (context, objectives, and expected results), as well as an interview in which we asked the same two key questions noted above. In answer to the first question, respondents expressed that they thought school practices and teaching, as well as the laws and regulations related to education in Rwanda, had likely contributed to social divisions and conflict. In response to the second question, which consisted in identifying values that should be taught in Rwandan schools in order to bring about social cohesion, each of the values was explained in order to help us understand the meaning attributed to the value.

Data analysis

Data were processed using the techniques of qualitative research. Question one was mainly answered through interviews and information categorised accordingly. Data analysis indicates that there are two distinct points of view as elaborated in sections one and three.

For question two, values as well as their explanations collected through individual interviews, focus group discussions with pupils, and the first consultations with teacher educators were merged in one file and processed using the techniques of qualitative research. We present a classification of the values respondents think should be integrated into the school curriculum as a means of preventing future conflicts and bringing about social cohesion. (See Appendix 3.) According to this classification, the process of curriculum review should aim at

1. intellectual development (knowledge, and the ability to think critically);
2. physical development;
3. personality development;
4. attitudes that are required for the best social relationships;
5. feeling of belonging (patriotism, participation, and engagement);
6. fundamental principles of life in a society; and
7. appropriate pedagogy.

Below we present some of the fundamental principles regarded as important for a curriculum for social cohesion as well as an appropriate pedagogy. More details on these values are given in Appendix 1.

Fundamental principles

Equality between citizens

Inequalities in Rwanda are the result of the fact that some people have been holding too much more power and wealth than others. Inequalities have developed all over the course of Rwandan history, and have been based on individual or group characteristics. Some groups continue to be victims of such inequalities. (We can mention, among others, the plight of handicapped people in Rwanda.)

According to our respondents, curriculum change should emphasise the elimination of inequalities and structural discriminations based on ethnic differences, in order to create a community of equal rights and equity. It should focus on social relationships by proposing pedagogic strategies centred on teamwork and the pursuit of common objectives. Learning activities must be meaningful for students in order for them to effectively develop harmonious relationships based on equality, human rights, and democratic norms. The change should aim to overcome the exacerbation of ethnic differences and focus on the social integration of all Rwanda citizens. To reach social cohesion, it is necessary to build a society driven by universal values and principles, but through a social contract, not ethnic differences, as was the case in the former regimes.

Social cohesion requires a fundamental principle of equality between citizens. Conflicts and social divisions in Rwanda occurred because of a lack of equality between social groups, where one group has been the victim of prejudices and historical stereotypes that hindered it to participate fully to the shaping of the nation. Rwandan children need to learn that each individual is entitled to equality and personal development as a human being, without consideration of his social, physical, psychological, and intellectual attributes. The curriculum should then include the defence of the principle of equality of rights and duties of all citizens.

Unity and reconciliation

The issue of social cohesion has been most striking in Rwandan political orientations. It is a response to a history of violence and massacre that culminated in the 1994 genocide. This concern has been translated into many activities, such as the creation of the National Commission for Unity and Reconciliation. It is through this commission's policies and practices that the government of Rwanda wants to establish the foundations of social cohesion and citizenship. Former regimes had always ruled on the basis of ethnicity and the refusal to grant one social group full citizenship.

Peace building

Peace has been associated with social cohesion. Our respondents think that curriculum change should create the appropriate conditions for a lasting peace. The process of this change needs to involve peace-building education, which will help to make youth capable of valuing the peaceful resolution of conflicts. Peace is essential to social cohesion because there is no violence, rejection, discrimination, and intolerance. Social cohesion implies a society where there is

- a refusal to be violent in the course of human interaction;
- a resolution of conflicts by means of dialogue and compromise, which allows the discovery of others, their recognition, the acceptance of differences, and the cooperation between opposed interests; and
- a rejection of inequalities.

Our respondents suggest that Rwandan youth should be educated in human rights as a mediator of social relationships. Human rights constitute a fundamental reference to individual and social life. Peace is seen as synonymous with social cohesion because it guarantees the application of human rights and their fundamental principles: equality of rights, freedom, equity, and dignity. Justice is seen as a remedy to all social and individual conflicts; it protects individual rights and hinders conflicts. *Without justice, there is no peace. Justice helps to avoid impunity.*

Peace building should not only be reflected in the disciplinary contents, but also be supported by all (inside and outside) school practices. It was suggested by our respondents that in order to break with the culture of violence and impunity that have characterised Rwandan society since the 1960s, the youth should learn the modalities of individual and social conflict resolution by means of dialogue, compromise, negotiation, and nonviolence.

Social cohesion is based on values and principles of justice, equality, dignity, the recognition and respect of others, the respect for life, and freedom. These values and principles are clearly very important, but Rwandans also should have the will to reconcile and unite.

Fraternity and human relationships

Social cohesion calls upon social relationships based on love, fraternity, friendship, sociability, and ethics. Love is perceived as essential. *Without love, all other values will not be easy to apply. It is the foundation of unity.* Love helps to develop empathy, solid human relationships, peace, and respect for others. With love, individuals feel like brothers and sisters.

Legitimate social and political institutions

Social cohesion is linked to legitimate social and political institutions that make the appropriate conditions of its fulfilment. These institutions are characterised by good governance, impartiality, incorruptibility, and transparency.

Pedagogy

Under normal conditions, education helps people to avoid conflicts; something went very wrong in education in Rwanda. Today, people assume that something "prevented people of Rwanda from thinking critically and [they] became blind." What needs to change is pedagogy. All our respondents agreed that the acquisition of intellectual knowledge, skills, and attitudes depends on a pedagogic approach that combines discourse and practice—that is, a pedagogic approach that offers students the possibility to acquire knowledge, attitudes, and values.

According to our respondents, to be efficient, the curriculum should control the practices that occur in classrooms. Thus, social divisions that characterised the former curriculum were less apparent in the content of official documents than in classroom and teacher practices. This means curriculum may be good but still not fulfil the objective of social cohesion, unity, and reconciliation, if it does not control what is effectively occurring in the classrooms. Indeed, violence and the promotion of inequalities between students were practiced by teachers in a daily way. Other respondents maintain: "What was in the former curriculum was neutral." But the educators were not, in fact, neutral. Until now in Rwanda, pedagogy has not been given priority. This needs to change. In Rwanda, there is no school or department dealing with classroom behaviour. There should be *at least* a whole department dealing with classroom behaviour. Offering new curricula and new material or just changing teaching material will not be enough; it is pedagogy itself that must change.

> You can change the curriculum but this will give nothing if the approach does not change. Inversely, you may succeed by changing the approach.

Teachers tend to reproduce the methods they went through themselves, but they now need to learn new methods. They must learn to change.

We must also question teaching methods:

> How to teach well with old materials . . . use old texts in different ways? . . . Up to now, in our classrooms, the teacher is still the boss. It is assumed that he/she knows every thing. This kind of pedagogy should change.

The curriculum must take into account the training of teachers and head teachers:

> You have to train head teachers. . . . There is a need to develop head teachers. . . . Teacher training is a big thing.

Books that go to schools and are then used there should be on the agenda of teacher training in the universities or any other institutions dealing with teacher training. "As you develop your curriculum, the teachers should be aware of that." There must be coordination in teaching.

> When teachers teach, they have to have all the qualities of the curriculum in order to translate them into each individual subject. . . . You teach Algebra, you must know how to integrate all the values in Algebra. . . . OK. I am teaching Maths. What other kinds of values can I integrate?

Almost all the respondents we met agreed on an integrated curriculum. They also think that the realisation of this integrated curriculum is absolutely dependent on political will backed by policies and a plan of action.

Pedagogic approaches must be appropriate. The curriculum should implement active pedagogy that allows students to develop their critical thinking, sense of action, and openness of mind, solidarity, tolerance, and acceptance. Curriculum should encourage cooperation rather than competition, solidarity rather individualism, a long-term intellectual investment rather than short-term achievement. Our respondents suggested that active pedagogy encourages interactions between students, participation, sharing, respect of different points of view, and individual abilities. These approaches propose learning situations in which students can discuss and argue; where they can make decisions, and develop social projects and the rules of school life. The curriculum should focus on pedagogy like cooperative learning, projects, discovery, and any other strategies that allow openness to others, dialogue, cooperation, negotiation, and collective construction. In the words of one respondent: "The classroom must be a location of analytical and critical thinking, and problem-solving."

Values and attitude training cannot be limited to one subject or to what is occurring in a classroom. Our respondents proposed an integrated pedagogic approach that should be used in all subjects, including arts and sciences. Life skills must not be learned in only a single subject; it must transcend the whole curriculum. Furthermore, all school practices (in and out of classrooms) should reflect the values and attitudes leading to social cohesion. They should all be coherent with this national phenomenon.

Finally, to teach these values and attitudes, curriculum should create appropriate learning conditions. It should avoid exclusion of some students and create appropriate conditions for the inclusion of all Rwandan children in the development of thinking.

Whatever approach is taken, it must be appropriate to Rwandan culture. There are many examples of democracy in Rwandan culture, and it is possible to tie the culture of schools to the traditional culture of Rwanda and thereby integrate the school with the community. Our respondents suggested, to this end, looking into the genres of Rwandan proverbs (*imigani*) and poetry (*ibisakuzo*).

To summarise this section, our respondents suggested a multitude of positive values that could be integrated into the curriculum in order to bring about social cohesion. An analysis of content shows that these values can be regrouped in fewer categories. The capacity to work for social cohesion is related to the integral development of the individual. Such an individual is characterised by an ability to think critically and creatively, a sound personality, positive attitudes toward others, a feeling of belonging and responsibility, and good physical and mental health. Furthermore, curriculum change should lead students to adopt particular behaviours driven by some fundamental principles like equality, unity and reconciliation, peace, dignity, fraternity, freedom, and others. Social cohesion requires good governance and transparency, for it is within these kinds of institutions that the appropriate conditions for social cohesion are created.

Most of our respondents went beyond the issue of values and stated that the inclusion of all those values into the curriculum will not be enough for social cohesion unless an appropriate pedagogy and better school practices are developed.

Sensitive issues

Teaching the history of Rwanda

In the teaching of history, there are sensitive issues that teachers do not teach even if they are indicated in the syllabus. Some of these are related to

- the population settlement in Rwanda;
- the ethnic composition (Hutu, Tutsi, and Twa) of Rwandan society;
- the events of 1959;
- land ownership; and
- the question of citizenship.

The National University of Rwanda is currently studying the issue of Rwandan history as it applies to curriculum change.

The issue of ethnicity

In the course of our research, we found that our respondents think that in Rwanda, the issue of ethnicity has become taboo. People feel uncomfortable with using the terms "Tutsi," "Hutu," and "Twa" in daily conversation and are reluctant to even disclose their ethnic belonging. However, other people feel that since the issue of ethnicity is central to the social divisions in Rwanda, and probably still active in the minds of many if not all Rwandans, the issue should not be avoided. Our respondents maintain that when an issue leads to social divisions and violent conflict, it cannot just be ignored. The diversity of our respondents' views is reflected in the following statements:

- Some maintain that it is not in the "nature" of things to be a Hutu, a Tutsi, or a Twa.
- Others believe that there is no reason to hide one's "ethnic" belonging: "These days people fear to say what ethnic group they belong to. Whether one is Tutsi or Hutu, there is nothing to be ashamed or proud of. This is a 'complex' among people. It must stop."
- Finally, "ethnic group" identity as a social identity could be illustrated by the view that "a Hutu is any one who has the conscience to be a Hutu and a Tutsi is also any one who has the conscience to be a Tutsi."

We would like to argue that it is not the existence or nonexistence of ethnic groups that is important. The problem is that people believe in them and then behave accordingly. Therefore, if Rwandans want to find solutions to social divisions, it is important to talk about ethnic categorisations, ethnicity, and ethnic groups, in order to express a consensus as to the truth about them as they are experienced and defined.

The issue of language

According to the students interviewed, the speakers of different languages (French, English, and Kinyarwanda) behave as if they were different social groups. The students indicated that the curriculum should pay attention to this issue, since it may create social divisions in Rwanda and hinder national unity and reconciliation.

The students maintain that the problem in school is that members from the Anglophone and Francophone communities are somehow separated from each other. They have very limited relationships, and there is sometimes mistrust between them. The students think that in such a situation language may be a source of division.

Additional suggestions on a curriculum for social cohesion

Curriculum change should involve activities that teach children to live together in harmony. These activities should be interesting enough that the youth will engage in them with pleasure. They should promote discussion and debate without being compulsory. The students stated that the approach used in discussions is not efficient. Generally, the sensitisation is done through very long discourses, when it is easy to use theatre, songs, and other activities that allow students' participation and empowerment. One student observed that

> If education is the source of knowledge, then it should involve teachings on community life. Knowledge in mathematics and in other disciplines is very relevant but it is also very important to know how to live together in harmony.

Teaching nationalism and patriotism

The curriculum should teach all Rwandan children to consider themselves as Rwandans first and not Hutu, Tutsi, or Twa. Patriotism should also be taught to teachers. Curriculum should inculcate values of Rwandan citizenship. The curriculum change should also lead to the formation of a Rwandan citizenship founded on the diversity of gender, age, social status, wealth, and individual characteristics. Citizenship education should allow citizens to assume their social and political obligations, and to indulge in critical thinking and judgement. It should allow citizens to learn to act on their own.

History

The teaching of history should be revised, and should be objective. Parents need to be involved and endeavour to tell the truth to their children. Books and other teaching materials that carry messages of hatred and social division should be removed from the school syllabus. Scientific research on the history of Rwanda is needed in order to invalidate the hermitic theory that presents Tutsi as foreigners and invaders. This research should be based on scientific arguments, methods, and new paradigms more elaborated than the hermitic theory. The truth should be put to light.

For issues related to sensitive events, our respondents said that history consists of both good and bad events. History should cover all of these, including negative events; what should be avoided is the distortion of information to suit one group or the other.

Critical thinking

The curriculum should emphasise critical thinking. One university lecturer interviewed observed that the existing programmes focus on disciplinary courses and not on the formation of the mind. He suggested the changing of pedagogic approaches to allow students to participate and reason, through debate, on the relevance of arguments, ideas, and opinions that take place in their environment.

CONCLUSION

Rwanda is in a period of great curriculum reform. All Rwandans believe that education is a means that will help them develop and live together in harmony. Even though highly educated Rwandans did take part in the massacres and genocide, Rwandans still believe education is the source of unity and reconciliation. They believe it can make a difference, and can lead to an inclusive society—a society for *all* Rwandans—as long as the process of education remains focussed on essential positive values. Thus, curricula should take into account such a necessity.

Curriculum reform should go hand in hand with the training of teachers, improved teaching materials and methods, and good classroom and school management practices. Education must be free from stereotypes and prejudices. It must train a free human being endowed with critical thinking and skills for problem-solving and decisionmaking. Curriculum should involve positive values in order to break with the culture of violence that has characterised the Rwandan past. Students need to learn to tolerate and accept others. Curriculum change should be driven by the Rwandan culture and should emphasise moral education, life skills, and the values essential for the building of the nation.

An efficient curriculum should involve all stakeholders in the education of youth, teachers, parents, and the society at large. Formal education has been seen as important but inadequate on its own; the system needs to work with parents and the community. This mechanism has already been set in motion. It can only get better, and move faster, in the important process of facilitating social cohesion in Rwanda.

Endnotes

[1] Editor s note: Credible sources have also suggested that it might be worth bearing in mind that "ethnic" discrimination against Hutu children may have also taken on violent forms as practiced by some missionaries prior to 1959.

[2] Editors note: expert comment on final draft of this study.

[3] In 2002, an estimated 400,000 children in the seven-to-twelve age group were still out of school.

[4] In 2000–01, 45 percent of first-grade pupils had repeated. An estimated 36 percent of all pupils in 2003 will have repeated at least one year of primary schooling. (Education for All Plan of Action, 2003.)

[5] Out of a total of 376 secondary schools throughout the country, 190 are privately owned. In the private sector, education is largely provided through religious organisations.

[6] Other principles related to personal, social, and economic development, which the curriculum will address are:

- promote life skills, including health education and HIV/AIDS prevention;
- be a continuous and flexible process, responding to changes in government policy and practice and to the changing needs of learners, society, and employers;
- take account of other prevailing Ministry of Education policies;
- promote the role of women in society and the education of girls in school;
- promote positive traditional and modern Rwanda customs, culture, and skills;
- promote respect and understanding of the mentally and physically disabled and those suffering from emotional distress, etc.;
- ensure that every school leaver is literate and numerate;
- support the acquisition of scientific and ICT skills;
- integrate the learning of life skills across all subjects;
- provide an adequate preparation of lifelong learning;
- provide content that encourages girls to have a developed sense of self-worth and to be ambitious about their role in society;
- provide content that links the world of the child's family and community with other in-school and out-of-school activities; and
- provide content that will ensure a smooth transition from schools to the labour market via careers guidance, prevocational education, etc.

[7] Obura, 2003.

[8] The thematic groups include: nursery and preschool education, access and retention in primary education, improvement of the quality of education, reduction of inequalities in education, vocational training for young people and adults, literacy and education for adults, and HIV/AIDS.

[9] The government of national unity has also created a number of forums where the people of Rwanda can debate issues related to "living together harmoniously." Many programmes through the media have provided an opportunity to people from different background to discuss and debate issues that may be controversial, or any other issues that affect the lives of Rwandans. This is evident in the Sunday 10 O clock Phone-In Question and Answer Programme, which is always televised live for live debate.

References

African Rights. (2001.) *The Heart of Education: Assessing Human Rights in Rwanda's Schools.* London.

———. (1998.) *Rwanda: The Insurgency in the Northwest.* London.

———. (1994.) *Resisting Genocide.* London.

Dahrandorf, R. (1995.) *Economic Opportunity, Civil Society and Political Liberty.* Discussion Paper vol. 58. Geneva: UNRISD.

Duckitt, J. (1992.) "Prejudice and Behaviour: A Review," *Current Psychology* 4.

Du Prez, W. (1994.) *Genocide: The Psychology of Mass Murder.* London: Boyars.

Gamson, W. A. (1995.) "Hiroshima: The Holocaust and the Politics of Exclusion," *American Sociological Review* 60: pp. 1–20.

Goldhagen, D. J. (1996.) *Hitler's Willing Executioners: Ordinary Germans and the Holocaust.* New York: Alfred A. Knopf.

Haralambos. M., and Holborn, M. (1995.) *Sociology: Themes and Perspectives.* London: Collins Educational.

Horowitz, D. L. (1985.) *Ethnic Groups in Conflict.* Berkeley and Los Angeles: University of California.

Merton, R. K. (1968.) *Social Theory and Social Structure.* New York: Free Press.

Moore, R. I. (1987.) *The Formation of a Persecuting Society.* Cambridge: Blackwell.

Mulinda, C. K. (2002.) "La généalogie de l'idée du peuplement du Rwanda: consideration sur l'autochtonie ou l'allochtonie des rwandais," in Cahiers du Centre de gestion des conflits no. 5, *Peuplement du Rwanda. Enjeux et Perspectives.* Université Nationale du Rwanda: Editions de l'Université Nationale du Rwanda, pp. 49–72.

Obura, A. (2003) *Never Again: Educational reconstruction in Rwanda,* Paris: UNESCO International Institute for Educational Planning.

Prunier, G. (1995.) *The Rwanda Crisis: History of a Genocide.* Kampala: Fountain Publishers.

Republic of Rwanda. (March 1999.) *Gazette Official.*

Republic of Rwanda Ministry of Education, Technology and Scientific Research. (2002a.) *Curriculum Policy.*

———. (2002b). *Education for All (EFA) Plan.* Draft.

———. (2002c). *Education Sector Policy.* Draft.

————. (2002d.) *Textbook Policy*.

Republic of Rwanda Ministry of Finance and Economic Planning. (2002a.) *National Poverty Reduction Programme*. Rwanda: Poverty Reduction Strategy Paper.

————. (2002.) *Vision 2020*.

Ross, M. (1993.) *The Culture of Conflict: Interpretations and Interests in Comparative Perspective*. New Haven and London: Yale University Press.

Simpson, G. E., and Yinger, J. M. (1953.) *Racial and Cultural Minorities: An Analysis of Prejudice and Discrimination*. 3rd ed. New York: Harper and Row.

Staub, E. (1990.) "Moral Exclusion: Personal Goal Theory and Extreme Destructiveness," *Journal of Social Issues* 46(1).

UNESCO: IBE. (2002.) "Curriculum Change and Social Cohesion in Conflict-Affected Societies." Unpublished project proposal document, Geneva.

Uvin, P. (1998.) *Aiding Violence: The Development Enterprise in Rwanda*. Connecticut: Kumarian Press.

Appendix 1: Proposed Curriculum for Social Cohesion

Intellectual development

In addition to the organised knowledge, the curriculum should include abilities and attitudes that lead to efficient and rational thinking. Our respondents observed that the education system has been relying on disciplinary knowledge rather than on training to think. This should change, allowing students to participate and debate the relevance of ideas and arguments. They should learn ethics, values, logical reasoning, problem-solving, and other things that help them to think critically. From this perspective, education is seen as a value that improves behaviours in society, broadens the mind, encourages good judgement, and promotes openness to others.

The development of thinking capacity will allow students to rigorously analyse factors that create social divisions, bring about social cohesion, and establish relationships among citizens based on respect for life and dignity in order to develop a plan of returning to social order and national unity. Students will be able to understand the relevance of social cohesion and the possibilities to bring it about. The search of explanations and solutions will focus on the present situation, as well as on its historical, psychological, and cultural foundations. They will imagine different perspectives to social divisions. Development of thinking requires students to be able to open up to different alternatives. If the education system seeks to encourage independent judgement, it must first develop the capacity of reasoning through logical thinking—the capacity of forming hypotheses, analysing information, and formulating appropriate conclusions and decisions.

During our process of investigation, critical thinking was proposed as one of the strategies to train students to think critically. According to our respondents, critical thinking will allow students to function adequately in a democratic society, to analyse and assess information coming from their environment, and to compare it with other sources of information.

> People need to evaluate the source of information. . . . The development of the ability to evaluate information is fundamental. They are many ways to encourage people to make their independent thinking . . . teachers should not be dictators. The class must be democratic.

With critical thinking, students learn how to protect themselves from manipulations of all kinds, to be conscious of political and social manipulations that can occur at any one time.

> Rwanda is a compliant society. If the big boss says do this, he will do that. When the Rwandans will be able to say "No, I am not going to kill," then the social cohesion will be possible.

Training in critical thinking calls for appropriate attitudes such as openness of mind and intellectual honesty. It equally calls for the capacity to reason and undertake logical investigation. Critical thinking is reflective thinking oriented or directed toward problem resolution.

Using critical thinking, students can apprehend the present situation, assess the validity (soundness) of theories proposed to explain it, and have the capacity to accept or to reject it. As critical thinkers, students will be able to reason and deliberate and try to look more into the situation. Critical thinking allows students to question the choices made by some individuals. It calls on some abilities like discernment of the situation with precision.

Training for critical thinking allows students to analyse themselves, their behaviours, and those of others, and also analyse and assess ideas contained in school materials or transmitted by teachers or politicians.

Critical thinking will teach students to develop attitudes and abilities that are essential to analyse and master information characterising the current social context, to develop autonomy of thinking and a questioning and distance toward divisionist messages, as it helps them understand how these messages are produced and transmitted. Students will be able to analyse objectively any assertion, source, and belief and assess their precision, relevance, and accuracy, and make decisions in an autonomous manner, while respecting others, understanding the situation, and appreciating the quality (soundness and weakness) of the arguments, their acceptability, and their foundations. They can change their way of thinking, functioning, and attitudes.

Training for efficient thinking will allow students to understand the present situation of social divisions, the underlying theories and explanations, the core elements that have been maintaining such a situation. They will also understand how these theories have led to violence and genocide.

Personality development

To achieve social cohesion at the national level, curriculum change should emphasise personality development. Indeed, social cohesion requires group members of some attributes and particular behaviours. Among others, our respondents mentioned that a personality predisposed to social cohesion is characterised by

- courage,
- determination,
- firmness,
- hope,
- humility,
- integrity, and
- honesty.

A person disposed to social cohesion is someone who has simplicity, who is flexible. He or she is humble, so they can listen and understand others. According to our respondents, if "you develop humility in students, this helps to develop the abilities to negotiation and to have sound social relationships based on mutual respect."

Curriculum change should emphasise impartiality. The training for impartiality inculcates honesty, uprightness in students, and the willingness to fight against cruelty and instil fairness. Personality development also involves the development of

- Incorruptible citizens, who have a firm personality, "a critical thinking that helps them to avoid influences that hamper social harmony."
- Honest citizens, with good manners, know-how, and self-control.
- Flexible citizens, who can accept others' points of view and show comprehension, tolerance, and mutual understanding.
- Patient citizens, who can take time, listen, and try to understand others, their forces and weaknesses: "For social cohesion one should be patient . . . patience allows to achieve a

good result." Patience applies to waiting one's turn: "society cannot provide everything to everybody at the time it is wanted." It is the quality of waiting with the hope of a better result. It helps to shape positive social relationships between citizens.

Honesty was also mentioned as a key value for social cohesion. Indeed, honesty excludes the trend by which the "unlawful benefit at the expense of the group." It refers to the sense of uprightness, a lack of trickery, and the absence of lies.

> Social cohesion is a union of people, it cannot be achieved if there is no reliability . . . when there is no honesty, and there is loss of confidence in all dishonest persons.

Honesty helps to maintain a mood of reliability between citizens: "a reliable person is a person who you are sure is consistent and dependable."

Self-control is another tenet that the school may instil. "It refers to the ability to come to a point and be able to say: if I go beyond this point I may harm somebody else." According to our respondents, given what happened in Rwanda, self-control could have limited the massacres in the sense that people could have asked, "Why go out and kill?" Thus self-control can be developed in a classroom.

Attitude toward others

As indicated in Appendix 3, social cohesion calls upon a number of attitudes that allow individuals to live in harmony. Curriculum should then shape these attitudes at an early age. Rwandan youth should know that to sacrifice oneself for the sake of others is a factor of social cohesion. The curriculum should instil attitudes such as courtesy, compassion, devotion, flexibility, and sympathy.

Communication and dialogue

The challenge of living together involves dialogue and communication between citizens. Communication and dialogue as factors of social cohesion will allow children to build a common culture based on shared values. It will be at school that Rwandan children should start to learn the principles and rules of collective life and cooperation. The curriculum should therefore create the conditions of exchange, dialogue, and communication through which they discuss rules and ideas and agree on common reference points. Children communicate and construct ideas together about the society in which Rwandans could live harmoniously. From this perspective, the curriculum may be an agent of social cohesion or social division.

Social cohesion is based on respect of rules of social life. However, this respect cannot in itself grant "a better living together." Communication between different groups is necessary. Respect for others does not on its own allow for unity, living together, and building a united and reconciled nation. With communication and dialogue, there is mutual understanding, conviviality, and listening that, according to our respondents, is a key factor of peace, humility, and collaboration. It helps to fight against segregation, and to develop reliability. Communication and dialogue allows the exchange of ideas between people who share the same social space and thus leads to comprehension.

Helpfulness and sharing

Helpfulness and sharing imply the idea of helping someone else. This can be inculcated in young people. Schools should give Rwanda children the opportunity to help others. In a poor country like Rwanda, people need to be able to cooperate with each other. The idea of helpfulness is not yet embedded in people's minds. In the view of our respondents, helpfulness constitutes the key attitude for the "better living together."

Solidarity

Solidarity is seen as a channel of social energy. With solidarity, people unite their efforts toward a common, positive goal.

> One must not be supportive of bad things or a wrong person . . . solidarity contains all positive values: helpfulness, love of others, generosity, goodness, sincerity, fidelity, sociability, honesty, and responsibility.

Our respondents said, "it is clear that without solidarity, a society could not solve its major problems, and work requiring efforts of many people could not be done." Other respondents confirmed that solidarity leads to achieving common objectives and interests. It brings understanding, exchange of experiences, and cooperation. Solidarity was seen by our respondents as a key factor of unity and social and national harmony. It requires the commitment of every citizen, the recognition of others, complementarity, and interdependence.

Respect for others

Respect for others is considered the basis of social relationships. It allows bypassing of differences and accepting individuals with their differences. Respect of others leads to harmony, consideration, and tolerance. Lack of respect is a cause of divisionist practices and denial. Respect facilitates understanding and the acceptance of different ideas, and avoids labelling individuals and groups. *Respect is the starting point of unity and reconciliation and hence of social cohesion.*

Acceptance and tolerance

Tolerance and acceptance refer to the diversity of ideas, opinions, religion, and origin. Tolerance means "live and let others live." Tolerance is seen as an attitude that leads to peace and social cohesion by allowing different people to live together without aggression; it makes easy a common existence, it encourages reconciliation and peace, communication and dialogue. Tolerance allows fighting against revenge. For social cohesion, each person should know that none is perfect, that individuals have their weaknesses and forces and differences, and that should not be a cause of violence.

But tolerance is only a minimum for peace. People have to accept each other so they can communicate and build a cohesive society. The acceptance of others in their physical, psychological, or attitudinal differences is essential for social cohesion. It cannot be imposed by decree or legislation. It results from an education that emphasises values that underlie social relationships in democratic societies. *In this world, everybody should know that none is perfect; everybody has got their own strength and weakness. We have to accept each other.* Curriculum change should then inculcate in Rwandan youth not just an attitude of acceptance of differences but also a recognition that differences are important for a nation's development.

Citizenship

Our respondents suggested that curriculum should lead children to become responsible citizens. Social cohesion is associated with a sense of responsibility toward the community. Responsibility here refers to one's ability to be self-reliant, to care for his or her family, to work, and to study. "Everybody assumes their responsibilities and the social organisation is facilitated." Curriculum should encourage personal and collective responsibility. It should aim at

- bringing each individual student to self-reliance in all spheres of life;
- developing skills to make him or her a master of the surrounding environment;
- instilling self-reliance in the minds of youths;
- creating a character of reliability and dependability on oneself; and
- creating a sense of leadership.

Work and production

Social cohesion is not only limited to the issues of rights and freedoms of citizens; it must also take into account economic issues. It recognises the problems of poverty, unemployment, and revenue distribution among citizens. Social divisions result from a social fracture. If there are economic gaps between social groups, this is the antithesis of social cohesion. These gaps call into question the principles of equality, freedom, and human dignity, which are the basis of a democratic organisation. Work and production are seen as a means of self-reliance and participation. Also, curriculum should prepare students for involvement and participation in local, regional, and national development as well as develop a willingness to participate. Critical thinking, judgement, and decisionmaking will help them to engage in this national development.

The curriculum needs to integrate students in the core national projects, such as Vision 2020, now the guiding policy of Rwanda. Our respondents observed that Vision 2020 is not currently reflected in the classroom.

Another value mentioned was patriotism. It needs to be emphasised in teaching.

> With a spirit of patriotism, we are citizens ... patriotism also calls for the love of our country. ... A patriot aspires to be a national hero.

A patriot promotes collective interest at the expense of individual or partisan interests. He avoids all trends to divisionism, selfishness, and discriminations of all kinds. "It means the love of the country, and consequently all the Rwandans are considered as brothers and sisters belonging to the same nation." A patriot is virtuous; he has good relationships and fights against criminality, intolerance, and revenge. Curriculum should then lead students to love their country, to be loyal to their motherland. Some of our respondents insisted, "Patriotism should not lead to negative things such as cheating, killing."

Curriculum should reinforce or place students in their own cultural context. This dimension of social cohesion is important, as students could identify themselves as belonging to one and same nation. This will reinforce their social relationships within the community. Culture contains social values that are promoted by the society. Culture is defined as a factor of social cohesion. It allows one to understand and be understood, to communicate and to feel in communion with others. Culture offers common references that facilitate social exchanges and communications.

Health and physical development

Health is a state of physical and psychological well-being. It is also a resource that allows individuals to assume their social duties. For school-age children, a state of health allows them to go to school and develop the knowledge required for their development. Rwandan children should thus be trained to maintain themselves in a state of good health. Health covers two dimensions. Our respondents mention values related to both physical and mental health. The state of health is determined by biological and environmental factors both physical and socioeconomic. It is also determined by individual behaviour. To be healthy, children should learn how, for example, to stay clean. Cleanliness, hygiene, and sport were all mentioned as factors that influence a good state of physical health. With regard to mental health, our respondents evoked factors like nobility of mind as well as nobility of conscience.

Children should eat a balanced diet, and the government should provide mechanisms and a conducive environment that promotes the availability of healthy food and medical care to children in order to allow them to study well and fulfil their responsibilities as citizens.

Appendix 2: Resource persons consulted as part of the study

Table 1: Number of Participants from Teacher Training Colleges (TTCs)

Province	College	Number of participants
Butare	TTC Save	2
Gitarama	TTC Kavumu	3
Gikongoro	TTC Mbuga	3
Byumba	TTC Byumba	3
Gisenyi	TTC Gacuba	3
Kibuye	TTC Rubengera	3
Cyangugu	TTC Mururu	3
Kibungo	TTC Zaza	2
Umutara	TTC Mutara	3
Ruhengeri	TTC Kirambo	2
Kigali Ngali	TTC Bicumbi	3
Kigali City	LNDC	3
Total	**12**	**33**

Teachers (14) interviewed from a total of 14 primary schools in Kigali

Table 2: Participants from the Ministry of Education

Department	Number of participants
NCDC	5
Information Service	1
Directorate of Primary Education	1
Directorate of Secondary Education	1
Inspection	2
Total	**10**

Table 3: Participants from Religious Organisations

Organisation	Number of participants
SDA (Adventist)	1
SNEC (Catholic)	1
CPR (Anglican)	1
Total	**3**

Appendix 3: Total Number of Evoked Values

Category 1	Category 2	Category 3	Category 4	Category 5	Category 6
Comprehension	Cleanliness	Assertion	Abnegation	Care of oneself	Dignity
Critical thinking	Health	Calm	Altruism	Citizenship	Good governance
Decision	Hygiene	Courage	Assistance	Cohesion	Equality
Development	Nobility of heart	Determination	Availability	Engagement	Equity
Discernment	Nobility of mind	Firmness	Charity	Entrepreneurship	Ethics
Education	Sport	Frankness	Collaboration	Exemplary	Fraternity
Education to		Happiness	Communication	Heroism	Freedom
diversity		Hope	Compassion	Innovation	Friendship
Education-life		Humility	Complementarity	Patriotism	Human relation
Epistemology		Insurance	Confidence	Production	Humanism
Initiative		Integrity	Consideration	Responsibility	Human rights
Instruction		Kindness	Cooperation	Self-reliance	Impartiality
Intelligence		Optimism	Courtesy	Vision 2020	Incorruptibility
Logic		Patience	Devotion	Work	Justice
Openness of mind		Pride	Dialogue	Work (hard)	Love
Political education		Prudence	Empathy	Work (love of)	Nondiscrimination
Precision		Respect-oneself	Fidelity		Nonviolence
Reasoning		Self-confidence	Flexibility		Peace
Science		Self-control	Forgiveness		Peace building
Thought		Simplicity	Generosity		Peaceful resolution
Wisdom		Softness	Helpful		of conflicts
		Uprightness	Honesty		Respect-life
			Hospitality		Reconciliation
			Listening		Sincerity
			Respect of others		Sociability
			Sharing		Sociality
			Solidarity		Transparency
			Sympathy		Truth
			Tolerance		Union
			Mutual		Unity
			understanding		
			User-friendliness		

Appendix 4: List of Persons Consulted

Ministry of Education, Science, Technology and Scientific Research

- Minister of Education, Science, Technology and Scientific Research
- Minister of State, Ministry of Education, Science, Technology and Scientific Research
- Director of higher education
- Director of secondary education
- Director of primary education
- Executive Secretary, National Examinations Board
- Regional Inspector of Education
- Two curriculum developers

Lycée de Kigali

- Head teacher
- Group discussion with teachers
- Group discussion with students (Forms 5 and 6)

National University of Rwanda

- Professor, Faculty of Education
- Coordinator, Centre for Conflict Management

DfID

- CfBT coordinator
- Curriculum adviser

UNESCO

- Representative

Appendix 5: Fact Sheet - Rwanda

Total population:	8.1 million (94 % rural)
Population under age 15:	45.3%
Life expectancy at birth:	38.2 years
Adult literacy rate (15+):	68%
Youth literacy rate (age 15–24) :	84.2%
Net primary enrolment ratio:	97%
Net secondary enrolment ratio:	7%
Children reaching grade five (2000):	39%
Gross domestic product (in billions):	US$ 1.7
Purchasing Power Parity GDP per capita:	US$1,250
Public expenditure on education (2001):	2.8%
Education system structure:	6+3+3

Compulsory education: Schooling is free and, in principle, compulsory for children aged seven to thirteen. However, in 2002, an estimated 400,000 children of this age group were still not in school.

Types of schools: Out of a total of 376 secondary schools throughout the country, 190 are privately owned. In the private sector, education is largely provided through religious organisations.

Ethnic groups: Hutu (approximately 86%); Tutsi (14%); Twa (1%).

Official languages: Kinyarwanda, French, and English.

Religion: 50% Roman Catholic, 10% Muslim, 10% Protestant.
(The remainder of the people follow traditional religions.)

Sources: The authors, the UNDP Human Development Report 2003, and
http://www.mapzones.com/world/africa/rwanda/rwanda.php

Note: All data for 2001 unless otherwise specified.

Chapter 8

Education Reform and Political Violence in Sri Lanka

Lal Perera

Swarna Wijetunge

A. S. Balasooriya

About the Authors

The three authors are senior professionals who have been associated with the development of school and teacher education curriculum over the last three decades. Two members of the study team, professor Lal Perera, dean of the Faculty of Education, and Swarna Wijetunge, professor of Educational Psychology in the Faculty of Education, are senior academics at the University of Colombo, Sri Lanka, who have worked very closely with the National Institute of Education and the Ministry of Education. Mr. A. S. Balasooriya is a former chief project officer of the National Institute of Education whose contribution has been in the areas of education management development and curriculum development in peace and values education. All three authors have been closely associated over the years with both general education and teacher education curriculum development. They served in advisory and curriculum development capacities in the formulation and implementation of the 1997 curriculum reforms. Professor Perera, in his capacity as the additional secretary of the Ministry of Education responsible for School Education, spearheaded the 1997 curriculum reforms' implementation. Professor Wijetunge has served continuously as a curriculum consultant for the subject of social studies in secondary grades. The authors are following through with their work in the area of social cohesion and civic education by playing a key role in current national initiatives. The National Education Research and Evaluation Centre, headed by Professor Perera, will shortly be conducting the IEA Civic Education study with ninth graders in Sri Lanka. Professor Wijetunge will serve as team leader of this research project. The NEREC, affiliated with the Faculty of Education at the University of Colombo, designs research to investigate (among others) conflict-related issues, the impact of teacher education programmes on conflict resolution, the importance of the hidden curriculum, and the role of nonformal approaches in pursuing ethnic harmony. Mr. Balasooriya will also lead a study titled "A Review of Current School Level Initiatives to Promote Respect for Diversity, Peace Building, Good Citizenship and Democratic Governance."

Acknowledgements

The theme of the present case study is a controversial one, with many differing viewpoints and interpretations of data as presented and analysed in different sources. In order to obtain and present a comprehensive and balanced record, and to analyse the events that have taken place in the country during the past twenty-five years with respect to ethnic and other conflicts, we tried primarily to access printed documents that present different analyses of the incidents. Regarding the curriculum changes that have occurred in the last few years, we consulted and interviewed the relevant persons and authorities to obtain their views and opinions concerning how curriculum changes were effected in order to foster social cohesion and peace in the country. The team wishes to extend their gratitude to the following for their support and cooperation in providing the valuable information that has allowed us to produce this study:

- officers in charge of curriculum planning and development at the National Institute of Education;
- commissioner and deputy commissioner of the Educational Publications Department;
- secretary of the Book Development Board;
- commissioner general of examinations and other officers;
- chairman of the University Grants Commission;
- director, National Integration Programme Unit;
- dean, Faculty of Law, University of Colombo;
- director, Consortium of Humanitarian Agencies;
- director, Human Rights Commission;
- director, Peace Education Unit, the Ministry of Education;
- vice chairperson of the National Education Commission and the dean of the Faculty of Education at the Open University, for providing guidance;
- Mr. Peter Colenso, educationist of the World Bank Resident Office of Sri Lanka, and Dr. Gerhard Huck, project manager of GTZ, Kandy;
- Dr. Sobhi Tawil and Ms. Alexandra Harley of UNESCO: IBE, Geneva, for assigning us the task of writing the case study and providing continuous guidance and direction to make this work a success;
- senior lecturer, Niwala College of Education;
- the teachers who participated in the surveys we conducted; and
- those who assisted us by providing valuable documents and books they possessed to facilitate the work.

Lal Perera
Swarna Wijetunge
A. S. Balasooriya

List of Acronyms

ADB	Asian Development Bank
BECARE	Basic Education for Children in Affected Areas
BESP	Basic Education Sector Programme
CHA	Consortium of Humanitarian Agencies
CSHR	Centre for the Study of Human Rights Education
DAC	Development Assistance Committee
E&CA	Education and Cultural Affairs
EPD	Education Publications Department
G.C.E. (A/L)	General Certificate of Education (Advanced Level)
G.C.E. (O/L)	General Certificate of Education (Ordinary Level)
GEP	General Education Programme
GISP	Governance and Institutional Strengthening Project
GTZ	Gesellschaft für technische Zusammenarbeit (German Technical Cooperation)
HRE	Human Rights Education
IBE	International Bureau of Education (UNESCO: IBE)
ICES	International Centre for Ethnic Studies
ILO	International Labour Organisation
IPKF	Indian Peace Keeping Forces
ITAK	Ilankai Thamil Arasu Kadchi (Ceylon Tamil State Party)
JVP	Janatha Vimukthi Peramuna (People's Liberation Front)
LTTE	Liberation Tigers of Tamil Eelam
MHRD	Ministry of Human Resources Development
NEC	National Education Commission
NEREC	National Education Research and Evaluation Centre
NIE	National Institute of Education
NIPU	National Integration Programme Unit
OECD	Organisation for Economic Co-operation and Development
PCIA	Peace and Conflict Impact Assessment
PPTE	Primary Pre-service Teacher Education
SLMC	Sri Lanka Muslim Congress
TNT	Tamil New Tigers
UNESCO	United Nations Educational, Scientific and Cultural Organization
UNICEF	United Nations Children's Fund
VERP	Vanni Education Rehabilitation Programme

INTRODUCTION

In the course of the previous century, Sri Lanka saw not only thirty years of civil war, initially concentrated in the southern parts of the country, but also an additional twenty years of war in the north and east. These latter twenty years of violent clashes between the government's army and the militants of the Liberation Tigers of Tamil Eelam (LTTE) since 1982 have brought untold suffering to all communities living on the island. Furthermore, they have brought the country's economy to the verge of collapse. Only recently have the participants in the conflict become seriously engaged in the process of negotiating for peace. More than a year has passed since the signing (February 22, 2002) of the Memorandum of Understanding between the government of Sri Lanka and the LTTE, with no major or drastic violations of the ceasefire conditions agreed upon by the two parties to date. In spite of varying vicissitudes in the political climate in the country—the most recent being the power politics played by the president while the prime minister was on a state visit in Washington, and the aftermath to her actions—all parties have reiterated their commitment to the peace process. The final outcome of the peace that is currently still being negotiated will have a significant bearing on all facets of the process of education and curriculum reform addressed in this chapter.

Generally, the intense internal armed conflict is understood as being an ethnic conflict between the Sinhalese and the Sri Lankan Tamils. We would like to point out, however, that to characterise it as such is somewhat superficial, as it is a complex and multidimensional conflict, with its genesis in ideological, historical, social, political, and economic factors. The purpose of this study is to examine how the education system of Sri Lanka has responded to the problem of violent conflict, through curriculum change, to bring about social cohesion.

BACKGROUND TO THE CONFLICT

The nature of social composition

Sri Lanka is an island located between the sixth and tenth north latitudes and the eightieth and eighty-second east longitudes, and separated from southern India by a strip of sea about forty kilometres wide. It has a land area of 65,525 square kilometres (see Map 1). The island has a population of over 18.7 million.

Map 1: Ethnic Communities and Religions in Sri Lanka

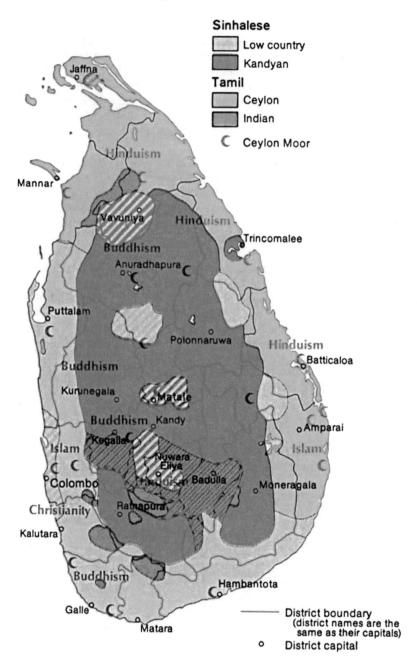

Source: http://www.lib.utexas.edu/maps/islands_oceans_poles/sri_lanka_charts_76.jpg

In 1991, a national census could not be conducted, because of the prevailing conditions in the country, nor could the next census, carried out in 2001, cover the entire island. Data collection was completed in only eighteen of the island's twenty-five administrative districts, with the partial results coming from the northern and eastern provinces. The 2001 census figures estimated the present population of Sri Lanka to be 18,732,255, based on the collected data and projections made from the statistics of the 1981 census. The Department of Census and Statistics released the Census of Population and Housing in 2001, in which the actual demographic composition of the population was computed using only the information from the eighteen districts in which the collected data were complete.

Table 1 shows the composition of the population, using the figures from the 1981 census plus the 2001 numbers.

Table 1: Population of Sri Lanka by Ethnic and Religious Group

Ethnic groups	Percent of total population
Sinhalese	81.9
Sri Lankan Tamil	4.3
Indian Tamil	5.1
Muslim (Moor)	8.0
Other	0.2
Religious groups	**Percent of total population**
Buddhist	76.7
Hindu	7.9
Islamic	8.5
Catholic	6.1
Christian	0.8
Other	0.1

Source: Based on 2001 census data.

Sri Lanka is administratively divided into nine provinces, with a concentration of Sri Lankan Tamils in the northern and eastern provinces. A considerable percentage of the Sri Lankan Tamil population also live among the Sinhalese in the south, where the Sinhala provinces are predominant. Two of these southern provinces, Central and Uva, additionally reflect the strong presence of the Indian Tamil population, who were brought to Sri Lanka by British colonialists between 1930 and the beginning of the twentieth century. Muslims live scattered throughout almost all parts of the country, although there are several Muslim-dominant areas, especially in the east. Catholics and other Christians belong to both the Sinhalese and Tamil communities.

The two main languages spoken in Sri Lanka are Sinhala and Tamil. Sinhala is the mother tongue of the Sinhalese, and Tamil the mother tongue of the Tamils. A majority of Muslims speak Tamil as their mother tongue, but a fair percentage of Muslim students study in schools where the medium of instruction is Sinhala. The Constitution of the Republic of Sri Lanka[1] specifies Sinhala and Tamil as the official languages of Sri Lanka, with Sinhala, Tamil, and English all recognised as national languages (and we will observe this distinction throughout this paper with regard to the use of those two terms). English is the official link language, as stipulated by the Official Languages Act of 1990.

Historically, caste and class divisions have played a significant role in how both intra- and inter-group social relationships emerged. The caste systems among the Sinhalese and the Sri Lankan and Indian Tamil communities are intricately and inextricably interwoven into the fabric of their respective social group formation. Along with parallel class divisions, they impact significantly on many of the issues discussed in the present study. Many scholars argue that the ideological fabrication of ethnic identities by the three conflicting communities (Sinhalese, Sri Lankan Tamil, and Muslim) is more socially constructed than inherent. Nevertheless, differing historical antecedents are used in attempts to establish legitimacy for these identities. The Sinhalese community, for example, claim descent from the first Aryan settlers, who came to the island in the fifth century BC from Orissa in India. The Sri Lankan Tamil community likewise trace their origins to India, and claim that their ancestors arrived in Sri Lanka prior to the Aryans. The Indian Tamils of Sri Lanka are differentiated from the Sri Lankan Tamils, who live in the northern parts of the country, by origin, caste, and even by regional variations in the Tamil language they speak. They trace their origins to the Dravidian groups in the parts of the Indian subcontinent from which they came, and they are the descendants of the southern Indian migrants who came to Sri Lanka during British colonial rule. Although a majority of the Indian Tamil population reside in and have citizenship status in Sri Lanka, they continue to be categorised as Indian Tamils. The people who make up the Muslim community originally arrived in Sri Lanka as traders, from the Arab world (Moors) and from other regions such as parts of India and the Malayan archipelago (Malays). The term "Muslim" is used in Sri Lanka to give a common name to these various groups, even though they may differ in geographic origin and in cultural and other traditions. In this study, "Muslim" is used as broadly inclusive of all such groups.

The Indian Tamil population have, by and large, not been directly involved in the conflict, remaining neutral over the years. The Central and Uva Provinces, in which the majority of them live, are not located near the conflict zones. However, the Indian Tamils, and in particular the youth, are mobile and live scattered in all parts of the country, particularly in cities, where they often go in search of employment. The leadership of the Indian Tamil community has neither actively promoted linking with the Tamil militants nor championed the cause of a Tamil homeland, although some of their leaders have occasionally expressed sympathy for the Tamil cause in general.

The Sinhalese and, in particular, the Sri Lankan Tamils, through continuously reminiscing about the glorious eras of their respective monarchies, construct exclusive identities of "Sinhalaness" and "Tamilness." The conflict has intensified ethnic consciousness and collective identification, promoting these exclusive ethnic identities to an unprecedented degree of intensity. To some degree, the historical emphasis on locality and differing representations of national spaces are likewise ideological manifestations, which are backed by territorial discourses and, eventually, by sanctions and military force.

The nature of the conflict

The history of the conflict in Sri Lanka can be separated into three stages:

1. the pre-independence stage (prior to 1948);

2. the post-independence stage (from 1948 to the early 1970s); and

3. the stage comprising the island's history as it has been marked by the protracted nonethnic and ethnic conflicts spanning the last three decades.

In tracing the conflict's history over the course of a century, historians and other analysts have identified and assessed the tapestry of factors that have significantly contributed to the conflict: its progression as marked by landmark events; the roles played by key actors and institutions; the emerging forms of so-called nationalism, ethnicity, and territoriality; and the complexities of the political scene. These scholars have contributed to an extensive available discourse about the conflict.[2] For the purposes of this study, we will attempt only a brief sketch of this extremely complex web of multiple strands, focusing on the interconnections that form the patterns of the conflict. The progression of the conflict as laid out in the above stages is described only as relevant to the present analysis.

The Sinhalese-Tamil "ethnic" conflict—the two periods of armed insurgency, in 1971 and 1987–89—suggests a different aspect of the armed struggle. The Janatha Vimukthi Peramuna (JVP—People's Liberation Front) is the party of the radical Sinhala political movement, whose members tend to be young political activists, primarily of rural origin. Their popularly labelled "insurgencies" have been acutely violent sociopolitical struggles aimed at capturing state power. These social or overtly "class" conflicts (devoid of ethnic characteristics), coupled with the "ethnic" conflict in the north and the east, have transformed the island's rural society in both Sinhalese and Tamil communities into a source of continuing political conflict, marking a major trend in Sri Lanka's political evolution in recent decades.

The pre-independence stage of the conflict is set against the backdrop of two factors: first, the emerging nationalist movement, which was increasingly critical of British colonial rule; and second, the apprehensions of the "minority" groups—who occupied a favourable position under colonialism—concerning the imminent majority Sinhalese rule that would characterise post-independence Ceylon.[3] Led by the Sri Lankan Tamil elite political leadership of the time, and fed by the policy of divide and rule initiated by the colonial masters, the undercurrents of the emerging conflict became increasingly evident through the overt manifestations of intense political power plays within the Legislative Council. The Sri Lankan Tamils, who then comprised 11 percent of the population—compared to the Sinhalese, who comprised 69.4 percent[4]—were apprehensive of rising Sinhalese nationalism and the emerging threat to the existing balance of power, which had been favourable to them. The relative advantage enjoyed by the Sri Lankan Tamils included: a disproportionate share of high-ranking positions in the civil service and in the prestigious professions of medicine, law, and engineering; and better-quality schooling in the English medium, due to the relatively larger number of missionary schools set up in the northern and eastern provinces compared to the number in the other provinces. The growing fear of Sinhalese ascendancy and a sense of imminent threat to the supremacy enjoyed by the Sri Lankan Tamil elite was fuelled by the Sinhalese elite political leadership, who adopted measures to "correct the existing imbalance."

Initiatives to forge minority solidarity, engendered by this fear of Sinhalese majority rule, began as far back as 1885, the year in which the Tamil representative in the Legislative Council made overtures to bring the Muslim political leadership under the umbrella of the Tamil leadership. The Muslims, however, rejected the proposition. Further key actors and events in the history of the development of Tamil nationalism during the first stage of the conflict are represented by the following:

- the formation, in 1921, of the first communal party in the country's history, namely, the Tamil People's Society;

- Tamil political leader and member of the Legislative Council G. G. Ponnambalam's proposal to the Soulbury Commission on Constitutional Reform (1945) for equal representation (50 percent representation for the Sinhalese, 50 percent for minorities); and

- Tamil political leader S. J. V. Chelvanayaga's call for a separate Tamil state, and his formation, in 1949, of the federal Ceylon Tamil State Party (ITAK).

Ever since this first Tamil nationalist demand, the following refrain has been typed on the ITAK statement:

> We believe that the only means of ensuring that Tamils are guaranteed their freedom and self respect by law, and of solving their problem in a just and democratic manner is to permit them to have their own autonomous state guaranteeing self government and self determination for the Tamil nation in the country and to work indefatigably for the attainment of this objective.
>
> (As cited in K. M. de Silva, 1998)

The emergence of Sinhalese nationalism, which precipitated and fuelled Tamil nationalism, is likewise marked by a series of key events during the pre-independence stage. The emergence of Sinhalese Buddhist nationalism and its concept of space—which rested on a claim to the island in terms of an essential relationship between Buddhism, the territoriality of Lanka, and the Sinhala people—became manifest both in measures adopted by the elite Sinhala political leadership of the Legislative Council and in the form of state-aided colonisation schemes in the 1960s. The latter involved the resettlement of Sinhalese peasantry in predominantly Tamil and Muslim areas in the north and east, often claimed as being "Tamil homelands." The perception of the Sinhalese that they were a "disadvantaged majority"—due in part to the relative advantages enjoyed by the Sri Lankan Tamils in such areas as education and jobs in the public sector, among others—played a significant role in the turn of events after independence, when political power came to be in their hands.

The development of Muslim nationalism and an exclusive ethnic identity by the Muslims in Sri Lanka has been most significantly impacted by the conflict. As noted above, the mother tongue of the majority of the Muslims in Sri Lanka is the Tamil language, and this and other shared cultural bonds with the Tamils (such as customs and traditions) had seen the two communities living amicably together. But as the conflict progressed, the Muslim community began to turn inward, purging itself of any identification with the Tamils, a phenomenon that is contributing significantly to the development of Muslim nationalism and an exclusive Muslim ethnic identity. The most recent move on the part of the divided Muslim political leadership to come together was shown when they requested an independent Muslim delegation at the peace talks, which marks the current stage in the emergence of Muslim nationalism.

By and large, the Muslims had coexisted peacefully with both the Sinhalese and Tamils, were aligned with the main political parties, and wielded considerable political power and influence. Nevertheless, with the militarisation of the conflict and, in particular, the ambivalent position of the Tamil political and militant leadership vis-à-vis the political position of the Muslims in the east (the proposed Tamil homeland), ethnic tensions mounted. The simmering frictions exploded into Tamil-Muslim violence in the 1980s. Given this history, the political agenda of the currently ongoing peace talks contains the following significant factors and issues:

- the displacement of Muslims from lands they had occupied in the north;
- the insecurity of Muslims in the eastern districts, where there are a preponderance of Tamils;
- the transforming demographic patterns in villages in terms of the relative numbers of Tamils and Muslims and Sinhalese and Muslims; and
- the role played by the powerful Muslim political party, the Sri Lanka Muslim Congress (SLMC), in giving leadership to the Muslims in the east.

In the post-independence stage—with S. W. R .D. Bandaranaike's government coming into power, riding on the crest of a wave of Sinhalese nationalism; and the passing of the Official Languages Act, which made Sinhala the official language of the island, in the face of vehement opposition by the Tamils—the conflict enters the phase of militarisation. The Official Languages Act in particular triggered a series of events that culminated in the communal riots of 1958. These riots were arguably the precursor to the ethnic riots and wars waged between the Tamil militants and government armed forces during the last two decades of the twentieth century. Communal sentiments ran high in the racial riots of 1958, causing death and destruction in the various parts of the country to which the riots spread. In the aftermath of the Official Languages Act, the ITAK presented the Bandaranaike-Chelvanayagam pact, which proposed a system of Regional Councils for the north and east, with devolved political power. The pact had to be abandoned, however, under the pressure of the Sinhala nationalist forces. In retaliation, the Tamils under the ITAK made what is known as the Vadukkodai declaration, reiterating their intention to separate from the Sri Lankan state.

The third phase of the conflict began with Prime Minister Sirimavo Bandaranaike coming to power after the assassination of S. W. R. D. Bandaranaike in 1959. A left-radical insurrection (of a nonethnic nature) began in the south in 1971, headed by the JVP. This acutely violent social and political conflict was suppressed by the state with enormous human cost to the JVP. This first insurrection was of relatively short duration, lasting only a few weeks. The second JVP insurrection was more of a nationalist or patriotic war, in part a reaction against the extreme forms of state militarism such as the repression of the freedom of expression and the general domination of civil society.

The second insurrection was more prolonged than the first, beginning in July 1987 and lasting a little over two years, until November-December 1989. Although exact statistics are not available, during the 1971 insurrection approximately twenty thousand of JVP's members and supporters had been killed, with an equal number thrown in jail. The second insurrection in 1987–89 was a longer and bloodier one, and the number of JVP members and sympathisers killed during the rebellion is estimated to be in the region of forty or fifty thousand. The estimated civilian loss of life and destruction to public and private property by the equally ruthless insurgents is considered to be equivalent to the losses incurred by the JVP.

The capacity for calls for radical political transformation to endure and continue to have an impact on the country's political process is clear in the JVP's ability to regenerate, and offers a frame of reference for some of the continuing contradictions in the island's post-colonial process of change. Among the perplexing manifestations of these contradictions is the fact that Sinhalese as well as Tamil societies have sponsored movements of radical insurrectionary resistance and rebellion whose object has been the seizure of state power. Leaving aside the ethnic factor, the economic crisis in Sri Lanka and the subsequent crisis of the welfare state had significant consequences, including low economic growth and joblessness. The dire economic situation contributed to these movements, since it blunted any expectations for social emancipation and generated social despair and anger, particularly among youths, for whom doors had been seemingly opened in 1944 with the granting of free primary, secondary, and post-secondary education. Neither the state nor private capital had been able to set in motion macroeconomic processes that could provide new opportunities for the masses of rural youth and allow them to enter the mainstream of economic and social advancement. Ethno-nationalist politics effectively harnessed the antisystem impulses of these disaffected youth, giving the conflict a pronounced ethnic dimension that has tended to colour interpretations of the nature of the conflict.

Tamil militant youth organisations emerged in the north that shared antisystem impulses with Sinhalese youth in the south, views generated by the context of their times and propelled by Tamil nationalist separatist political rhetoric. Led by the aggressive campaigner and nationalist Tamil leader and politician Amirthalingam, who broke away from the Federal Party (ITAK) to form the Tamil Liberation Front, militant youth in the north and east formed numerous liberation organisations. Between 1981 and 1984, there were thirty-six of these Tamil paramilitary groups. Prabhakaran, later the leader of the LTTE, was a member of such a militant group, Tamil Manavi Peravi (Tamil Youth Front), from which he subsequently broke away to form the Tamil New Tigers (TNT) in 1975, later renamed the Liberation Tigers of Tamil Eelam (LTTE).

The leader of the opposition, Amirthalingam, intensified the canvassing of international opinion on behalf of the Tamils, a process that had begun during the regime of J. R. Jayawardhane, who came to power in 1977. In 1983, an ethnic riot of unprecedented ferocity was unleashed on Tamils, triggered by the killing of fourteen soldiers by the LTTE in the north. The event became known as "Black July," and significantly swayed international opinion in favour of the Tamil cause. The riot erupted first in Colombo and quickly spread to other locations, unrestricted by government intervention in its first few days. The fury of the mobs, who mercilessly killed, burned, and otherwise destroyed the lives and property of Tamil civilians, was unprecedented. In the course of Black July, there was a mass exodus of Tamils seeking refugee status from the south of the island to the north, and to destinations overseas, particularly to neighbouring India and countries in the Western world such as the United Kingdom, Canada, Australia, and the United States. This event effectively tarnished the image of the Sinhalese and the Sinhala state as no other single event in the history of the conflict has. The burning of the Jaffna Library by a mob of government security forces also impacted symbolically on the Tamil psyche, further polarising the ethnic divide between the two warring groups.

The nature of the peace

Black July brought legitimacy and sympathy for the LTTE, not only from the Tamil community living on the island and abroad, but also from the international community. Expatriate Tamil intellectuals and others in Western countries formed various pro-LTTE organisations, in order to provide funds and support for the LTTE. India also sympathised with the Tamil militants, offering them a safe haven on Indian soil, facilitating military training, and providing funds. President Jayawardhane intensified the government military operations in the north in an attempt to crush the LTTE, but, under pressure from India, the government finally agreed to peace talks. The Indian government's 1983 peacekeeping efforts marked the first direct external intervention in the conflict. Thimpu, Bhutan, was selected as the venue for the peace talks, with India as mediator. The negotiations failed, mostly due to the non-negotiable conditions laid down by the LTTE:

1. the acceptance of the principles of a distinct Tamil nation;

2. an exclusive Tamil homeland;

3. the right to self-determination and political autonomy in the homeland (north and east); and

4. full citizenship and fundamental rights to be granted to all Indian Tamils.

The government considered that the acceptance of the first three conditions would be tantamount to the granting of Eelam—the Tamil state—a situation it deemed unacceptable, and the negotiations broke down. However, India insisted on a resolution of the conflict and proposed the devolution of political and administrative power from the central government to the provincial level through a system of provincial councils, modelled on Indian state governments (such as that of Tamilnadu). Indian prime minister Rajiv Gandhi and President Jayawardhane signed an accord to this effect in 1986. The Sri Lankan government agreed to a temporary merger of the Tamil-predominant north and east, and to combine the two provinces as a single administrative unit. The Thirteenth Amendment to the Constitution took effect in 1987, devolving power to the provinces. India sent peacekeeping forces (IPKF) to monitor the implementation of the conditions stipulated in the accord.

Within three months of signing the agreement, the LTTE turned aggressor and fought with the IPKF, totally rejecting the devolution package. Furthermore, they began assassinating key people who had been instrumental in bringing about the accord (most notably Rajiv Gandhi, who was killed in May 1991). In spite of the LTTE's rejection of the package, the government proceeded with the devolution.

The outcome of the second attempt at peace talks—initiated by President Premadasa, who came to power after President Jayawardhane—saw the government play into the hands of the LTTE, which capitalised on the president's attempts at reconciliation to further its own ends. In 1990, the Tamil language was granted official language status on a par with the Sinhala language, and English was declared to be the link language. President Premadasa even supported the LTTE in their fight against the IPKF, and India had to withdraw their forces, having suffered significant losses. In spite of the extended hand of friendship to the LTTE manifested through conciliatory measures adopted by President Premadasa, the LTTE killed him in 1995 using a suicide bomber.

The third attempt at peace talks was initiated in 1997, during the first presidency of Chandrika Bandaranaike Kumaratunga, with whom the LTTE signed an agreement for a mutual cessation of hostilities for a period of six months. The long, drawn-out negotiations, during which there were allegations of hostility by both parties, ultimately ended when the LTTE resumed military action. Some allege that the LTTE had strategically utilised the respite offered by the ceasefire to strengthen and build up its military.

The fourth initiative at negotiating peace, with Norwegian mediation, is currently ongoing. Following a change of government in 2001, and under Prime Minister Wickramasinghe, the government and the LTTE signed a ceasefire agreement in 2002. The government then removed the existing proscription of the LTTE, a condition demanded by the LTTE for the peace talks. The current peace talks are focused on seeking an agreement for the resolution of contentious issues such as, among others,

- the form of self-governance for the north and east;
- the laying down of arms by the LTTE;
- the withdrawal of government forces from what are termed the "high-security zones" in the north and east;
- the resettlement of displaced populations; and
- the rehabilitation and rebuilding of the north and east.

The issues that are being currently negotiated in the political realm are couched in the old understanding of the historiography of the three ethnic groups in the conflict. But even though the discussions are articulated in historical terms, the main determinant today is the military balance between the Sri Lankan state and the dominant military group, the Liberation Tigers of Tamil Eelam. A recent announcement by LTTE spokesman Dr. Balasingham—that the LTTE would not demand a separate state as long as the government was prepared to give them self-autonomy to the north and east, and that a federal form of governance would be acceptable as long as it fulfils Tamil aspirations—was then contradicted by LTTE leader Prabhakaran, who in his Heroes Day speech declared that "the thirst of the Tamils was for nothing but Eelam, only the means had been changed, due to circumstances." Likewise, the LTTE has yet to prove its honesty in the peace process, either through conforming to the conditions of the ceasefire or in keeping to its promise to the international community (and, in particular, to UNICEF) of not conscripting children as combatants while the current peace negotiations are in progress. The demands of the Sinhalese nationalist pressure groups, and Muslim concerns, are other critical and sensitive considerations in the peace process.

The costs of war

The costs of war to humanity, in terms of human development, social cohesion, and peaceful coexistence, are never measurable in quantitative terms. Thus, the human costs of the conflict in Sri Lanka can be termed the most tragic legacy that both present-day and future Sri Lankans will inherit, whether they live in Sri Lanka or elsewhere.

The costs of the war, which has spanned a twenty-year period, have been variously estimated, in terms of lives lost and incapacitated, the escalation of the defence budget, the GDP, Sri Lankan rupees, and other indicators. Dr. Balasingham has cited a death toll figure of twenty-five thousand government soldiers and seventeen thousand LTTE soldiers. The number of civilian casualties has been estimated as being between twenty and thirty thousand. The costs to life and property of the two insurgencies have been mentioned above. The Institute of Policy Studies in Colombo produced a report on the economic cost of the war (January 2000), which attempts to calculate the cost from 1982 to 1996.

According to this report, the defence budget, which was 3.1 percent of the total government expenditure in 1986, gradually rose to 21.6 percent by the year 1996. The total number of government forces in 1986 was 58,660, rising to 235,000 in 1996. The general number of the LTTE cadre was estimated at three thousand. The report says the military expenditure incurred by the LTTE was 10 percent of the expenditure incurred by the government.

Nearly 53,000 families had been displaced as of 1996. Of this number, twelve thousand sought refuge in India. Nearly 56,000 houses were completely damaged, and 34,000 were partially damaged. The destruction to commercial and government property, roads, bridges, irrigation systems, industrial plants, and firms was immense. The government has spent 21 billion Sri Lankan rupees (US$ 218 million) providing dry rations, food, and compensation to displaced citizens between 1987 and 1996. This amounts to 3 percent of Sri Lanka's GDP. The cost of the damage to infrastructure in the north and east was close to 90 billion rupees (US$ 934 million). The cost of the damage to property in the Greater Colombo region was 4.5 billion rupees (US$ 47 million). Together, the total cost of the lost infrastructure amounted to 13.5 percent of Sri Lanka's GDP. The report estimates the total cost of the war for both parties, as of 1996, as 1,429,144 million rupees (US$ 15 billion). This includes the government's and the LTTE's military expenditures, government relief services, infrastructure costs, lost income due to forgone public investment and reduced tourism, lost earnings from foreign investment, and the displacement and loss of human capital due to death and injury.

How children have been affected

As a general fact of war, children are the most affected group. The direct and indirect effects on the everyday life of a country at war apply to all children indiscriminately, and especially to those living in the war zones and border villages. According to UNICEF sources, 900,000 children in the north and east have been directly affected by the war as of 1998. An estimated 380,000 children have been displaced; of these, 250,000 remain displaced. Thousands of children living in all parts of the country suffered the loss of a parent or parents, and family members were separated from loved ones and lived in constant fear and suspense. Education of children in the north and east, and in the border villages, was disrupted. Some schools were occupied by the armed forces. Recruitment of child soldiers by the LTTE deprived those children of their right to education and emotional and physical well-being. Many schools could not function properly due to poor student attendance, lack of teaching staff, and poor or destroyed facilities. Children living in fear demonstrated psychological dysfunction such as a loss of concentration in their studies and social withdrawal behaviours.

Generations of children in the north and east have known nothing but war. They learned fear, prejudice, hatred, and violence, and came to demonise the enemy and idealise martyrdom. Children living in other parts of Sri Lanka, even those unaffected directly by the war, learned some of those same lessons. The relatively recent phenomenon of emerging violence in extreme forms, taking place in schools and universities and engaged in by both individuals and groups of students, indicates something of the nature of children's learning in a culture of war. Sociologists point out that schools and universities are not islands; they naturally reflect the violence of the larger society. A report by Somasundaram (1996), a psychiatrist who worked in the Jaffna hospital, gives a clinical account of the psychological disturbances children manifest as a result of taking part in war as soldiers. He questions their mental fitness to be responsible future citizens. The vivo5 evaluation report (2003) on the psychosocial/counselling component of the GTZ/BECARE Vanni Education Rehabilitation Programme (VERP) validates the findings of a school-based epidemiological survey of children's mental health conducted by GTZ/vivo in 2002 in the Vanni region. The report indicates that 92 percent of the children surveyed have experienced severely traumatising events, and that about a quarter of the interviewed children suffer from severe and chronic post-traumatic stress disorder (PTSD).

BACKGROUND TO THE EDUCATION SYSTEM

The structure of the school system

The system of education in Sri Lanka has evolved over the centuries, originating with an indigenous system of vernacular education provided in temples and higher seats of learning. A network of village schools and ancient universities provided education to the society's elite groups. Colonial rulers and missionaries also set up schools, with the result that one key aspect of Western colonisation—beginning with the Portuguese, in 1505, followed by the Dutch, and then later the British, in 1802—was the establishment of a parallel system of education. Under British rule, education was provided in these schools, in the English medium, to the local elite. A nationalist revival during the pre-independence period witnessed the establishment of a significant number of Buddhist and Hindu schools modelled on the missionary schools and providing education in the English medium. An unprecedented expansion of education was witnessed in 1944, with the provision of free education from kindergarten to university and the network of Central schools set up on the basis of one for each electoral district, to provide good schools to rural areas. Scholarships were offered to high achievers on a needs basis, and hostel facilities were provided to enable children from any part of the country to benefit from the educational facilities provided in these schools. The switch to swabhasha—schools taught in the Sinhala or Tamil medium—in the 1950s and 1960s and the state takeover of denominational schools in 1964 were both measures adopted to bring about a unified system. These measures succeeded in constructing a strong public system and formal schooling which today is, thus, predominantly state owned and managed, with only 3 percent of Sri Lankan children attending private schools.

Table 2: The Number of Government Schools by Medium of Instruction

Province	Sinhala Medium	Tamil Medium	Both Media
Western	1266	117	28
Central	940	520	30
Southern	1116	39	05
Northern	19	848	—
Eastern	258	691	01
North Western	1100	152	03
North Central	687	83	—
Uva	638	193	01
Sabaragamuwa	956	194	02
Total	**6980**	**2837**	**70**

Source: 2001 School Census.

The schools, 9,887 in total, are categorised by medium of instruction, with 6,980 in the Sinhala medium, 2,837 in the Tamil medium, and seventy schools featuring both media. A majority of Muslim students attend Tamil medium schools, although a fair percentage of them attend Sinhala medium schools. Schools that provide instruction in both Sinhala and Tamil are predominantly located in urban areas. In effect, the 2001 School Census presents a statistical picture parallel to that of the 2001 Population Census: the ratio of students who attend Sinhala medium schools to Tamil medium schools is roughly three to one.[6]

The nature of the management system of school education

The Ministry of Human Resources Development, Education and Cultural Affairs, under the direction of a cabinet minister, and the Ministry of School Education, under the direction of a minister, are at the apex of the formal education structure, and the management of schools is within the purview of these two bodies. The main function of these ministries (in conjunction with the Ministry of Tertiary and Vocational Education) is the administration and development of general, tertiary, and vocational education at a national level, under the policy guidelines of the National Education Commission (NEC).

The overarching national policy is to provide equal educational opportunities for all students of school-going age. Beyond this enduring principal policy objective, in practice policies are influenced by the vision of the political party in power, changing global educational trends, and public opinion. In spite of the fact that the NEC is the entity responsible for developing general education policy guidelines, central government ministers in charge of education occasionally change the policy direction to be in line with their own personal or political party agenda. There is a marked tendency on the part of governments that come into power, for example, to either change or deemphasise whatever the previous government had been doing. Accordingly, from time to time many programmes are discontinued not only with a change of government, but even with a change of ministers within the same government.

Since the devolution of power to the provinces in 1990, the provincial minister and the provincial council's Ministry of Education have headed the educational management structure in each province. They do so along with the National Institute of Education (NIE), whose function is to advise the minister on matters of: education, research and development; curriculum design and development; teacher education; and the development of school management. The NIE is the key institution of the central government's Ministry of Education and is responsible for implementing national education policy at the level of general education and teacher training throughout the island. The NIE is also responsible for curriculum design and development for the general education sector, in accordance with the policy guidelines set down by the NEC. In carrying out this work, the NIE draws on the expertise of experienced teachers, subject specialists, and university academics. The draft curricula are submitted to the NIE's Academic Affairs Board for scrutiny and comment by its membership, which is composed of eminent educationists, subject specialists, and representatives of ethnic and religious groups. Once the Academic Affairs Board approve the curricula, they are submitted to the Council, the governing body of the NIE, for discussion and final sanction.

Power devolved to the provinces

The Thirteenth Amendment devolved substantial power over education to the provinces. At the time, Sri Lanka had approximately 10,200 schools, with a student population of 4.2 million. The Central Ministry opted to retain 238 schools as National Schools in order to ensure standards of education throughout the island. The main functions devolved to the provincial councils are specified in the list below:

1. *Provision of schooling* with the authority to: open and upgrade schools; construct and maintain educational buildings; procure and distribute furniture and equipment; control school admissions, time tables, the duration of the school year, and student discipline; register and supervise preschools; and provide staff for schools and for school zones within the approved cadre. The above functions need to be carried out in accordance with the national policies formulated by the Central Ministry. The cadre is also to be determined by the Central Ministry. Finally, it is the Central Ministry that is responsible for building the National Schools and any special education schools in each province.

2. *Personnel administration* with the authority to: recruit teachers who have earned recognised teaching qualifications (diplomas and degrees) from Colleges of Education and universities; appoint principals; supervise education officers; transfer and exercise disciplinary control over all educational personnel; and to appraise staff performance. The Central Ministry establishes the recognised teaching qualifications for recruitment eligibility.

3. *General management, supervision, and financing of schools* (other than the National Schools), including: planning, supervision, monitoring and evaluation, and budgeting. The national and other specified schools are to be managed and supervised in collaboration with the Central Ministry.

4. *School curriculum and co-curriculum and examinations* with the authority to: implement curriculum and the use of concomitant evaluation material; propose and implement local variations of primary curriculum and selected subjects in the secondary schools; produce textbooks and course guides after approval of the manuscript by the National Ministry; organise sports and other co-curricular activities; and conduct local

examinations that have been approved by the National Ministry. The Central Ministry is responsible for setting the guidelines for regional boards of examination.

5. *Nonformal, special education, and* pirivenas *(Buddhist monks' schools)*, with the authority to implement nonformal education programmes and special education programmes.

6. *Teacher training and support services* with the authority to: conduct in-service training programmes with the approval of the National Institute of Education; implement guidance and counselling programmes; implement library services; and develop school libraries. The administration of certain English teacher training courses is to be in collaboration with the Central Ministry. The courses are to be designed nationally.

The Central Ministry's functions relative to the above lie mostly in the formulation of policy, the setting of guidelines, and the specification of technical standards in order to maintain national standards and policies. These centralised functions were seen as necessary in light of maintaining national cohesion as well.[7]

Achievements of devolution

It took a few years for the newly set up provincial councils to realise the power vested in them and feel established in their new roles. In the meantime, it was a phase of role confusion, true for the authorities in the Central Ministries as well. Only a few research studies have been conducted to evaluate the effectiveness of devolution in the area of education. De Silva (1999) observes strong hierarchical organisations emerging in provinces, essentially replicating the former centralised structure. Perera (1987) points out the possibility of complete curricular devolution leading to the parochialisation of education on the basis of cultural and ethnic identity. This has in fact already been observed in the north and east, where the LTTE has recently introduced a localised version of the country's history.

Initially, the quality of teacher in-service training in the provinces after devolution was seen to suffer. However, many initiatives have since been put into place, such as the island-wide establishment of a system of Teacher Centres, special projects for the enhancement of subject teaching, and projects for overall general education and teacher education sector development.8 As a result of these initiatives, a difference is being made in the enhancement of quality in education in general, and in teacher in-service training in particular. Nevertheless, regional imbalances are a continuing systemic feature of concern. What could be concluded here is that the development of education in the provinces is dependent on the degree of ownership, commitment, and enthusiasm of the directing trio, namely, the education minister, the chief minister, and the provincial director of education.

How education has contributed to the conflict

The island's education system, in the beginning of the twentieth century, was notable for its bifurcation between a privileged English education sector, to which access was limited, and the vernacular schools, which formed the larger sector of the school system. The privileged English-educated and English-speaking elite, who were the products of missionary schools (a significant number of which were situated in the Jaffna peninsula relative to their numbers in other parts of the island), held the monopoly on all important positions in public life and in the bureaucracy. In 1944, the first Sri Lankan minister of education, Dr. C. W. W. Kannangara, pioneered a network of Central schools throughout the island, especially in rural areas, in order to provide free education from kindergarten to university.

The expansion in education, and the switch in the 1950s and 1960s to swabasha, resulted in increased access, in relative numbers, to the majority community. Consequently, there was a significant increase in the numbers of Sinhalese students entering the two universities in the system at the time. The Sri Lankan Tamil students who had enjoyed a dominant position in the science-based faculties of the then University of Ceylon found their numbers decreasing. Taking effect in 1973, a system of standardisation of marks by language media was adopted for deciding on university admissions. The Committee on the Reorganisation of Higher Education (1971) recommended standardisation as a temporary measure until educational facilities were more equitably distributed.

In 1974, the District Quota Scheme was introduced, setting university entrance quotas for students in rural areas and educationally disadvantaged districts. The Tamils considered these changes deliberately discriminatory and adversely impacting the then prevailingly Tamil university population. The media-wise standardisation of marks was discontinued in 1978 in consideration of the vehement opposition. Subsequently, the formula for university admission has been modified on several occasions, causing the relative percentage of students to be admitted under the categories of merit, district quota, and underprivileged quota to fluctuate. Currently, the formula of the District Quota Scheme is 40 percent on merit, 55 percent on district quotas, and 5 percent on underprivileged quotas.

Historically in Sri Lanka, the phenomenon of segregation of children by medium of instruction existed as a consequence of the geographical distribution of ethnic groups. This was the case even during precolonial times, when the majority of the island's schools conducted education in the vernacular—Sinhala in predominantly Sinhala areas, and Tamil in predominantly Tamil areas. Under British rule, English medium denominational schools were set up in some of the multiethnic urban areas to cater to an elite group of multiethnic composition. However, the majority of Sri Lankan children continued to study in vernacular schools, invariably segregated by the medium of instruction.

After the switch to the swabhasha medium and the state takeover of the denominational schools, the segregation by language medium became more pronounced. Unfortunately, even at the university level, most students still remain segregated by medium of instruction. Except for the courses offered in the English medium, segregation of students by their ethnicity persists, due to the fact that all other courses are conducted separately in the two official languages, Sinhala and Tamil. This pattern is noted in the Colleges of Education that conduct teacher training as well; the National Colleges of Education that conduct preservice teacher education courses in the two official languages automatically segregate trainees by ethnicity vis-à-vis the language of instruction. The differing religious affiliations of the schools have also served to segregate children to some degree. Today there are Sinhala, Tamil, Muslim, Buddhist, Hindu, Catholic, and Christian schools, a situation that encourages ethnic and religious segregation of children in schools.

PROCESS OF CURRICULUM POLICY CHANGE

Education reforms

During the years of conflict, three sets of education reforms were implemented at the national level: in 1972, 1981, and 1997. The reforms were initiated in response to the sociopolitical crises that surfaced in the course of the war. However, the reforms do not appear to reflect a conscious effort to address the issue of social cohesion and national integration, through curriculum change or otherwise, with the exception of the 1997 reforms. Other than an attempt to deal with the imbalances in educational provision in rural and urban areas in terms of equity and access, the 1972 reforms did not seek to address, either directly or indirectly, the major divisive systemic features such as segregation of children by ethnicity, the need to enable children to become bilingual and thereby facilitate communication among them, and the need to introduce a multicultural perspective in designing curriculum. The change in curricula and methods of teaching and learning at the primary level and the introduction of pre-vocational subjects at the secondary level were both hailed as innovative features of the 1972 reforms.[9] Nonetheless, they failed to incorporate a much-needed social harmony and national integration perspective at the levels of the conceptualisation, design, and implementation of these initiatives. Based on the rationale of enabling schools to share resources, the 1981 reforms attempted to bring schools together in "school clusters." Ideally, this innovative clustering of schools at the regional level could have been used to bring together the schools that were segregated by medium of instruction within a cluster, and to consciously build in a component of social harmony. This was potentially feasible, given the relative numbers of Sinhala and Tamil medium schools in most provinces, yet no such objectives were indicated in the reform rationales.

The *Presidential Commission on Youth Unrest* report (1990), which became the basis for both the 1992 and 1994 National Education Commission Reports and the 1997 reforms, highlighted some of the systemic features that had not been addressed in the educational system or any of its introduced reforms. The National Education Commission Report of 1992 proposed nine national goals, which were also considered to be the goals of education. The goals reflect the expectations of the nation. Three of these goals (numbers one, two, and six) specifically aim at the achievement of social cohesion:

- the achievement of national cohesion, national integrity, and national unity;
- the establishment of a pervasive pattern of social justice; and
- the active partnership in nation-building activities to ensure the continuous nurturing of a sense of deep and abiding concern for one another.

Five basic competencies on which education was to be founded were also identified. The competencies related to communication, ethics, and religion, in particular, complement the three national goals mentioned above and, if consciously pursued, would address the most critical concerns of social cohesion.

A comprehensive proposal for reform was presented in 1997, covering the entire spectrum of general education from primary to junior and senior secondary levels, with the expected outcome of achieving the national goals and the five competencies. Changes were proposed in

- the system of teaching-learning;
- student guidance and counselling;

- subject curricula at all levels of schooling;
- the design, production, and provision of textbooks;
- school-based evaluation processes;
- teacher education; and
- procedures for the effective management of schools to facilitate the implementation of reform (see Appendix 2).

To what extent the reforms (as conceptualised, designed, and implemented) consciously address the national goals and competencies with regard to social cohesion needs to be researched systematically.

The effectiveness of the implementation of this set of reforms has already been researched to some degree. However, the specific objective of investigating the extent to which the reforms have been designed to facilitate, and have actually facilitated, the achievement of the national goals and competencies for social cohesion has not been examined adequately and qualitatively. In the analysis to follow, some of the aspects of these reform initiatives and the issues that have surfaced in their implementation are discussed, providing useful insights on key issues and systemic constraints, and indicating guidelines for the identification of future scenarios and much-needed research agendas.

Rationales for curriculum policy change and the selection of "legitimate knowledge"

Systematic curriculum development in Sri Lanka commenced in the late 1960s with the establishment of the Curriculum Development Centre, prior to which curriculum development was handled by the Ministry of Education as part of its routine work. When the National Institute of Education was established in 1986, it took over responsibility for curriculum development and design. The document entitled The National Curriculum Policy and Process Plan (2000) intends to provide a nationally accepted framework and guidelines to all school curriculum developers and education practitioners in Sri Lanka. It takes into consideration definitions of curriculum such as: "a structured series of intended learning outcomes," "all contrived experiences within the school environment," and, from a more comprehensive and practical perspective, "a course of study provided in school to include the aims, objectives, content, teaching strategies, evaluation and essential learning resources to facilitate learning and teaching of a given discipline." In the present study, these definitions of curriculum, as appropriate, have guided the writers.

The section of the document indicating main principles and considerations states that the broad curriculum framework should serve the needs of a multicultural, pluralistic, but nationally integrated society, in addition to learners from varying home and community environments. In content, there can be no bias in relation to ethnicity, religion, gender, or economic deprivation. Although there is a provision for local adaptation (see the above discussions about devolution), such variations in the primary curriculum and selected subjects in the secondary curriculum will be permitted only with the approval of the National Institute of Education.

The process adopted by the National Institute of Education in curriculum design has already been discussed above. The NIE engages a similar process for the design of totally new curriculum as it does for revisions of already existing curriculum. To recap, the basic curriculum structure and content are initially agreed upon by the consultants and curriculum committee drawn up for a particular subject. Ethnic, religious, and gender representation is ensured in drawing up subject committees. This representative resource group then designs the curriculum. For some subjects such as language and religion, the respective groups would proceed to develop the curricula in the different language media, within the agreed-upon common curriculum structure.

The Education Publications Department (EPD) is entrusted with the responsibility of producing national textbooks. In Sri Lanka, the government's provision of one standard textbook for each subject in the curriculum has been the longstanding practice. Textbooks are produced nationally in the two official language media, Sinhala and Tamil, although the language textbooks are produced in the three media, with English texts provided for each grade. However, as of 2004, and beginning with grade six, schools and students will be given the option of selecting from among multiple textbooks (i.e., other than the one nationally prescribed text) to be used in parallel with the prescribed text.

The Curriculum Process Plan specifies that the national curriculum should be designed while keeping in mind that children are unique, and that they come from different communities and backgrounds. Reference is made to a Quality Control Mechanism—with units to be set up at the NIE and the Education Publications Department (EPD)—to ensure that there is no bias in the curriculum against ethnicity, religion, gender, and socially and economically disadvantaged groups. Curriculum is to be pretested among groups where different languages and ethnicities are represented.

Mirroring the global trend for reviews of school textbooks to identify biases, if any, a content analysis and review of the national texts was undertaken in the context of the ongoing conflict. One outcome is that reviews of social studies and history, language, religion, environmental studies, and science textbooks have become the focus of debate, controversy, and wide public awareness. A number of reports on the subject have been available since the 1980s, with an increased number of reports and articles as a result of more intensive academic and public scrutiny in the 1990s, pointing out that school texts contained a series of biases. Mono-ethnic and mono-religious biases, gender biases, an imbalanced portrayal of cultural heritages, and many factual and contextual errors were documented as having been committed in the process of writing school texts. Both language groups have complained about factual, grammatical, and spelling mistakes in textbooks, alleging that even in spite of wide publicity, the errors have not been corrected. In addition, process issues such as the ethnic composition of the advisory boards and panels that write and review textbooks, and the practice of translating texts from Sinhala to Tamil, have been considered discriminatory and not in conformity with the processes being advocated globally.

In response, the EPD has adopted (effective since January 2003) an "evaluation system" to be used by textbook evaluation boards and technical committees to evaluate draft manuscripts of the books that will be reviewed by panels. The evaluation system has eight factors, each assigned a maximum number of points of either five or ten. Factor eight defines sensitivity guidelines:

- To what extent does the book portray persons and events in an objective way?
- Are all groups represented in a way that is fair to them and their beliefs?
- Is the material likely to promote harmony and understanding, or could it evoke fear and hostility?

A required minimum score is stipulated for each of the eight factors. Factors one and eight, which check conformity to the requirements of the curriculum and which define sensitivity guidelines, respectively, must each receive at least three points out of the possibly allotted five (maximum). The other six factors do not have a required minimum score stipulated. After receiving their sensitivity evaluation, the books would be subject to a further review in order to assess their "respect for diversity," for which the formation of a panel was to be effective as of January 2003.

The envisioned system to ensure that all textbooks conform to the set sensitivity guidelines and further demonstrate respect for diversity is presently in place. The EPD has assembled a review panel, which includes people from beyond the ministry/NIE and from outside Colombo, and is multiethnic and multidenominational in composition. The EPD put together these review teams after having acknowledged that even textbooks published during the year 2000 had to be expunged of "offensive parts." By sensitising textbook writers and monitoring conformity to sensitivity criteria at the stage of textbook writing, the EPD aims to work toward reaching the ideal of an intrinsic and self-regenerating evaluation system.

TRANSLATING CURRICULUM POLICY CHANGES INTO ORGANISATION OF LEARNING CONTENT

In this section, we will discuss directions of both emerging and implemented curriculum change. We will devote particular attention to the newly introduced subject of "life competencies" to the school curriculum, which replaced the subject "life skills." We do this in order to analyse how curriculum change—which was initiated in the context of a generalised concern for social cohesion and national integration, but was not consciously formulated or implemented to effect such change—has failed to utilise the potential to bring about the critically needed transformation. The changes in language policy and the teaching of language in the curriculum, and the structural alterations brought about to effect such changes, are also discussed, in order to analyse how effectively the potential of language teaching in the curriculum is being harnessed to bring about much-needed social cohesion and national integration. The status of the subjects of history, religion, and civics in the school curriculum have been addressed in the section on restructuring and reorganising school knowledge and challenges posed by sensitive learning content, as it is more appropriate to locate the discussion in that section. Educating teachers, a priority area of concern in the context of effective implementation of curriculum change is, however, included in this section, for the emerging scenario indicates that the direction of curriculum change hinges critically on the vital factor of teacher training.

Life competencies: Lessons learned at the level of implementation

The reforms introduced the new subject of life competencies, assigned two periods weekly from grades seven to nine. Life competencies was established to strengthen the efforts of education to develop the total personality of the child, a goal that cannot be achieved through examination-oriented subject teaching alone. (Therefore, the new subject was excluded from examination.) The group of competencies that were selected to be developed through this subject are deemed necessary for every individual, both personally and socially, to lead a productive and full life. The subject aims at strengthening children as individuals through developing their self-esteem, mental alertness, and vision of life. This new subject, if creatively utilised, could directly serve the objective of social cohesion and national integration, by students' achievement of these dual national and educational goals. It also allows teachers ample creative freedom in order to innovate and experiment within the given framework.

The subject of life competencies is made up of four units:

- **Unit one**: Personal development through building self-esteem, identity, and goal-oriented life vision.
  Major themes: Sensitiveness; understanding emotions; understanding one's potentials and skills; and differentiating between helpful and destructive social forces.
- **Unit two**: Competencies in positive interpersonal-relationship building.

  Major themes: Accepting diversity; equality; communication and working in groups; active listening and assertive behaviour; gender sensitivity; and conflict resolution.
- **Unit three**: Competencies in productive learning.

  Major themes: Self-organising practices; planning; time management; decisionmaking skills; and the ability to research necessary information.
- **Unit four**: Vocational guidance and selection of vocations.

  Major themes: Understanding the diversity of the working world and the dignity of labour.

At the level of implementation, some challenges have surfaced:

- the question of which category of teachers should be entrusted with the teaching of the new subject;
- the absence of either a students' textbook or predetermined lessons and content material to guide teachers through this unfamiliar territory;
- methodological issues;
- the challenge of teaching a subject that was not going to be "examined" and therefore would not have the competitive edge that other high-priority subjects had acquired in the system in general; and
- issues of student motivation.

Some school principals entrusted the subject to teachers who had previously taught the subject of life skills, which the new subject replaced. However, life skills was a subject that sought to equip learners with practical skills at a technical or craft level, whereas the teaching of life competencies demands a complex repertoire of sensitivities, understandings, and intra- and interpersonal skills. Moreover, to facilitate their students' meaningful learning, teachers have to engage in this subject creatively.

Teachers experience of teaching life competencies

In the absence of any broad evaluative research findings on the implementation of the life competencies curriculum, the authors conducted a small-scale opinion survey of a sample of forty-seven teachers of the new subject, in the Western Province (in one education zone of the Colombo district).

The sample consisted of teachers from rural, semi-urban, and urban schools in the zone. In this sample there were twenty-one trained teachers, four trained graduates, six graduates, and sixteen postgraduate diploma holders. Thirty-two of the teachers had experience in teaching the subject for at least two to four years. On average, the experienced teachers had participated in four to twelve days' worth of training in the subject. The rest of the teachers were new to the subject. An in-depth group interview was conducted after they had filled out a questionnaire that requested their views and evaluation of the subject.

Most of the respondents found the subject's themes too abstract to understand as presented in the syllabus. As a result, they would like a revision of the syllabus with better explanations of the concepts. The teachers demonstrated considerable variation in their levels of understanding of the curriculum's objectives. The majority thought that the primary objective was to develop the child's skills in facing and solving life's challenges and problems. The discussion revealed that they needed not only to deepen their understanding of the goals and their contextual relevance, but also should have a more profound grasp of the relationship between the concepts and the teaching methods. For instance, many teachers had adopted a teacher-centred and patronising approach in teaching life competencies.

Those teachers who handled the subject well said that they saw positive changes in children along the lines of

- the development of group spirit and positive attitudes toward the natural environment;
- manners and discipline;
- positive life attitudes;
- interpersonal skills;
- conflict-resolution skills;
- self-esteem;
- creativity;
- a sense of responsibility; and
- presentation skills.

The teaching of life competencies is a classic example of curriculum change that had significant potential to bring about social cohesion but failed to do so because the objective was only presented as a generalised expectation and was never spelled out in clear terms. Consequently, inadequate attention was paid to significant process factors that should have been addressed prior to introducing the new curriculum, resulting in a lack of systemic support to sustain the initiative.

Teaching of languages in school curriculum

In all government schools in Sri Lanka, the two official languages are to be taught to all children, as part of the core curriculum. At the junior secondary level (grades six to ten), Sinhala and Tamil (Tamil for Sinhala students and Sinhala for Tamil students) are to be taught as subjects in the core curriculum, to all students. At the senior secondary level (grades ten to eleven), the "other," alternate official language is an elective subject. This initiative had, in various forms, been previously introduced to the system, but had never been consistently sustained. The system's ability to provide teachers proficient enough to teach the alternate language in all Sri Lankan schools is a key factor and, in the short term, calls for innovative interventions. The ability to offer all electives in all schools is a luxury that the system can ill afford. The basic reality is that unless a subject is among the compulsory core, the urgency and commitment to make the necessary provision for the teaching of that subject in both languages and in all schools nationwide gets diluted.

The push and pull factors that motivate or demotivate the teaching and learning of the official languages in schools need to be recognised and addressed. The following factors would be among the principal ones to consider in earnest:

- the political will and determination to sustain the initiative of teaching both official languages to all children;
- the incentives and directives given to the school system and to students that would influence the preference a student (or parent) might have for learning the "other" official language;
- the nature of the school climate for teaching and learning in these languages; and
- the motivation of teachers to teach the languages.

These factors are in clear contrast to the initiative of teaching English as a link language, which is not constrained by the same factors due to the fact that English is clearly recognised as the language for economic advancement and global citizenship and is therefore in strong demand. Ultimately, political will plays a significant role in the critical decisionmaking about where the limited available finances will be channelled. For example, all the remaining money from a substantial loan negotiated by the government from the World Bank for the education sector has been diverted to English education, IT education, and educational rehabilitation in the north and east.

It is our contention that a strong link with the outcomes of the peace process may give the official language teaching initiative the drive it seems to lack, for in the final analysis, macro-level decisionmaking in the political realm emerges as the arbiter of what change will take effect at the school and curriculum level. We would further like to argue that the critical issue of bringing about social cohesion by means of all students learning the two official languages is only superficially being addressed, constrained no doubt by systemic inadequacies and a generalised faith in the power of the link language to remedy all ills. It is not apparent, in other words, that tapping the power of bilingualism in the official languages for sustainable social cohesion is being genuinely pursued. Currently the debate seems to be more focused on the medium of instruction (and its technical or planning implications) and concerned with the following questions:

1. Should school knowledge be imparted in the official languages or in the link language?

2. When looking at issues of access and equity, what are the implications of a switch to using the link language as the medium of instruction (something that is currently being attempted, on a pilot scale)?

3. Finally, and in more fundamental terms, what is the medium in which learners best acquire and make meaning of knowledge?

The National Education Commission sees education as a means of engineering social change—in particular, social harmony—in Sri Lanka. Undoubtedly, there is significant potential for the achievement of national cohesion, national integration, and national unity (i.e., the national goals as set by the NEC) by strengthening the position of English as a link language between communities. A common means of communication might then play its part in promoting genuine understanding among students from different groups. In practical terms, for English to serve as a link language between children of different ethnic groups, the students must coexist on the same school premises and come together during English periods (an arrangement that exists in some of the few schools that provide instruction in both languages) and during other subjects as well if they are offered in the English medium (which is already occurring in schools that have opted to teach a number of subjects at the secondary level in the English medium). The government school system has initiated the teaching of advanced (senior secondary) subjects in the English medium, beginning with science and mathematics, providing another opportunity for a multiethnic composition of students in these classes.

Amity schools

In 2001 the central government proposed to establish so-called "amity schools" nationwide. Initially, the aim of these schools would be to allow high-achieving students representing different ethnic groups to grow up in an amicable atmosphere, studying and working together, using a common link language to forge common thinking and learning, and, in doing so, harnessing core values of goodwill for the country. With this objective, the best performers of the year five scholarship examination from the Sinhala and Tamil streams were to be selected. The idea was to ensure that amity schools could be set up with a consistent proportion of ethnic diversity in all education zones wishing to accommodate them. All students would be trilingual at graduation, since instruction in core subjects was to be in English, and students would study Sinhala and Tamil either as their compulsory first language or their second official language. The side benefits of this initiative would be

- the experience of selecting students on the basis of merit;
- the provision of quality inputs, both in terms of human and material resources, in the promotion and development of amity schools as centres of excellence; and
- the development of materials in English, which could be shared with any school wishing to use them, thereby making such materials broadly available particularly in educationally disadvantaged areas.

The progress reported thus far of the amity school programme (such as that recorded on February 17, 2003) indicates that what is being implemented is a far cry from the originally articulated concept of these schools. In practice, education authorities gave schools that opted to offer classes in the English medium a green light, but little else has been accomplished in terms of setting up these schools. A status report does show that classes in the English medium have begun in schools that responded positively, as has teacher training and the translation of textbooks. However, as it is currently being implemented, the realisation of the envisaged objectives and outcomes expected of the amity school initiative may be at best incidental. One may hope that the ideal amity school as originally conceived may still be achieved, but it will only happen if a conscious effort is made to admit students from all ethnic groups.

A prototype amity school already exists in the form of international schools, and others going by different names, such as the Sri Lankan English Medium School, which have been around for some time and have considerably increased in number over the past few years. The ethnic mix desired through the establishment of amity schools already exists to varying degrees in the international schools. We therefore considered it useful to obtain views of informants from these schools on the nature of amity that exists among their students from different ethnic groups. We conducted a cursory survey of educators in three international schools and one Sri Lankan English Medium School to gain insights on the experience of schools who use English as the medium of instruction. Specifically, we requested that either the principal or a senior teacher make a written submission on the social harmony being fostered among students.

According to them, social cohesion is more of a cumulative by-product of "all contrived experiences within the school environment" than a direct outcome of the formal curriculum. The focus of these respondents was on how the whole ethos of the school was facilitating peace and harmony irrespective of students' ethnic or other group affiliation. A particularly interesting bit of information from one respondent was the speculative observation linking acquired language proficiency to increased intergroup socialisation. They note that in the lower grades (lower and upper kindergarten and grades one and two), when English proficiency is still limited, students tend to keep to their own "groups," but as children move on to the higher grades and improve their English proficiency, this pattern changes. The prospects for the original amity school concept are promising, therefore, if implemented island-wide, on a pilot basis, and monitored and nurtured with commitment.

Reorganising and restructuring of school knowledge: Challenges posed by sensitive learning content

In the present scenario, many difficult and critical issues are being debated on school knowledge as it is currently organised and structured in the form of subjects. Numerous stakeholders, from varying ideological standpoints, engage in the multifaceted debate of the perennial philosophical question that asks, "What knowledge is of most worth?" and its adjunct, "And for what purpose?" In terms of school curriculum, many decisions still need to be made concerning the subjects of history and social studies, religion, language, and civics. The challenges posed by some of the most contentious issues seem to threaten the very foundation of the curriculum framework, indicating that the processes of negotiation and consensus building in the political realm will be crucial, in the final analysis, to how decisionmaking is dealt with at the level of reorganising and restructuring school knowledge.

History

History is the subject with the most contentious issues. In the aftermath of the conflict, the content of the history curriculum has been debated with such intensity by all stakeholders that reaching consensus on some of the fundamental and most sensitive questions—Whose history is it? Who should get to select it? For what purpose?—seems well nigh impossible. The one aspect on which all stakeholders agree is that history should be reinstated in school curriculum as a subject in its own right. Such consensus was the result of stakeholders' resisting the integration of history into the thematic area of social studies, after this had been briefly done following global trends. As a concession, the subject as it presently appears in the curriculum is entitled "History and Social Studies."

Historiography has significantly influenced the conflict, and the painful collective memories and group animosities that have become increasingly polarised over time stand in the way of reconceptualising or rewriting history as a school subject that could facilitate social cohesion and national integrity. Creative solutions may need to be sought, building on the flexibility already existing within the system for regional variations, the option of choosing from among multiple textbooks, and so on.

The critical comments made as a result of the content analysis of history textbooks over the last two decades should also be taken into consideration as the subject of history is reorganised and restructured. Reviewers contend that the history of Sri Lanka and its people and land is not portrayed objectively in the texts, and that such partiality and imbalance go against the grain of cultivating social cohesion. They have also critiqued how history has been conceptualised, interpreted, and portrayed in textbooks, enumerating the following shortcomings:

- it has been written in a narrative style that is focused on tracing *continuity* from pre-historic times to the present;
- it is event centred rather than problem centred;
- it is prescriptive rather than encouraging of a multiplicity of possible interpretations;
- it disregards the fluidity of identities and fails to mention the lack of certainty about categories in presenting all cultural identities;
- it does not discuss objectively the complex dynamics that created the ethno-cultural mosaic of contemporary Sri Lanka; and
- it avoids issues such as ethnicity, ethnic conflict, and war.

Religion

There is considerable focus on the subject of religion in the school curriculum in terms of its potential for social cohesion. However, the traditional mode of organising and structuring religion as school knowledge in the form of religious instruction is very strongly entrenched, and jealously guarded. Because of this, reorganising and restructuring these sensitive learning contents in terms of comparative religion or the culture of religions, which would be particularly conducive to a multicultural pluralist society, may well be an impossible proposition in the current context, given the nature of the resistance to be envisaged from the stakeholder community.

A content analysis of the textbooks used for the subject of religion at the secondary level (grades six to eleven), which was undertaken as part of an ongoing research project at national level for the National Education Commission, clearly indicates the nature of the transformation that is needed if the subject of religion is to be effectively enlisted in the cause of forging social cohesion. These are issues currently being addressed—somewhat tentatively—as academic and theoretical exercises and pilot projects at the school level undertaken by the intellectual community as researcher practitioners. The real test will be at the level of negotiation and consensus building for the eventual transformation of the teaching of religion into "culture of religions" or "comparative religions."

Civics

The content of civics as a subject in the school curriculum was long ago integrated into other subjects such as social studies, and has not been taught as a separate subject in the curriculum for a considerable length of time. However, given the current context, the need to reintroduce civics independently in the school curriculum is being seriously considered. The initiatives to institutionalise Human Rights Education in the school and teacher education curricula can be considered as measures to fill an existing vacuum in this area that was created by removing the subject civics. The National Education Commission will shortly be proposing that civics be given its rightful place in the school curriculum.

Language

Finally, language as a school subject is no less controversial, but the degree and intensity of the issues that arise concerning language as a subject in school curriculum are less contentious relatively in terms of sensitive learning content. It is, however, a vital policy issue with a broader impact than a discreet subject area and was, for this reason, analysed separately above.

IMPLEMENTATION

Teacher education

The 1997 reforms proposed that the curriculum for teacher education be revised to equip teachers with necessary competencies for effective delivery of school curriculum. Teacher education was to emphasise education for human values, human rights, national cohesion, gender rights, and the environment. Student teachers as well as those in service were to be provided facilities to improve their competency in the official languages and in the link language (English). The reforms envisaged the integration of concepts of national cohesion, peace, and conflict resolution into teacher education programmes of principles of education, classroom management, sociology of education, and counselling and guidance. These concepts also contributed to enrich the general education subjects of life competencies, religion, and culture.

To cite the example of the teacher education curriculum of the National Colleges of Education, in the syllabus for the course on principles of education, which was revised in accordance with the reforms, we find the following themes:

- education for national cohesion;
- education as a human right;
- values education;
- equal opportunities in education;
- children's rights;
- and the role of the teacher.

The teachers' guides suggest that these themes be covered mostly through discussion, debate, literature, and field surveys, and other creative activities. Under the theme, "role of the teacher," trainees are expected to develop skills of empathetic listening, democratic leadership, developing children's self esteem, and conflict resolution through role-playing. The colleges are instructed to organise and implement projects for learning human rights, children's rights, and conflict resolution as co-curricular activities, with a view to enhancing the learning of the related themes. In carrying out the projects, trainees conduct surveys and observational studies through activities such as visiting neighbourhood orphanages and schools, organising guest lectures at the college, and implementing programmes in schools to raise the awareness of students, teachers, and parents.

Preparing teachers for a pluralist society—that is, educating teachers who become able to manage curriculum-related teaching and learning by adopting a multicultural perspective—would require a more concerted and systematic orientation. The Basic Education Sector Programme (BESP) cited in the concluding section of this chapter is an example of a project that is designed along the lines envisaged.

RESEARCH AND EVALUATION

Currently, there is a significant positive trend to incorporate research and evaluation as a critical factor in conceptualising, designing, and implementing curriculum change.[10] This was evident in the processes adopted with respect to the most recent initiative for curriculum reform at the national level. The reforms were the end product of a series of extensively documented research initiatives. Furthermore, a significant number of research studies have been commissioned to evaluative the effectiveness of the reform's implementation, some of which have already been completed and others which are still ongoing. There is considerable system-wide interest and focus on the findings of these research studies. The centralised, national-level focus of the research, however, is a cause for concern, because it limits the capability and commitment of school personnel to analyse their own practice. Continuous analysis and assessment of implemented reforms should ideally be built into an ongoing process that includes school-level initiatives. Sri Lanka must still work toward the goal of establishing a system that is characterised by an institutionalised research culture.

The extent to which the reforms have focused on bringing about social cohesion and national integration through curriculum change remains to be investigated, through systematically designed research that would analyse the process of such curriculum change as well as the implementation of reforms to bring about the intended change.

The *piloting* of reforms is, however, an institutionalised feature. A clear example of this followed the 1997 primary level reform initiative. The reforms were immediately piloted in one selected district, beginning with grade one and progressively introduced over subsequent years until the reform at the primary level was complete. Another notable feature is the involvement of independent research bodies in the evaluation of current reforms. For example, the National Education Research and Evaluation Centre (NEREC), at the Faculty of Education, University of Colombo, is heavily involved in researching reform implementation at the national level. The findings of evaluation studies conducted by the NEREC provide useful feedback to those who are implementing and those who are designing the reforms. What is still needed is for micro-level follow-up research to be conducted based on the NEREC findings and for action research that could contribute to qualitative enhancement of the reform initiatives.

In the research studies that have been conducted, the degree of stakeholder receptivity and resistance in the implementation of curriculum reforms is evident to a considerable degree. For example, research evidence indicates that there is a fair amount of resistance on the part of teachers to the current reform initiative that looks to institutionalise school-based assessment in post-primary classes. The result is that this assessment is reduced to the level of a routine chore that teachers carry out with little conviction. In contrast, at the primary level there is considerable stakeholder receptivity to most of the features of the reform initiative, such as activity-based and interactive student-centred learning. In implementation, however, the conscious or unconscious resistance on the part of teachers to this change in the focus of student learning has been documented in recent research findings (NEREC). This receptivity/resistance dichotomy in the system is symptomatic of what implementers of curriculum change for social cohesion have to be conscious of and alert to, in attempting to reorganise and restructure school knowledge in areas of sensitive learning content.

KEY AREAS OF OUTSTANDING ISSUES

Hypotheses/scenarios for the future

We would like to present the preconditions for future scenarios and the hypotheses we see emerging from the present analysis:

1. At the macro level, identifying and dealing honestly with the major constraining systemic features and contextual factors that have dominated the past and continue to dominate the present scenario, and which have either not been addressed or have merely been tinkered with for reasons of political expediency, will be fundamental to meaningful and sustainable change.

2. A mindscape shift from a macro- to a micro-level search for solutions with wider stakeholder participation and greater tolerance of diverse perspectives and paths to proposed solutions may facilitate the reform process more effectively than dogged reliance on paths that have been habitually followed, which are considered sacrosanct.

3. In the sphere of curriculum reform and change, there needs to be a more serious focus on the first national goal of national cohesion, national integrity, and national unity, in addition to the competencies that will enable the child achieve those goals meaningfully.

Priority areas to follow up

The priority areas to follow up are numerous. The areas that come immediately to mind are

- the glaring inadequacies in the teacher education system that constrain the curriculum reform process in general, and the reform's implementation in particular, in both the short and the long term;
- the dearth of teacher educators who have a specialisation in curriculum studies;
- the need to initiate action research at the school level and strengthen the feedback loop between policy and practice; and
- the networking necessary to enable Sri Lanka to learn from the experiences and solutions of other countries.

SOCIAL COHESION THROUGH CURRICULUM: SOME EXEMPLARS

In this section, selected exemplars of initiatives in place, either in the form of specific projects or as examples of institutions specifically focused on bringing about social cohesion through curriculum, are presented. The projects have been selectively identified by sectors: general education, higher education, and teacher education. The chosen institutions are from the public and other sectors. We would like to clarify that the contributions of international government and semi-government funding organisations, non-governmental organisations, and other voluntary bodies are broadly and inclusively categorised as nonpublic.

The initiative for peace education through cross-curricular integration and co-curricular projects in the school system and the Basic Education Sector Project (BESP, GTZ) focus directly on the general and teacher education sectors. The recent higher education sector initiative to incorporate a social harmony component in undergraduate education is illustrative of the proactive participation of the higher education sector in seeking creative solutions through curriculum. Likewise, an innovative Human Rights Education programme conducted by the Centre for the Study of Human Rights Education (CSHR) at the University of Colombo, in collaboration with the National Institute of Education, is presented. The programme aims to strengthen and enrich the CSHR outreach programmes being conducted in schools, and achieve its goal of institutionalising HRE in the school system, by incorporating HRE in the preservice and in-service training of teachers. A curriculum development initiative for HRE by the Human Rights Commission has been selected, to focus on the feasibility of collaborative networking among providers. Sri Lanka as a conflict-affected country has attracted international as well as local initiatives for peace education in substantial measure, thus strengthening, providing a broad base for, and adding to government efforts. Two of the most longstanding and proactive contributors to the peace initiative in Sri Lanka—UNICEF and Sarvodaya—have been selected, in the category of institutions. These two groups have already contributed significantly to social cohesion, either by conducting their own peace education programmes or processes or by supporting the government's programmes.

Peace education in school through cross-curricular integration

The need to build peace awareness in children has been strongly felt and consciously addressed at an official level within the system, as a corollary to the conflict. The situation brings to mind what Maria Montessori pointed out at the dawn of the last century, in her book *Peace Education* (1930):

> Those who want war prepare young children for war; but those who want peace have neglected young children and adolescents so that they are unable to organize themselves for peace.

Peace education was introduced to the curriculum as early as 1991. The National Institute of Education, in collaboration with UNICEF, compiled a syllabus and learning activities in the form of a book, along with several teacher guides. These materials have been widely distributed to all provinces. The peace education curriculum was based on the themes of peace, positive thinking, empathy, inner peace, cooperation, assertiveness, critical thinking and decisionmaking, conflict resolution, nonviolence, community peace building, caring for the planet, and intercultural understanding. It was to be delivered through the cross-curricular integration of the formal subjects. A large number of teacher guides have been developed. Schools were encouraged to develop and implement co-curricular projects and activities like organising intercultural events, interschool friendship camps, peace seminars, and peace dramas, to further peace education.

An empirical study is yet to be conducted on how these initiatives for peace education through curriculum have taken effect. Evidence of co-curricular projects on the theme of peace education being undertaken in schools and efforts to build bridges between ethnic groups by bringing children of different ethnic and religious groups together through playful activities, organising multiethnic cultural events and student exchange programmes (between the north, the east, and provinces in the south), and so on are being attempted sporadically. However, the extent to which the envisaged cross-curricular integration and, in particular, the raising of teachers' awareness as peace educators has been effected, by reorienting teacher education programmes "to ensure the professionalisation of every teacher and teacher educator as a peace teacher" (UNESCO regional seminar on curriculum development for peace education, Colombo, Sri Lanka, January 3–5, 2001), needs verification. The systemic pressure on teachers and students to concentrate on core syllabus contents for examination purposes generally tends to defeat most other purposes for which school curriculum is geared. In sum, the implementation of peace education through cross-curricular integration deserves further research investigation.

Programmes conducted by Peace Education Special Unit, Ministry of Education

A special unit at the Ministry of Education attempts to raise peace awareness among schoolchildren through a number of different programmes. It organises an annual National Peace Week in all schools across the country. Schools are encouraged to organise programmes in various capacities, such as supporting children affected by war and arranging community development activities and seminars on civic themes. The unit runs education programmes on peace, active nonviolence, national integration, and students' leadership development. It also arranges intercultural appreciation programmes, art exhibitions on peace themes like human rights, and school link programmes to bring children of various communities together. Furthermore, it publishes resource materials for resource persons to use in the provinces. In addition to the central ministry, some provincial ministries (e.g., North Central Province) take a keen interest in peace education. The climate of acceptance and facilitation for these special unit initiatives by the respective provinces is a significant factor in whether and how effectively they are implemented at the provincial level.

National Integration Programme Unit (NIPU)

This is a semipublic government organisation attempting to build ethnic unity and understanding through various educational and cultural programmes. It conducts seminars, issues publications, and provides training to resource persons in peace education. The content analysis of school textbooks conducted under the auspices of NIPU made a significant contribution toward textbook revision and raising awareness among education sector personnel concerning the need for sensitivity criteria to guide textbook writing.

A higher education sector initiative for social harmony

At present, the University Grants Commission is actively pursuing the design of a social harmony component in undergraduate education in the Universities of Sri Lanka, with pre-implementation support by the government of the Netherlands for the design of the social harmony concept. An inaugural conference was held in November 2002, followed by a training course in March 2003 for members of the academic staff who are engaged in the implementation of the social harmony component (inclusive of Peace and Conflict Studies) in the teaching programme. This recent initiative is a direct response for proactive intervention through the higher education curriculum by the university sector.

A collaborative higher education, general education, and teacher education sector initiative

A higher education sector initiative to institutionalise Human Rights Education (HRE) in the formal education curriculum, an outreach programme of the University of Colombo's Centre for the Study of Human Rights, is cited here, showing the potential for creative collaborative links between the higher education, general education, and teacher education sectors.

Presently, there is no explicit government policy on HRE, but rather a commitment to integrate HRE into school curricula, albeit in a limited manner. Currently it is addressed directly at the advanced level (AL) classes (through the subject of political science, and as an optional topic) and indirectly at the primary level, where it is integrated into environment-related studies. A recent study on HRE in Sri Lanka, commissioned by the Asia Foundation, underlines the need to support the subject and highlights that "the most glaring gap—in HRE in Sri Lanka's school system—is the non-inclusion of teacher training colleges (TTCs) in planned activities to institutionalise human rights in the schools." The report goes on to say that "making human rights part of teacher training both in pre-service and in-service will accelerate the institutionalisation of HR in the school system."

The Centre for the Study of Human Rights (CSHR), a service-oriented, nonprofit institution in the Faculty of Law at the University of Colombo, has been working closely with the National Institute of Education in promoting the institutionalisation of HR in the formal education curriculum. Its twin mandates of education and research in human rights combine to reinforce its longer-term goal of building a culture of human rights in the country. In 2001, the CSHR entered into an agreement with the Human Rights Research and Education Centre of the University of Ottawa and the chief executive of the Governance and Institutional Strengthening Project (GISP), whereby GISP provides a contribution to the CHSR to strengthen the capacity of Colleges of Education (preservice) in Sri Lanka in order to enhance awareness of teacher trainees on human rights. The aim of the program was to enhance the capacity of teacher trainees (once they are teaching) to assist secondary-level students in their human rights projects, and to instil in these prospective teachers both their responsibility to protect the rights of others and the values and attitudes necessary for them to assist in constructing a more civic conscious society. This project has now been extended to cover in-service teacher training colleges.

A curriculum development initiative for Human Rights Education, including the formal education sector—by the Human Rights Commission

Parallel with the CSHR initiative, an ambitious project has been initiated by the Sri Lankan Human Rights Commission to develop curricula that would be introduced sector-wide, including the formal education sector. Modules have been developed for the training of human rights educators such as principals, teachers, and preschool, primary, and secondary school children, in the formal education sector. The feasibility of a combined HRE initiative—which would capitalise on the outreach of the CSHR and the link it has forged with the NIE, and utilise the curricular material developed by the HRC (in module format and with methodological strategies outlined for its use at the different levels of the formal education system)—merits serious consideration. In accordance with the curriculum policy and process plan, the institutionalisation of curricula in the formal education sector can only be effected with NIE collaboration. Therefore, networking among sectors to identify feasible collaborative initiatives would be mutually advantageous, and enable efficient and cost-effective educative processes to be set in motion.

The Basic Education Sector Programme (GTZ)

Among several organisations working in collaboration with the Ministry of Human Resources Development, Education & Cultural Affairs (MHRD, E&CA), in its efforts for social cohesion, the German Technical Cooperation (GTZ) is worth mentioning here. The German government (Federal Ministry for Economic Cooperation and Development) funds, through the GTZ, the Basic Education Sector Programme (BESP) and implements it in close collaboration with the MHRD, E&CA, and eight principal ministries, within the context of the recent education reforms designed by the Sri Lankan government. Since the inception of the programme in 1999, BESP has endeavoured to bring about quality improvement in primary education through preservice and in-service training of primary teachers. The aim of improving quality is done through training primary school teachers, who may serve as a support to the peace process between Sinhala, Tamil, and Muslim communities in Sri Lanka. The programme seeks to empower all pupils who have completed the primary level and children and adolescents who have completed basic education, for lifelong learning and living in a multicultural and pluralistic society.

It also aims to offer an appropriate basic education for children and youths who were unable to complete the primary level. Instead of the mere provision of knowledge and skills, the programme emphasises attitudinal changes in the target groups by incorporating peace concepts, conflict resolution, and conflict transformation into the training materials and training, as cross-cutting issues. In addition, the programme contributes to the rehabilitation of the education system in the North East Province and in disadvantaged areas.

The preservice component of the programme has focused on developing a new Primary Pre-service Teacher Education (PPTE) course, paying special attention to the development of new language curricula in five subjects, namely: mother tongue Sinhala, mother tongue Tamil, second national language Sinhala, second national language Tamil, and English. The objective is to allow Sri Lankan primary school teachers to develop language proficiency and language teaching skills, and enable them to be conversant in the three languages to be used in all primary schools. This approach recognises the importance of communication for social cohesion in a multiethnic society. Preservice training of prospective primary school teachers, with a view to preparing them for the real learning-teaching situations in the classrooms, supplemented by a new internship programme, is operating countrywide in twelve National Colleges of Education.

The second component is the Teacher In-Service Project (TIP), which is focused on the training of practicing teachers in the Sri Lankan education system. The TIP trains provincial master trainers and in-service advisers (ISAs) using a set of five manuals that address the basic needs of primary teachers and ISAs, as identified by baseline surveys. Themes that are relevant for social cohesion, such as conflict transformation, and understanding and protecting the child, feature significantly in these manuals. Using a cascade training model and school-based training approaches, the project aims to reach all primary school teachers and principals. The TIP, which started its activities in the northeast and in the Central Province in 1999, will gradually extend its reach to all other provinces in Sri Lanka.

The third component, Basic Education for Children in Disadvantaged Areas, aims to improve the basic education of war-affected children and dropouts by extending coverage and reaching out-of-school children. It further pays special attention to the strengthening of psychosocial counselling capacities in order to establish a school-based psychological service. The peace process in place has facilitated the opening up of the Vanni region, which was under the control of LTTE, and the programme runs the Vanni Education Rehabilitation Programme (VERP), in order to rebuild basic education in this region, which has been hardest hit by the ethnic conflict.

UNICEF

As early as 1991, UNICEF pointed out the need for peace education for Sri Lankan children. Since that time, it has been providing funding to the ministry in charge of subject education and the National Institute of Education, for the development of peace education/education for conflict resolution curricular materials, and for quality improvement in primary education. It funds many organisations working on the protection of children's rights. It has stood sternly against child recruitment into the armed forces by the LTTE and has exerted pressure to stop the practice. UNICEF also provides funding for the welfare of child refugees in the country.

Sarvodaya

Sarvodaya is one of the largest NGOs in Sri Lanka. Even prior to the ethnic conflict, and certainly since the organisation's inception, Sarvodaya has been working to raise the peace consciousness of the people, stressing the fact that no party can "win" the present ethnic conflict. Throughout the country, in villages and towns, Sarvodaya runs a large number of programmes,[11] which aim to reawaken people for total development, addressing all major facets of life and society including programmes for economic development, delivery of preschool education, human resource development for youth, children's rights education, women's rights programmes, legal aid for human rights, and so on. A relatively recent initiative is the launching of peace consciousness, which aims to awaken people through inter-religious meditation sessions, transcending ethnic and religious divisions. Large numbers of people of all ethnic and religious groups participate in these sessions.

The above analysis illustrates the system-wide focus on seeking creative solutions to facilitate social cohesion through the educative process, interpreting curriculum in a wide and inclusive sense as incorporating all "structured series of intended learning outcomes," be they in conventional institutionalised education settings or elsewhere. The projects and other initiatives selectively identified for inclusion in this section provide insights by way of their lessons learned, their constraints and limiting factors, and their potential to serve as models to be adopted in the search for solutions to an extremely critical global concern of violence and social exclusion that engulfs not merely the "conflict-affected" societies but all humanity as an all-pervasive, destructive global phenomenon.

Endnotes

[1] See chapter iv, sections 32 and 33.

[2] A comprehensive selection of these analyses are included in the "Sources for Further Reference" of Appendix 4.

[3] Ceylon is the name under which the island of Sri Lanka was formerly known.

[4] Statistics taken from the 1946 census.

[5] Vivo is an independent nonprofit organisation working to assist individuals and communities affected by violence to overcome and prevent the consequences associated with traumatic stress.

[6] The total population of students in government schools island-wide, in grades one through thirteen, is 4,184,957. Of this number, 3,167,188 students attend Sinhala medium schools, and 1,017,769 attend Tamil medium schools.

[7] Editors' note: It has been suggested by others that the new devolution has resulted in duplications, placing additional strains on meagre resources, causing operational delays, and provoking in-fighting for power and recognition at the expense of quality and efficiency. Whereas previously there was one secretary of education, there are now nine, one for each province. Those occupying high-level positions worked, at least initially, without the training, exposure, and experience typically necessary for such posts. Whether or not this short-term dilution of the quality of administrative services in the country will persist remains to be seen.

[8] See, for example, the discussion of the Basic Education Sector Programme in the final section of this chapter.

[9] Editors' note: To complement the information given here, it has also been suggested by others that the reforms introduced in 1972 were a radical landmark in the history of education in Sri Lanka. The reforms are considered to have been particularly positive in the following ways. First, they changed the teaching-learning process, bringing the child to the centre of it for the first time, which also effected a change in methods of evaluation. Secondly, they provided an enabling base for subsequent changes creating a culture of reform in the field of education. The repercussions of this were particularly evident insofar as a new mindset was created, manifest through attitudinal change, both among the general public and educationists. The perceived need for occasional education reform became linked to recognising and attempting to integrate changing socioeconomic and cultural realities both nationally and globally. Finally, educationists gained confidence and competence from these reforms, allowing them to address broad systemic needs for change rather than focusing on isolated initiatives. One of the critical problems noted concerning the reforms was that school principals were left out of the reform process.

[10] Editors' note: Prior to the 1980s, the research culture in Sri Lanka was not well established. Typically, it was limited to a university setting and did not produce any comprehensive data that might have been useful for taking action in the field of education. Research acquired a more vital position with the establishment of the National Institute of Education, and the creation, in 1986, of a research department under its supervision. The newly established National Education Research and Evaluation Centre was another important development to reinforce research in Sri Lanka.

[11] Significantly, Sarvodaya is one of the few national NGOs that managed to carry on its work in the north and east even during the height of ethnic war in these regions.

References

Balasooriya, A. S. (2002.) *Learning the Way of Peace*. New Delhi: UNESCO.

———. (1996.) *The Challenge of Terrorism*. 1674/1C, Malambe Road, Kottawa. Pannipitiya, Sri Lanka.

———. (1994.) *Teaching Peace to Children*. (In Sinhala and Tamil.) Maharagama, Sri Lanka: Peace Education, National Institute of Education.

———. (1993.) *Peace Education*. (In Sinhala and Tamil.) Maharagama, Sri Lanka: National Institute of Education.

Bastian, S. (1972.) "Education and Racial Prejudice," *Logos* 16(6) (December 1972).

Department of Census and Statistics. (2001.) *Census of Population and Housing (2001) Preliminary Release*.

De Silva, C. R. (1999.) "Role of Education in Ameliorating Political Violence in Sri Lanka," in Rotberg, ed., *Creating Peace in Sri Lanka*. Massachusetts: World Peace Foundation.

De Silva, K. M. (1998.) *Reaping the Whirlwind—Ethnic Conflict, Ethnic Politics in Sri Lanka*. Penguin Books India (Pvt.) Ltd.

First Report of the National Commission of Education. (1992.) Government Publications.

Graca, M. (1996.) *Impact of Armed Conflict on Children, Selected Highlights*. New York: UNICEF.

Gunaratna, Rohana. (1987.) *War & Peace in Sri Lanka*. Sri Lanka: Institute of Fundamental Studies.

Gunasekara, S. L.(1996.) *Tigers and Moderates and Pandora's Package*. Self-published.

Gunawardana, R. (1995.) *Sri Lanka's Ethnic Crises and National Security*. South Asia Network on Conflict Research, Wijitha Yapa, Colombo 4.

Hayes, D. (1995.) *Language, Textbooks and Perspectives on Social Harmony in Sri Lanka*.

Horowitz, D. L. (1985.) *Ethnic Groups in Conflict*. London: University of California Press.

Mayer, Markus, Rajasingham-Senanayake, Darini, and Thangarajah, Yuvi, eds. (2003.) *Building Local Capacities for Peace: Rethinking Conflict and Development in Sri Lanka*. India: Macmillan.

Ministry of Education and Higher Education, Sri Lanka. (2001.) *School Census (Preliminary Report)*.

National Institute of Education, Sri Lanka. (1998.) *Life Competencies Syllabi, Grades 7, 8, 9*.

————. (1997.) *Education Reforms and Restructure, Policy and Programmes of Action.*

National Institute of Education and Ministry of Education & Higher Education, Sri Lanka. (June 2000.) *Curriculum Process Plan, for GEP-2/WB.*

————. (June 2000.) *National Curriculum Policy of Sri Lanka, for GEP-2/WB.*

Perera, Sasanka. (1987.) *The Structure and Content for Education.* International Institute for Ethnic Studies.

Rasanayagam, Y., and Palaniappan, V. (1999.) *Education and Social Cohesion, Analysis of Potential Ethno-Cultural and Religious Bias in the School Text Books of History and Social Studies for Year 7, 8, 10 and 11.*

Thirteenth Amendment to the Constitution. (1987.) Sri Lanka Government Publication, Government Press, Colombo.

Towards Social Harmony in Education—Sri Lanka. (2000.) For the Department for International Development and World Bank.

Wickramasinghe, N., and Perera, S. (1999.) *Assessment of Ethno-Cultural and Religious Bias in Social Studies and History Texts of Years 7, 8, 10 and 11.*

Appendix 1: List of Key Informants

Prof. Swarna Jayaweera
Vice Chairperson of the National Education Commission

Mr. M. Wijayasiri
Commissioner General of the Department of Examinations (National Education Testing Service)

Mr. S. L.Gunawardhene
Commissioner General of the Educational Publications Department

Mrs. Ranjani Senanayake
Additional Commissioner of the Educational Publications Department

Mrs. Sudharma de Silva
Secretary of the Educational Publications Advisory Board
Director of the National Integration Programme Unit (NIPU)

Prof. B. R. R. N. Mendis
Chairman of the University Grants Commission

Prof. Chandra Gunawardhene
Dean of the Faculty of Education, Open University of Sri Lanka

Mr. N. Selvakkumaran
Dean of the Center for the Study of Human Rights,
Faculty of Law, University of Colombo, Colombo 3

Mr. Nimal Hapuarachchi
Director of Education & Special Programmes, Human Rights Commission, Sri Lanka

Mr. Jeevan Thiagarajah
Executive Director of the Consortium of Humanitarian Agencies

Mr. Danesh Jayatilaka
Project Coordinating Officer

Dr. Gerhard Huck
Project Manager of the Basic Education Sector Programme, GTZ

Mr. Peter Colenso
Educationist at the World Bank, Resident Office

Appendix 2: The Reforms in 1997

The reform in 1997 was another step in taking further the thinking of the Report on Youth, the national goals, and the five competencies. Taking up the challenge of reform through education requires the ability to identify correctly the existing problems of society with vision, foresight, courage, and innovativeness. In Sri Lanka, educational change is a politically sensitive affair. Suspicion of motives arises from political, ethnic, religious, and other standpoints. In developing the vision, principles, and strategies for the recent reforms, the ministry consulted experts and experienced educators. Discussions were held with various relevant interest groups, teachers as well as students. The president appointed an education task force, consisting of thirteen committees, under the leadership of the minister of education, to design the reforms.

Sri Lanka regards primary education to be of prime importance. The 1999 reforms aim to lay a firm foundation for development of the personality of the child through primary education to enable him or her to face the challenges of life successfully as a future citizen.

The five competencies are stressed in all the subjects at both the primary and secondary levels. In fact, they form the integrative principles of the whole curriculum. The new primary curriculum was introduced in grade one in 1999, successively introduced to the next grade annually, and culminated in grade five in the year 2003. The reforms aim at correcting the ills of present society through developing children's interpersonal skills, broad vision, empathy, and competencies for peaceful living so they will respect not only their own culture but also others' cultures and points of view, and can live to learn in harmony with others as patriotic citizens of Sri Lanka.

Any educational reform can be considered as an attempt to interpret and suggest solutions to the existing social problems in the country concerned. They will be meaningful only in the context of the existing political, economic, ethnic, and cultural milieu of the society. The NEC in 1997 presented a paper proposing a series of reforms to the system of education. They are presented below in a summary form.

1. Education for all

Education for all has been Sri Lanka's goal since 1944. The provision of functional literacy to all citizens in the country was one of Sri Lanka's objectives, from the beginning. To achieve this it was necessary to ensure that students finish the period of schooling up to completion of general education. To meet this target, the school dropout rate needs to be minimised. It was expected to make basic education from grade one to nine (ages five to fourteen) compulsory by introducing new regulations. A programme for raising parents' awareness and motivation for sending children to school and completing general education was to be initiated. Early identification of the children who tend to drop out, in order to actively help them to stay in school, was necessary as a preventive measure.

In addition to normal schools, a set of new schools called functional or open schools were to be established for those children who wanted a more flexible type of schooling. These schools were to be open to all children beyond fourteen years of age. Facilities for special education were also to be extended.

For the first time, the Ministry of Education showed an interest in maintaining quality in preschools. The private organisations running preschools were expected to get approval from the Child Rights Protection Authority to ensure that basic standards were maintained. The training of preschool teachers was also to be improved and extended.

2. Primary education

The quality of education from grade one to five was to be improved. Primary education was to be delivered through a combination of play method, experiential learning, and academic learning, with a view to helping children in their total and balanced growth. One of the problems the schools had was the overcrowding of students in classrooms, especially in popular urban schools. The reforms limited the student enrolment in a class to thirty as an ideal size. Classrooms were to be constructed with adequate space for activity learning, and with suitable and necessary equipment and furniture.

3. Junior secondary education

The quality of education from grade six to nine was to be improved. A competency-based teaching and learning approach was to be developed. Academic learning should be coupled with practical competency and skill development. Necessary resources were to be provided to facilitate the process. It is also necessary to help the child to identify her or his talents and potentials. Students who have had an integrated curriculum in the primary grades find it difficult to adapt themselves to the level expected at grade six. This changeover phase needs to be facilitated by reducing the difficulties.

Statistics show that a large number of students leave school at grade nine. Therefore, the secondary curriculum should be reformed to provide the tools for students to be competent citizens. Schools were expected to open an activity room for the pupils in the junior secondary stage, where they could engage freely in technical skill development such as in electronics, information technology, cooking, dancing, beauty makeup, and so on of their own free choice during the school hours, whenever they found extra time.

The reforms also introduced a new subject called life competencies to help students' self-development, including important aspects of moral and citizenship education like skills in conflict resolution and peaceful living.

4. Senior secondary education: G.C.E. (Ordinary Level)

Grades ten and eleven should cover the syllabus for the G.G.E. (O/L.) The co-curriculum includes six subjects:

- first language;
- English 1 or English 2;
- mathematics 1 or mathematics 2;
- science 1 or science 2;
- social studies and history; and
- religion.

In addition, students have to select four subjects as electives from the following list:

- studies in development or planning and technology;
- aesthetics (drawing, music, dancing, drama);
- Sinhala or Tamil (i.e., Tamil for Sinhalese students and Sinhala for Tamil students, as a second language);
- international or classical language;
- health science and physical education;
- technical subject;
- history;
- geography; and
- literature (Sinhala, Tamil, English)

There are two streams for mathematics, science, and English, from which students can select one according to their level of achievement.

5. Senior secondary education: G.C.E. (Advanced Level)

There are three streams at G.C.E. (A/L), namely: arts, science, and commerce. A new technical stream consisting of subjects such as agriculture, engineering, production, and services is being proposed.

The requirement of four subjects to enter university was reduced to a minimum of three in order to reduce students' burden of studies, about which parental concerns had been expressed.

G.C.E. (A/L) courses are of two years' duration. Suitable practical study projects were introduced in all subjects.

There were proposals for revision of curriculum at the G.C.E. (A/L). The practical side of learning was to be improved.

6. English language

The English language was to be introduced from grade one. Previously it has been taught from grade three. However, at the beginning both the children and teachers were to be eased into the subject through the informal introduction of spoken English. Primary teachers were to be trained for this innovation.

The facilities to learn English at the A/L were to be developed.

7. Organisational development of schools

Each local government region in the country will have at least one school where all subject streams are taught. Accordingly, three hundred schools were to be developed in the first phase. In the second phase, another three hundred schools were to be developed. The present schools were expected to be restructured in order to form two categories. The first category consists of primary and junior secondary grades. The second category will have schools with G.C.E. (O/L) and A/L grades.

In the total education system the basic management unit is the school. The principal is the frontline manager. The school's foremost responsibility is to make optimum use of the available resources.

The central ministry and education officers intervene only to help improve effectiveness and efficiency and to ensure provision of necessary resources.

A performance appraisal scheme to evaluate the performance of teachers, principals, and education officers will be introduced.

Schools will be selected for development on the basis of a school mapping exercise. Physical resources, the provision of infrastructure facilities, will be standardised.

Principals will be trained to be efficient and effective school managers.

The performance of the present national schools will be assessed along with the development of the three hundred schools.

A special functional unit will be established in the Ministry of Education and Higher Education under a director general of education.

8. School textbooks and other curricular materials

Three types of curricular materials are supplied to schools. They are:

    a.   materials that direct students for self-studies;
    b.   workbooks for furthering subject knowledge; and
    c.   books for extra reading, which helps critical examination and broadens knowledge.

The ministry will recruit or encourage experts to prepare curricular materials. Writing extra curricular books for G.C.E. (A/L) is also encouraged.

9. Assessment

A system of school-based evaluation will be introduced. It attempts to

    a.   motivate students to achieve practical skills in the subject areas;
    b.   provide feedback to teachers and students;
    c.   help identify learning difficulties; and
    d.   facilitate teachers' performance evaluation.

Evaluation at the primary level aims at developing teamwork and cooperation.

In the junior secondary grades, students' progress reports will be maintained to record their activities in the subject learning and co-curricular learning. In the senior secondary grades, evaluation will be done on the basis of their study projects. Students leaving after grade nine will be issued certificates after a formal evaluation.

Scholarship examinations will be conducted on completion of all the stages of learning in school. The purposes of such examinations are to identify students who need support for furthering their learning, and to direct and instruct schools to identify a pool of gifted students for developing and establishing schools for them at the national level.

The assessment programme intends to

a. prepare model instruments and identify methods for school-based assessment;
b. train principals and teachers in school-based assessment practices;
c. prepare formats for recording students' achievement; and
d. establish provincial centres of school-based evaluation.

10. Teacher education

A national authority for teacher training will be established for quality assurance and improvement and validation of all teacher training, and programmes conducted by universities, colleges of education, and teacher centres. All recruits for teaching will be given preservice training before sending them to schools. Facilities will be provided for them to develop their potentials, acquire full professional qualifications, and update their knowledge.

Curriculum for teacher education will be revised to equip teachers with necessary competencies for effective delivery of school curriculum. Teacher education will emphasise education for human values, human rights, national cohesion, and gender rights and environment. Student teachers as well as those in service will be provided facilities to improve competency in the English language.

A professional Teacher Educators Service will be established to further the development of teacher education.

An intensive programme to train teachers for the delivery of the new curriculum will be started, taking each grade year by year and going upward. One teachers' college will be developed with all the equipment and expert staff for teachers to acquire practical skills in relevant technological subjects.

11. Educational guidance and counselling

All schools will provide education and vocational guidance to students. Teachers will be trained for this service. Students will be helped by guidance to improve and adjust learning according to their developmental needs during various stages of growth. Parents are also helped in the process for better decisionmaking with regard to children's furthering of learning.

School leavers will be helped to find suitable job opportunities through maintaining a vocational information service in the school, including lists of vocational training centres, organisations, resource persons, and so on. Teachers will be trained for the above service.

12. Immediate action steps

Raising public awareness of the present education reforms is necessary. Without the public's understanding and cooperation, it is difficult to achieve reform success.

A study of the system of legal and administrative regulations of the present education procedure was to be conducted to suggest changes, if necessary, for the implementation of the intended education policies and reforms.

Appendix 3: Sources for Further Reference

Abeysekara, C., and Gunasinghe, N., eds. (1998.) *Facets of Ethicist in Sri Lanka*.

ACCORD. (1998.) *Demanding Sacrifice: War and Negotiation in Sri Lanka*, Issue 4.

Alles, A. C. (1976.) *Insurgency (1971): An Account of the April Insurgency in Sri Lanka*. Colombo: Colombo Apothecaries.

Amnesty International. (1991.) *Sri Lanka—The Northeast: Human Rights Violations in a Context of Armed Conflict*. London.

———. (1990.) *Sri Lanka: An Update on Human Rights Concerns*. London.

Anon. (1999.) *Statistical Information of Northeast Province*, Planning Secretariat, NEPC.

———. (1993.) *The Land of the Singing Fish*, Chief Secretary, North-Eastern Province, Trincomalee.

Arasaratnam, S. (1994.) "Sri Lanka's Tamils: Under Colonial Rule," in C. Manogaran and B. Pfaffenberger, eds., *The Sri Lankan Tamils: Ethnicity and Identity*. Boulder: Westview Press.

Bastian, S. (1999.) *The Failure of State Formation, Identity Conflict and Civil Society Responses —the Case of Sri Lanka*. Bradford Peace Studies Working Papers.

———. (1998.) "Development NGOs and Ethnic Conflicts," in M. Tiruchelvam and C. S. Dattathreya, eds., *Culture and Politics of Identity in Sri Lanka*. Colombo: International Centre for Ethnic Studies

———. (1997.) "Development NGOs and Ethnic Conflicts—Conceptual Challenges," *Nethra* 1(3) (April-June 1997).

Bastian, S., and Bastian, N. (1996.) *Assessing Participation: A Debate from South Asia*. New Delhi: Konark.

Bauer, E., et al. (1999.) *Food Security and Conflict: A Participatory Development Concept for the Integrated Food Security Programme (IFSP), Trincomalee, Sri Lanka*. Berlin: Schriftenreihe des Seminars für ländliche Entwicklung, S183.

Bush, K. (2000.) "The Logic of PCIA," *Consortium for Humanitarian Agencies Newsletter* 4(6) (November/December 2000).

———. (1999.) *The Limits and Scope for the Use of Development Assistance Incentives and Disincentives for Influencing Conflict Situations*. Case Study: Sri Lanka. Paris: OECD/ DAC Informal Task Force on Conflict, Peace and Development Co-operation.

———. (1998.) *Peace and Conflict Impact Assessment (PCIA) of Development Projects in Conflict Zones*. Working Paper no. 1, Peace Building and Reconstruction Program Initiative and Evaluation Unit.

Chandraprema, C. A. (1991.) *Sri Lanka: The Years of Terror, the JVP Insurrection 1987–1989*. Colombo: Lake House Bookshop.

Committee for Rational Development, ed. (1984.) *Sri Lanka: The Ethnic Conflict: Myths, Realities and Perspectives*. New Delhi: Navrang.

Cox, D. (1998.) "The Post-Conflict Situation: Importance of a Comprehensive Approach," *CHA Newsletter* 2(10): pp. 7–23. Colombo: Consortium of Humanitarian Agencies.

Daniel, V. E. (1996.) *Charred Lullabies: Chapter in an Anthropography of Violence*. Princeton: Princeton University Press.

———. (1984.) *Fluid Signs: Being a Person the Tamil Way*. Berkeley: University of California Press.

Daniel, V., and Thangarajah, Y. (1995.) "Form, Formation, and the Transformation of the Tamil Refugee," in V. Daniel and J. Knudser, eds., *Mistrusting the Refugee*. Berkeley: University of California Press.

De Silva, C. (1988.) "The Impact of Nationalism on Education: The Schools Take-over (1961) and the University Admissions Crisis, 1970–75," in M. Roberts, ed., *Sri Lanka: Collective Identities*. Colombo: Marga Institute, pp. 103–31.

———. (1984.) "Sinhala-Tamil Ethnic Rivalry: The Background," in R. B. Goldman and A. J. Wilson, eds., *From Independence to Statehood*. New York: St. Martin's Press.

De Silva, G. V. S. (1998.) "Socialism or Barbarism," in C. Abeysekara, ed., *Collected Writings of G. V. S. de Silva*. Colombo.

De Silva, K. M. (1998.) *Reaping the Whirlwind*. India: Penguin Books.

Department of Census and Statistics. (1994.) *Statistical Abstract—1994*. Colombo.

Dissanayake, A. (1997.) *Last Resort of the Resourceless: A Clash of Cultures*. Unpublished dissertation.

———. (1993.) *JVP Prabavaya, Vikashaya and Deshapalanaya (JVP, Its Origins, Evolution and Politics)*. Colombo: Diyesa Publishers.

Divakalala, S. (1998.) *Educational Problems and Challenges in Conflict Areas in Sri Lanka*. Ministry of Education Culture and Sports, North East Province Sri Lanka, Colombo.

Dunham, D. (2000.) *Policy Impact Analysis in Contemporary Sri Lanka*. Research Studies, MIMAP—Sri Lanka Series no. 1, Institute of Policy Studies, Colombo.

Dunham, D., and Jayasuriya, S. (2000.) "Equity, Growth and Insurrection: Liberalization and the Welfare Debate in Contemporary Sri Lanka," *Oxford Development Studies* 28(1).

———. (2000.) "Liberalisation and Political Decay: Sri Lanka's Journey from a Welfare State to a Brutalised Society," *Pravada* 7(7).

Farmer, B. H. (1957.) *Peasant Colonisation in Ceylon*. Cambridge: Cambridge University Press.

Foster, Y. (2000.) *Sri Lanka: Donor Policy in a Complex Political Emergency*. Working Paper for International Alert.

Fuglerud, O. (In press.) "Space and Movement in the Sri Lankan Conflict," in J. Schijvers and G. Frerks, eds., *Refugees and the Transformation of Societies*. London: Berghan Books.

———. (2001.) "Time and Space in the Sri Lanka-Tamil Diaspora," *Nations and Nationalism* 7(2): pp. 195–215.

———. (1999.) *Life on the Outside: The Tamil Diaspora and Long-Distance Nationalism*. London: Pluto Press.

Gamage, S., and Watson, I. B., eds. (1997.) *South Asia–Conflict and Community in Contemporary Sri Lanka*. Special Issue (vol. 20), South Asian Studies Association.

Gilles, D. (1992.) "Principled Intervention: Canadian Aid, Human Rights and Conflict in Sri Lanka," in R. Miller, ed., *Aid as Peacemaker: Canadian Development Assistance and Third World Conflict*. Ottawa: Carleton University Press.

Goodhand, J. (2001.) "Aid, Conflict and Peacebuilding in Sri Lanka." Second draft, September, DFID-study.

Goodhand, J., and Lewer, N. (1999.) "Sri Lanka: NGOs and Peace-Building in Complex Political Emergencies," *Third World Quarterly* 20(1): pp. 69–87.

Government of Sri Lanka. (1990.) *Report of the Presidential Commission on Youth*.

Gunaratna, R. (1998.) *Sri Lanka's Ethnic Crisis and National Security*. South Asian Net Work on Conflict Research, Colombo.

———. (1991.) *Sri Lanka: A Lost Revolution*. Institute of Fundamental Studies, Kandy.

Gunasinghe, N. (1996.) "A Sociological Comment of the Political Transformation in 1956 and the Resultant Socio-Political Processes," in S. Perera, ed., *Newton Gunasinghe: Selected Essays*. Colombo: Social Scientists' Association.

Gunatilleke, G. (1993.) *Development and Liberalisation in Sri Lanka, Trends and Prospects*. Marga Institute, p. 15.

Hettige, S.T. (2000.) "Dilemmas of Post-Colonial Society after 30 years of Independence: A Critical Analysis," in S. T. Hettige and M. Mayer, eds., *Sri Lanka at Crossroads: Dilemmas and Prospects after 50 Years of Independence*. India: Macmillan.

———. (1998.) "Pseudo Modernization and the Formation of Youth Identities in Sri Lanka," in S. T. Hettige, ed., *Globalization, Social Change and Youth*. Colombo: German Cultural Institute.

————. (1996.) *Unrest or Revolt: Some Aspects of Youth Unrest in Sri Lanka.* Colombo and Sri Lanka: Goethe Institute and American Studies Association.

Hettige, S. T., and Mayer, M. (2000.) *Sri Lanka at Crossroads: Dilemmas and Prospects after 50 Years of Independence.* New Delhi: Macmillan.

ILO. (1971.) *Matching Employment Opportunities and Expectations: A Programme of Action for Ceylon.* Geneva.

International Centre for Ethnic Studies. (1997.) *Sri Lanka: The Devolution Debate.* Colombo.

Ivan, V. (1979.) *71 Kerella: Janatha Vimukthi Peramune Arambhaya ha Vikashaya.* (The Insurgency 71: The Origin and Evolution of Janatha Vimukthi Peramuna.) Colombo: Lake House Investments Ltd.

Jeyanathan, P. (1998.) "eelam.com: Place, Nation, and Imagination in Cyberspace," *Public Culture* 10(3): pp. 515–28.

————. (1998.) "In the Shadow of Violence: Tamilness and the Anthropology of Identities in Southern Sri Lanka," in T. J. Bartholomeusz and D. R. de Silva, eds., *Buddhist Fundamentalism and Minority Identity in Sri Lanka.* New York.

Jeyanathan, P., and Ismail, Q. (1995.) *Unmaking the Nation: The Politics of Identity and History in Sri Lanka.* Colombo: SSA.

Kapferer, B. (1988.) *Legends of People, Myths of State Violence, Intolerance and Political Culture in Sri Lanka.* London.

————. (1988.) *Legends of People, Myths of State: Violence, Intolerance and Political Culture in Sri Lanka and Australia.* Washington, DC.

Keerawella, G. B. (1980.) "The Janatha Vimukthi Peramuna and the 1971 Uprising," *Social Science Review* 2: pp. 1–55.

Kelegama, S. (1990.) "Economic Costs of Conflict," in R. I. Rotberg, ed., *Creating Peace in Sri Lanka Civil War and Reconciliation.* Washington: Brookings Institution Press.

Kloos, P. (1997.) "The Struggle between the Lion and the Tiger: The Relevance of Inter- and Intra-Ethnic Conflict for the Construction of Ethnic Identities in Sri Lanka," in C. Govers and H. Vermeulen, eds., *The Politics of Ethnic Consciousness.* London.

Kukabalan, K. (1996.) *Jaffna Migration.* Colombo: Admiral Graphics Press.

Lawrence, P. (1998.) "Grief in the Body: The Work of Oracles in Eastern Sri Lanka," in S. Gamage and I. B. Watson, eds., *Conflict and Community in Contemporary Sri Lanka.* India: Sage Publications.

Liyanage, S. (1998.) *Interventions in the Devolution Debate.* Colombo.

Manogaran, C. (1994.) "Colonization as Politics: Political Use of Space in Sri Lanka's Ethnic Conflict," in C. Manogaran and B. Pffafenberger, eds., *The Sri Lankan Tamils: Ethnicity and Identity*. Colorado: Westview Press.

———. (1987.) *Ethnic Conflict and Reconciliation in Sri Lanka*. Honolulu.

Mayer, M. (2000.) "Life Opportunities and Youth Conflict in Sri Lanka: Challenges for Regional Development Planning," in S. T. Hettige and M. Mayer, eds., *Sri Lanka at Crossroads: Dilemmas and Prospects after 50 Years of Independence*. New Delhi: Macmillan, pp. 156–68.

McGilvray, D. B. (1982.) "Mukkuvar Vannimai: Tamil Caste and Matriclan Ideology," in Batticaloa, Sri Lanka," in D. McGilvray, ed., *Caste Ideology and Interaction*. Cambridge: Cambridge University Press.

———. (1973.) "Caste and Matriclan Structure in Sri Lanka: A Preliminary Report on Fieldwork in Akkraipattu," *Modern Ceylon Studies* 4(1&2): pp. 5–20.

Ministry of Education. (1998a.) *North East Province: Six-Year Primary Education Plan (1999–2004)*. Colombo.

———. (1998b.) *An Appraisal of the Education System in the Vanni Areas of Sri Lanka*. Colombo.

Moore, M. (1985.) *The State and Peasant Politics in Sri Lanka*. Cambridge: Cambridge University Press.

National Peace Council of Sri Lanka. (2000.) *The Cost of the War*. Colombo.

———. (1998a.) *Children: Zones of Peace, a Call for Action (Promoting and Protecting the Rights of Children Affected by Armed Conflict in Sri Lanka)*. Colombo.

———. (1998b.) *Don't Wage War on Our Behalf*. Report of National Peace Delegates Concentration, Colombo.

NEC. (1997.) National Education Commission–Sri Lanka: Reforms in General Education, Maharagama.

Nissan, E., and Stirrat, R. L. (1990.) "The Generation of Communal Identities," in J. Spencer, ed., *Sri Lanka: History and Roots of Conflict*. London and New York, pp. 19–44.

Nordstorm, C. (1992.) "The Dirty War: Civilian Experience of Conflict in Mozambique and Sri Lanka," in K. Rupesinghe, ed., *Internal Conflict and Governance*. London: St. Martin's Press.

Obeysekere, G. (1974.) "Some Comments on the Social Background of the April 1971 Insurgency in Sri Lanka," *Journal of Asian Studies* 33(3): pp. 367–84.

Peebles, P. (1995.) *Social Change in Nineteenth Century Ceylon*. New Delhi: Navrang Books.

————. (1990.) "Colonization and the Ethnic Conflict in the Dry Zone of Sri Lanka," *Journal of Asian Studies* 49(1): pp. 30–55.

Perera, S. (1999.) *Stories of Survivors: Socio-Political Contexts of Female Headed Households in Post-Terror Southern Sri Lanka*, vol. I. Colombo: Women's Education and Research Centre.

————. (1998a.) *Political Violence in Sri Lanka: Dynamics, Consequences and Issues of Democratization*. Colombo: Centre for Women's Research.

————. (1998b.) "The Other Victims," in *Culture and Politics of Identity in Sri Lanka*. Colombo: International Centre for Ethnic Studies.

————. (1995.) *Living with Torturers and Other Essays of Interventions: Sri Lankan Society, Culture and Politics in Perspective*. Colombo: International Centre for Ethnic Studies.

Pfaffenberger, B. (1994.) "The Sri Lanka Tamils," in C. Manogarnan and B. Pfaffenberger, eds., *The Sri Lankan Tamils: Ethnicity and Identity*. Colorado: Westview Press.

Presidential Task Force on General Education—Sri Lanka. (1997.) General Education Reforms, Colombo.

Rajanagam, H. D. (1994.) "Tamils and the Meaning of History," in C. Manogarnan and B. Pfaffenberger, eds., *The Sri Lankan Tamils: Ethnicity and Identity*. Colorado: Westview Press.

Rajasingham-Senanayake, D. (2002.) "Identity on the Borderline: Modernity, New Ethnicities, and the Unmixing of People in Lanka," in *A Hybrid Island*. Sri Lanka: Social Scientist's Association.

————. (2001.) "Transformations of Legitimate Violence and Civil-Military Relations," in M. Alagappa, ed., *Coercion and Governance*. Stanford: Stanford University Press.

————. (1999a.) "Democracy and the Making of Bi-Polar Ethnic Identity," in J. Pffaff Czarnecka et al., eds., *Ethnic Future: The State and Identity Politics in Asia*. New Delhi: Sage.

————. (1999b.) "The Dangers of Devolution: The Hidden Economies of Armed Conflict," in R. I. Rotberg, ed., *Creating Peace in Sri Lanka: Civil War and Reconciliation*. Washington, DC: World Peace Foundation and Belfer Center for Science and International Affairs, pp. 57–70.

————. (1999c.) "Unmaking Multiculturalism: The Fetishism of Ethnicity in Conflict Analysis and Anthropology," in K. Rupesinghe, ed., *Culture and Identity*, Washington, DC: Sasakawa Peace Foundation.

Ranugge, S. (2000.) "State, Bureaucracy and Development," in S. Hettige and M. Mayer, eds., *Sri Lanka at Crossroads: Dilemmas and Prospects after 50 Years of Independence*. India: Macmillan, pp. 50–62.

Rotberg, R. I., ed. (1999a.) *Creating Peace in Sri Lanka: Civil War and Reconciliation.* Washington, DC: World Peace Foundation and Belfer Center for Science and International Affairs.

————. (1999b.) "Sri Lanka's Civil War: From Mayhem Toward Diplomatic Resolution," in R. I. Rotberg, ed., *Creating Peace in Sri Lanka: Civil War and Reconciliation.* Washington, DC: World Peace Foundation and Belfer Center for Science and International Affairs, pp. 1–16.

Samarasinghe, G. (1998.) "Some Thoughts on the Sri Lankan Family Exposed to Armed Conflict and the Impact on the Psychological Well-being of Youth," in S. T. Hettige, ed., *Globalization, Social Change and Youth.* Colombo: German Cultural Institute.

Senaratne, J. P. (1997.) *Political Violence in Sri Lanka, 1977–1990: Riots, Insurrections, Counterinsurgencies, Foreign Intervention.* Amsterdam: VU University Press.

Seneviratne, L. H., ed. (1997.) *Identity, Consciousness and the Past Forgoing of Caste and Community in India and Sri Lanka.* Delhi: Oxford University Press.

Shanmugaratnam, N. (2001.) "Linking Peace and Development in Sri Lanka," *Pravada* 7(3): pp. 14–20.

Shastri, A. (1994.) "The Material Basis of Tamil Separatism: The Tamil Eelam Movement in Sri Lanka," *Journal of Asian Studies* 45(1): pp. 56–77.

————. (1983.) "The Political Economy of Intermediate Regimes: The Case of Sri Lanka," *South Asia Bulletin* 3(2): pp. 1–14.

Sivarajah, N. (1998.) *School Aged Children in Jaffna District.* Save the Children Fund (UK) and UNICEF.

Somasundaram, D. (1998.) *Scarred Minds.* India: Sage Publications.

Somasundaram, M., ed. (1999.) *Re-Imagining Sri Lanka Northern Ireland Insights.* Colombo: International Centre for Ethnic Studies.

Sorbo, G. M., Brochmann, G., Dale, R., Moore, M., and Whist, E. (1987.) *Sri Lanka: Country Study and Norwegian Aid Review.* Bergen: Centre for Development Studies, University of Bergen.

Spencer, J. (1990.) *A Sinhalese Village in a Time of Trouble: Politics and Change in Rural Sri Lanka.* Bombay: Oxford University Press.

Spencer, J. (Hg.) (1990.) *Sri Lanka: History and Roots of Conflict.* London and New York.

Tambiah, S. J. (1997.) *Levelling Crowds: Ethno-Nationalist Conflicts and Collective Violence in South Asia.* New Delhi: Vistaar Publications.

————. (1996.) *Levelling Crowds: Ethnonationalist Conflict and Collective Violence in South Asia.* Berkeley: University of California Press.

———. (1992.) *Buddhism Betrayed: Religion, Politics and Violence in Sri Lanka*. Chicago: University of Chicago Press.

———. (1986a.) *Ethnic Fratricide and the Dismantling of Democracy*. Chicago: University of Chicago Press.

———. (1986b.) *Sri Lanka: Ethnic Fratricide and the Dismantling of Democracy*. Chicago and London: University of Chicago Press.

Thangarajah, Y. (2000.) "The Genealogy of Tamil Nationalism in Post-Independent Sri Lanka," in S. T. Hettige and M. Mayer, eds., *Sri Lanka at Crossroads: Dilemmas and Prospects after 50 Years of Independence*. Delhi: Macmillan, pp. 119–38.

———. (1997.) *State Violence, Ethnicity, and Identity in Eastern Sri Lanka*. Ph.D. dissertation, Department of Anthropology, University of Rochester, Rochester, New York.

———. (1989.) "Tamil-Muslim Tensions in the East Coast." Proceedings of the Sri Lanka Conference, Paris.

Thiruchandran, S. (1999.) *The Other Victims of War: Emergence of Female Headed Households in Eastern Sri Lanka*, vol. II. Colombo: Women's Education and Research Centre.

UNDP. (2000.) *Human Development Report—Sri Lanka Country Report*.

———. (1997.) *Project Proposal for Resettlement of IDPs in the Jaffna Peninsula*.

University Teachers for Human Rights (Jaffna). (1997.) *A Vision Skewed*. Special Report no. 9.

UTHR (1993.) *Land, Human Rights and the Eastern Predicament*. Report no. 11, Colombo.

———. (1991.) *The Clash of Ideologies and the Continuing Tragedy in Batticaloa and Ampara Districts*. Report no. 7, Colombo.

———. (1990.) *August, a Bloody Stalemate*. Report no. 5, Colombo.

Uyangoda, J. (2001.) "Sri Lanka's Left: From Class and Trade Unions to Civil Society and NGOs," in R. Philips, ed., *Sri Lanka: Global Challenges and National Crises*. Proceedings of the Hector Abhayawardhana Felicitation Symposium, Social Scientists' Association, Colombo.

———. (2000.) "A State of Desire? Some Reflections on the Unreformability of Sri Lanka's Post-Colonial Polity," in S. T. Hettige and M. Mayer, eds., *Sri Lanka at Cross Roads: Dilemmas and Prospects after 50 Years of Independence*. New Delhi: Macmillan.

———. (1999.) "Post-Independence Social Movements," in W. D. Lakshman and C. A. Tisdell, eds., *Facets of Development of Sri Lanka Since Independence: Socio-Political, Economic, Scientific and Cultural*. Brisbane: University of Queensland Press.

———. (1998.) "Dharmasiri Bandaranayake's 'Echoes of War': Peace Please," *Lanka Guardian* 10(23).

————. (1994.) "The State and the Process of Devolution in Sri Lanka," in *Democracy and Development*. Colombo: ICES.

Van Brabant, K. (December 1997.) "The Coordination of Humanitarian Action: The Case of Sri Lanka," in *Relief and Rehabilitation Network Paper*. London: Overseas Development Institute.

Weisberg, W., and Hicks, D. (1999.) "Overcoming Obstacles to Peace: An Examination of Third-Party Processes," in R. I. Rotberg, ed., *Creating Peace in Sri Lanka: Civil War and Reconciliation*. Washington, DC: World Peace Foundation and Belfer Centre for Science and International Affairs, pp. 143–56.

Wickremasinghe, N. (2001.) *Civil Society in Sri Lanka, New Circles of Power*. New Delhi: Sage Publications.

————. (1994.) *Ethnic Politics in Colonial Sri Lanka*. New Delhi: Vikas.

Wilson, A. J. (1998.) *The Break-Up of Sri Lanka: The Sinhala Tamil Conflict*. London: C. Hust and Co.

————. (1988.) *The Break-Up of Sri Lanka: The Sinhalese-Tamil Conflict*. Honolulu: University of Hawaii Press.

Woost, M. D. (1994.) "Developing a Nation of Villages: Rural Community as State Formation in Sri Lanka," *Critique of Anthropology* 14(1): pp. 77–95.

World Bank. (2000.) *Sri Lanka: Recapturing Missed Opportunities*. World Bank Country Report, Washington, DC.

Yalman, N. (1967.) *Under the Bo Tree: Studies in Caste, Kinship and Marriage in the Interior of Ceylon*. Berkeley: University of California Press.

Zvelebil, K. (1996.) "Some Features of Ceylon Tamil," *Indo-Iranian Journal* 9: pp. 113–38.

Appendix 4: Fact Sheet - Sri Lanka

Total population: 18.8 million

(The 1991 national census could not be conducted, due to prevailing conditions in the country. The 2001 census enumeration was carried out completely in only eighteen of the twenty-five administrative districts on the island. In the northern and eastern provinces, enumeration was carried out only partially. The 2001 enumeration is therefore based on the enumerated data and projections from the statistics of the 1981 census.)

Population under age 15:	25.5%
Life expectancy at birth:	72.3 years
Adult literacy rate (age 15 and above):	91.9%
Youth literacy rate (age 15–24):	96.9%
Net primary enrolment ratio:	97%
Gross domestic product (in billions):	US$ 15.9
Purchasing Power Parity GDP per capita:	US$ 3,180
Public expenditure on education:	3.1%
Education system structure:	5 + 3 + 3 + 2
Compulsory education:	5–14 years of age, free at all levels.

Types of schools: Predominantly state owned and managed, with approximately 3% of children attending private schools. In 1996, Sri Lanka had 9,554 elementary schools, of which most were government institutions.

Language: The Constitution of the Republic of Sri Lanka specifies Sinhala and Tamil as the official languages of Sri Lanka, and Sinhala, Tamil, and English as the national languages. English is the official link language, as stipulated by the Official Languages Act of 1990.

Ethnic groups: Sinhalese (81.9%), Sri Lankan Tamil (4.3%), Indian Tamil (5.1%), Muslim (Moor) (8.0%), other (0.2%).

Religion: Buddhist (76.7%), Hindu (7.9%), Islamic (8.5%), Catholic (6.1%), Christian (0.8%), other (0.1%)

Sources: The authors and the UNDP Human Development Report 2003

Note: All figures for 2001 except if otherwise stated.

Designed and printed by TYPHON